A POLITICAL AND ECONOMIC DICTIONARY OF LATIN AMERICA

A POLITICAL AND ECONOMIC DICTIONARY OF LATIN AMERICA

Peter Calvert

FIRST EDITION

Europa Publications
Taylor & Francis Group

LONDON AND NEW YORK

First Edition 2004
Europa Publications
11 New Fetter Lane, London EC4P 4EE, England
(A member of the Taylor & Francis Group)

ISBN 1 85743 211 8

Development Editor: Cathy Hartley
Copy Editor and Proof-reader: Simon Chapman

Typeset in Times New Roman 10/13.5

Typeset by AJS Solutions, Huddersfield • Dundee
Printed and bound in Great Britain by MPG Books Ltd, Bodmin, Cornwall

FOREWORD

Latin America, in the first decade of the 21st century, remains as exciting, interesting and unpredictable as ever. In 2004 Haiti, the first Latin American country to gain its independence, celebrated its second centenary. But although the structure and organization of government, politics, production, international relations and trade in the region are by now well established, important changes are under way, and the Latin American countries are becoming more important than ever before in world politics as a bridge between the USA and the rest of the world. This *Political and Economic Dictionary of Latin America* seeks to provide an overview of the region based on the most up-to-date information available at the time of writing.

Latin America, for the purposes of this book, encompasses all of the countries in the Americas South of the Rio Grande/Río Bravo, which separates the USA from Mexico, and includes the Greater and Lesser Antilles.

Entries in the dictionary are designed to stand on their own in providing definitions and essential facts, with coverage of recent developments, and, wherever possible, full contact details. The broad scope of the dictionary ranges over political groups (both legal and illegal), institutions, main government leaders and prominent individuals, trade unions, financial and trade bodies, ethnic groups, countries, territories and principal cities, as well as essential terms and concepts. Cross-referencing between entries is indicated by the simple and widely familiar device of using a bold typeface for those words or entities which have their own coverage. The longest individual entries in the book are those for the region's individual countries and territories, giving a succinct description and historical survey to place recent events in context. For all but the smallest economies, the country entry is followed by a separate entry on that country's economy, again combining up-to-date basic data with a short overview and a focus on recent issues and developments.

I am most grateful to Matthew Beech for the help he has given me on this project.

Chandlers Ford, April 2004

THE AUTHOR

Peter Calvert is Emeritus Professor of Comparative and International Politics at the University of Southampton. He has written on Latin American politics, comparative politics in the third world, and environmental politics. His most recent publications include: Peter Calvert and Susan Calvert, *Politics and Society in the Third World*, 2nd edition (2001), Peter Calvert, *Comparative Politics: an Introduction* (2002) and Peter Burnell and Peter Calvert, editors, *Civil Society in Democratization* (2004).

ABBREVIATIONS

Apdo	Apartado (Post Box)	ha	hectare
Av., Avda	Avenida (Avenue)	Km	Kilometre(s)
Ave	Avenue	kph	Kilometres per hour
b.	born	Lic.	Licenciado
Bldg	Building	Lt	Lieutenant
Blvd	Boulevard	Ltd	Limited
Capt.	Captain	m	metre(s)
CEO	Chief Executive Officer	m.	million
Chair.	Chairman/person/wo-man	Maj.	Major
		Man.	Manager
Co	Company	MBA	Master of Business Administration
Col	Colonel		
Col.	Colima; Colonia	Mgr	Monseñor
Corpn	Corporation	mph	miles per hour
CP	Case Postale, Caixa Postal, Casella Postale (Post Box)	No(.)	Number; numéro; número
		NW	North-West
DC	District of Columbia; Distrito Capital; Distrito Central	NY	New York
		OECD	Organisation for Economic Co-operation and Development
DF	Distrito Federal		
Dir	Director	Of.	Oficina (Office)
DN	Distrito Nacional	PO(B)	Post Office (Box)
Edif.	Edificio (Building)	PPP	purchasing-power parity
esq	esquina (corner)	PR	Puerto Rico
Exec.	Executive	Pres.	President
f.	founded	Prof.	Professor
FL	Florida	Rd	Road
Fr	Father	rtd	retired
Gen.	General	RJ	Rio de Janeiro
GNI	Gross National Income	Sec.	Secretary
Gov.	Governor	Sgt	Sergeant

Abbreviations

SP	São Paulo	UN	United Nations
Sq.	Square	US(A)	United States
St	Street; Saint		(of America)
Sta	Santa		

INTERNATIONAL TELEPHONE CODES

The code and relevant telephone number must be preceded by the International Dialling Code of the country from which you are calling.

Anguilla	1 264	Guyana	592
Antigua and Barbuda	1 268	Haiti	509
Argentina	54	Honduras	504
Aruba	297	Jamaica	1 876
Bahamas	1 242	Martinique	596
Barbados	1 246	Mexico	52
Belize	501	Montserrat	1 664
Bermuda	1 441	Netherlands Antilles	599
Bolivia	591	Nicaragua	505
Brazil	55	Panama	507
British Virgin Islands	1 284	Paraguay	595
Cayman Islands	1 345	Peru	51
Chile	56	Puerto Rico	1 787
Colombia	57	Saint Christopher and Nevis	1 869
Costa Rica	506	Saint Lucia	1 758
Cuba	53	Saint Vincent and the	
Dominica	1 767	Grenadines	1 784
Dominican Republic	1 809	Suriname	597
Ecuador	593	Trinidad and Tobago	1 868
El Salvador	503	Turks and Caicos Islands	1 649
Falkland Islands	500	United States of America	1
French Guiana	594	United States Virgin Islands	1 340
Grenada	1 473	Uruguay	598
Guadeloupe	590	Venezuela	58
Guatemala	502		

A

Acción Democrática (AD)
Democratic Action, Venezuela

Social democratic party. F. 1936 as Partido Democrático Nacional by **Rómulo Betancourt**, one of the small group of men exiled by the dictator, Juan Vicente Gómez, who met at Barranquilla, Colombia, in 1931 to concert opposition to the dictatorship. Between 1935 and 1937 they tried to put together the nucleus of a Popular Front government, but in 1937 left-wing activity was banned, and the party suppressed. At the change of government in 1941 the party obtained legal recognition under its present name, and in 1945 members played a key role in the junta that overthrew Gen. Isaías Medina Angarita. In 1948, in the first elections held under the Constitution of 1947, the AD candidate for President, the novelist and thinker Rómulo Gallegos, was successful and, though he was deposed a few weeks later, the experience of the *trienio* was to guide both Betancourt and the AD when they returned to power after the popular uprising that overthrew Marcos Pérez Jiménez in 1958. Since that time it has remained the dominant political party in Venezuela, though eclipsed by the **Movimiento V República** in 1998.

    Leadership: Henry Ramos Allup

    Address: Casa Nacional Acción Democrática, Calle Los Cedros, La Florida, Caracas 1050

    E-mail: informacion@acciondemocratica.org.ve

    Internet: www.acciondemocratica.org.ve

Acción Democrática Nacionalista (ADN)
Nationalist Democratic Action, Bolivia

The ADN was formed as a vehicle for former dictator Gen. (retd) **Hugo Bánzer Suárez** (1971–78) for the July 1979 general election, in which he came third with

14.9% of the vote. In the 1980 general election his share of the vote increased slightly, to 16.9%, and the ADN won 30 congressional seats, which were finally taken up when Congress was recalled in September 1982. The ADN initially supported the July 1980 coup led by Gen. Luis García Meza, but in April 1981 this backing was withdrawn. A month later Bánzer was arrested on a charge of plotting a counter-coup.

The general election of July 1985 resulted in Bánzer winning the largest share of the vote (28.6%) in the presidential contest, while the ADN obtained 51 seats in Congress. However, because no presidential candidate had obtained a clear majority, a centre-left alliance in Congress elected **Víctor Paz Estenssoro** of the **Movimiento Nacionalista Revolucionario** (MNR) as President. For the May 1989 election the ADN entered into an alliance with the Partido Demócrata Cristiano. Bánzer, the alliance's joint candidate, won 22.7% of the vote in the presidential contest and was narrowly outpolled for second place by the MNR candidate, Gonzalo Sánchez de Lozada. Personal enmity between the two candidates precluded an ADN–MNR pact and ensured that neither was elected President by Congress, which opted for Jaime Paz Zamora of the **Movimiento de la Izquierda Revolucionario** (MIR). The resultant Acuerdo Patriótico (AP) coalition Government led by the ADN and the MIR assumed power in August 1989. In return for the presidency, Jaime Paz Zamora awarded the ADN 10 out of 18 ministerial posts, including the most important portfolios of finance, defence and foreign affairs. Bánzer personally took the chairmanship of the Political Council of Convergence and National Unity, a post which gave him effective control over government policy.

In March 1992 MIR leaders ratified Bánzer as the AP's 1993 presidential candidate. However, although the AP secured 43 seats in the Chamber of Deputies and eight in the Senate, Bánzer himself could only manage second place in the presidential election, victory going to Sánchez de Lozada of the MNR. The AP was consequently dissolved in August 1993, with Bánzer resigning as ADN leader in November. In February 1995, however, Bánzer returned to the leadership of the ADN.

In August 1997 Bánzer again became President, having headed the popular polling in June with 22.3% of the vote and secured election in a congressional vote with the support of an ADN-headed 'mega-coalition' which included the MIR, Conciencia de Patria and the Unión Cívica Solidaridad. In the June 1997 congressional election the ADN headed the poll, winning 33 Chamber seats and 13 in the Senate. The party was therefore dominant in the resultant coalition Government. In August 2001, announcing that he was suffering from cancer, Bánzer resigned both the state presidency and the party leadership, and was succeeded in both positions by Vice-President Jorge Fernando Quiroga Ramírez.

The ADN is an associate member of the International Democrat Union.

Leadership: Jorge Fernando Quiroga Ramírez (leader, former President of the Republic); Ronald Maclean (2002 presidential candidate)

Address: c/o Cámara de Diputados, La Paz, Bolivia

Internet: www.bolivian.com/adn

Acción Popular (AP)
Popular Action, Peru

Moderate right-wing party founded by **Fernando Belaúnde Terry** to contest the presidential election of 1980, which he won with 44.5% of the votes cast. His ineffectiveness in combating the threat posed by **Sendero Luminoso** led to his defeat by Alan García of the **Alianza Popular Revolucionaria Americana** in 1985. In the 2001 presidential election the party did not field a candidate and won only three seats in the Chamber of Deputies.

Leadership: Fernando Belaúnde Terry (Leader), Luis Enrique Gálvez de la Puente (Sec.-Gen.)

Address: Paseo Colón 218, Lima 1

Telephone: (1) 332-1965

Fax: (1) 332-1965

E-mail: ap_sgn@telefonica.net.pe

Internet: www.accionpopular.org.pe

Acción por la República—Nueva Dirigencia (AR—ND)
Action for the Republic—New Leadership, Argentina

Right-wing electoral alliance formed in Argentina in 1997 between Acción por la República and Nueva Dirigencia, the latter a centre-right party founded in 1996 by dissident Peronist Gustavo Béliz. Obtained nine seats in the Chamber of Deputies at the mid-term election in 2001.

Leadership: Caro Figueroa (Leader)

E-mail: accionrepublic@geocities.com

Internet: www.ar-partido.com.ar;www.nuevadirigencia.org.ar

Agencia Chile Noticias (ACN)
Chilean News Agency

> *Leadership:* Jeanete Franco N. (Dir)
> *Address:* MacIver 233, Of. 117, Santiago
> *Telephone:* (2) 638-3188
> *Fax:* (2) 638-3188
> *E-mail:* prensa@chilenoticias.cl
> *Internet:* www.chilenoticias.cl

Alexander VI
Rodrigo Borgia or Borja (1432–1503), as Pope Alexander VI (1492–1503), established the Line of Demarcation between the Spanish and Portuguese territories in the Indies, which was subsequently fixed at a meridian 370 leagues west of the Cape Verde Islands by the Treaty of Tordesillas of 1494.

¡Alfaro Vive! ¡Carajo! – *see* Izquierda Democrática (ID)

Algemeen Verbond van Vakverenigingen in Suriname 'De Moederbond' (AVVS)
General Confederation of Trade Unions, Suriname

The principal trade union organization in Suriname, with 15,000 members.
> *Leadership:* Imro Grep (Pres.)
> *Address:* Verlengde Coppernamestraat 134, POB 2951, Paramaribo
> *Telephone:* 463501
> *Fax:* 465116
> *E-mail:* moederbond51@hotmail.com

Alianza por Chile
Alliance for Chile

Right-wing alliance of political parties founded in 1996; originally named the Unión por Chile (Union for Chile), it adopted its present name in 1999. Its presidential candidate, Joaquín Lavín, of the Unión Demócrata Independiente, obtained 47.5% of the first-round votes in the election of December 1999, but was defeated in the second round.
> *Leadership:* Joaquín Lavín Infante (Leader)

Alianza Democrática–Movimiento 19 de Abril (AD–M-19)
Democratic Alliance–M-19, Colombia

Alliance of left-wing groups which was formed to support the M-19 campaign for elections to the National Constituent Assembly in 1990.

Leadership: Diego Montaña Cuéllar (Leader)
Address: Transversal 28, No. 37–38, Santafé de Bogotá, DC
Telephone: (1) 368-9436
E-mail: alianzademocraticam19@hotmail.com
Internet: www.alliancefordemocracy.net

Alianza Nacional Popular (ANAPO)
National People's Alliance, Colombia

Right-wing populist political movement founded in 1971 to support the candidature of former dictator Gustavo Rojas Pinilla; now led by his daughter.

Leadership: María Eugenia Rojas de Moreno Díaz (Leader)
Address: Carrera 18, No. 33–95, Santafé de Bogotá, DC
Telephone: (1) 287-7050
Fax: (1) 245-3138

Alianza Popular Revolucionaria Americana (APRA)
American Popular Revolutionary Alliance, Peru

Founded by **Víctor Raúl Haya de la Torre** in exile in Mexico 1924; established in Peru as the Partido Aprista Peruano in 1930, but banned in 1932; legalized in 1945 but repeatedly denied election victory by the armed forces until the election of Alan García as President in 1985. Democratic, left-wing populist party; claims 700,000 members. In the 2001 presidential election the party's candidate, Alan García, despite his dismal record as President, came second to Alejandro Toledo of **Perú Posible**, with 25.78% of the votes cast. In the concurrent legislative election APRA emerged as the second largest party, winning 27 seats in the 120-seat, single-chamber Congress.

Leadership: Alan Gabriel García Pérez
Address: Avda Alfonso Ugarte 1012, Lima 5
Telephone: (1) 428-1736
Internet: www.apra.com.pe

Alianza Republicana Nacionalista (ARENA)
Nationalist Republican Alliance, El Salvador

Right-wing party founded in 1981 by Maj. Roberto D'Aubuisson to fight terrorism and resist pressure for change; initially closely linked to 'death squads', it contested the election for the Constituent Assembly in March 1982 with limited success, but in the election in April 1984 right-wing support coalesced behind d'Aubuisson who obtained 46.4% of the votes cast, compared to 53.6% for the successful Christian Democratic candidate, José Napoleon Duarte. The election of Alfredo Cristiani in 1989 ushered in a long period of ARENA dominance.

Leadership: José Salaverria
Address: Prolongación Calle Arce 2423, entre 45 y 47 Avda Norte, San Salvador
Telephone: 260-4400
Fax: 260-5918

Allende, Salvador

Salvador Allende Gossens, President of Chile in 1970–73, was born in Valparaíso in 1908. The son of a lawyer, he studied medicine and graduated from the University of Chile in 1932, after a brief interval in which he had been excluded from the University for political activity. Being known as a relative by marriage of Marmaduque Grove, he was arrested after the fall of the Socialist Republic, but was finally acquitted of all charges. In 1933 he was a founder member of the **Partido Socialista de Chile**, of which he became secretary-general in 1943. Elected a deputy in 1937, he helped organize the presidential campaign of Pedro Aguirre Cerda, who appointed him Minister of Health, in which post he established both health insurance and compensation for victims of industrial accidents. In 1945 he was elected for the first time to the Senate, where he remained until 1970, being re-elected on three occasions. However, in his first campaign for the presidency in 1952 he obtained only 6% of the votes cast. In 1958 he won 29% and in 1964 39%, but it was only in 1970, when he obtained 36.2%, that he was elected as President as the candidate of the Unidad Popular coalition. According to custom, the Chilean Congress agreed to confirm his election, but only after he had undertaken to respect the Constitution. Despite this, he immediately launched a far-reaching programme of social reform, including nationalization of the copper mines and other strategically important industries, and a programme of land reform, which, however, soon got out of control as the country became increasing polarized. Although his coalition gained support at the congressional elections, on 11 September 1973 he was overthrown in a military coup led by Gen. **Augusto Pinochet Ugarte**. After the air force had bombed La Moneda, the presidential palace, and had set it on fire, Allende ensured that his supporters left the building safely and then shot himself.

Alliance for Progress
Alianza para el Progreso

Programme of economic aid for Latin America launched in 1961 by the (John F.) Kennedy Administration in the USA, intended to counter the influence of **Fidel Castro**'s Cuba. The Declaration of the Peoples of America and the Charter of Punta del Este, which established the alliance, were formally adopted by the Economic and Social Council of the **Organization of American States** on 17 August 1961. The US Government was committed to funding about one-half of the US $20,000m. over 10 years that was to be devoted to long-range development plans submitted by member states, with emphasis on land reform and land-tax changes. Political changes, however, meant that few governments availed themselves of this funding, and after 1963 the impact of the programme gradually fell away.

Alliance of Small Island States (AOSIS)

Ad hoc intergovernmental grouping founded in 1990 to defend the interests of small island states and low-lying coastal developing states. Forty-three states (not all of them islands) are members, of which the following are in the Caribbean area: Antigua and Barbuda, the Bahamas, Barbados, Belize, Cuba, Dominica, Grenada, Guyana, Haiti, Jamaica, St Christopher and Nevis, St Lucia, St Vincent and the Grenadines, and Trinidad and Tobago. Observer states in the region are: Netherlands Antilles, and the US Virgin Islands.

Leadership: Jagdish Koonjul, Mauritius (Chair.)

Address: c/o 800 Second Ave, Suite 400d, New York, NY 10017, USA

Telephone: (212) 599-6196

Fax: (212) 599-0797

E-mail: mauritius@un.int

Internet: www.sidsnet.org/aosis

Alternativa por la República de Iguales (ARI)
Alternative for a Republic of Equals, Argentina

The centre-right ARI was established in April 1997 by Domingo Cavallo, the former economy minister (1991–96) who had been responsible for the successful Convertibility Plan, as a vehicle to support his bid for a congressional seat in the October 1997 legislative election and for a possible candidacy in the 1999 presidential election. In the 1997 election the party secured three seats. In the presidential election of 1999 Cavallo secured 10.1% of the popular vote, while in the simultaneous legislative election the ARI increased its representation from nine seats to 12. Cavallo joined the *Alianza* government as economy minister in March 2001, but was unable to repeat his former success and was forced to flee on the resignation of President de la Rúa in December 2001. In the 2001 mid-term election ARI had won one seat in the Senate and increased its representation to 17 in the Chamber of Deputies.

Leadership: Armando Caro Figueroa (Chair., Exec. Cttee); José Luis Fernández Valoni (Sec.-Gen.); Domingo Cavallo (1999 presidential candidate); Alfredo José Castañón (congressional Pres.)

Address: Congreso de la Nación, 1835–1849 Buenos Aires 1089, Argentina
Telephone: (11) 4954-5541/4842
E-mail: ecarrio@diputados.gov.ar
Internet: www1.hcdn.gov.ar/dependencias/ari

Amazon Co-operation Treaty
Tratado de Cooperación Amazónica

The Treaty for Amazon Co-operation was signed in **Brasília**, Brazil, on 3 July 1978 by the foreign ministers of Bolivia, Brazil, Colombia, Ecuador, Guyana, Peru, Suriname and Venezuela. The object of the Treaty was to promote the harmonious development of the Amazon territories of the eight signatory states by joint efforts towards their common benefit; to protect the environment; to preserve and make rational use of natural resources; and to maintain full freedom of commercial navigation on the Amazon and other international rivers of the region as guaranteed by each signatory. Owing to the vast size of the region and the mutual suspicions of the countries involved, the agreement has had very little effect, although by entering into closer ties with Guyana, Brazil effectively checked Venezuela's ambitions to annex the Essequibo region and began the process of opening up direct road links to the Guyanan capital of Georgetown. In December 1995 the foreign ministers of the member states agreed to establish a regional secretariat in Brasília and signed the Lima Declaration on sustainable development.

Andean Community of Nations
Comunidad Andina de Naciones (CAN)

The Andean Pact, Andean Group (Grupo Andino) or Acuerdo de Cartagena, was the first major subregional organization in the hemisphere. The Group took its customary Spanish name from the Treaty of Cartagena, originally known as the Andean Subregional Integration Agreement, signed at Cartagena de Indias, Colombia, by Bolivia, Chile, Colombia, Ecuador and Peru on 26 May 1969. In February 1973 Venezuela joined the organization, but Chile withdrew from it on 21 January 1977, officially because of its hostility to foreign capital; in reality, because of the other members' criticism of, and unwillingness to work with, the dictatorial regime of Gen. **Augusto Pinochet Ugarte**. Even after the Mandate of Cartagena of May 1979, which advocated greater political and economic co-operation, local disputes continued to disrupt the working of the Group.

The purpose of the Andean Group was to promote economic integration between the member states, by progressive elimination of tariff barriers and the co-ordination of industrial development. Intra-Group trade grew significantly after its formation. The supreme authority of the Group was the Commission, made up of one ambassador from each member state. Foreign ministers met annually or as required to formulate external policy. The Andean Parliament (*Parlamento Andino*) of five members from each state had a purely advisory role, but the Court of Justice, established in 1984, settled disputes arising under the Treaty.

The Andean Pact led to the reduction of many tariffs and to some increase in intra-regional trade. Dissatisfaction with the rate of progress towards integration, however, led to the decision, taken at a summit meeting held in Cuzco, Peru, on 22–23 May 1990, to achieve free trade in goods by 1995. At a summit meeting in Venezuela in May 1991 heads of government approved the Declaration of Caracas, committing the five states to a free-trade zone by January 1992 and reaffirming the goal of a fully integrated common market by 1995. The military-backed coup in Peru in April 1992, however, threatened to bring the whole process of integration to a halt when Peru withdrew temporarily from the Pact. Nevertheless, in March 1993 the other four member states agreed to establish a customs union. In October tariffs were abolished altogether between Bolivia, Colombia and Ecuador. Peru subsequently rejoined the Pact, though it did not take part in negotiations leading to the creation of the unified market on 1 January 1995, and was not due to participate in the free-trade zone until mid-1996.

In March 1996 an agreement was signed, in Trujillo, Peru, to restructure the Pact into an Andean Community of Nations, thus strengthening regional integration. However, after the recurrence of border conflict with Ecuador, in April 1997 Peru announced its intention to withdraw from the Community and was not represented at the summit meeting held in Sucre, Ecuador, in that month. In the late 1990s, with Venezuela in economic crisis and Colombia affected by civil war, the Andean Community lost momentum. Two of its members, Chile and Bolivia, began to seek other ties and, in May 1999, the decision by the new Venezuelan Government of Lt-Col **Hugo Chávez Frías** to close Venezuela's frontier to Colombian long-haul lorries for one year was a clear breach of community rules.

Leadership: Guillermo Fernández de Soto (Colombia: Sec.-Gen.)
Address: Paseo de la República 3895, eq. Aramburú, San Isidro, Lima, Peru
Telephone: (511) 411-1400
Fax: (511) 221-33-29
E-mail: contacto@communidadandina.org
Internet: www.comunidadandina.org

Andean Development Corporation
Corporación Andina de Fomento (CAF)

The Andean Development Corporation, with headquarters in Caracas, Venezuela, was formed in 1968 to act as the development-financing arm of the Andean Group, mainly for industrial development and for the creation of basic services. The principal shareholders in the CAF are the members of the **Andean Community of Nations**: Bolivia, Colombia, Ecuador, Peru and Venezuela. There are in addition 11 regional partner shareholder countries. It defines its mission as being to promote the sustainable development of its shareholder countries and regional integration and it provides funding to both public and private sectors. In 2000 disbursements totalled over US $1,800m., of which 72% was directed to public-sector projects. In March 2002 the Andean Presidents agreed to increase the authorized share capital of the CAF from $3,000m. to $5,000m.

Officer: Enrique García Rodríguez (Exec. Pres.)
Address: Torre CAF, Avda Luis Roche, Altamira, Apdo 5086, Caracas, Venezuela
Telephone: (12) 209-2111

Fax: (12) 209-2444
E-mail: infocaf@caf.com
Internet: www.caf.com

Andean Pact – *see* Andean Community of Nations

Anguilla

An Overseas Territory of the United Kingdom, one of the most northerly of the Leeward Islands in the Lesser Antilles, Anguilla is the smallest island territory in the Caribbean. The main island, named by the French for its resemblance to an eel (*anguille*), is 91 sq km in area and the smaller island of Sombrero 5 sq km.

Area overall: 96 sq km; *capital:* The Valley; *population:* 12,446 (July 2002 estimate); *official language:* English.

Constitution: Under the British Overseas Territories Act of 2002, the Governor both represents the Crown and presides over the Executive Council and the House of Assembly. He himself is responsible for defence, external relations, the public service, the judiciary and the audit. The Executive Council consists of the Chief Minister and not more than three other ministers appointed by the Governor from the elected members of the House of Assembly, as well as two members ex officio, the Deputy Governor and the Attorney-General. The House of Assembly is elected for a maximum term of five years by universal adult suffrage, and consists of seven elected members, the two ex-officio members and two nominated members.

History: Anguilla was first settled by English settlers in 1650. In 1825 it was attached for administrative purposes to St Christopher (St Kitts) and Nevis. With it, it was part of the Leeward Islands Federation from 1871 until 1956, when it joined the short-lived West Indies Federation. When the Federation broke up, the inhabitants refused to return to rule from St Kitts, and in 1969 a detachment of the British Metropolitan Police was dispatched to the island to maintain order, though it was not formally constituted as a separate British Dependent Territory until 1980. The island lies in the main track of the hurricane belt and was severely damaged by 'Hurricane Luis' in 1995.

Latest elections: In the elections of March 2000 the Anguilla National Alliance (ANA) won three seats and the Anguilla United Party (AUP) two. The Anguilla Democratic Party (ADR) retained only one seat and the seventh seat went to an independent. Osbourne Fleming of the ANA became Chief Minister in succession to Hubert Hughes of the AUP, who had served as Chief Minister since 1994, latterly at the head of a coalition with the ADP.

International relations and defence: The United Kingdom government is responsible for both.

Economy: The territory has a prosperous middle-income economy, as defined by the **International Bank for Reconstruction and Development** (World Bank). Gross domestic product per head in 2001 was US $11,430. The main source is tourism. There is a limited amount of commercial fishing.

Antigua and Barbuda

Antigua and Barbuda lie slightly to the east of the main chain of the Leeward Islands, 43 km (27 miles) north-east of Montserrat. The third island in the group, Redonda, is uninhabited.

Area overall: 442 sq km (171 sq miles); *capital:* **St John's**; *population:* 77,426 (2001 census), many recent immigrants from Montserrat and the Dominican Republic; *official language:* English; *religion:* mainly Anglican, some Roman Catholic, other Protestant denominations.

Constitution: Antigua and Barbuda is a constitutional monarchy within the **Commonwealth**. The head of state is HM Queen Elizabeth II, who is represented by a Governor-General of local citizenship. Parliament consists of an appointed Senate of 17 members (at least one from Barbuda) and a 17-member, directly elected House of Representatives. The Barbuda Council is the local authority for that island.

History: **Christopher Columbus** landed on the main island and named it Santa María de la Antigua in 1493, but the first permanent European settlement on the island, in 1632, was by English settlers. In 1666 the island was briefly captured by France, but soon relinquished. **Sugar** cultivation by imported slaves was introduced in 1674, and remained the principal economic activity even after emancipation in 1834. English Harbour, which provided excellent shelter, had meanwhile become Britain's major naval base in the West Indies.

In 1871 Antigua became the seat of government for Britain's Leeward Islands Federation. This was dissolved in 1957 and Antigua and Barbuda, where universal suffrage had been introduced in 1951, joined the Federation of the West Indies. When it collapsed, negotiations to federate the smaller states were unsuccessful and in 1967 Antigua and Barbuda became a British Associated Territory, with full internal self-government under the leadership of Vere C. Bird, Sr, and the Antigua Labour Party (ALP), which had first come to power in 1950. Full independence was achieved on 1 November 1981, since when the Bird family and the ALP have continued to maintain tight control of Antiguan politics, aided by the distorting effects of the 'first-past-the-post' electoral system. At the general election held on 9 March 1999, at which Lester Bird and the ALP were returned to power, the results were: ALP 12 seats (17,417 votes), United Progressive Party (UPP) four seats (14,817 votes), Barbuda People's Movement one seat (418 votes).

Latest elections: In a general election held on 24 March 2002, the ALP was defeated, after 53 years in office under successive members of the Bird family. The UPP, led by Baldwin Spencer, won 14 seats in the House of Representatives and the ALP three seats. Turn-out at the election, monitored by Commonwealth observers, was 90%.

International relations and defence: Antigua and Barbuda is a member of the United Nations, the **Organization of American States**, the Commonwealth, the **Caribbean Community and Common Market** and the **Organization of Eastern Caribbean States**. The US Government leases two military bases on Antigua, which participates in the US-sponsored Regional Security System. It has a small defence force of 170 men.

Economy: The islands have a relatively prosperous economy by regional standards. With gross domestic product (GDP) per head of US $9,055 in 2001, Antigua and Barbuda ranked as a middle-income country. However, though the economy grew at an average rate of 5.3% in 1996–99, the rate fell to 2.5% in 2000, 1.5% in 2001 and 1.2% in 2002. This was largely as a result of stagnation in the country's chief industry, tourism, revenue from which was insufficient to cover the trade deficit. The government has maintained a deficit for many years, with the result that total external debt was equivalent to 79.6% of GDP in 2001. According to a March 2004 US State Department report, the island is of 'primary concern' for money-laundering and is an important transhipment point for South American cocaine.

Arias Sánchez, Oscar

Oscar Arias Sánchez, b. 1941, President of Costa Rica in 1986–90, was the youngest President in the country's history. He had studied abroad, at the London School of Economics and Political Science, before taking an active role in the **Partido de Liberación Nacional**. As President, he took a lead in persuading his fellow Central Americans to take matters into their own hands and discuss a peace plan, known as the Arias Plan, to end conflict and foreign intervention in Central America. Although any peace agreement that did not result in the fall of the Sandinista Government in Nicaragua was strongly opposed by the Reagan Administration in the USA, with support from Mexico, Colombia, Venezuela and

Panama, the Arias Plan eventually led to the Esquipulas II agreement, and Arias was awarded the Nobel Peace Prize for his work.

Argentina
República Argentina

Argentina, situated on the east side of the Andes in the southern part of South America, is the second largest country in Latin America and the ninth largest in the world.

Area: 2,780,000 sq km (1,073,518 sq miles), exclusive of the **Falkland Islands** and Antarctic territory claimed by Argentina; *capital:* **Buenos Aires**; *population:* 36,223,947 (2001 census), 85% European by extraction, the majority from Italy and Spain, most of the rest being of mixed European and native American descent; *official language:* Spanish (Italian is also spoken); *religion:* officially Roman Catholic (92%), many non-practising.

Constitution: The Constitution of 1994 is substantially the same as the Constitution of 1853 which it replaced. This, the oldest in Latin America, established a federal, presidential republic, loosely modelled on the USA. Executive power is vested in a President, directly elected by the people, who may serve more than one term. Other constitutional amendments effected in 1994 included the reduction of the presidential mandate from six years to four; delegation of some presidential powers to a chief of Cabinet; a run-off election for presidential and vice-presidential candidates when neither obtained 45% of the votes cast, or 40% when the nearest candidate gained less than 30% of the ballot; and the establishment of an autonomous government in the city of Buenos Aires with a directly elected mayor.

History: Much of Argentine history in the 19th century focused on the problem of constitutional organization, owing to the rivalry between Buenos Aires and the other Provinces. In 1853 a federal Constitution was created for the new Argentine Republic. Buenos Aires seceded from the federation, but in 1859 was defeated in a military confrontation with the other Provinces. Then, in 1861, it joined the union in order to dominate it, and, with its economic strength, finally triumphed in 1880, when the city of Buenos Aires replaced Rosario as the national capital. A new capital for the old Province of Buenos Aires was built at La Plata. The provincial *caudillos* made the transition to being more conventional politicians, though it was the great landowners, the *estancieros*, who dominated national life.

The next four decades were years of economic transformation as the combined impact of British investment, European immigration, the expansion of the railways and exploitation of corn and grain of the Pampas made Argentina by far the most advanced of the Latin American states. These developments initially benefited the landowners (cattle barons and commercial agriculturists) who dominated politics, but new classes of professionals (bankers, brokers and lawyers) and an urban working class emerged with the rapid growth of cities and began to challenge the hold of the ruling classes. As a result, in 1916 Hipólito Yrigoyen, nephew of the founder of the **Unión Cívica Radical** (UCR—Radical Civic Union), became Argentina's first popularly elected President. In 1928 Yrigoyen was elected to a second term, causing a split in the UCR. Before the effects of the 1929 depression were felt, Yrigoyen's reclusiveness made it possible for a small band of armed cadets to seize power in 1930, led by a retired general, José E. Uriburu.

From 1932 to 1943, a period known as the 'Infamous Decade', the oligarchy resumed power in the form of a loose coalition (the Concordancia) of Conservatives and anti-personalist Radicals, supported by the armed forces. It was their friends and supporters who benefited from the economic recovery. The Second World War divided Argentine society further. Some leaders were strongly pro-Allied, but others, not least in the armed forces, pro-Axis. In 1941 it seemed that the civilian politicians would install a pro-Allied President, and the army intervened again. Col **Juan Domingo Perón**, secretary of the army lodge that planned and executed the coup, became Minister of War and Secretary for Labour and Social Welfare in the military Government. He promoted labour reforms and encouraged unionization, becoming immensely popular with the masses, though not with the oligarchy. In 1946, in a free election, he won the presidency decisively. In 1949 he amended the Constitution to permit his immediate re-election and held power until 1955.

Perón's authoritarian regime rested on an alliance with trade unions and the popular support of the urban underprivileged, the *descamisados* (shirtless ones). Large welfare programmes brought real benefits to the poor and were dramatized by Perón's charismatic wife, Eva Duarte de Perón ('Evita'), who came to be regarded virtually as a saint. A staunch nationalist, Perón bought out the British-owned railways and other public utilities, greatly accelerated industrialization under strong government control, and increased the role of the state in the economy. In his foreign policy he sought a 'Third Position', later to be termed non-alignment, and the leadership of South America. However, he neglected the agricultural sector, formerly the basis of Argentina's export trade. Rural migration increased and serious economic imbalances developed. As inflation rose and agricultural output fell, the economy's growth slowed down. Eva Perón died in July 1952, depriving her husband of his strongest ally with the masses. However, the military had been alienated by her prominence, some officers were already tired of Perón himself, and in September 1955 Perón was deposed and went into exile in Spain. However, his legacy and his political movement survived, to form the fundamental divide in Argentine politics for the next three decades.

The critical factor was the antagonism between the armed forces and the Peronists, the former trying for 18 years to exclude both Perón and his supporters from national politics.

Between 1955 and 1983 Argentina's political history was very turbulent. In June 1973 Perón was allowed to return and in September he was elected as President, with his third wife, María Estela ('Isabela') Martínez de Perón, assuming the vice-presidency. Inevitably, the hopes of his supporters were disappointed. Perón, now a sick man of 78, was unable to meet the many conflicting demands made of him. On his death on 1 July 1974, his widow became Latin America's (and, indeed, the world's) first woman executive President. The Peronist movement was now not only divided, its extreme wings were, in fact, at war, and in March 1976 the armed forces again seized power, and, with the commander of the army, Gen. Jorge Videla, as President, began what the Government termed euphemistically the 'Process of National Reorganization' and others came to know as the 'dirty war', *la guerra sucia*—a concerted attempt to eradicate terrorism by the use of terror—in which some 30,000 are now believed to have died.

A right-wing nationalist, Gen. Leopoldo Fortunato Galtieri, took over in December 1981 as President and head of the junta, with a plan which, he believed, would guarantee his position. On 2 April 1982 Argentine forces seized the British-ruled Falkland Islands (*Islas Malvinas*) in the South Atlantic, title to which had long been disputed by Argentina. The tiny British garrison was rapidly overwhelmed by 10,000 Argentine soldiers. Initially, the seizure was a resounding success for the Government—even the Peronists supported it. However, the final defeat of the Argentine forces by British troops on 14 June was a catastrophe and a national humiliation. Galtieri was abruptly replaced, and an interim government formed, under cover of which the military could retreat from power.

An election held on 30 October 1983 restored civilian government by the victorious Raúl Alfonsín, of the UCR, a 57-year-old lawyer, who had courageously opposed the war and had a record of defending human rights. Alfonsín removed anti-democratic senior officers and replaced them with more co-operative ones. The defence budget was drastically reduced, for economic as well as for political reasons, and in the 1986 defence budget a start was made on reducing the traditional significance of the armed forces in the nation's economic life. In April 1987, however, military rebellions broke out in Córdoba and later at the Campo de Mayo itself. Although there were popular demonstrations in support of democracy, concessions were made to the military, despite the ensuing controversy, and there were further insurrections in January and December 1988. Meanwhile, however, the Government's attempts at achieving economic stabilization were unsuccessful; the deficit on the public-sector account worsened and inflation continued to increase. In early 1989 the **International Bank for Reconstruction and Development** (World Bank) suspended all of its financing in Argentina.

In the 1989 presidential election the Peronist candidate, **Carlos Saúl Menem**, the flamboyant former Governor of the inland Province of La Rioja, was victorious. Food riots, looting and bombings in several Argentine cities forced Alfonsín to impose a state of siege and to hand over presidential power to Menem five months early, on 8 July, in order to avoid a total breakdown of public authority. President Menem first entrusted the conduct of his anti-inflationary policies to economists of Argentina's only native multinational company, Bunge and Born. The attempt failed and the association with Bunge and Born ended in December 1989, after only five months. Meanwhile, a widespread lack of confidence was reflected in the collapse of the currency and a second wave of hyperinflation.

Then, in January 1991, Domingo Cavallo was appointed economy minister and proceeded to implement a far-reaching programme of economic stabilization. This had three main aims. The first was 'dollarization', whereby the Argentine economy was linked to the US economy by the establishment of a new currency, the peso, at parity with the US dollar. The second was an ambitious programme of privatization, reversing 40 years of Peronist policy. The third aim was to improve government finances by raising revenue and eliminating tax evasion, by means such as the 'fiscal pact' with an agricultural development association, the Argentina Rural Society. By the time of President Menem's state visit to the USA in November, he was celebrated as Latin America's leading free market reformer and US ally. As a result, in March 1992 the President secured a promise of debt reduction under the Brady Initiative (a plan for debt relief originally proposed by Nicholas Brady, the US Secretary of the Treasury, in 1989).

In 1995, in spite of the worsening economic situation and the Government's continuing austerity programme, President Menem became only the third Argentine President to achieve re-election, winning 49.9% of the votes cast in the first round of voting and thereby avoiding a second ballot. His second term, almost inevitably, was an anticlimax. Following his victory, President Menem showed increasing irritation at the power of Domingo Cavallo, who had been reappointed to the economy ministry, and in July 1996 Cavallo was dismissed from the Cabinet. His successor continued his policies and the financial position of the country was apparently unaffected. In 1997, however, recession set in and the Government's popularity was further undermined by widespread and sometimes violent social and industrial unrest, caused by discontent with the Government's economic austerity measures and reports of corruption. In mid-term elections held in October 1997 the Partido Justicialista (PJ) lost its overall majority in the Chamber of Deputies and in the presidential election held on 24 October 1999, Fernando de la Rúa, the *Alianza* candidate, defeated former Vice-President Eduardo Duhalde of the PJ, thus ending a decade of Peronist domination of the presidency. However, in the mid-term elections held in October 2001, in which 127 of the 257 seats in the Chamber of Deputies were contested, the PJ recovered strongly to win 66 seats, or 116 seats overall. In December the economic situation had deteriorated to such an extent that riots broke out, in which 25 people died. Faced with the prospect of further violence, President de la Rúa resigned on 20 December. In the space of the next 13 days Argentina had six Presidents, a degree of stability returning only when the Peronist Congress appointed Duhalde as interim President to serve out the current term. This he did with some success, the economy showing clear signs of recovery by early 2003.

Latest elections: In the presidential election held on 27 April 2003, three PJ candidates confronted one another. Néstor Carlos Kirchner Ostoic of the Front for Victory (Frente para la Victoria) faction of the PJ, backed by outgoing President Eduardo Duhalde, obtained 22% of the votes cast and was declared the winner following the withdrawal of former President Menem. Menem had stood as the candidate of the Front for Liberty (Frente por la Libertad), but obtained only 19.4% of the votes cast. In a concurrent congressional election, the PJ consolidated its dominant position.

International relations and defence: Argentina is a member of the United Nations, the **Organization of American States**, the **Latin American Integration Association**, the **Southern Common Market** and the **Rio Pact**. In the 1990s it abandoned non-alignment and emerged as a close ally of the USA and an active participant in multinational peace-keeping operations, signalling its intention to adopt a more prominent role in international affairs, despite economic constraints which forced reductions in the military budget and the strength of the armed forces. In April 1995 compulsory military service was discontinued. The total strength of the armed forces in 2002 was 69,900, consisting of an army of 41,000, a navy of 16,000 and an air force of 16,500. During an official visit in October 1997 US President Bill Clinton commended Argentina's participation in more than 12 UN missions of the preceding decade, including those in Bosnia and Herzegovina, Cyprus and Haiti, and announced that he would seek non-NATO (North Atlantic Treaty Organization) ally status for the country. This would allow Argentina access to certain military funding and to a wider range of surplus US and NATO weaponry. The announcement drew protests from neighbours, particularly Brazil and Chile, which claimed that it could lead to a regional imbalance.

Although Argentina restored full diplomatic relations with the United Kingdom in February 1990, and agreements were subsequently concluded on the protection of fish stocks and the reduction of military restrictions in the South Atlantic region, the question of the Falkland Islands' disputed sovereignty was not resolved. The new Constitution of August 1994 reiterated Argentina's claim to sovereignty over the Islands and, following his re-election in May 1995, President Menem reaffirmed his goal of recovering the *Islas Malvinas* by 2000 through peaceful negotiation. Nevertheless, relations between the two countries continued to improve and, following the installation of a new British government in May 1997, this *rapprochement* was demonstrated by an official visit by President Menem to the United Kingdom in October 1998. During that conciliatory visit the President paid tribute to the British servicemen who had died during the 1982 conflict and disavowed the use of force to resolve the sovereignty issue. Furthermore, one of de la Rúa's first statements after his election confirmed his intention to maintain existing policy on the Islands, and his successors have done the same.

Argentina, economy

Argentina, potentially one of the richest countries in the world, declined from 1997 onwards into an acute economic crisis, and in 1999 was classified by the **International Bank for Reconstruction and Development** (World Bank) as a highly indebted middle-income country. In November 2002 it became the first country ever to default on a loan from the World Bank.

GNI: US $260,994m. (2001); *GNI per caput:* $6,940 (2001); *GNI at PPP:* $412,000m. (2001); *GNI per caput at PPP:* $10,980 (2001), rank 63; *exports:* $26,655m. (2001); *imports:* $20,312m. (2001); *currency:* peso (formally nuevo peso argentino), plural pesos; US $1 = 2.80 pesos at 31 May 2003.

In 2001 agriculture accounted for 4.8% of gross domestic product (GDP) and industry for 17.0%. Some 12.1% of the land is arable, 0.4% under permanent crops and 51.0% permanent pasture. The main crops are wheat, maize, sorghum and soya beans; other important crops include **sugar** cane, rice, linseed, potatoes, tomatoes, **cotton**, tea and grapes (in the late 1990s Argentina became increasingly significant as an exporter of good quality wine). Livestock production and meat sales abroad remain important to the economy: cattle and sheep being raised for the export market, and pigs and poultry for internal consumption. The main mineral resources are iron, aluminium, zinc, lead, **copper**, silver, gold and boron. The principal industries are car and truck production, white goods, pharmaceuticals, cosmetics, electronic equipment, fibres, cement, rubber and paper and other wood products. Argentina is fully self-sufficient in energy and likely to remain so. The main energy source is natural gas, which supplies some 55.1% of domestic consumption. Oil production totalled 284m. barrels in 2002. Coal production has virtually ceased. The hydroelectric potential of the country is estimated at some 30,000 MW.

The main exports are food and live animals, which account for some 23.7% of total exports. Principal imports are machinery and mechanical appliances, chemicals, and electrical appliances. In 2001 Brazil was the main purchaser of exports, followed by the USA and Chile. Brazil was also the main supplier of imports, followed by the USA, Germany, the People's Republic of China, Italy and Japan.

Since July 1990 Argentina has actively participated in creating a **Southern Common Market**. A major trade dispute with Brazil about the creation of a balanced market for motor vehicles was resolved in March 2000. In the 1990s the country had made good progress in surmounting the economic problems of the 1980s. President **Menem**'s Government, after first repeating the mistakes of its predecessors, showed itself ready to recognize economic reality and deal with the country's deep-seated problems. The disastrous cycle of military intervention, economic crisis and ineffective civilian government which, in the period 1930–90, took Argentina from being the seventh richest country in the world to being the 77th, was ended. The 'dollarization' of the economy virtually eliminated inflation and brought financial stability and the repatriation of capital for productive investment. However, the trade and fiscal deficits, high levels of unemployment and an overvalued currency recurred in the late 1990s. The Government of President de la Rúa failed to take effective action to rein in government expenditure and was toppled by social unrest in December 2001, but, to its credit, the interim Government of President Eduardo Duhalde was much more successful than anyone had expected, successfully restraining central government expenditure and persuading the provincial governors to accept fiscal discipline.

At the end of 2000 the country's total external debt stood at US $146,172m. The debt-to-GDP ratio stood at 51.4% and debt service at 71.3% of exports of goods and services.

An average annual inflation rate of 25.9% was recorded in 2002 and an unemployment rate of 25%. An estimated 37% of the population were living in poverty.

Aristide, Fr Jean-Bertrand

Jean-Bertrand Aristide, b. 1953, President of Haiti 1991, 1994–96, 2002–04, as a priest in the Salesian order (1982–94) became known as a protector of the poor and an opponent of the dictatorship of **Jean-Claude Duvalier**, son of **Dr François Duvalier**. Despite the opposition of the church hierarchy, he was elected as President in 1990 with the support of the Lavalas Movement, and suspended from the exercise of his priesthood by the Vatican. Ousted by a military coup after only seven months in office, he was eventually restored to power for the balance of his term in 1994 with the help of US military intervention, and dissolved the army. However, distrusted for his radicalism, he received no effective financial support, and after the end of his term in 1996 it proved almost impossible to form an effective government. In 2002 he was elected to a second term, but early in 2004 violence broke out in the north of Haiti and spread to Port-au-Prince. He was rescued from his opponents by US forces and refused to recognize the interim President who replaced him.

Aruba

Aruba is the most westerly of the chain of islands in the southern Caribbean and lies 25 km north of the Venezuelan mainland.

Area: 193 sq km; *capital:* **Oranjestad**; *population:* 93,333 (2002 estimate), four-fifths of mixed Dutch and indigenous (Arawak) descent; *official language:* Dutch; *religion:* Roman Catholic 80%, Protestant 8%.

Constitution: Aruba is part of the Kingdom of the Netherlands together with the Netherlands Antilles, from which it was separated in 1986.

History: Aruba was claimed by the Spanish in 1499 and settled by them, but in the 17th century their position was challenged by the Dutch, who acquired the island from Spain by the Treaty of Munster in 1648. Between that date and 1828 the island was ruled by the Dutch West Indies Co. In 1845 it was attached to Curaçao for administrative purposes and slavery was abolished in 1863. Its modern prosperity dates from the discovery of oil in Venezuela and the decision in 1929 of a subsidiary of the Standard Oil Co to site an oil refinery there. In 1954 the Netherlands Antilles were granted the status of an autonomous federation. Resentment at what Arubans regarded as their exploitation by the other islands led to demands for independence, and separation in 1986 was intended to lead to independence 10 years later. However, following the closure of the Lago refinery in

1985 and the resulting economic downturn, in 1994 it was mutually agreed between the three parts of the Kingdom not to insist on independence for the time being.

International relations and defence: The Netherlands government is responsible for external relations and defence. As an Overseas Territory in association with the **European Union** it forms a co-operative union with the Netherlands Antilles in economic and monetary affairs. The Aruban government has observer status in the **Caribbean Community and Common Market**.

Economy: Since 1987 Aruba has been heavily dependent on tourism, which had already been in relative decline before the disruption caused by the terrorist attacks on the USA in 2001.

Asociación Nacional de Empresarios (ANDE)

National Association of Businessmen, Ecuador

Address: Edif. España, 60, Of. 67, Avda Amazonas 1429 y Colón, Casilla 17-01-
3489, Quito
Telephone: (2) 223-8507
Fax: (2) 250-9806
E-mail: ande@vio.satnet.net

Asociación Nacional Republicana—Partido Colorado (ANR—PC)

National Republican Association—Colorado Party, Paraguay

The right-wing Colorado ('Red') Party was founded in 1887 and has been a major force in Paraguayan politics ever since. It originated in a conservative faction created by Gen. Bernardino Caballero (President of Paraguay 1882–91) and it took its name from the faction's red banners.

The Colorados were in power from 1887 until 1904 when the Liberals replaced them in a popular uprising. They remained in opposition to Liberal governments until the brief Febrerista interlude in 1936–37 and the sudden death in an accident of the war hero Marshal José Félix Estigarribia in 1940. They opposed the pro-Axis regime of Higinio Morínigo, until a Colorado/Partido Revolucionario Febrerista (PRF) coalition Government was installed in 1946 after the USA put pressure on the regime to oust fascist sympathizers. A series of coups and fraudulent elections followed, the PRF were edged out and the Colorados were the only legal party between 1947 and 1963.

The military coup of 5 May 1954 marked the beginning of Gen. **Alfredo Stroessner**'s 35-year dictatorship. Then an army commander, he was officially elected as President in July 1954. In 1956 Stroessner reorganized the party after exiling his main Colorado rival, Epifanio Méndez Fleitas. The 1958 elections were, like all elections held under his rule, completely stage-managed. To give a semblance of democracy, after 1963 selected opposition parties or acceptable factions of parties were permitted to take part (and even win some seats in Congress from 1968 onwards). The manipulated results invariably showed overwhelming support for Stroessner, despite the reality of exile, arrests, long prison sentences and the torture of his political opponents. However, after 1979 an extra-parliamentary opposition, the National Agreement (Acuerdo Nacional), emerged, comprising the Partido Liberal Radical Auténtico (PLRA), the PRF, the Partido Demócrata Cristiano and the Movimiento Popular Colorado, an anti-Stroessner faction of the Colorados.

The violent coup of 3 February 1989 which toppled Stroessner took place shortly before his former close ally and son-in-law, Andrés Rodríguez, was due to be transferred from the position of First Army Commander to the passive role of defence minister. Rodríguez, as interim President, legalized most opposition parties and called a general election for 1 May 1989. As the Colorado Party's presidential candidate, Rodríguez won 78.18% of the valid votes cast and the party polled 72.8% of the vote in the congressional elections. Under the prevailing Constitution, however, the winning party automatically gained two-thirds of the seats in Congress. Promising that he would hold elections in 1993 and not stand for a second term, Rodríguez was sworn in on 15 May 1989 and retained his interim Cabinet.

The ensuing power struggle between the 'traditionalists' and the newly formed 'democratic' wing led, however, to a serious rift in the party. At an extraordinary Colorado convention in February 1993 the military-backed Juan Carlos Wasmosy defeated Dr Luis María Argaña for the party's presidential nomination. Following this rejection, Argaña campaigned against Wasmosy in the May 1993 general elections. Following the elections (won by Wasmosy), Argaña set up a new breakaway party called the Movimiento Reconciliación Nacional—MRN, which formed a rival legislative block with the PLRA and Encuentro Nacional. In late 1994 three generals accused Wasmosy of vote-rigging and officially called for his impeachment. This clash between the Colorado Party and the military continued into 1995, with Gen. Lino César Oviedo Silva emerging as the leader of the fight against Wasmosy. A new party faction was launched, fuelled by Oviedo, which began making overtures to the exiled Albert Stroessner, son of the former dictator, thus prompting the possibility of a new *stronista* faction within the Colorado Party.

In April 1996, however, Oviedo and his supporters attempted to launch a coup, which was defeated after the **Organization of American States** had made it clear that it would not be recognized.

Although imprisoned, Oviedo was chosen as the Colorado candidate for the presidency in 1998. Legally barred from running, he was then replaced by his proposed running mate, Raúl Cubas Grau, who was elected in May 1998 in an election generally regarded as free and fair. On taking office, Cubas commuted Oviedo's sentence and ordered his release. In March 1999 Vice-President Argaña was assassinated and it was widely believed that this was the result of a conspiracy between Cubas and Oviedo. After several days of mounting crisis, with widespread strikes and demonstrations and impeachment pending in Congress, Cubas fled to Brazil, where he was granted political asylum. He was succeeded as President by the President of the Senate, Luis González Macchi, who formed a government of national unity. In a special election held on 13 August 2000 to choose a new Vice-President, the Colorado candidate, Félix Argaña, the brother of the assassinated Vice-President, was narrowly defeated by the PLRA candidate. In the presidential election held on 27 April 2003 the ANR—PC candidate, Oscar Nicanor Duarte Frutos, was victorious. In concurrent congressional elections the Colorado Party obtained 16 seats in the 45-member Senate and 37 seats in the 80-member Chamber of Deputies.

Leadership: Oscar Nicanor Duarte Frutos (President of the Republic)
Address: 25 de Mayo 842, Calle Tacuary, Asunción
Telephone: (21) 44-41-37; 49-86-69
Fax: (21) 44-42-10
E-mail: anr@uninet.com.py

Association of Caribbean States (ACS)
Asociación de Estados del Caribe (AEC)

The ACS was established under a convention signed in Cartagena de Indias, Colombia, on 24 July 1994 to promote consultation, co-operation and concerted action in the Greater Caribbean Basin area by bringing together the Caribbean and Central American states. The member states are: Antigua and Barbuda, the Bahamas, Barbados, Belize, Colombia, Costa Rica, Cuba, Dominica, Dominican Republic, El Salvador, Grenada, Guatemala, Guyana, Haiti, Honduras, Jamaica, Mexico, Nicaragua, Panama, St Christopher and Nevis, St Lucia, St Vincent and the Grenadines, Suriname, Trinidad and Tobago, and Venezuela. There are also four associate members: Aruba, Netherlands Antilles, France (in respect of French Guiana, Guadeloupe and Martinique). The first Summit of Heads of State and/or Government of the ACS was held at Port of Spain, Trinidad and Tobago, on 17–18 August 1995. The 3rd ACS summit was held on 11–12 December 2001, on Margarita Island, Venezuela. A total of 26 countries signed the Margarita Declaration and Plan of Action, which sets out specific goals and targets for the next two years, with a mechanism for monitoring and implementation. The current primary focus is on the areas of trade, transport, sustainable tourism and natural disasters.

Leadership: Prof. Norman Girvan (Sec.-Gen.)

Address: 5–7 Sweet Briar Road, St Clair, PO Box 660, Port of Spain, Trinidad and Tobago

Telephone: (868) 622-9575

Fax: (868) 622-1653

E-mail: mail@acs-aec.org

Internet: www.acs-aec.org

Asunción

Capital city and principal town of Paraguay, situated on the right bank of the Paraguay river; population 513,399 (2002 census).

Autodefensas Unidas de Colombia (AUC)
United Self-Defence Forces of Colombia

A significant contributor to a rising death rate in Colombia in recent years has been the operations of the self-styled AUC, a confederation of right-wing paramilitary forces which was classified by the USA as a terrorist organization in 2001. It claimed at that time to have as many as 10,000 members. It first came to public notice when, following the studied insult to the President by the **Fuerzas Armadas Revolucionarias de Colombia** (FARC) in January 1999, right-wing death squads rampaged through villages across the country killing some 150 civilians. Operations were stepped up following the Los Pozos agreement on 9 February 2001, in the belief that the FARC was yielding to intensified military pressure. In April alone, 80 civilians died as a result of these operations, though in May one of the AUC's senior commanders, Francisco Javier Correa González, was captured by security forces. By June a FARC attack on the AUC headquarters in the Nudo de Paramillo highlands, which drew army units into a series of ambushes, had been succeeded by a nation-wide FARC offensive in which some 200 died. On 11 July the AUC murdered 16 businessmen in Boyacá, and when, on 27 July, the two alleged AUC leaders were arraigned in Bogotá, it was only on the formal offence of the theft and destruction of identity documents. In July 2002, following elections, the leader of the AUC, Carlos Castaño, regrouped his organization to purge it of the associations which had led the USA to classify it as a terrorist organization that financed its operations through drugs-trafficking, and promised to support the new Government if it was unable to fight the guerrillas alone. In April 2004 the Government ordered AUC forces to gather in 'concentration zones' where they could be kept under observation by the **Organization of American States**.

Leadership: Salvatore Mancuso (Leader), Carlos Castaño (Political Leader)

Internet: http://colombia-libre.org/colombialibre/pp.asp

B

Bahamas

The Commonwealth of the Bahamas

Although regarded as part of the Caribbean, the Bahamas lie outside the chain of the Greater Antilles, to the north of Cuba and to the east of Florida. They consist of almost 700 islands and 2,000 cays, though owing to the dry climate many of the islands are uninhabited.

Area: 13,939 sq km; *capital:* **Nassau**, on the largest of the islands, New Providence; *total population:* 304,913 (2001 census), some 85% of African descent, 12% North European and 3% Hispanic; *official language* (the main language in use): English.

Constitution: The Constitution of the Bahamas came into effect at independence in 1973. The head of state, Queen Elizabeth II, is represented by a locally-born Governor-General, who appoints the Prime Minister, and, on the Prime Minister's recommendation, the rest of the Cabinet. Nine of the 16 members of the Senate are appointed on the advice of the Prime Minister, four on the advice of the Leader of the Opposition and three on the advice of both. The representative House of Assembly, which was first established in 1729, has been chosen by universal adult suffrage since 1962, and has 40 members.

History: The island of San Salvador (formerly Watling Island) is traditionally believed to be the place where **Christopher Columbus** made his first landfall in the New World in 1492. Within two or three decades all of the native Lacayans had been enslaved and deported. Thereafter, the islands were uninhabited, except by pirates, until the first Puritan settlers arrived in Eleuthera in 1647. Nassau was founded in 1666, and a representative House of Assembly established in 1729. In the American War of Independence the colony was briefly captured by the colonists in 1776 and by the Spanish in 1782, but was restored to British rule after 1783, when a substantial number of settlers arrived from the mainland. Although black property-owners were allowed to vote as early as 1807, the colony was tightly controlled by the so-called 'Bay Street Boys' until the secret ballot was extended to the 'Out Islands' in 1949.

International relations and defence: The Bahamas are a member of the United Nations, the **Organization of American States**, the **Commonwealth**, the **Caribbean Community and Common Market**, and the **Rio Pact**. The US government remains very concerned at the extent to which the islands are used by drugs-traffickers to circumvent controls elsewhere, as well as at the standard of regulation of the financial services industry. Illegal immigrants from Haiti use the islands as a transit point. The islands' only defence is provided by the 860-strong Royal Bahamian Defence Force (coastguard) and 2,300 police officers.

Economy: The Bahamas are one of the most prosperous territories in the Americas, with gross domestic product (GDP) per caput in 2001 of US $16,250. The Bahamian dollar is fixed at par with the US dollar. Heavy foreign investment in tourism in the 1990s declined after the terrorist attacks on the USA in 2001. There is a limited amount of commercial fishing in the 'Out Islands', where economic activity varies widely. There is no personal income tax or corporation tax in the islands, the bulk of the government's revenues deriving from import duties, with some 11% from taxes relating to tourism. In recent years the government has run a deficit, the debt-service ratio being some 4.1% of the estimated total value of exports of goods and services in 2001.

Balaguer, Joaquín

Joaquín Vidella Balaguer y Ricardo (1907–2002), President of the Dominican Republic 1960–62, 1966–78, 1986–96, held a number of government offices during the dictatorship of Gen. Rafael Trujillo. As a trusted supporter of the regime, he was nominated as Vice-President to Trujillo's brother, Héctor, and became figurehead President when Héctor resigned, shortly before Trujillo himself was assassinated in 1961. Distrusted by all sides, Balaguer was soon deposed by the army. However, after the US intervention in 1965, he re-emerged as a candidate of the right and was elected as President in 1966. He was re-elected in 1970, after a term marked by steady economic growth and limited social reforms, and re-elected again in 1974. The elections in 1970 and 1974 were boycotted by the left, but with their participation in 1978 Balaguer was defeated. He returned to power in 1986, and though by this time almost completely blind, was re-elected in 1992, having presided over the building of a vast lighthouse to commemorate the quincentenary of the bringing of Christianity to the New World in 1492. This, his last term of office, was curtailed by two years owing to political violence and allegations of electoral fraud and corruption.

Bananas

The banana, *musa sapientum*, is not a tree, but a large herb, capable of attaining a height of 9 m. Cultivated varieties are seedless hybrids and are reproduced by planting out shoots from the main rhizome. They are fast-growing and can be ready to produce within a year. In 2002 Ecuador was the second largest banana-growing country in the world (after India) and the largest in the Western hemisphere, producing 6m. metric tons. Brazil was a close second, followed, at some distance, by Costa Rica and Mexico. Bananas are the main cash crop in St Lucia, Martinique, St Vincent and the Grenadines, Guadeloupe, Dominica, Ecuador, Honduras and Costa Rica, and are usually the second largest source of export revenue in Colombia after **coffee**. They are important to the economies of Belize and Panama, but contribute only a small proportion of Brazil's export earnings. Most (70%) of the bananas from the Windward Islands are exported to the United Kingdom and those from Guadeloupe and Martinique to France. However, in September 1995 the USA (which, unlike the **European Union** (EU), is not itself a banana-producer) lodged with the newly formed **World Trade Organization** (WTO) a formal complaint against the EU quota system for bananas from the Windward Islands, in support of the US companies which trade in bananas from Latin America. In 1999 the WTO, for only the second time in its history, authorized the USA to levy punitive sanctions on the EU and it was not until 2001 that a compromise was reached, allowing Latin American producers a larger share of the European market.

Banco Central de Bolivia
Central Bank of Bolivia

Central bank of issue of Bolivia; f. 1911 as Banco de la Nación; present name adopted 1928; nationalized in 1952.
 Leadership: Dr Juan Antonio Morales Anaya (Pres.)
 Address: Avda Ayacucho, esq. Mercado, Casilla 3118, La Paz
 Telephone: (2) 237-4151
 Fax: (2) 239-2398
 E-mail: vmarquez@mail.bcb.gov.bo
 Internet: www.bcb.gov.bo

Banco Central do Brasil
Central Bank of Brazil

Central bank of issue of Brazil; f. 1965; operates under the supervision of the Conselho Monetário Nacional.

Leadership: Henrique Meirelles (Pres.)

Address: Q03, Bloco B, CP 04-0170, 70074-900 Brasília, DF

Telephone: (61) 414-2401

Fax: (61) 321-9453

E-mail: cap.secre@bcb.gov.br

Internet: www.bcb.gov.br

Banco Central de Chile
Central Bank of Chile

State-owned bank of issue; f. 1926; granted autonomy 1989.

Leadership: Vitttorio Cobbo (Pres.)

Address: Agustinas 1180, Santiago

Telephone: (2) 670-2000

Fax: (2) 670-5094

E-mail: mforno@bech.cl

Internet: www.bancoestado.cl

Banco Central de Costa Rica
Central Bank of Costa Rica

Leadership: Eduardo Lizano Fait (Pres.)

Address: Avdas Central y Primera, Calles 2 y 4, Apdo 10.035, 1000 San José

Telephone: 233-4233

Fax: 233-5930

Internet: www.bccr.fi.cr

Banco Central de Cuba
Central Bank of Cuba

State-owned sole bank of issue; f. 1997.

Leadership: Francisco Soberón Valdez

Address: Calle Cuba 402, Aguiar 411, Habana Vieja, La Habana
Telephone: (7) 33-8003
Fax: (7) 66-6601
E-mail: plasencia@bc.gov.cu
Internet: www.bc.gov.cu

Banco Central del Ecuador
Central Bank of Ecuador

Sole bank of issue; f. 1927.
  Leadership: Mauricio Yépez (Pres.)
  Address: Avda 10 de Agosto y Briceño, Plaza Bolívar, Casilla 339, Quito
  Telephone: (2) 258-2577
  Fax: (2) 295-0158
  E-mail: uweb@uio.bce.fin.ec
  Internet: www.bce.fin.ec

Banco Central de Honduras (BANTRAL)
Central Bank of Honduras

Bank of issue; f. 1950.
  Leadership: María Elena Mondragón (Pres.)
  Address: Avda Juan Ramón Molina, 7a Avda y la Calle, Apdo 3165, Tegucigalpa
  Telephone: 327-2270
  Fax: 237-1879
  Internet: www.bch.hn

Banco Central de Nicaragua
Central Bank of Nicaragua

Sole bank of issue and government fiscal agent; f. 1961; nationalized 1979.
  Leadership: Dr Mario Alonzo Icabalceta (Pres.)
  Address: Carretera Sur, Km 7, Apdos 2252/3, Zona 5, Managua
  Telephone: (2) 65-0500
  Fax: (2) 65-0651
  E-mail: bcn@bcn.gob.ni
  Internet: www.bcn.gob.ni

Banco Central del Paraguay
Central Bank of Paraguay

Sole bank of issue; f. 1952.
Leadership: Juan Antonio Ortiz Vely (Pres.)
Address: Avda Federación Rusa y Avda Sargento Marecos, Casilla 861, Barrio
Santo Domingo, Asunción
Telephone: (21) 61-0088
Fax: (21) 60-8149
E-mail: ccs@bcp.gov.py
Internet: www.bcp.com.py

Banco Central de la República Argentina
Central Bank of the Argentine Republic

Central reserve bank of the Argentine Republic; f. 1935, with right of note issue; all
capital held by the State.
Leadership: Alfonso Prat-Gay (Pres.)
Address: Reconquista 266, 1003 Buenos Aires
Telephone: (11) 4348-3500
Fax: (11) 4348-3955
E-mail: sistema@bcra.gov.ar
Internet: www.bcra.gov.ar

Banco Central de la República Dominicana
Central Bank of the Dominican Republic

Bank of issue; f. 1947.
Leadership: José Luis Malkun
Address: Pedro Henríquez Ureña, esq. Leopoldo Navarro, Apdo 1347, Santo
Domingo, DN
Telephone: (809) 221-9111
Fax: 687-7488
E-mail: info@bancentral.gov.do
Internet: www.bancentral.gov.do

Banco Central de Reserva de El Salvador
Central Reserve Bank of El Salvador

Sole bank of issue; f. 1935; nationalized 1961.
  Leadership: Luz María de Portillo (Pres.)
  Address: Alameda Juan Pablo II y 17 Avda Norte, Apdo 01-106, San Salvador
  Telephone: 281-8000
  Fax: 281-8113
  E-mail: comunicaciones@bcr.gob.sv
  Internet: www.bcr.gob.sv

Banco Central de Reserva del Perú
Central Reserve Bank of Peru

Bank of issue; f. 1922; refounded 1931.
  Leadership: Javier Silva Rueta (Pres.)
  Address: Jirón Antonio Miró Quesada 441-115, Lima 1
  Telephone: (1) 427-6250
  Fax: (1) 427-5880
  Internet: www.bcrp.gob.pe

Banco Central del Uruguay
Central Bank of Uruguay

Sole bank of issue; responsible for oversight of banking system; f. 1967.
  Leadership: Julio de Brun (Pres.)
  Address: Avda Juan P. Fabrini 777, Casilla 1467, 11100 Montevideo
  Telephone: 5982-1967
  Fax: (2) 902-6578
  E-mail: secgral@bcu.gub.uy
  Internet: www.bcu.gub.uy

Banco Central de Venezuela
Central Bank of Venezuela

  Leadership: Diego Luis Castellanos Escalona (Pres.)
  Address: Avda Urdaneta, esq. De las Carmelitas, Caracas
  Telephone: (212) 801-5111

Fax: (212) 861-0048
E-mail: info@bcv.org.ve
Internet: www.bcv.org.ve

Banco Centroamericano de Integración Económica (BCIE)
Central American Bank for Regional Integration

The Bank was founded in 1961 to promote the economic development and integration of the Central American states. Member states are: Costa Rica, El Salvador, Guatemala, Honduras and Nicaragua; non-regional members are: Argentina, the People's Republic of China, Colombia and Mexico. The Bank operates within the Central American Economic System (**Sistema de la Integración Centroamericana**) and has an authorized capital of US $2,000m.

Leadership: Pablo Schneider (Pres.)
Address: Blvd Suyapa, contigua a Banco de Honduras, Apdo 772, Tegucigalpa, Honduras
Telephone: 228-2182
Fax: 228-2183
E-mail: jarevalo@bcie.org and webmail-hn@bcie.org
Internet: www.bcie.hn

Banco de Guatemala
Bank of Guatemala

State central bank; f. 1946.
Leadership: Lizardo Arturo Sosa López (Pres.)
Address: 7a Avda 22-01, Zona 1, Apdo 2306, Guatemala City
Telephone: 230-6222
Fax: 253-4035
E-mail: webmaster@banguat.gob.gt
Internet: www.banguat.gob.gt

Banco Hipotecario Nacional
National Mortgage Bank, Panama

Government-sponsored bank; f. in 1973 to fund small-scale building projects; oversees the national savings system.

Leadership: Miguel Angel Cárdenas (Pres.); Waldo Arrocho (Gen.-Man.)
Address: Edif. Peña Prieta, Avda Balboa y Calle 40, Bella Vista, Apdo 222, Panamá 1
Telephone: 227-0055
Fax: 225-6956
E-mail: bhn@sinfo.net

Banco de México (BANXICO)
Bank of Mexico

State central bank of issue; f. 1925; granted autonomy 1994.
Leadership: Guillermo Ortiz Martinez (Pres.)
Address: Avda 5 de Mayo 2, Apdo 98 bis, 06059 México, DF
Telephone: (55) 5237-2000
Fax: (55) 5237-2370
E-mail: sidaoui@banxico.org.mx
Internet: www.banxico.org.mx

Banco de la Nación Argentina
Bank of the Argentine Nation

Government-owned commercial bank, the largest in Argentina with 617 branches; f. 1891.
Leadership: Horacio Ernesto Pericoli (Pres.)
Address: Bartolome Mitre 326, 1036 Buenos Aires
Telephone: (11) 4347-6000
Fax: (11) 4347-6316
E-mail: gerencia@bna.com.ar
Internet: www.bna.com.ar

Banco Nacional de Desarrollo Agrícola (BANDESA)
National Bank of Agricultural Development, Guatemala

State bank for the promotion of agricultural development; f. 1971.
Leadership: Gustavo Adolfo Real Castellanos (Gen.-Man.)
Address: 9a Calle 9–47, Zona 1, Apdo 350, Guatemala City
Telephone: 253-5222
Fax: 253-7927

Banco Nacional de Fomento
National Development Bank, Paraguay

State bank founded in Paraguay in 1961 to take over the deposit and private banking activities of the Banco del Paraguay. It now has 52 branches.

Leadership: Lic. Germán Rojas Irigoyen (Pres.)
Address: Independencia Nacional y Cerro Corá, Casilla 134, Asunción
Telephone: (21) 44-3762
Fax: (21) 44-4502
E-mail: correo@bnf.gov.py
Internet: www.bnf.gov.py

Banco Nacional de Panamá
National Bank of Panama

Government-owned bank of issue, f. 1904. Under legislation passed in 1998 it and all other banks in Panama operate under the supervision of the Superintendencia de Bancos, originally founded in 1970 to license and control all banking activities on and from Panamanian soil. The balboa's parity with the US dollar means that, to all intents and purposes, the dollar is the local currency. Hence, the Bank can effectively only issue currency for local use and has little control over the money supply, other than by creating credit against existing monetary resources.

Leadership: Roosevelt Thayer G. (Pres.)
Address: Torre BNP, Vía España, Apdo 5220, Panama 5
Telephone: 263-5151; 263-7901
Fax: 269-0091
E-mail: bnpvalores@cwp.net.pa
Internet: www.banconal.com.pa

Banco de la República
Bank of the Republic, Colombia

Sole bank of issue; f. 1923.

Address: Carrera 7a, No. 14–78, 5°, Apdo Aéreo 3551, Santafé de Bogotá, DC
Telephone: (1) 343-1111
Fax: (1) 286-1686
E-mail: wbanco@banrep.gov.co
Internet: www.banrep.gov.co

Bank of Guyana

Central bank of issue and regulatory authority for the banking sector; f. 1965.
  Leadership: Dolly S. Singh (Gov.), Lawrence T. Williams (Man.)
  Address: 1 Church St and Ave of the Republic, PO Box 1003, Georgetown
  Telephone: (22) 63250-9
  Fax: (22) 72965
  E-mail: communications@bankofguyana.org.gy
  Internet: www.bankofguyana.org.gy

Bank of Jamaica

Central bank of issue and regulatory authority for the banking sector; f. 1960.
  Leadership: Derick Milton Latibeaudière (Gov.)
  Address: Nethersole Pl., POB 621, Kingston
  Telephone: 922-0752
  Fax: 922-0854
  E-mail: info@boj.org.jm
  Internet: www.boj.org.jm

Bank van de Nederlandse Antillen
Bank of the Netherlands Antilles

F. 1818 as the Curaçaosche Bank; adopted present name 1962.
  Leadership: Ralph Palm (Chair.), Emsley D. Tromp (Pres.)
  Address: Simon Bolivar Plein 1, Willemstad, Curaçao
  Telephone: (9) 434-5500
  Fax: (9) 461-5004
  E-mail: info@centralbank.an
  Internet: www.central bank.an

Banque de la République d'Haïti
Bank of the Republic of Haiti

F. 1911 as the Banque Nationale de la République d'Haïti; renamed 1979; sole bank of issue.
  Leadership: Venel Joseph (Pres.)

Address: angle rues du Magazin de l'Etat et des Miracles, BP 1570,
        Port-au-Prince
Telephone: 299-1200
Fax: 299-1045; 299-1145
E-mail: brh_adm@brh.net
Internet: www.brh.net

Bánzer Suárez, Hugo

Hugo Bánzer Suárez (1926–2001), *de facto* President of Bolivia from 1971 to 1978, was born in Santa Cruz de la Sierra. The son of a military hero of the Chaco War and the grandson of German immigrants, he was educated at the Military College in **La Paz**, and was chosen for further training at the School of the Americas, Panama Canal Zone, in 1955 and the Armoured Cavalry School, Fort Hood, Texas, USA, in 1960, reaching the rank of colonel in 1961. He served as Minister of Education in the Government of Gen. René Barrientos until posted as military attaché to Washington, DC, in 1967. On the death of Barrientos in 1969 he was recalled to serve briefly (1969–70) as director of the Military College.

The armed forces at the time were seriously divided by political faction, and early in 1971 Gen. Juan José Torres seized power in a military coup, proposing a radical, left-wing programme with a strong resemblance to that of neighbouring Peru. After only four months, he in turn was overthrown in a coup led by Bánzer, with the support of the **Movimiento Nacionalista Revolucionaria**, the Frente Popular Nacionalista and, no less importantly, of the Brazilian military Government. Bánzer became *de facto* President. Then, in 1974, he carried out a so-called coup within the coup (*autogolpe*), imposing an authoritarian military regime which forcibly repressed political dissent, even among the farm workers who had hitherto supported his Government. The brief economic boom which followed soon gave way to rising inflation and growing debt, and in 1978 Bánzer yielded to pressure from the USA to hold elections, which, in the event, were so fraudulent that there was widespread unrest. In response, Bánzer's electoral protégé, Gen. Juan Pereda, denounced his mentor and overthrew him.

For almost 20 years Bánzer, with the backing of his party, the right-wing **Acción Democrática Nacionalista**—ADN, *Nationalist Democratic Action)* sought to return to power. In the 1985 presidential election he headed the poll, but was denied office by Congress. In 1997 he was finally successful, and returned to office as constitutional President. In August 2001, however, he was diagnosed with terminal cancer and resigned, being succeeded by Vice-President Jorge Fernando Quiroga Ramírez.

Barbados

Barbados, the most easterly of the Lesser Antilles, lies to the east of the main island chain, in the Atlantic, 160 km (100 miles) east of St Vincent and the Grenadines.

Area overall: 430 sq km (166 sq miles); *capital:* **Bridgetown**; *population:* 276,607 (2002 estimate), comprising Africans 89%, Europeans 3%; *official language:* English; *religion:* mainly Anglican, 40%, Pentecostalists 8%, Methodists 7%, Roman Catholics 4%. The synagogue stands on the site of one of the first two synagogues established in the Americas.

Constitution: Barbados is a constitutional monarchy within the **Commonwealth**, the present Constitution dating from independence on 30 November 1966. The head of state is HM Queen Elizabeth II, who is represented by a Governor-General. There is a bicameral legislature consisting of a Senate of 21 appointed members (12 appointed on the advice of the Prime Minister, two on the advice of the leader of the opposition, and seven representing various interests) and a House of Assembly of 30 members elected by universal adult suffrage. The Prime Minister is chosen by the Governor-General with regard to his likely ability to command a majority in the House of Assembly and chooses a Cabinet that is accountable to the House.

History: By 1627, when the first English setters arrived, the island had already been depopulated. The first settlers were smallholders, but after **sugar** was introduced in the 17th century many more slaves were imported, accounting for 47% of the population in 1655 and 77% in 1712. Slave revolts in 1675, 1692, 1702 and 1816 were forcibly suppressed. The House of Assembly was first established in 1639 and its powers were confirmed by the Charter of Barbados granted in 1652. This, however, acted as a brake on reform in the 19th century, and it was only in the 1930s that the rise of the labour movement enabled poorer Bajans to have an outlet for their political aspirations. After the serious riots of 1937, in which 14 people were killed, the Barbados Progressive League was formed, gaining its first five seats in the House in 1940. Universal adult suffrage was granted in 1950 and, following the collapse of the West Indies Federation in 1962, Barbados gained full independence in 1966.

International relations and defence: Barbados is a member of the United Nations, the **Organization of American States**, the Commonwealth and the **Caribbean Community and Common Market**. The Barbados Defence Force has a total strength of 610, including coastguard units, and there is a small reserve force.

Economy: Barbados is a relatively prosperous middle-income country, with an estimated gross domestic product per caput of US $9,444 in 2001. As a result of falling production, Barbados was unable in 1991–95 to meet the **European Union** quota for sugar under the Lomé Convention, and its US sugar quota was cut in 1995. The mainstay of the economy is now tourism and there is a significant financial services sector. In 2002 Barbados was removed from the OECD list of 'tax havens' after protests that it had been unfairly included in the first place.

Barbuda – *see* Antigua and Barbuda

Basse-Terre

Basse-Terre, founded 1643, capital of the French Overseas Department of Guadeloupe, is situated on Basse-Terre on the south-west part of the island of Guadeloupe, and had a population of 14,000 in 2002. The main settlement on the island, which had a population of some 100,000, was Pointe-à-Pitre on Grande-Terre adjoining the Sallée river, which separates it from Basse-Terre.

Basseterre

Basseterre is the chief town of St Christopher (St Kitts) and capital of the federated state of St Christopher and Nevis. A seaport, it is situated on the south-western coast of the island and had a population of 14,000 in 2002. It was founded in 1627, as a result of the first British settlement in the Caribbean.

Batlle Ibáñez, Jorge

Jorge Luis Batlle Ibáñez, President of Uruguay since 2000, was born in **Montevideo** in 1927. He took his law degree in 1956 and was elected to the National Assembly in 1958. He first contested the presidency in 1966, without success, under the old system of *lemas* (fractions of parties competing under the same banner). Though not a supporter of the Tupamaro guerrillas, he was a strong critic of the Bordaberry Government and was detained for a time in 1972, before all political activity was suspended by the military in the following year. With the return of democracy in 1984 he was elected as a Senator and in 1989 was chosen as the presidential candidate of the Partido Colorado, but was defeated by **Luis Alberto Lacalle** of the **Partido Nacional** (PN). Nudged out by a fellow-Colorado in 1994, in 1999, in the first presidential election to be held under the new, two-stage system, he came second in the first round of voting, but emerged as the winner in the second, and, in face of the serious economic crisis, formed a coalition government with strong PN representation. By October 2002 the first report had been published by the commission that Batlle had promised would investigate the fate of Uruguay's 'disappeared' and, despite union protests, the austerity measures he introduced were sufficient to carry Uruguay through the effects of the economic crisis in neighbouring Argentina, which at one stage had threatened to push the country into default.

Batlle y Ordóñez, José

José Batlle y Ordóñez (1856–1929), President of Uruguay 1903–07 and 1911–15, was the social reformer who laid the foundations for the Uruguayan welfare state and consolidated Uruguayan democracy. In his first term he successfully (1904) defeated the last of the military coups that had plagued the country in the 19th century, and in his second he introduced the concept of a collegiate executive which was later adopted. The dominance of the **Partido Colorado** in the 20th century owed much to the principles of *batllismo*.

Bauxite

The most important ore from which aluminium is recovered, consisting of aluminium oxide or aluminium hydroxide in various proportions mixed with other minerals. Named after the town of Les Baux in France, it is found widely throughout the world, but is costly to transport other than by sea and requires large quantities of electrical energy to extract the metal. Bauxite was first exploited in Guyana in the 1920s and the country dominated the market for bauxite between 1960 and 1980, when its share declined owing to competition from the People's Republic of China and Brazil. In 2001 Brazil was the world's third largest producer (after Australia and Guinea) and the largest in Latin America, followed closely by Jamaica. The mineral is Suriname's largest source of foreign exchange. Argentina, Brazil, Mexico and Venezuela are the largest producers of aluminium in Latin America.

Belaúnde Terry, Fernando

Fernando Belaúnde Terry (1912–2002), President of Peru 1963–68 and 1980–85, was born in Arequipa, brought up in an upper middle-class family, and qualified as an architect at the University of Texas in 1935. Architecture spurred his interest in politics, and in 1945–48 he served as a member of Congress. On the military coup of Gen. Odría in 1948, however, Congress was dissolved and Belaúnde returned to architecture, serving as Dean of architecture at the National Engineering University from 1955 to 1960. Military intervention in 1962 to forestall an electoral victory by the **Alianza Popular Revolucionaria Americana** left the way open for the election of Belaúnde in the 1963 elections. However, his failure to deal adequately with the problem of illegal oil leases led to his overthrow in 1968 and the imposition of a reforming military government under Gen. **Juan Velasco Alvarado**. With the restoration of civilian government in 1979, however, traditional voting patterns reasserted themselves and Belaúnde was elected to a second term. On the day of his inauguration, however, Lima was plunged into darkness by the guerrilla movement **Sendero Luminoso**, and over the next five years, while the movement grew and spread, measures to counter it appeared wholly ineffectual.

Belize

Belice

Belize, the second smallest state in Central America in area and the least populous, lies on the Caribbean coast of the Central American isthmus, bounded to the north by Mexico, and to the west and south by Guatemala (which maintains a territorial claim to the southern part of Belize).

Area: 22,965 sq km (8,867 sq miles); *capital:* **Belmopan**; *population:* 257,310 (2001 estimate), comprising mestizos 46%, creoles 28%, Amerindians 10%, Garifuna 6%, and recent immigrants 10%; *official language:* English (owing to heavy recent immigration, Spanish is now widely spoken); *religion:* Roman Catholic 51%, other Christian denominations 27%.

Constitution: Belize is a constitutional monarchy within the **Commonwealth**. The present Constitution came into effect at independence on 21 September 1981. The head of state is HM Queen Elizabeth II, who is represented by a Governor-General. The National Assembly consists of two houses, a nominated Senate of eight members and a House of Representatives of 29 members directly elected by universal adult suffrage. The Prime Minister is the member of the House of Representatives chosen by the Governor-General as most likely to command a majority, and appoints the other members of the Cabinet. The Cabinet is accountable for its actions to the House.

History: By the time that Spanish explorers arrived in what is now Belize, it had been all but abandoned by its original Mayan inhabitants. The first European settlers in the bay area, therefore, were British buccaneers, who made use of the many inlets and cays along the coast to mount profitable raids on Spanish ships. Eventually, in 1763, the settlers gained the right to cut logwood and from 1786 onwards the area, then known as British Honduras, was governed by British administrators. Finally, by the Treaty of Amiens in 1802, Spain recognized British sovereignty, and in 1862 British Honduras was designated a Crown Colony.

Unfortunately, after gaining independence from Spain, Guatemala began to claim the area as part of its national territory, though in fact it had not at any time formed part of the former Spanish province of that name. In 1859, however, Guatemala recognized the colony's boundaries and Britain undertook to build a cart road from the coast to link up with one from Guatemala City. The road, however, was never built and in 1945 Guatemala used this as a pretext to abrogate the 1859 Treaty, having tried unsuccessfully in 1940 to persuade the other American states to agree to it taking possession of the territory in the event of British defeat by Germany, which the then dictator of Guatemala, Jorge Ubico, confidently expected.

Britain, however, was not defeated and in 1954 elections were held in the colony under universal suffrage for the first time, in which the People's United Party (PUP), led by George Price, was victorious. However, in 1961 Belize, the capital, was devastated by a **hurricane** so severe that it was decided to construct a new administrative capital inland at Belmopan. In 1964 self-government was granted, prompting Guatemala to break off diplomatic relations with the United Kingdom, and in 1972 the new capital was occupied. In the following year the name Belize replaced that of British Honduras as the name of the territory as a whole. Though Guatemala still remained firmly opposed, Price was successful in winning support for the self-determination of Belize from the other Caribbean states and, in 1980, by an overwhelming majority, from the UN General Assembly. In spite of Guatemala's last-minute withdrawal of its acceptance of this decision, Belize became independent on 21 September 1981.

In the elections of 1984 the PUP was defeated by the United Democratic Party (UDP), led by Manuel Esquivel, who became Prime Minister. The UDP, with its strength in the south of the country, opposed concessions to Guatemala, but was defeated in 1989, when Price returned to power. In 1991 a new Guatemalan government officially recognized the right of the people of Belize to self-determination and established diplomatic relations; in return, Belize granted Guatemala access to its ports on the Caribbean coast. However, after the British garrison had been run down and the PUP defeated in the 1993 elections, in March 1994 Guatemala formally reaffirmed its claim to Belize.

Latest elections: In a general election held on 5 March 2003 the PUP, led by Said Musa, won 53.2% of the votes cast and 22 seats in the House of Representatives. The opposition UDP, meanwhile, received 45.6% of the votes cast and won seven seats in the House.

International relations and defence: Belize is a member of the United Nations, the **Organization of American States** (OAS), the Commonwealth, the **Latin American Integration Association** (*Asociación Latinoamericana de Integración*) and the **Sistema de la Integración Centroamericana** (*Central American Integration System*). The Belize Defence Force, founded in 1978, has a regular strength of 1,050, with 700 reserves. In 1994 the British garrison forces were withdrawn from Belize, leaving a small contingent of some 30 instructors in jungle warfare. As a member of the OAS, Belize is entitled to draw on the support of the Organization in the event of an attack by Guatemala.

Belize, economy

GNI: US $727m. (2001); *GNI per caput:* $2,940 (2001); *exports:* $269.1m. (2001); *imports:* $460.5m. (2001); *currency:* Belizean dollar, plural dollars; US $1 = BZ $2 since May 1976.

In 2001 agriculture, forestry and fishing accounted for 15.5% of Belize's gross domestic product (GDP), industry for 13.0% and services for 87.1%. Some 2.8% of the land is arable, 1.7% under permanent crops, 2.2% permanent pasture and most of the remainder forest and woodland. The main cash crops are **sugar** cane, citrus fruits and **bananas**; rice, maize, beans and other vegetables are grown for local consumption. The timber industry has been in decline for some years. Livestock are raised for domestic use only. The only mineral resource to be worked is limestone. The principal industries are sugar refining, brewing and production of citrus concentrate and soft drinks. The main energy source is hydroelectric power, though dam construction has been delayed because of environmental concerns. Only very small amounts of petroleum have been located despite many years of exploration. In 2002 tourism was the country's second largest earner of foreign exchange, accounting for some 22% of GDP.

Main exports are food and live animals. Principal imports are food and live animals, mineral fuels and lubricants and manufactured articles. In 2002 the United Kingdom was the principal market for Belize's exports, followed by the USA. The USA was the greatest supplier of imports, followed by Mexico. With the downturn in world trade in 2000, the deficit on the current account has widened significantly. Agriculture and forestry, which, together with tourism, constitute the mainstay of the Belizean economy, have suffered severely in recent years from the impact of '**Hurricane** Keith' in October 2000 and 'Hurricane Iris' in October 2001. Annual GDP growth was 12.1% in 1999, and 8.9% in 2000. In 2001 the annual growth rate declined to 4.6%, but rose to 6% in 2002. The average annual rate of inflation in 2001 was 1.2%. Unemployment stood at about 13% in 2003.

Belmopan

Belmopan, the capital of Belize since 1971, had a population of 8,130 at the 2000 census.

Bermuda

Bermuda is situated in the North Atlantic, 900 km (560 miles) east of Cape Hatteras, North Carolina, USA, and north-west of the Bahamas, and comprises some 138 islands of which only 20 are inhabited.

Area overall: 53.3 sq km (20.59 sq miles); *capital:* **Hamilton**, on Great Bermuda; *population:* 65,545 (2001 census), comprising Africans 58%, Europeans 36%; *official language:* English; *religion:* Anglican 28%, African Episcopalian Methodists.

Constitution: Bermuda is a Crown Colony of the United Kingdom, and is the oldest British colony, established in 1684. The Constitution of 8 June 1968 gave it full internal self-government. The head of state is HM Queen Elizabeth II, who is represented by a Governor, who retains responsibility for external affairs, defence and internal security. The legislature consists of two houses: a nominated Senate of 11 members and a House of Assembly of 36 members directly elected for a term of up to five years by universal adult suffrage. The Governor appoints the majority leader in the Assembly as Premier and the Premier chooses the other members of the Cabinet, which is accountable for its actions to the House. All British citizens over the age of 18 who have established the necessary residence requirements are entitled to vote.

History: Bermuda takes its name from a Spanish sailor who visited the islands in the early 16th century. British settlement began in the 17th century.

Latest elections: At elections held on 23 July 2003 the Progressive Labour Party, led by Premier W. Alex Scott, retained power, winning 22 seats in the 36-member House. The United Bermuda Party, meanwhile, won 14 seats.

International relations and defence: The Bermuda Regiment is raised locally by selective conscription and had a strength of approximately 650 in 1999.

Economy: In 1999–2000 Bermuda's gross domestic product (GDP) amounted to US $2,623.9m., while GDP per head totalled US $34,600, one of the highest per caput rates in the world, reflecting the island's status as a luxury tourist destination. In addition to tourism, financial services also contribute to the high level of national income, 87.1% of the labour force working in the services sector in 2000. Manufacturing and construction accounted for less than 10% of GDP in 2000. The island has no significant exports and, as a consequence, maintains a substantial deficit on its visible trade. The main imports are food, beverages and tobacco, machinery and fuel.

Betancourt, Rómulo

Rómulo Betancourt (1908–81) was provisional President of Venezuela in 1945–48, and President in 1959–64. Born in Guatire, Department of Miranda, Betancourt was educated at the Liceo Caracas and took part in the student protests of 1928 against the dictatorship of Gen. Juan Vicente Gómez. After a brief spell in prison he escaped to Colombia and remained active in politics, joining the Communist Party in 1930. After the death of Gómez in 1936 he returned to Venezuela to take part in left-wing agitation and was again exiled in 1939. In 1941 he returned to Venezuela and founded **Acción Democrática** (AD), which, in 1945, in alliance with junior army officers, led the revolt that toppled Gen. Isaías Medina Angarita. The provisional Government established thereafter carried out significant social reforms, wrote a new constitution and held the country's first direct presidential elections. These gave the AD candidate, the novelist Rómulo Gallegos, a large majority, but he was overthrown by the armed forces within months and a new dictatorship was established. It was not until January 1958 that Gen. Marcos Pérez Jiménez (1948–58) was overthrown by a military coup, and Betancourt returned from exile to try to establish a stable democracy. Under the Pact of Punto Fijo the three main political parties agreed to share power, thus combining to defeat the threat from the right of renewed military intervention and, from the left, of a Cuban-style uprising backed by radical insurgents in the armed forces. In 1964 Betancourt handed over power peacefully to his elected successor, inaugurating 30 years of stable democracy in Venezuela.

Betancur Cuartas, Belisario

Belisario Betancur Cuartas, President of Colombia in 1982–86, was born in 1923 in Amagá, Department of Antioquia, into an extremely poor family. He studied for the priesthood and though expelled for lack of vocation he eventually won a scholarship to the Universidad Pontificia Bolivariana, where he studied law. In 1946 he was elected a deputy for the **Partido Conservador Colombiano**, but being active in the opposition to the dictatorship of Gen. Rojas Pinilla, he was imprisoned on several occasions and was chosen as Conservative candidate for the presidency for the first time in 1962. After three further vain attempts to gain the presidency, he was successful in 1982 owing to a split in the dominant **Partido Liberal Colombiano**. As President he worked tirelessly to bring peace and was successful in reaching an accord with three of the four guerrilla movements then active in the country (the **Fuerzas Armadas Revolucionarias Colombianas** (FARC), Movimiento 19 de Abril (M-19) and the Ejército Popular de Liberación), which included not only an opening to legal participation in politics but also a far-reaching programme of social reform. Betancur's foreign policy, which incorporated support for the Contadora peace process and a *rapprochement* with Cuba, was equally innovative. However, when the FARC tried to reconstitute itself as a legal political party, the Unión Patriótica, its only senator and many of its candidates were assassinated. Then, in December 1985, the M-19, tiring of the dialogue, seized the Palace of Justice and took more than 100 hostages, most of whom died when the army stormed the building. Though the peace process lingered on under later Presidents, the opportunity for a lasting settlement had been lost.

Bogotá, Santafé de

Santafé de Bogotá (more generally known simply as Bogotá) is the chief city and capital of Colombia. It is situated in its own Capital District area . It lies on a high plateau east of the Andes within the Department of Cundinamarca and had a population estimated at 5,132,000 in 2002. The present city, founded in 1538, bears a variant of the name of its predecessor, Bacatá, the chief site of the Chibcha Indians. As the former capital of the Spanish Viceroyalty of New Granada, it became the capital of the confederation of Gran Colombia and later of New Granada and modern Colombia and remains an important cultural centre with significant industrial and commercial development.

Bolívar, Simón

Simón Bolívar (1783–1830), 'the Liberator', led the revolutions against Spanish rule in New Granada (now Colombia, Venezuela, and Ecuador), Peru, and Upper Peru (now Bolivia), and served as President of both Colombia (1821–30) and Peru

(1823–29), without being paid for either job. Born in Venezuela and educated in Europe, he joined the movement for independence in 1811 but was forced into exile at the Spanish reconquest in 1814. He returned in 1819 to make a daring attack on New Granada, leading some 2,500 men over routes previously considered impassable and taking the Spanish by surprise. With the help of Antonio Sucre, he liberated Ecuador in 1822, and Peru in 1824, while Sucre went on to free Upper Peru (renamed Bolivia in his honour) in 1825. He was, however, unable to persuade the new republics to unite and died on board the ship that was to take him into exile in 1830.

Bolivia
República de Bolivia

Bolivia is the fifth largest country in South America. It is situated in the centre of the continent, some two-fifths of its area lying on the Andean plateau and most of the remainder in the Amazon Basin. It is bounded on the north-west by Peru, on the north and east by Brazil, on the south-east by Paraguay, on the south by Argentina and on the south-west by Chile, to which it lost its coastal province of Antofagasta in 1879.

Area: 1,098,581 sq km (424,164 sq miles); *administrative capital* and largest city: **La Paz**, the highest capital in the world (3,640 m); *legal capital*, seat of the judiciary: **Sucre**; *population:* 8,400,000 (2002 estimate); *official languages:* Spanish, Quechua, Aymará; *religion:* Roman Catholic 80%, evangelical Protestant sects.

Constitution: The present Constitution dates from 1947. Executive power is vested in a President who is directly elected by full adult suffrage for a term of five years (four years until 1997), and who is not eligible to serve two consecutive terms. If no presidential candidate emerges from the election with an absolute majority, the newly elected Congress appoints a President. The President appoints the Cabinet, the nine departmental prefects and the country's diplomatic representatives, and nominates archbishops and bishops. In the event of the death or incapacity of the President the Vice-President assumes office, or, failing that, the President of the Senate. Legislative power is vested in a bicameral Congress, consisting of a Senate of 27 members, three from each of the country's nine Departments, and a Chamber of Deputies of 130 members, both chosen by the list system of proportional representation. Universal suffrage was established after the 1952 revolution, when women and illiterates over the age of 21 were granted the vote and the age of suffrage for married people was reduced to 18. Voting is compulsory. Non-participation can result in loss of certain legal rights, such as the use of banks, for up to three months.

History: In the colonial period what is now Bolivia was known as Upper Peru, and its mines were the richest source in the Spanish Empire of the silver which had attracted the conquerors. It claimed independence from Spain in 1825 and its first Constitution was written in November 1826 with the approval of 'the Liberator', **Simón Bolívar**, from whom the country takes its name. In the 19th century its politics were extremely turbulent and economically the country stagnated. In the War of the Pacific (1879) the country lost its sea coast province of Antofagasta to Chile and with it the rich nitrate fields. After a brief period of relative stability at the beginning of the 20th century, the Chaco War (1932–37) with Paraguay erupted, with a heavy cost in lives. In the post-war period, still cut off from access to the sea, Bolivia was almost entirely dependent on the deep-mining of tin, of which it was the world's second largest producer. Then, in 1943, the old oligarchy was ousted by a military coup, only to return briefly when Maj. Gualberto Villroel (President 1943–46) suffered defenestration at the hands of a crowd and his body was hanged from a lamp post.

After their electoral victory in 1951 had been forestalled by yet another coup, in 1952 a popular revolution brought to power a reforming civilian Government in the form of the **Movimiento Nacionalista Revolucionario** (MNR)—later the MNR (Histórico)—led by **Víctor Paz Estenssoro** (1952–56, 1960–64, 1985–89). The franchise was extended to all, the mines nationalized and an agrarian reform programme launched. However, the Bolivian economy remained dangerously weak and in 1964 Col René Barrientos led a successful coup to forestall the inauguration of a new President. Bolivia subsequently fell under the rule of military-led juntas almost continuously between 1964 and 1982. Barrientos was the first Bolivian President to speak Quechua; ironically, it was under his rule that **Che Guevara**'s attempt to make Bolivia the revolutionary centre of South America was defeated and Guevara himself killed. In 1970–71, for a brief period, a left-wing military Government held power, led by Gen. Juan José Torres González. Torres was soon deposed and was murdered in Buenos Aires in 1976 by the Argentine military Government as part of 'Operation Condor'. In November 1999 the Argentine Government agreed to pay US \$224,000 in compensation to his widow. He was deposed by Col (later Gen.) **Hugo Bánzer Suárez**, who established Bolivia's longest-ever spell of traditional dictatorship between 1971 and 1978, but when pressed to hold elections he was defeated. Bánzer was backed by Brazil, but was unable either to manage the economy or to do a deal on access to the sea with his fellow dictator, Gen. **Augusto Pinochet Ugarte** of Chile.

A junior officers' coup began the process of returning Bolivia to civilian rule. Elections, however, were indecisive and the army was unwilling to surrender power. President **Hernán Siles Zuazo** (1952, 1956–60, 1982–85) inherited an economy devastated by the final collapse of the tin market. Many turned instead to the illegal cultivation of **coca**, a plant grown naturally for local consumption in Bolivia's high altitudes for centuries. Gen. Luis García Meza Tejada (1980–81), who had intervened to cancel the democratic elections of 1980, remained in power for long enough to make the illegal cultivation of coca the mainstay of the economy. Since that time the USA, in pursuit of its policy of combating the drugs trade at its source, has deployed teams in the country to help eradicate illegal coca cultivation, generating strong local hostility and consolidating support for the legal coca growers (the *cocalero*).

In the first round of the 1997 presidential election no candidate received a majority of the popular vote. Gen. (retd.) Hugo Bánzer Suárez of the **Acción Democrática Nacionalista** (ADN) won a congressional run-off vote on 5 August 1997, after forming a 'mega-coalition' with the Movimiento de la Izquierda Revolucionaria, Unión Cívica Solidaridad, Conciencia de Patria, Nueva Fuerza Republicana and the Partido Demócrata Cristiano. In concurrent congressional elections, the ADN-led coalition won overwhelming majorities in both the Chamber of Deputies and the Senate. The MNR's presidential candidate, Juan Carlos Durán Saucedo, won only 17.7% of the vote, while in concurrent congressional elections the party's representation was reduced to 26 seats in the Chamber of Deputies and three in the Senate. President Bánzer resigned because of mortal illness in August 2001 and was succeeded by Vice-President Jorge Fernando Quiroga Ramírez.

Latest elections: In the presidential election held on 30 June 2002, former head of state Gonzálo Sánchez de Lozada of the MNR won 22.5% of the votes cast. Unexpectedly, Evo Morales, of the Movement towards Socialism (*Movimiento al Socialismo*—MAS), leader of the *cocalero*, came a strong second, receiving 20.9% of the votes cast, but the newly elected Congress, mandated under the Constitution to select the winning candidate, chose Sánchez de Lozada by 84 votes to 43. In the concurrent legislative elections the MNR had won 11 seats in the Senate and 36 seats in the Chamber of Deputies, making it the largest party in each house and giving it effective control of the outcome.

International relations and defence: Bolivia is a member of the United Nations, the **Organization of American States**, the **Latin American Integration Association** (LAIA—*Asociación Latinoamericana de Integración*), the **Andean Community of Nations**, and the **Rio Pact**. It is an associate member of the

Southern Common Market. Its army numbers 25,000, its navy 6,000 and its air force 3,000. A selective system of military service (one year) operates and the majority of the army are conscripts. The National Police (*Policia Nacional)*, numbering 31,000, has a paramilitary capability.

Bolivia, economy

The **International Bank for Reconstruction and Development** (World Bank) classes Bolivia at the lower end of the world's lower-middle-income countries. It is the poorest country in mainland Latin America.

GNI: US $8,044m. (2001); *GNI per caput:* $950 (2001); *GNI at PPP:* $19,000m. (2001); *GNI per caput at PPP:* $2,240 (2001), rank 155; *exports:* $1,457m. (2001); *imports:* $1,849m. (2001); *currency:* boliviano, plural bolivianos; US $1 = B7.620 at 31 May 2003.

In 2001 agriculture accounted for 14.9% of Bolivia's gross domestic product (GDP), mining and quarrying for 6.8%, industry for 27.2% and services for 57.9%. Only 2.6% of the land is arable; 0.2% is under permanent crops, 30.8% permanent pasture, 53% forest and woodland and 21% other terrain, mostly mountain. The main crops are maize, wheat, rice, potatoes and cassava (manioc), grown for domestic consumption, though grain imports have been needed since the late 1980s to supplement domestic production. In recent years there has been a sharp increase in the amount of soya cultivated and this is now the country's largest legal agricultural export. Bolivia is the world's third largest cultivator of **coca** and in recent years has produced approximately one-third of the cocaine illegally traded. Sheep, cattle, llama, alpaca, chickens and cavies are raised for domestic use. The collapse of the International Tin Agreement in 1985 has deprived Bolivia of income from its main mineral resource, deep-mined tin, which remains uncompetitive. Meanwhile, the mining sector, led by the state mining corporation, COMIBOL, has diversified into gold, silver, zinc and lead. Large deposits of iron ore at Mutún remain unexploited. The principal industry is the manufacture of durable consumer goods. Bolivia is effectively self-sufficient in energy, the limited domestic demand being supplied by petroleum (61%), natural gas (25%) and traditional combustibles. Demand from Argentina for Bolivian natural gas has not yet been fully replaced by sales to Brazil. Hydroelectric potential is vast but as yet hardly exploited.

The principal exports are metals (17.1%), food and live animals (16.9%), machinery and transport equipment (13.3%) and basic manufactures (10.4%). Principal imports are machinery and transport equipment (36.8%), basic manufactures (19.0%), chemicals (14.0%) and food and live animals (9.7%). In 2001 the

51

USA was the main market for Bolivia's exports (24%), followed by Colombia (13%), the United Kingdom (12%), Brazil (11%) and Switzerland (11%). The USA was also the principal supplier of Bolivia's imports (24%), followed by Argentina (15%), Brazil (14%) and Chile (8%).

Bolivia's economic problems stem from two causes: the collapse of tin production and the debt burden accumulated in the 1980s. The former resulted in rapid monetary growth and 'hyperinflation'. In August 1985, amid growing budget deficits, goods shortages and devaluations, Bolivia's annualized inflation rate reached 16,000%. In that month President **Víctor Paz Estenssoro** introduced the New Economic Policy (NEP), an economic austerity programme which caused considerable social hardship and unrest but reduced inflation to double figures within a few months. In 1987 a new currency, the boliviano, was adopted, equivalent to one million pesos. Average annual inflation in 1985–95 was 18.4%. The NEP reduced the number of public-sector employees and their wages and salaries; it also abolished many trade restrictions, price controls and subsidies, thus further reducing state-sector expenditure.

Successive governments maintained these austerity measures. Since a large proportion of public revenue came from taxes and royalties from the mining and energy sectors, which were vulnerable to fluctuations in demand and prices, efforts were also made to broaden the tax base. Value-added tax on consumer goods was introduced in 1986. Tax revenue represented 11.8% of GDP in 1995, compared with 17.5% in 1989. However, the fiscal deficit rose to 3% in 1997, largely as a result of the introduction of a new pension scheme.

In recognition of the progress made over a decade in macroeconomic stabilization, in September 1998 the World Bank and the **International Monetary Fund** (IMF) approved a debt-relief package worth some US $760m. Bolivia became the first country in Latin America to receive debt-service relief under the terms of the World Bank-led Heavily Indebted Poor Countries (HIPC) programme. It has since qualified for HIPC II and since 1999 has been regarded as a pilot country for the World Bank- and IMF-sponsored Comprehensive Development Framework, a programme which is intended, in part, to complement debt reduction plans. In June 2001 the IMF and the World Bank agreed to reduce Bolivia's debt-service burden by $120m. per year over the next 10 years and in July the 'Paris Club' of donor nations agreed to write off some $262m. of the country's national debt.

Meanwhile, Bolivia was expected to continue to encourage private-sector investment and to stimulate private-sector capital inflows, and further efforts would undoubtedly be made to encourage non-traditional exports. There was still significant need for expansion and improvement of the country's infrastructure. The outlook for metals was not encouraging, but the prospects for hydrocarbons had improved markedly, even though it was estimated that some 50% of the country's gas production was still going to waste. Moreover, the US-funded coca-eradication programme had sharply reduced the national income while, at the same time, encountering determined resistance from rural interests which threatened to escalate into outright insurrection. Although there was consistent economic growth in the 1990s, it was still insufficient to make a significant impact on poverty, which continued to present the major challenge to the Government. Unemployment was officially 11.4% at the end of the decade, but this figure clearly understated the extent of underemployment. The sustained austerity measures, wage controls and taxation increases of the late 1980s and early 1990s stabilized the economy but reinforced Bolivia's position as mainland Latin America's poorest country.

Annual GDP growth averaged 3.5% in 1990–2001. In 2001 the GDP growth rate of 1.2% represented a net decline in real terms. In 2002 the annual inflation rate averaged 0.9%. The official rate for urban unemployment was 12.9% in October 2002.

Bolsa de Bogotá
Bogotá Stock Exchange

F. 1928; the principal stock exchange in Colombia; there are also stock exchanges in Medellín and Cali.

Leadership: Augusto Acosta Torres (Pres.)
Address: Carrera 8a, No. 13–82, 4°-80, Apdo Aéreo 3584, Santafé de Bogotá
Telephone: (1) 243-6501
Fax: (1) 281-3170
Internet: www.bolsabogota.com

Bolsa Boliviana de Valores, SA
Bolivian Stock Exchange

Leadership: Lic. Luis Felipe Rivero Mendoza (Pres.)
Address: Edif. Zembrana P. B., Calle Montevideo 142, Casilla 12521, La Paz
Telephone: (2) 244-3232
Fax: (2) 244-2308
E-mail: info@bolsa-valores-bolivia.com
Internet: www.bolsa-valores-bolivia.com

Bolsa de Comercio de Santiago

F. 1893.
  Leadership: Pablo Yrarrázaval Valdés (Pres.)
  Address: La Bolsa 64, Casilla 123-D, Santiago
  Telephone: (2) 399-3000
  Fax: (2) 380-1959
  E-mail: fledermann@bolsadesantiago.com
  Internet: www.bolsadesantiago.com

Bolsa Mexicana de Valores, SA de CV
Mexican Stock Exchange

F. 1894.
  Leadership: Lic. Manuel Robleda Gonzales de Castilla (Pres.)
  Address: Paseo de la Reform 255, Col. Cuauhtémoc, 06500 México, DF
  Telephone: (55) 5276-6794
  Fax: (55) 5276-6836
  E-mail: cinforma@bmv.com.mx
  Internet: www.bmv.com.mx

Bolsa de Valores de Lima
Lima Stock Exchange

F. 1860.
  Leadership: Rafael D'Angelo Serra (Exec. Pres.)
  Address: Pasaje Acuña 106, Lima 100
  Telephone: (1) 426-0714
  Fax: (1) 426-7650
  Internet: www.bvl.com.pe

Bolsa de Valores de Montevideo
Montevideo Stock Exchange

  Leadership: Ignacio Rospide (Pres.)
  Address: Edif. Bolsa de Comercio, Misiones 1400, 11000 Montevideo
  Telephone: (2) 916-5051

Fax: (2) 916-1900
E-mail: info@bolsademontevideo.com.uy
Internet: www.bolsademontevideo.com.uy

Bolsa de Valores do Rio de Janeiro
Rio de Janeiro Stock Exchange

F. 1845; deals principally in government bonds and foreign exchange.
Leadership: Edson Figueiredo Menezes (Pres.)
Address: Praça XV de Novembro 20, 20010-010 Rio de Janeiro, RJ
Telephone: (21) 2514-1010
Fax: (21) 2514-1023
E-mail: info@bvrj.com.br
Internet: www.bvrj.com.br

Bolsa de Valores de São Paulo (BOVESPA)
São Paulo Stock Exchange

The principal stock exchange of Brazil and the most important in South America; 550 companies listed in 1997; the BOVESPA index is the main index of industrial activity in Brazil.
Leadership: Raymundo Magliano Filho (Pres.)
Address: Rua XV de Novembro 275, CP 3456, 01013-001 São Paulo
Telephone: (11) 3233-2000
Fax: (11) 3242-3550
E-mail: bovespa@bovespa.com.br
Internet: www.bovespa.com.br

Bonaire

Bonaire is situated in the southern Caribbean, some 80 km north of the Venezuelan mainland. Politically it forms part of the Netherlands Antilles.
Area: 288 sq km; *capital:* Kralendijk; *population:* 14,169 (1996 estimate); *official language:* Dutch.

Brasília

Brasília, the capital of Brazil, is situated in its own Federal District (Distrito Federal—DF). At the 2000 census it was the sixth largest city in the country, with a population of 2,051,146.

Brazil

República Federativa do Brasil—Federative Republic of Brazil

Brazil is the largest country in Latin America and the fifth largest country in the world. It is situated in the east of South America, extending west through Amazonia to Peru and south on the coast to Uruguay.

Area: 8,547,404 sq km (3,300,171 sq miles); *capital:* **Brasília**, which was designed and built inland to draw the population away from the coast, and replaced **Rio de Janeiro**, the country's second largest city (population 5.9m.), as capital in 1960. The largest city and main industrial and commercial centre is São Paulo, with a population of 10.1m.; *population:* 174,632,960 (2002 estimate), 55% being regarded as of principally European descent, 6% of African origin, 22% mixed European and African (mulatto) and 12% mixed European and Amerindian; *official language:* Portuguese (more than 100 indigenous languages are also spoken); *religion:* 90% nominally Roman Catholic, though in recent years evangelical protestant sects have made many converts.

Constitution: Brazil is a federative republic. Under the 1998 Constitution, legislative power is vested in the National Congress, which has two houses: the Chamber of Deputies, elected by universal suffrage for four years, and the Federal Senate. The Senate consists of three members from each state and from the Federal District, elected for eight years, of whom one-third retire after four years in office and two-thirds after eight years. Executive power is vested in a President of the Republic, elected for four years and (since 1997) eligible for re-election. He chooses the Ministers of State, who must countersign his acts and decrees. Voting is compulsory for all literate citizens over 18 and under 69 years of age, and optional for the illiterate, those aged 16–17 and those aged over 70. The President-elect takes office on 1 January of the year following his election.

History: Brazil was probably discovered by the Portuguese as early as the 1480s, and had been assigned to Portugal by the Treaty of Tordesillas of 1494 before Cabral returned to claim it in 1500. In the 17th century the Dutch made a determined effort to annex the chain of coastal settlements the Portuguese had established, but the settlers themselves had repelled them by 1658. By then they had already begun to enjoy great prosperity by importing African slaves to grow **sugar**. In 1808 the Portuguese royal family took refuge in Rio de Janeiro from Napoleon's forces. At the end of the wars in Europe the crown prince remained in Brazil, and, in 1822, proclaimed Brazilian independence, first as a kingdom and then as an empire. However, the decision to free the slaves in 1888 led to the fall of the empire and the proclamation of the republic in the following year.

The 'Old Republic' was an oligarchy of wealthy landowners dominated by two large states, São Paulo and Minas Gerais. The first substantial movement of settlers into Amazônia led to the rubber boom, which came to a sudden end when commercially farmed rubber became available. **Coffee** then emerged as the basis of a new boom, until it became clear that more coffee had been planted than the rest of the world could drink. Until this time power had been shared by the élites of the two biggest states, São Paulo and Minas Gerais. When Getúlio Dornelles Vargas, from the southern cattle-ranching state of Rio Grande do Sul, polled well but failed to win in the presidential election of 1930, he and his supporters launched a revolt and the armed forces offered him the presidency.

Vargas established a strongly centralist government, suspending Congress, the state legislatures and local government, before holding elections in 1934 that both confirmed him in power and gave him greatly increased powers. A state oil company, PETROBRÁS, was established, while the Volta Redonda project gave Brazil a strong steel industry and laid the foundations for further industrial development. The government also played a key role in establishing an international regime to support the prices of its two main export crops, coffee and sugar. By extending the vote to all literate men and women over the age of 18, Vargas mobilized working-class support behind his Government, and when it was challenged from the left, he postponed the 1937 elections and proclaimed the Estado Nôvo ('New State'), modelled on Mussolini's Italy and Salazar's Portugal. The powers of Congress were further reduced, though in fact it did not meet again until 1945. Meanwhile, Vargas ruled by decree.

Though Vargas was deposed in 1945, he was soon elected to the Senate, and in 1950 was re-elected to the presidency and the Partido Trabalhista Brasileiro (PTB) to power. However, disillusion with the corruption and intrigue that surrounded his Government led the armed forces to demand his resignation and he committed suicide rather than resign in August 1954. Juscelino Kubitschek (1956–61) was elected on the promise of rapid industrialization and modernization, but inflation was already reaching alarming levels when Jânio Quadros, an independent, succeeded Kubitschek in 1961. Within seven months Quadros had resigned, abruptly, plunging the country into crisis, when the armed forces refused to accept in his place the left-wing Vice-President, João Goulart (1961–64), unless his powers were restricted.

On 1 April 1964 the armed forces again assumed power, this time intending to keep it until they had succeeded in bringing about the modernization of the country. Though they kept the Congress in session, held regular elections and wrote a new (strongly authoritarian) Constitution in 1967, the five military Presidents who held office between 1964 and 1985 ruled by decree, denied left-wingers political rights and tried to compress political debate into an official two-party system. However, the 1973 petroleum crisis hit Brazil particularly hard, and after relatively open elections in 1974 had unexpectedly given the opposition party (the Movimento Democrático Brasileiro) a majority, the regime embarked on a long period of 'decompression'.

In 1985 civilian government was restored, but the presidential candidate elected, Tancredo Neves, was taken ill on the day of his inauguration and died a month later without having been sworn in. **José Sarney**, who took his place, lacked his popularity, but, as promised, began to carry out his programme. Elections for the new Congress took place successfully in 1986, but the Government failed to implement the Cruzado Plan to end hyperinflation and the urge to reform was soon lost. In 1989 the electorate chose as President an outsider, a television personality from the remote state of Alagoas, who, in an increasingly fragmented party system, lacked an effective political base in Congress. Despite this, Fernando Collor de Mello (1990–92) embarked on a radical reform programme, and, as part of a plan to liberalize trade, took a leading role in establishing the **Southern Common Market** (Mercosul) with Argentina, Paraguay and Uruguay. Accusations of corruption against his associates, however, led to his impeachment by Congress in 1992.

Fortunately, Itamar Franco (1992–94) backed his Minister of Finance, Fernando Henrique Cardoso, in his efforts to stabilize the economy, and his Real Plan, which introduced a new currency pegged to the US dollar, was so successful in restraining inflation and increasing real incomes that Cardoso was the obvious choice to succeed Franco in 1995. Cardoso's election for a second term in 1998 was without precedent. By then, however, it was already clear that the government faced a significant challenge from Luiz Inácio da Silva ('Lula'), the presidential candidate of the left-wing Partido dos Trabalhadores (PT), and from landless peasants organized as the Movimento dos Sem-Terra (MST).

Latest elections: In the first round of the presidential election held on 6 October 2002, Luiz Inácio da Silva failed to win an overall majority, receiving slightly less than 46.4% of the votes cast, compared to the 23.2% cast for the government candidate, José Serra, 17.9% for Anthony Garotinho and 12% for Ciro Gomes. The withdrawal of both Garotinho and Gomes from the second round of voting, held on 27 October, allowed da Silva to secure a decisive victory, 61.2% of the votes cast being for him, compared with only 38% cast for Serra. Though in the concurrent legislative elections the PT became the largest party in the Chamber of Deputies, winning 91 of the 513 seats, the remainder were divided between the Partido da Frente Liberal (84), the Partido do Movimento Democrático Brasileiro (74), the Partido da Social Democracia Brasileira (71), the Partido Progressista Brasileiro (49), the Partido Liberal (26), the Partido Trabalhista Brasileiro (26), the Partido Socialista Brasileiro (22), the Partido Democrático Trabalhista (21), the Partido Popular Socialista (15), the Partido Comunista do Brasil (12) and eight minor parties (22). The PT also only won three governorships, those of São Paulo and Minas Gerais going to the President's PSDB. Though Cardoso could justifiably claim to have been, perhaps, Brazil's most successful President, in the end what had mattered to the voters was their feeling that they were no better off. Though the currency remained stable, the economy shrank by 0.2% in 2003 and average earnings fell by 12%, increasing pressure on the PT Government to fulfil its pledges to its supporters.

International relations and defence: Brazil is a member of the United Nations, the **Organization of American States**, the **Latin American Integration Association** (LAIA—*Asociación Latinoamericana de Integración*), the Southern Common Market (Mercosul), and the **Rio Pact**. It is by far the most powerful country in South America in military terms, though rivalled in the hemisphere as a whole by Cuba. The army has a strength of 189,000, including 40,000 conscripts. The navy numbers 48,600 and the air force 50,000. There are more than 1.1m. reservists at the government's disposal, with a further 385,600 in state militias known as Public Security Forces. Military service is compulsory for men aged 18–45 and lasts for one year.

Brazil, economy

Brazil has one of the world's largest economies. However, though diversified, its development is uneven, it remains excessively dependent on foreign capital and is marked by great disparities both between regions and between rich and poor. Balance-of-payments problems, persistent inflation and an equally persistent public-sector deficit continue to present challenges.

GNI: US \$528,900m. (2001); *GNI per caput:* \$3,070 (2001); *GDP at PPP:* \$1,219,000m. (2001); *GNI per caput at PPP:* \$7,070 (2001), rank 86;

exports: $60,362m. (2002); *imports:* $47,232m. (2002); *currency:* real, plural reais; US $1 = R$2.9660 at 31 May 2003.

In 2001 agriculture accounted for 8% of Brazil's gross domestic product (GDP), mining and quarrying for 2% and industry for 31%. Some 6.5% of the land is arable, 0.9% under permanent crops and 23.0% permanent pasture. Forest and woodland covers much of Amazônia. The main crops grown for export are soya beans, **coffee**, oranges and **bananas**. Rice, beans and maize are grown for domestic consumption, while the cultivation of **sugar** cane, once the basis of the export economy, expanded again in the 1990s, for distillation into alcohol for fuel. Cattle, pigs, sheep and chickens are raised for domestic consumption. Brazil is the world's largest exporter of iron ore and concentrates. Other main mineral resources are manganese, tin and gold, much of the last produced illegally by *garimpeiros*. The principal industries are ethanol distillation, steel production, manufacture of vehicles and components and agricultural chemicals. The main energy source is hydroelectric power, which meets some 95% of the country's electricity requirements. Oil was not discovered until 1974, but by 2002 the country was meeting 80% of its domestic petroleum requirements with the aid of the PROALCOOL distillation programme. Natural gas is also produced, though much is now imported from Argentina and Bolivia.

Main exports are metals, ores and concentrates, soya beans, aircraft, passenger cars and radios. Principal imports are crude petroleum, motors, generators and electrical equipment, motor vehicle parts, pharmaceuticals and electronic components. In 2002 the USA was the main market for exports, followed by the Netherlands and the People's Republic of China. The USA was the also the principal supplier of imports in that year, followed by Argentina and Germany.

The civilian Government of Juscelino Kubitshek promised 50 years of progress, but its legacy was an economy that was seriously overheated and the high level of inflation that, generally, has plagued Brazil ever since. In 1964 the armed forces took power with the intention of retaining it for as long as was necessary to build a modern economy. In the first few years of military rule average growth rates of 9% were achieved. The opening-up of the Amazon by the construction of the Trans–Amazon highway, the completion of the Itaipú Dam and the Carajás iron ore project and the development of nuclear and space industries all formed part of a systematic programme of state-led economic development. However, all petroleum had still to be imported and when the first 'oil shock' occurred in 1973, the fateful decision was taken to fund continued development by massive borrowing. By 1982 the size of Brazil's national debt was second only to that of Mexico, and the return to civilian rule in 1985 left successive civilian governments struggling to contain persistently high rates of inflation without the support of a divided and fractious Congress. In

1993 the rate of inflation was some 2,500%. Though the implementation of the Real Plan in 1994 brought about a sharp fall in the rate of inflation, it also transformed a trade surplus into a persistent deficit, which grew to reach 4.5% of GDP in 1998. Devaluation in 1999 was followed by a move away from the strict monetary policy which had characterized the 1990s, and GDP grew by 0.8% in 1999 and 4.5% in 2000. In 2002, however, the economy was still in serious crisis and in 2003 the da Silva Government surprised the world by introducing a policy of strict austerity which it hoped to be able to temper with meaningful social change before popular patience was exhausted.

Bridgetown

Bridgetown, capital and chief port of Barbados, is situated on the south-west coast of the island. In 2001 the UN estimated its population at 136,000.

British Virgin Islands

The British Virgin Islands are an Overseas Territory of the United Kingdom situated in the Caribbean Sea at the north-western end of the chain of the Lesser Antilles, immediately adjoining the US Virgin Islands and some 100 km (60 miles) east of Puerto Rico. They consist of more than 40 islands, islets and cays, only 16 of which are inhabited.

Area overall: 153 sq km (59 sq miles); *capital:* Road Town, on Tortola; *population:* 21,000 (2001 estimate), mainly of African descent (83%); *official language:* English; *religion:* Christian (Methodists 33%, Episcopalian 17%, Roman Catholic 10%).

Constitution: The British Virgin Islands have had a representative assembly since 1774. Under the June 1977 Constitution, the head of state is HM Queen Elizabeth II, who is represented by a Governor, who retains responsibility for external affairs, defence and internal security. The Executive Council consists of the Governor, the Attorney-General ex officio, the Chief Minister appointed by the Governor from the members of the Legislative Council together with four other ministers appointed on the advice of the Chief Minister. The Legislative Council consists of a Speaker, the Attorney-General, and 13 members directly elected for a term of up to five years by universal adult suffrage.

History: The islands were sighted and named by **Christopher Columbus** in 1493. Originally settled by the Dutch, they were captured by Britain in 1666, and were governed with the aid of an elected Assembly from 1773. They did not join the

West Indies Federation but were incorporated as a separate British Dependent Territory in 1960 and a British Overseas Territory in 1998. In 1967 the Virgin Islands Party (VIP) formed a government with H. Lavitty Stoutt as the islands' first Chief Minister.

Latest elections: In the general election held on 16 June 2003, the ruling VIP was defeated by the National Democratic Party (NDP), led by Orlando Smith; results being: NDP 52.4%, eight seats; VIP 42.2%, five seats; others 5.4%, no seats.

International relations and defence: Britain is responsible for both. Royal Air Force patrols operate from the islands to interdict drug smuggling.

Economy: The mainstay of the islands' economy is financial services; 360,000 foreign businesses were registered at the end of 2002. US currency is used for all purposes. Tourism has suffered from the downturn since 2001, however, and accounted for only 14% of GNI in 2002. Such agriculture as there is is entirely geared to production for the local market. GNI per head in 2001 was US $36,034.

Buenos Aires

The city of Nuestra Señora de los Buenos Aires (Our Lady of Fair Winds) was first established in 1536, but was refounded in 1580. After the formal proclamation of independence in 1816, it remained aloof from the confederation of the United Provinces of the Río de la Plata, but was finally united with it in 1870, when a new capital was established for the Province of Buenos Aires at La Plata. Today the city officially consists of the Federal District, which had a population of 2,768,772 at the 2001 census, but the greater metropolitan area comprises as much as two-fifths of the total population.

Buenos Aires Herald

English-language newspaper published daily; f. 1876; the only Argentine newspaper to carry information about the excesses of the military Government of 1976, its reporting at that time led to the arrest of its editor, Andrew Graham-Yooll, and his subsequent deportation; independent.

Leadership: Andrew Graham-Yooll (Editor-in-Chief)
Address: Azopardo 455, 1107 Buenos Aires
Telephone: (11) 4349-1500
Fax: (11) 4349-1505
E-mail: info@buenosairesherald.com
Internet: www.buenosairesherald.com

bureaucratic-authoritarianism

Term invented by the Argentine Guillerm O'Donnell to explain the emergence of military regimes in Latin America in the 1960s, e.g. Brazil 1964, Argentina 1966 and 1976, Uruguay 1973, Chile 1973. It envisages three stages of political development: in the oligarchic stage the popular sector is neither mobilized nor incorporated; in the populist stage the popular sector is mobilized and incorporated; in the bureaucratic-authoritarian stage the popular sector is demobilized and excluded. The model is derived specifically from the experience of Argentina between 1966 and 1973 and fits it closely; it fits the other examples less well.

Burnham, Forbes

Forbes Burnham (1923–1985) was born in Kitty, British Guiana, and educated as a lawyer. With **Cheddi Jagan** he helped found the **People's Progressive Party** (PPP) in 1950. He served as its first chairman and was elected to the House of Assembly in 1953, serving briefly as Minister of Education. In 1955 he left the PPP and two years later founded the rival **People's National Congress** which he led until his death. As Prime Minister after 1964, however, he took an equally nationalist course, nationalizing the key **bauxite** and **sugar** industries and taking an active anti-colonialist position. In 1980 he became Executive President in an election widely believed to have been rigged.

C

Cable & Wireless Jamaica Ltd

Company formed in 1989 to manage Cable & Wireless interests in Jamaica; 79%-owned by Cable & Wireless (United Kingdom); in 1995 merged with Jamaica Telephone Co Ltd, and Jamaica International Telecommunications Ltd.

Leadership: E. Miller (Pres.)
Address: 97 Church Street, Kingston
Telephone: 926-9450
Fax: 929-9530
Internet: www.cwjamaica.com

Caldera Rodríguez, Rafael

Rafael Caldera Rodríguez, President of Venezuela 1969–74 and 1994–99, was born in San Felipe, Yaracuy, in 1916 and educated in the Colegio San Ignacio de Loyola and the Central University, graduating in law and political science in 1939. As a student he took an active part in politics, founding the National Student Union in 1936 to promote Christian social principles. In 1945 he was invited to join the **Acción Democrática** Government as Attorney-General, but he resigned from it in 1946 to found the Partido Social-Cristiano, coming second in the 1947 presidential elections. He was arrested and finally exiled for his opposition to the dictatorship of Marcos Pérez Jiménez, on whose fall he concluded with **Rómulo Betancourt** the Pact of Punto Fijo to maintain the restored democracy. In December 1968, at his fourth attempt, he was elected as President. In office he adopted a conciliatory stance, recognizing the Soviet Union and legalizing both the Partido Comunista de Venezuela and the Movimiento de Izquierda Revolucionaria. After the serious decline of the Venezuelan economy in the 1980s, he was again elected to the presidency in 1994, running in opposition to his old party under the banner of Convergencia Nacional, but was unable to change the system he had helped create.

Cámara Argentina de Comercio
Argentine Chamber of Commerce

F. 1913; 1,500 members.
　Leadership: José Chedier (Pres.)
　Address: Florida 1, 40°, 1005 Buenos Aires
　Telephone: (11) 4331-0813
　Fax: (11) 4331-9116
　Internet: www.cac.com.ar

Cámara de Comercio de Costa Rica
Costa Rica Chamber of Commerce

F. 1915; 900 members.
　Leadership: Emilio Bruce Jiménez (Pres.)
　Address: POB 4946-1000, San José
　Telephone: 221-0005
　Fax: 233-7091
　E-mail: biofair@sol.racsa.co.cr

Cámara de Comercio, Industrias y Agricultura de Panamá
Chamber of Commerce, Industry and Agriculture of Panama

F. 1915; 1,300 members.
　Leadership: Iván Cohen (Pres.)
　Address: Avda Cuba y Ecuador 33a, Apdo 74, Panamá 1
　Telephone: 227-1233
　Fax: 227-4186
　E-mail: infoccia@panacamara.com
　Internet: www.panacamara.com

Cámara Nacional de Comercio
National Chamber of Commerce, Bolivia

F. 1890.
> *Leadership:* Guillermo Morales Fernández (Pres.)
> *Address:* Edif. Cámara Nacional de Comercio, Avda Mariscal Santa Cruz 1392,
> 1° y 2°, Casilla 7, La Paz
> *Telephone:* (2) 237-8606
> *Fax:* (2) 239-1004
> *E-mail:* cnc@boliviacomercio.org.bo
> *Internet:* www.boliviacomercio.org.bo

Cámara Nacional de Comercio, Producción y Servicios (PERUCAMARAS)
National Chamber of Commerce, Production and Services, Peru

The national association of chambers of commerce of Peru; the Lima Chamber was founded in 1888.
> *Leadership:* Samuel Gleiser Katz (Pres.)
> *Address:* c/o Cámara de Comercio de Lima, Avda Gregorio Escobedo 398, Jesús
> María, Lima 11
> *Telephone:* (1) 463-3434
> *Fax:* (1) 463-2837
> *E-mail:* cholguin@rey.com.pe
> *Internet:* www.perucam.com

Cámara Nacional de Comercio y Servicios del Paraguay
National Chamber of Commerce and Services of Paraguay

F. 1898 as the Cámara y Bolsa de Comercio; adopted present name in 2002.
> *Leadership:* Raul Ricardo dos Santos (Pres.)
> *Address:* Estrella 5 40-550, Asunción
> *Telephone:* (21) 49-3221
> *Fax:* (21) 44-0817
> *E-mail:* infor@ccparaguay.com.py
> *Internet:* www.ccparaguay.com.py

Cámara Nacional de Comercio, Servicios y Turismo de Chile
National Chamber of Commerce, Services and Tourism of Chile

F. 1858.
   Leadership: Fernando Luis Concha (Pres.)
   Address: Merced 230, Santiago
   Telephone: (2) 365-4000
   Fax: (2) 365-4001
   Internet: www.cnc.cl

Cámara Nacional de Comercio y Servicios del Uruguay
National Chamber of Commerce and Services of Uruguay

National Chamber of Commerce, f. 1867; 1,500 members.
   Leadership: Horacio Castells Montes (Pres.)
   Address: Edif. Bolsa de Comercio, Rincón 454.2°, Casilla 1000, Montevideo
   Telephone: (2) 916-1277
   Fax: (2) 916-1243
   E-mail: info@cncs.com.uy
   Internet: www.cncs.com.uy

Cambio-90 (C-90)
Change 1990, Peru

Organization of political independents formed to support the candidature of **Alberto Keinya Fujimori** in the 1990 Peruvian presidential elections. Entered into coalition with Nueva Mayoría to contest the 1992 elections to the constituent assembly. Supported the candidature of Fujimori for re-election in 1995 and again in 2000, when he was generally considered to be constitutionally debarred from running. Contested the 2001 congressional elections under new leadership.
   Leadership: Pablo Correa (Leader)
   Address: Jr Santa Isabel 590, Urb. Colmenares, Pueblo Libre, Lima
   Telephone: (1) 944-1739

Caracas

Caracas, chief city and federal capital of the Bolivarian Republic of Venezuela, is situated in central coastal highlands, above but close to its port town, La Guaira. At mid-2000 the population of the city was estimated at 1,975,787 and that of the Federal District at 2,284,921.

Cárdenas, Lázaro

Lázaro Cárdenas del Río (1895–1970), President of Mexico 1934–1940, was born in Michoacán and as a youth enlisted in the Constitutionalist forces, rising to the rank of General. Elected Governor of the state of Michoacán in 1928, he was a popular choice for the presidential nomination in 1934. Once in power, he immediately implemented the programme of reform for which he is famous, distributing some 20m. ha of land, supporting the trade unions in their struggle for better pay and, in 1938, nationalizing the foreign-owned oil companies, an action still celebrated in Mexico as a demonstration of economic independence. In retirement he remained a popular hero of the Left, speaking in support of **Fidel Castro** and the Cuban Revolution. He is buried under the Monument to the Revolution in Mexico City.

Cárdenas Solórzano, Cuauhtémoc

Cuauhtémoc Cárdenas Solórzano, son of former Mexican President Lázaro Cárdenas del Río, was born in 1934. In 1985 he became leader of the Corriente Democrático within the ruling **Partido Revolucionario Institucional**, and, following his expulsion from the party, unsuccessfully contested the 1988 presidential elections, widely believed to have been rigged. As leader of the Partido Revolucionario Democrático he was again unsuccessful in 1994, and subsequently decided to run for the newly created post of Mayor of Mexico City. Though at his third attempt to win the presidency, in 2000, he achieved a substantial majority of the votes cast in the federal capital, the right-wing opposition candidate, **Vicente Fox Quesada**, was nevertheless the ultimate victor.

Cardoso, Fernando Henrique

Fernando Henrique Cardoso, President of Brazil 1994–2002, was born into a wealthy military family in São Paulo in 1931. In the 1960s he taught sociology at the University of São Paulo and was a prominent member of the left-wing intellectual opposition when Brazil was under military rule. In 1965–67 he worked in the UN Latin American Institute for Social and Economic Planning in Santiago, Chile, co-authoring (with Enzo Faletto) the widely influential *Dependency and*

Development in Latin America (*Dependencia y desarrollo en América Latina,* 1971). After the return of democracy to Brazil in 1985, he was elected senator from his native state and in 1993 was appointed finance minister. In that capacity he introduced the Real Plan, a plan to counter inflation by creating a new currency, the real, pegged to the US dollar. His success in curbing inflation and stabilizing the economy helped him win the presidency in 1994. As President he lacked a broad base of political support, but proved highly successful in engineering majorities in congress for a wide range of centrist policies, including the privatization of state-owned companies and increased foreign investment. In 1998 he became the first President in Brazilian history to be elected for a second term.

Caribbean Community and Common Market (CARICOM)

CARICOM was formed in 1973 by the Treaty of Chaguaramas to replace the Caribbean Free Trade Association, which had been founded in 1965. There are 15 member states: Antigua and Barbuda, Bahamas (of the Community, not the Common Market), Barbados, Belize, Dominica, Grenada, Guyana, Haiti, Jamaica, Montserrat, St Christopher and Nevis, St Lucia, St Vincent and the Grenadines, Suriname, Trinidad and Tobago. Anguilla, Bermuda, the British Virgin Islands, the Cayman Islands and the Turks and Caicos Islands are associate members. The Heads of Government Conference is the final decision-making authority of the Community and meets annually, or more often as required. Since 1998 the Council of Ministers, consisting of the ministers responsible in each member state for Community affairs, has met to develop plans for Community co-operation and integration. The Secretariat provides services to the Conference and the Council. The process of integration made little progress until the 1990s, however. The attempt to foster intra-regional commerce through the creation of a free-trade area within the Community, which had a population of 5,500,000, had been hampered persistently by political disputes and by the maintenance of import restrictions in an effort to protect the domestic economies of individual island countries. In the 1990s, however, Caribbean leaders became increasingly concerned about the impact on their small and often fragile economies of other regional and global developments, such as the consolidation of powerful regional trading blocs through the single European market and the **North American Free Trade Agreement**, and globalization and trade liberalization under the **World Trade Organization**. CARICOM has sought, in the face of problems of commitment and implementation, to lower barriers to trade between member states and set common external tariffs. A particular area of anxiety has been the continuation of preferential access to European markets for Caribbean **bananas** (a staple of several economies) in the face of intense competition from lower-cost 'dollar bananas' originating from the larger (often US-owned) plantations of Central America.

Leadership: Edwin W. Carrington (Sec.-Gen.), Trinidad and Tobago

Address: Bank of Guyana Bldg, POB 10827, Georgetown, Guyana

Telephone: (2) 226-9280

Fax: (2) 226-7816

E-mail: carisec1@caricom.org

Internet: www.caricom.org

Caribbean Development Bank

The Bank was founded in 1969 to promote regional economic growth in the Caribbean region by supporting agriculture, industry, transport, tourism and education. The membership comprises the member states of the **Caribbean Community and Common Market** and a number of associate members: Canada, the People's Republic of China, Colombia, France, Germany, Italy, Mexico, the United Kingdom and Venezuela.

Leadership: Prof. Compton Bourne (Pres.)

Address: POB 408, Wildey, St Michael, Barbados

Telephone: (246) 431-1600

Fax: (246) 426-7269

E-mail: info@caribank.org

Internet: www.caribank.org

Castries

The chief town and capital of St Lucia, Castries, which with its suburbs had a population estimated at 57,000 at mid-2001, is situated on the north coast of the island and overlooked by Mount Fortune.

Castro, Fidel

Fidel Castro Ruz, Prime Minister (1959–76) and President (1976–) of Cuba, was born at Mayarí, Oriente province, Cuba, on 13 August 1926. The second son of a wealthy sugar planter who had emigrated to Cuba from Spain, he was educated in Santiago de Cuba and at the Jesuit Colegio Belén, **Havana** (La Habana), before studying law at the University of Havana (1945–50). When Fulgencio Batista seized power in 1953 Castro organized a revolt based on the seizure of the Moncada

Barracks in Santiago; the attempt was a disastrous failure and many of his colleagues were hunted down and shot. Captured several weeks later, he was tried and sentenced to imprisonment on the Isle of Pines. Amnestied in 1954, he travelled to Mexico and in December 1956 sailed from Tuxpam on the *Granma* to overthrow Batista. The expedition was ambushed and only a few of its members escaped with Castro to the Sierra Maestra, where in July 1957 he signed the Manifesto of the Sierra Maestra, promising liberal democracy, free elections, freedom of the press and land reform. At the end of 1958 the Batista regime collapsed and on 1 January 1959 the insurgents entered Havana.

Castro appointed his former judge, Manuel Urrutia Lleo, as President of a provisional government, but, impatient to see progress, on 15 February 1959 took over the post of Prime Minister himself. A land reform programme was decreed. However, relations with the USA deteriorated soon after Cuba had demanded more economic aid than the entire US aid budget. When, in 1960, the US Government cut the Cuban **sugar** quota, the Soviet Union stepped in to take it instead. On 6 July 1960 the Castro Government decreed the expropriation of the US-owned sugar mills. In October Cuban enterprises were also nationalized. Then, in April 1961, the Kennedy Administration in the USA sponsored a landing by US-trained exile forces at the Playa de Largos (Bay of Pigs), on the south coast of Cuba. Castro seized the strategic moment and declared his revolution 'socialist' on 16 April. On 1 December 1961 he stated publicly: 'I am a Marxist-Leninist and I shall continue to be one until the last day of my life.' In April 1961 the Soviet Union formally recognized Cuba as being engaged 'in the construction of socialism' and shortly afterwards agreed to send intermediate-range ballistic missiles to Cuba, thus triggering the Cuban Missile Crisis of October 1962.

Since then Castro has taken personal charge of the series of national projects by which Cuba has sought to modernize along socialist lines. In the early 1960s a determined effort was made to industrialize and to diversify the economy. At the same time, important gains were made in literacy and public health. However, sugar remained the mainstay of the economy and in 1970 it was attempted to secure a harvest of 10m. metric tons for the first time. In the event, the harvest totalled 8.3m. tons, itself a record, but from then on there was increasing pressure from the Soviet Union for Cuba to follow Soviet methods. Under the Soviet-style Constitution adopted in 1975, Castro was elected President in 1976 and has been regularly re-elected since then.

Since the collapse of the Soviet Union in December 1991, Castro has continued to maintain a Soviet-style regime in Cuba with only minimal concessions to economic necessity—see also **special period in time of peace**.

Castro Ruz, Lt-Gen. Raúl

Raúl Castro Ruz (b. 1931), **Fidel Castro**'s younger brother, fought with him in the Sierra Maestra. Since 1976 he has combined the post of Second Secretary of the Cuban Communist Party with the governmental post of Minister of the Revolutionary Armed Forces. He is Fidel Castro's designated successor.

Cayenne – *see* French Guiana

Cayman Islands

A British Overseas Territory in the Caribbean, located 290 km (180 miles) north-west of Jamaica, between Cuba and Honduras. It consists of three islands, Grand Cayman, Cayman Brac and Little Cayman. Total population at the 1999 census was 39,410. The capital, George Town, on Grand Cayman, had a population of 20,626. Eighty per cent of the islanders are of mixed African and European descent, but foreigners generally account for one-third of the population. The sole language in use is English.

Constitution: The most recent revision of the Constitution was in 1994. The Governor is chief executive and chairman of the Executive Council, which comprises three official members and five who are chosen by the Legislative Assembly from among their own number. The Legislative Assembly has 15 elected and three official members. In 1999 the Caymans were redesignated a British Overseas Territory.

History: Grand Cayman was first settled in 1670, and the two smaller islands in1833. Until 1959 all three islands were a dependency of Jamaica. Before 1991 there were no political parties, but in 1992 a loose coalition, termed the National Team, won 12 of the 15 elective seats in the legislature and retained nine in 1996.

Latest elections: In the elections of November 2000 the ruling National Team, led by Truman Bodden, was heavily defeated, losing six of its nine seats. The new Assembly chose Kurt Tibbets of the Democratic Alliance as Leader of Government Business, but when the United Democratic Party (UDP) was formed in November 2001 he was ousted by nine votes to five and McKeeva Bush, of the UDP, was elected in his place. In May 2002 Tibbets was chosen as leader of the new opposition party, the five-member People's Progressive Movement.

International relations and defence: The major problem for the islanders, drugs-related crime, led to the signature in 1986 (ratified in 1990) of a Mutual Legal Assistance Treaty with the USA. More recently the islands' status as one of the major offshore financial markets of the world has led to pressure from both the UK government and the **European Union** (EU) to prevent 'money-laundering'. The territory became an Associate Member of the **Caribbean Community and Common Market** in May 2002.

Economy: The Cayman Islands are one of the world's largest offshore markets. In 2002 there were 527 banks and trust companies and 4,077 funds registered and the sector contributed some 36% of the islands' gross domestic product (GDP). Since 1986 they have had a treaty for the mutual exchange of information with the USA which was extended in 2001 in response, partly, to the revelation that the US company, Enron, had used 692 island companies to avoid US tax liabilities. The Cayman Islands have, however, resisted EU pressure to disclose details of private savings accounts as long as that is not required of EU member states. Tourism, which contributes some 25% of GDP and accounts for one-half of all employment, slowed after 2001 so that GDP, which grew in 1999 by 5.4%, and in 2000 by 3.2%, grew by only 1.5% in 2001 and 1.7% in 2002. The currency is the Cayman Islands dollar, pegged to the US dollar at CI$1 = US $1.20.

Central American Integration System
Sistema de la Integración Centroamericana (SICA)

F. 1991 by the Protocol of Tegucigalpa, an agreement between the heads of state of six Central American states to create a new framework for Central American integration and to revive the Central American Common Market, created in 1960.

Leadership: Dr Oscar Alfredo Santamaría (Sec.-Gen.)
Address: Blvd Ordén de Malta 470, Urb. Santa Elena, Antiguo Cuscatlán, San Salvador
Telephone: 289-6131
Fax: 289-6124
E-mail: sgsic@sicanet.org.sv
Internet: www.sgsica.org

Central Bank of Trinidad and Tobago
The central bank of issue of Trinidad and Tobago; f. 1964.

Leadership: Ewart S. Williams (Gov.)
Address: Eric Williams Plaza, Independence Sq., POB 1250, Port of Spain
Telephone: 625-4835
Fax: 627-4696
E-mail: info@central-bank.org.tt
Internet: www.central-bank.org.tt

Central Obrera Boliviana (COB)
Bolivian Workers' Confederation

Bolivia's main trade union confederation; f. 1952; it includes the three most powerful unions in the country: the peasant farmers' union, Confederación Sindical Unica de los Trabajadores Campesinos, the mineworkers' union, the Federación Sindical de Trabajadores Mineros de Bolivia and the oil workers' union, the Federación Sindical de Trabajadores Petroleros de Bolivia; the COB was the principal force behind the Bolivian revolution of 1952, which brought the **Movimiento Nacionalista Revolucionario** to power, and it has continued to play a significant role in Bolivian politics, even after the collapse of the tin industry of 1985; it reports 800,000 members.

Leadership: Alberto Camacho Pardo (Exec.-Sec.)
Address: Edif. COB, Calle Pisagua 618, Casilla 6552, La Paz
Telephone: (2) 228-3220
Fax: (2) 228-0420

Central de Trabajadores de Cuba (CTC)
Confederation of Cuban Workers

F. 1939, the CTC is the sole trade union confederation in Cuba, with 19 affiliated trade unions.

Leadership: Pedro Ross Leal (Gen.-Sec.)
Address: Palacio de los Trabajadores, San Carlos y Peñalver, Havana
Telephone: (7) 78-4901
Fax: (7) 55-5927
E-mail: digital@trabajo.cip.cu
Internet: www.trabajadores.cubaweb.cu

Central Unica dos Trabalhadores (CUT)
Sole Workers' Confederation, Brazil

F. 1983; the main trade union confederation of Brazil; affiliated to the International Confederation of Free Trade Unions and the Organización Regional Interamericana de Trabajadores.

Leadership: Vincente Paulo da Silva (Pres.)
Address: Rua Caetano Pinto 575, Brás, 03041-000 São Paulo, SP

Telephone: (11) 2108-9200
Fax: (11) 2108-9310
E-mail: duvaier@cut.org.br
Internet: www.cut.org.br

Central Unitaria de Trabajadores (CUT)
Sole Confederation of Workers, Colombia

F. in 1986; the Confederation takes in 50 smaller federations and claims four-fifths of all trade unionists in Colombia.
  Leadership: Carlos Rodríguez Diaz (Pres.)
  Address: Calle 35, No. 7–25, 9°, Apdo Aéreo 221, Santafé de Bogotá
  Telephone: (1) 323-7550
  Fax: (1) 323-7550

Central Unitaria de Trabajadores de Chile (CUT)
Sole Confederation of Chilean Workers

F. 1988; the largest of Chile's trade union confederations, with some 411,000 members; affiliated to the International Confederation of Free Trade Unions and the Organización Regional Interamericana de Trabajadores.
  Leadership: Arturo Martínez Molina (Pres.)
  Address: Alameda 1346, Santiago
  Telephone: (2) 361-9452
  Fax: (2) 361-9452
  E-mail: presidencia.cut@entelchile.net and cut@cutchile.cl
  Internet: www.cutchile.cl

Centrale Bank van Suriname
Central Bank of Suriname

Government central bank of issue; f. 1957.
  Leadership: Andre E. Telting (Pres.)
  Address: 18–20 Waterkant, POB 1801, Paramaribo
  Telephone: 473741
  Fax: 476444
  E-mail: info@cbvs.sr
  Internet: www.cbvs.sr

Chamber of Commerce of Puerto Rico

The main association of Chambers of Commerce in Puerto Rico; f. in 1913; 1,800 members.

Leadership: Ricardo d'Acosta (Pres.)
Address: 100 Calle Tetuan, POB 9024033, San Juan, PR 00902-4033
Telephone: (787) 721-6060
Fax: (787) 723-1891
E-mail: camarapr@camarapr.net
Internet: www.camarapr.zonai.com

Chamorro, Violeta Barrios de

Violeta Barrios was born into a wealthy Nicaraguan family in 1931 and married Pedro Joaquín Chamorro, editor of *La Prensa*, and a member of the conservative Chamorro family which dominated Nicaraguan political life until the rise of the Somozas. His murder in 1978, which was universally believed to have been ordered by **Anastasio Somoza Debayle**, was the trigger for Sandinista-led revolution and the fall of the dictatorship. In 1979 she was invited to become one of the five members of the ruling junta of the provisional Government, but withdrew after a few months and emerged as a leading political opponent of **Daniel Ortega Saavedra**, who was elected President in 1985. In a country weary of the devastation caused by the long US-sponsored *contra* war, as candidate of a coalition of 14 parties (including the Communists), however, she defeated Ortega in the 1990 presidential election. As President, her Government was handicapped both by the failure of the US Government to give it adequate financial support, and by the difficulties of demobilizing both the Sandinistas and the *contras*, and Nicaragua has remained the poorest country on the mainland of the Americas.

Chávez Frías, Hugo

Hugo Chávez Frías, President of Venezuela since 1999, was born in 1954 in Sabaneta, Barinas. Together with three colleagues, in 1982 he founded a military lodge, Movimiento Bolivariano Revolucionario 200 (MBR-200), in opposition to the political system created by the 1958 Pact of Punto Fijo and the impact of neo-liberal economics. In February 1992, at a time of widespread social unrest, he and MBR-200 led an unsuccessful coup against the Government, following which he was arrested and imprisoned; a second coup in November 1992, organized by elements in sympathy with their objectives, helped to dislodge President Carlos Andrés Pérez, who was found guilty of misuse of public funds in 1996 and sentenced to two years' imprisonment. Meanwhile, in 1993 Chávez and his colleagues were pardoned by President Caldera. Chávez was not, however, allowed to re-enter the army, and devoted his time instead to political organization and founding the **Movimiento V República** (MVR—Fifth Republic Movement) in 1997. Despite an attempt by the traditional parties to prevent Chávez's election by bringing forward the date of the congressional elections, he successfully contested the presidential election in December 1998 and took office in February 1999.

In April 1999 a national referendum voted to convene a constituent assembly to write a new, Bolivarian, constitution, which was approved by a large majority in a further referendum in December. By that time increasing concern at the President's authoritarian tendencies, and his evident desire to use military personnel as administrators, had led Francisco Arias Cárdenas and five other former colleagues of Chávez to issue the Declaration of Maracay, which criticized him for abandoning democracy. However, despite a severe economic crisis brought about by falling oil revenues, in new elections in May 2000 Chávez defeated Arias as well as the candidates of the traditional parties, consolidated his support among the less well-off members of society and gained a substantial majority in Congress, which later granted Chávez the right to legislate by decree for one year. From then on there was growing unrest as the trade union movement resisted attempts to sideline it; the unrest spread throughout the oil sector as Chávez led the **Organization of Petroleum Exporting Countries** in a successful attempt to force up world oil prices. In April 2002 the US Government greeted with enthusiasm a coup to displace him. This, however, was ultimately unsuccessful. Subsequently, a coalition of business and trade union interests concentrated on trying to force a referendum to oust him.

Chile
República de Chile

Chile is situated on the west coast of South America, isolated from the rest of the continent by the cordillera of the Andes. It is 4,329 km (3,000 miles) long and approximately 180 km (120 miles) wide. Towards the south the country breaks up into a number of sub-Antarctic islands, of which the best-known is Cape Horn (Cabo de Hornos), and it also includes a number of Pacific islands of which the best known, and most remote, is Rapa Nui (Easter Island), 3,790 km west of the mainland. Like its neighbour Argentina, Chile claims a sector of Antarctica which it counts as part of its national territory.

Area: 756,096 sq km (291,930 sq miles); *capital:* **Santiago** (sometimes termed Santiago de Chile to distinguish it from Santiago de Cuba); *population:* 15.1m. (2002 census), some 90% of mixed European and native American descent; *official language:* Spanish; *religion:* most Roman Catholic, some 12% being regarded as Protestants.

Constitution: The Constitution of 1981 was extensively amended in 1989 to facilitate the return of democratic government. There is a bicameral legislature, consisting of an upper house, the Senate, and a lower house, the Chamber of Deputies. The Senate is made up of 38 senators elected by popular vote for an eight-year term, together with all living ex-Presidents and nine nominated members. The 120 deputies are elected for four years. Executive power is in the hands of a President elected by the people for a term of six years.

History: Isolated from most of its neighbours by the Andes, Chile was liberated by the forces of Bernardo O'Higgins and José de San Martín in 1818 and was able to establish a stable oligarchy after 1833. In 1889, in the War of the Pacific, Chilean forces defeated both Peru and Bolivia and seized the valuable nitrate fields of Antofagasta. However, when Congress refused to ratify the budget presented by President José Manuel Balmaceda (1886–91), who had angered the big landowners by his insistence on reform, civil war followed. In 1891 the congressional forces, based on the navy, defeated the presidential forces, based on the army. Balmaceda committed suicide and the victorious Congress established a semi-parliamentary regime, in which the President remained as a figurehead but a Prime Minister and Cabinet responsible to Congress actually governed. Meanwhile, the country enjoyed an economic boom which reached a peak during the First World War, generating a powerful labour movement and a series of strikes. At the war's end, the discovery of cheap artificial nitrates brought about a sharp slump. Unfortunately, Arturo Alessandri, the 'Lion of Tarapacá' (President 1920–24, 1924–25), lacked a parliamentary majority and in 1924 the armed forces stepped in and removed him. A short period of coups and successive counter-coups culminated, in 1932, in a short-lived 'Socialist Republic' led by Col Marmaduque Grove before a presidential republic was restored. Even then the strength of the left was such that between 1938 and 1941 Chile had a 'popular front' government and both communists and socialists remained in the government throughout the Second World War.

With the onset of the Cold War, however, tensions increased and in 1948, after a number of strikes, the Communist Party was banned. This, however, merely had the effect of strengthening its keenest rival, the Socialists. Marxism was widely popular and enjoyed significant working-class and trade union support. In the 1964 presidential election the Socialist candidate, a country doctor called **Salvador Allende**, came a close second to the Christian Democrat candidate, Eduardo Frei Montalva. In 1970 the younger members of the Christian Democrats pressed for the nomination of a more radical candidate than Frei, who was constitutionally debarred from succeeding himself. However, the more right-wing members deserted their candidate, Radomiro Tomic, and Allende was elected at the head of an Unidad Popular coalition.

US corporations sought intervention by the Nixon Administration to prevent Allende from taking power. An abortive coup did take place, in which the military commander, a keen supporter of the constitutional order, was killed. The Christian Democrats demanded guarantees that the Constitution would be upheld, and, when these were forthcoming, ratified Allende's election. Sadly, Allende failed to realize the contradictions inevitable in trying to carry out a revolutionary programme within a constitutional framework. Though the programme was popular with the voters, who gave the UP a narrow majority in the 1972 congressional elections, the country was already sliding into economic chaos as the Movimiento de la Izquierda Revolucionaria backed illegal land occupations in the countryside. The Chilean middle-class began to resist, a national truckers' strike brought the country to a standstill and on 11 September 1973 the armed forces, led by Gen. **Augusto Pinochet Ugarte**, took power.

Troops apprehended thousands of suspects and incarcerated them in the National Stadium and other centres. Many were summarily executed, while others died after torture. Within a year the junta had made Pinochet head of state and from then until 1990 he ruled as a dictator. At first all representative organizations had been dissolved. In the second stage of the dictatorship, under the influence of the so-called Chicago Boys, Chile became the venue for a mass experiment in free market economics, backed by the sanction of military force. Then, a pseudo-constitutional regime was established; Pinochet was confirmed in power for nine years by a plebiscite. However, the economic boom ended in the early 1980s, there was a spate of bankruptcies and, in a second plebiscite, which was intended to grant him another nine-year term of office, Pinochet was defeated. He was obliged to honour the promise he had given to call elections, in which the Christian Democrat leader, Patricio Aylwin, won the presidency, and a broad cross-party coalition, the Concertación, obtained a majority in the Chamber of Deputies.

Latest elections: In the first round of voting in the elections in December 1999, Gladys Marín Millie, the Partido Comunista de Chile candidate, gained sufficient votes (3.2%) to deny Ricardo Lagos Escobar (with 48.0%) a first-round victory against his right-wing opponent Joaquín Lavín Infante (47.5%) of the Partido Unión Demócrata Independiente. Lagos was a former socialist Minister of Public Works, briefly detained in 1986 following the unsuccessful assassination attempt on Gen. Pinochet, and founder in 1987 of the Partido por la Democracia. He had defeated the President of the Senate, Andrés Zaldívar, of the President's Partido Demócrata Cristiano, in the presidential primary for the nomination of the ruling Concertación coalition. In the second round of voting, held on 16 January 2000, Lagos defeated Lavín and became Chile's first socialist President since the overthrow of Salvador Allende Gossens in 1973.

International relations and defence: Chile is a member of the United Nations, the **Organization of American States**, the **Latin American Integration Association** (LAIA—*Asociación Latinoamericana de Integración*), and the **Rio Pact**. It is an associate member of the **Southern Common Market**, and has tried, so far unsuccessfully, to join the **North American Free Trade Agreement**. It has four armed services: the army with a strength of 45,000 (just under one-half conscripted), the navy 23,000, the air force 12,500 and the *carabineros* 36,000. Military service is compulsory for men from the age of 19, and lasts for one year in the army or for 22 months in the navy or air force.

Chile, economy

GNI: US $70,600m. (2001); *GNI per caput:* $4,590 (2001); *GDP at PPP:* $136,000 (2001); *GNI per caput at PPP:* $8,840 (2001), rank 76; *exports:* $18,340m. (2002); *imports:* $15,830m. (2002); *currency:* peso, plural pesos; US $1 = 710.1 pesos at the end of May 2003.

In 2002 agriculture accounted for 6.0% of Chile's gross domestic product (GDP), mining and quarrying for 8.9% and industry for 37.8% (2001). Some 2.6% of the land is arable, 0.4% under permanent crops and 17.0% permanent pasture. Forest and woodland covers much of the south of the country. The main crops are wheat, maize, barley, oats, rice, rye, potatoes and other vegetables. Chilean wine is celebrated for its high quality and is in great demand abroad. The country has more than one-half of the world's temperate rainforests, though 80% has been damaged, and forestry products are the country's second largest export earner. Stock rearing is not a major contributor to the economy, but fishing has expanded rapidly. The main mineral resources are **copper** (of which Chile is the world's largest producer), nitrates, selenium, molybdenum, iodine and gold. The principal industries are textiles, motor cars, chemicals, rubber products, cement and consumer goods. The main energy sources are hydroelectric power and petroleum: Chile's total potential generating capacity is estimated at 18,700 MW. Oilfields in Tierra del Fuego and Magallanes supply 45% of Chile's petroleum needs; the rest has to be imported.

Main exports are copper, copper ores and concentrates, wood products, vegetables and fruit and fish products. Principal imports are machinery and transport equipment and other manufactured products. In 2001 the USA (19.4%) was the biggest market for Chile's exports, followed by Japan (12.1%), the United Kingdom (6.9%) and the People's Republic of China (6.0%). Argentina (17.8%) was the principal supplier of imports in that year, followed by the USA (16.8%), Brazil (8.7%) and the People's Republic of China (6.1%).

Between 1880 and 1920 Chile benefited hugely from the export of nitrates, but after the First World War artificial nitrates became available and copper became the mainstay of the economy. Chile, which had suffered a sharp recession in the early 1920s, suffered even more from the Great Depression, and after 1945 the country's efforts at state-led development culminated in the wholesale nationalization of all major productive enterprises under Dr **Salvador Allende** (1970–73) and the major economic crisis which facilitated the dictatorship of Gen. **Augusto Pinochet Ugarte**. Under him, trade unions were suppressed, wages driven down and Chile became the first country in Latin America to adopt the currently fashionable free-market economic model. However, though rapid economic growth took place in 1974–81, the overvaluation of the currency and other factors led to a sharp recession in 1981 and the virtual collapse of the banking system in 1983, by which time the foreign debt was equivalent to 71.1% of the country's GDP. The banks were supported by massive state intervention and Chile began a further period of rapid economic growth, averaging 6.2% during the civilian government of Patricio Aylwin (1990–94). Though not rating as a 'tiger' economy, growth continued into the early 21st century, fuelled by a steady inward flow of foreign investment and successful diversification of export markets. Chile has applied to join the **North American Free Trade Agreement** and is an associate member of the **Southern Common Market**.

Annual GDP growth averaged 3.0% in 1981–90, and 6.6% in 1990–2000; in 2002 GDP grew by 2.1%, and the inflation rate was 2.8%; in 2003 22% of the population were living below the poverty line.

Coca

The coca plant, *erthroxylum coca*, is a hardy shrub which grows naturally and is legally cultivated in the Andes. Drinking an infusion of the leaves (a *maté de coca*) is an effective remedy for altitude sickness and the local inhabitants have long chewed the leaves to counter hunger pangs and stimulate them for hard physical work. The main centres of legal cultivation are Colombia, Peru and Bolivia. Since the 1980s the US government has preferred to try to prevent the illegal cultivation of coca in South America rather than to stop it entering the USA. At a meeting with US President George Bush at Cartagena, Colombia, in 1989, therefore, several Latin American Presidents were forced to agree to the presence of US anti-drug squads on their territory and to the use of aerial crop-spraying and other methods to destroy illegal coca sites and processing laboratories. This policy, which still continues, has been conspicuously unsuccessful and has earned the USA a disproportionate amount of ill will, especially in poverty-stricken Bolivia.

Cocalero
Association of Coca-growers

Under the US-led campaign to end illegal **coca** cultivation in Bolivia (the 'Dignity Plan'), coca production for the manufacture of cocaine was drastically reduced during the 1990s. There was, however, strong opposition to the policy from a combination of indigenous groups and small farmers, resulting in rural unrest and demonstrations, the issue meshing with a range of other grievances, and protests continued after the new government of Jorge Quiroga took office.

On 15 January 2002 farmers at Sacaba, Department of Cochabamba, attempted to reopen a coca leaf market closed by presidential decree; subsequently, at the end of January, seven people were killed in a clash nearby. On 9 February, after mediation by religious leaders, the Government agreed to allow the markets to stay open for legal dealings in coca leaf. Meanwhile, legislators had voted on 24 January to strip the president of the *Cocalero* (coca-growers' association), Evo Morales, of his parliamentary immunity from prosecution for alleged incitement. However, in response to increasing military activity in Chaparé, there were clashes between troops and *cocaleros*, which led the Government to transfer coca eradication efforts to the National Police.

Morales, running as the candidate of the Movimiento al Socialismo, subsequently took 20.94% of the vote in the presidential election held on 30 June 2002, winning strong support from the indigenous peasant class. In his campaign he pledged to expel US Drug Enforcement Administration officers from Bolivia and US government officials warned that aid to Bolivia would be cut off if he were elected, branding him a left-wing ideologue and apologist for terrorism. In August 2002, therefore, Congress chose Gonzálo Sánchez de Lozada as the new President. However, in an important concession to the indigenists, on 1 September the decision was reported to redistribute some 500,000 ha of agricultural and 700,000 ha of forestry land to 11,000 landless families. The programme would cost an estimated US $2,500m.

Leadership: Evo Morales (Pres.)

Cocoa

Cocoa (*theobroma cacao*) is native to tropical America and was first cultivated in Mexico (*c.* AD 600), where the seeds were used as currency. The trees, which can grow to a height of 14 m and require a minimum of four years' cultivation before economic production, need good soil, tropical heat and high rainfall. They are very vulnerable to pests. The pods they produce contain a large number of seeds ('cocoa beans') which are cut out, separated, fermented to develop the flavour and then dried and bagged for export. Nine-tenths of the cocoa produced is used in the manufacture of confectionery. Brazil is the world's fifth largest and Latin America's largest producer of cocoa beans. In 2002 it was followed in Latin America by Ecuador, the Dominican Republic, Colombia and Mexico. An International Cocoa Agreement (ICCA) was first negotiated in 1972, under UN auspices, with the objective of stabilizing prices; though prices had been low for many years, it was renewed for the sixth time in 2001, with effect from 1 January 2002.

Coffee

Coffee (*coffea arabica, coffea canephora*) is a small evergreen tree or large shrub. It is indigenous to tropical Asia and Africa, but is now the major cash crop of much of Latin America. Cultivars are normally pruned to a maximum height of 3 m for convenience of picking the seeds ('beans'), which, when dried, roasted and ground, are infused with water to produce the world's most popular non-alcoholic drink. It takes 3–5 years for a tree to begin bearing fruit and six years before it reaches maximum yield. Yields begin to decline after 25 years and become uneconomic by 30. Since the 1960s occasional frosts, previously unknown, have devastated the crop in Brazil, where it was formerly the most valuable agricultural export, and though a record 29.3m. bags (of 60 kg) were exported in 2002–03, its relative importance to the economy has declined and Brazil's main export crop is now soya beans. Colombia, which grows a high-quality arabica coffee, produced 11.3m. bags in 2002–03, much of it exported to the USA, the world's largest consumer. Coffee is still usually the most important export crop in El Salvador, Guatemala, Haiti, Mexico, Nicaragua and Peru, and the second most important export crop in Costa Rica, the Dominican Republic, Ecuador, Honduras and Puerto Rico.

Colombia
República de Colombia

Colombia is situated in the north-west of South America, with coastlines on both the Pacific and the Caribbean. Its national territory includes a number of islands, notably the island group of San Andrés and Providencia in the Caribbean, sovereignty over which is disputed by Nicaragua. It is divided into 32 Departments.

Area: 1,141,748 sq km (440,831 sq miles); *capital:* **Santafé de Bogotá** (commonly known as Bogotá), situated in its own Capital District (DC) in the Department of Cundinamarca; *population:* officially estimated in mid-2002 at 43.8m., but no census has been carried out in the country since 1985. Twenty per cent of the population is regarded as of European extraction, 1% native American, 58% mestizo, 14% mulatto, 4% African-American and 3% mixed African and native American; *official language:* Spanish (*Castellano*); *religion:* more than 90% Roman Catholic.

Constitution: The Constitution of 1991 retained the basic structure of its 19th century predecessor, but included many new provisions designed to promote civil rights and guarantee the independence of the judicial process. Executive power is vested in a President directly elected by the people for a four-year term. The legislature consists of a Senate of 102 directly elected members, in which a minimum of two places are reserved for representatives of the sparse indigenous population, and a House of Representatives (*Cámara de Representantes*) with 161 members.

History: Colombia was one of the few Latin American states not to have a military coup in the 1930s. Instead, the election of 1930 brought the Liberals to power; under Enrique Olaya Herrera (1930–34) and Alfonso López Pumarejo (1934–38) they carried out important social reforms. However, at the end of the Second World War pressure for further reforms divided the Liberals and the Conservatives returned to power in 1946 on a minority vote. The pressure for further reform remained strong, however, and many looked to the leader of the radical faction of the Liberals, Jorge Eliecer Gaitán, for change. Then, in April 1948, as the Inter-American Conference was meeting in Bogotá, he was assassinated. Three days of violent riots escalated into all-out civil war, which was succeeded by a

Conservative backlash and the election of the intransigent Laureano Gómez to the presidency (1950–53). While tens of thousands died in the period simply known as 'the violence' (*la Violencia*), Gómez sought a personal dictatorship. Instead, the commander of the army, Gen. Gustavo Rojas Pinilla, stepped in, and assumed the presidency himself (1953–57). Civilian government was not restored until Gómez had departed and an agreement between the Liberals and Conservatives to share power was negotiated.

Though Colombia experienced left-wing guerrilla movements for longer than any other country in the region, they never threatened the well-established competitive party system. Indeed, between 1982 and 1986 the Conservative President, Dr **Belisario Betancur Cuartas,** had some success in persuading the guerrillas to lay down their arms and re-enter competitive politics. Yet, under Betancur's Liberal successor, Dr Virgilio Barco Vargas (1986–90), political violence erupted again. It was contained, though at a heavy cost in terms of human rights, while rivalry between the two giant illegal drugs syndicates (the larger based in Medellín, the smaller in Cali) emerged instead as the most serious threat facing civil society. The creation of a new Constitution in 1991 offered the chance for many of the former armed opposition to find a place in democratic politics. Despite a series of political assassinations within their ranks, some did so and this did not incline the armed forces to intervene openly.

The credibility of civil government declined to its lowest level ever under the Government of President Ernesto Samper Pizano (1994–98). His own reputation never recovered from the arrest, on 27 July 1995, of his election-campaign treasurer, Santiago Medina, on charges of using drugs money in the 1994 campaign. He, in turn, implicated the Minister of Defence, Fernando Botero, who was forced to resign. In September President Samper appeared before a congressional committee to deny any personal association with the drugs cartels, and in December 1995 the committee concluded that there was insufficient evidence to impeach him. Under his successor, Andrés Pastrana Arango, elected in August 1998, Colombia's problems of lawlessness, civil unrest and poverty intensified, despite successive rounds of peace talks with guerrilla groups.

Latest elections: Promising tough action against the rebels, the 49-year old Alvaro Uribe Velez, running as candidate of the right-wing Colombia First coalition, secured 53.04% of the vote and an unprecedented outright win in the first round of the presidential elections held on 26 May 2002. The official candidate of the outgoing Partido Liberal Colombiano (PL), Horacio Serpa Uribe, received only 31.72%. The Partido Conservador Colombiano candidate, Juan Camilo Restrepo, had withdrawn after the legislative elections and the party then endorsed Uribe. On

11 June the PL agreed to support the new Government, ensuring it a large majority in both houses of Congress.

International relations and defence: Colombia is a member of the United Nations, the **Organization of American States**, the **Latin American Integration Association** (LAIA—*Asociación Latinoamericana de Integración*), the **Andean Community of Nations** and the **Rio Pact**. In its foreign policy it has traditionally followed the lead of the USA and it has only one unresolved boundary dispute, with Venezuela, offshore in Lake Maracaibo. Because of the ongoing civil unrest, Colombia's armed forces are exceptionally large, totalling 158,000 in 2002, including 75,000 conscripts. The regular army numbers some 158,000, the navy 15,000 and the air force 7,000. Between 12 and 18 months' military service is compulsory for all male citizens except students. The paramilitary National Police Force, which is heavily involved in counter-insurgency duties, numbers 104,000.

Colombia, economy

GNI: US $81,600m. (2001); *GNI per caput:* $1,890 (2001); *GNI at PPP:* $292,000m. (2001); *GNI per caput at PPP:* $6,790 (2001), rank 88; *exports:* $12,775m. (2001); *imports:* $12,267m. (2001); *currency:* peso, plural pesos; US $1 = 2,855.90 pesos at the end of May 2003.

In 2002 agriculture accounted for 14.2% of Chile's gross domestic product (GDP), mining and energy for 7.3%, manufacturing industry for 14% and construction for 4.7%. Some 2.2% of the land is arable, 1.5% under permanent crops and 36.7% permanent pasture. The main legal crops are **coffee**, of which Colombia is the world's third largest exporter, **bananas**, cut flowers and palm oil; potatoes, maize, beans, rice, plantains, cassava and citrus fruits are grown for domestic consumption. In the mid-1990s there was a substantial increase in the illegal cultivation of **coca** for processing, as production was diverted from Peru and Bolivia, and opium poppies were introduced in the south for the manufacture of heroin. Colombia is now the world's largest illegal producer of cocaine. The value of these illegal exports may amount to as much as 20% of GDP. Beef and veal production in the llanos has been disrupted by guerrilla activity. The main mineral resources are petroleum, coal, gas, nickel and emeralds. The principal industries are food and beverages, chemicals, car assembly and textiles, including clothing manufacture. Colombia has the largest coal reserves in Latin America and is the world's fourth largest producer and exporter. Hydroelectric power supplies about 70% of Colombia's electricity needs, with the balance met by thermal generation.

Main exports are petroleum, chemicals, coal, vegetable products, especially coffee, textiles and emeralds. Principal imports are mechanical, electrical and transport equipment and paper and paper products. In 2002 the USA was the greatest purchaser of exports, followed by Venezuela. The USA was by far the greatest supplier of imports in that year, followed by Venezuela.

Traditionally coffee dominated the Colombian export economy, until superseded by petroleum and, more recently, by coal. However for many decades, until 1990, the Colombian government encouraged import-substituting manufacturing industry, giving the country a relatively diversified economy by regional standards. The removal of tariffs and quotas in 1991 checked growth abruptly. Excessive central and local government expenditure in the mid-1990s, together with the disruption caused by rising guerrilla activity, paved the way for a sharp recession in 1998–99. In 1999 the economy contracted by 4.7%, but it revived in 2000. Owing to its inability to keep the fiscal deficit in check, Colombia lost its investment-grade debt rating in 1999 and was downgraded further in 2000. Annual GDP growth in 1990–2001 averaged 2.6%. In 2001 it was 1.6% and in 2002 1.8%. In 2001 the rate of inflation was 8.6%.

Colón, Cristóbal – *see* Columbus, Christopher

Colón Free Zone

The Colón Free Zone (CFZ) is the most important manufacturing zone in Panama. Occupying a strip of land between Panama City and the port of Colón, it covers an area of more than 400 ha, and houses more than 2,000 companies. Its imports come mainly from east and south-east Asia and its exports, most of which are to Latin American destinations, account for some 7% of Panama's gross domestic product. In 2001 earnings from re-exports totalled US $5,323m.

Columbus, Christopher
Cristóbal Colón

Cristoforo Colombo (1451–1506) was born in Genoa and had extensive experience at sea before he learnt, probably in Portugal, of the important geographical discoveries that were being made in the Indies and conceived the idea of sailing west instead of east. In 1492, in command of three ships, Pinta, Niña and his flagship, Santa María, funded by the Queen of Castile, he sailed from Palos in Spain and revictualled in the Canaries before making landfall, on 12 October 1492, at

Watling Island (San Salvador) in the Bahamas. Turning southward, he sighted Cuba and made landfall on Hispaniola, where the Santa María was wrecked. Leaving men behind to found a settlement, he took command of the Niña and set sail for Spain. His arrival early in 1493, coming so soon after the fall of Granada, caused a sensation and, in accordance with his agreement with the Queen, he was made Admiral of the Ocean Sea, confirmed as governor of the new territories and given command of a fleet of 17 ships to establish a permanent settlement in the Indies (as they were to be erroneously known). However, though his second voyage in October 1493 located the Lesser Antilles and Puerto Rico, the settlement he had founded had been destroyed, the new settlement he established in its place was badly planned and by 1496 he had to return to Spain to defend himself. A third voyage, in 1498, ended badly when a new governor arrived from Spain and sent him back in chains, and by the time of his fourth and final voyage his stubborn insistence that he had discovered the way to the Indies had already been disproved by other navigators. A disastrous legacy of his rule was his mistreatment of the native Americans, who were forced into slavery with the result that many of the islands were almost depopulated.

Comisión Ejecutiva Hidroeléctrica del Río Lempa (CEL)
Hydroelectric Executive Commission for the Río Lempa, El Salvador

State agency; f. 1948; responsible for the generation and transmission of electricity; privatization planned.

    Leadership: Guillermo A. Sol Bang (Pres.)
    Address: 9a Calle Poniente 950, San Salvador
    Telephone: 271-0855
    Fax: 222-9359
    E-mail: angular@cel.gob.sv
    Internet: www.cel.gob.sv

Comisión para el Esclarecimiento Histórico (CEH)
Historical Clarification Commission, Guatemala

The CEH was formed as part of the UN-brokered peace agreement reached in Oslo, Norway, in 1994 in order to record the impact on both sides of the 36-year Guatemalan civil wars and to promote internal reconciliation. Its report, published in February 1999, concluded that the US Central Intelligence Agency and US army advisers had financed and trained Guatemalan forces which had carried out 'acts of genocide' against the indigenous Mayan population. The Government, however, decided not to set up a commission to investigate the conduct of the army and security forces which had been responsible for 90% of the recorded deaths (three civilian members of security patrols were later convicted and sentenced to death).

Previously, in March 1998, after three years of work, the Catholic Church had released a report, entitled *Guatemala: nunca más*, which gave as much detail as could be found on more than 55,000 crimes committed during the civil war, including 25,123 murders and 3,893 'disappearances'. Four-fifths of the crimes had been committed by the armed forces and 92% of the victims were civilians. Almost immediately after the release of the report the Auxiliary Bishop of Guatemala and head of the archbishopric's human rights office, Mgr Juan José Gerardi Conadera, was bludgeoned to death, provoking a popular outcry. The extreme right-wing 'death squad', Jaguar Justiciero (Jaguar Justice), claimed responsibility for the attack.

Comité Coordinador de Asociaciones Agrícolas, Comerciales, Industriales y Financieras (CACIF)

Co-ordinating Committee of Agricultural, Commercial, Industrial and Financial Associations, Guatemala

Leadership: Jorge Briz (Pres.), Rafael Pola (Sec.-Gen.)
Address: Edif. Cámara de Industria de Guatemala, 6a Ruta 9–21, Zona 4, Guatemala City
Telephone: 231-0651

Commonwealth, The

The Commonwealth is a free association of member states, who accept HM Queen Elizabeth II as the symbol of their association and as the Head of the Commonwealth. It has no contractual obligations or written constitution, but members are expected to accept the Declaration of Commonwealth Principles approved in Singapore in 1971, and a number of later agreements. Members do not conduct formal diplomatic correspondence with one another and exchange High Commissioners not Ambassadors, with the intention of facilitating free exchange of views; meetings of Heads of Government, which take place in different locations every two years, are private and decisions are made by consensus not voting.

Meetings are also held regularly at ministerial and official level. All former British colonies in the Caribbean area are members, as are the UK dependencies.

Leadership: Rt Hon. Donald McKinnon, New Zealand (Sec.-Gen.)

Address: Commonwealth Secretariat, Marlborough House, Pall Mall, London
SW1Y 5HX, United Kingdom

Telephone: (20) 7839-3411

Fax: (20) 7747-6500

E-mail: info@commonwealth.int

Internet: www.thecommonwealth.org

Communism

Marxism did not have much of an impact in Latin America until the first decade of the 20th century. Chile's Partido Obrero de Chile, established in 1912 by Luis Emilio Recabarren and others, became the Partido Comunista de Chile (PCCh) in 1920 and, with the Partido Comunista de Argentina, was a founding member of the Third International (Comintern). By 1928 parties also existed in Brazil, Guatemala and Uruguay, as well as Mexico, where an unsuccessful revolt in 1929 made little impact. A major insurrection in El Salvador in 1932, however, was put down with heavy loss of life ('La Matanza') and the revolt of Luis Carlos Prestes in Brazil in 1935 only strengthened the growing authoritarianism in that country.

Under the new 'Popular Front' strategy, the Colombian party backed the reformist Liberal Government of Alfonso López Pumarejo and the PCCh joined with the Radicals and others to elect Pedro Aguirre Cerda as President in 1938. Communists also formed part of the coalition that elected Fulgencio Batista in Cuba in 1940. During the Second World War parties were legalized and gained support throughout the continent, and briefly, in 1945–47, the Partido Comunista do Brasil was the largest in the region. With the onset of the Cold War, however, it was banned in 1947 and the 'Bogotazo' of 1948 gave an excuse to other governments, notably that of Chile, to follow suit. Under the name of the Partido Guatemalteco del Trabajo, however, the Guatemalan party remained legal until the fall of Jacobo Arbenz in 1954 and Cuban deputies remained in Batista's Congress until 1959.

With the Cuban Revolution, the path of armed struggle again gained favour. Though the Communists had done nothing to help Castro's victory, they now gained power. Communist parties in Colombia and Venezuela also for a time supported insurgent movements, but by 1965 most had been suppressed and the Partido Comunista de Bolivia failed to support **Che Guevara**. Divided into pro-Soviet, pro-Chinese and pro-Cuban factions, Communists ceased to be of much significance thereafter except as useful bogeymen for the new, hardline military governments. An exception was the PCCh, which had remained committed to peaceful means and took part in the Popular Unity Government of Salvador Allende. For this it paid a heavy price after 1973, though its successor is still active in democratic politics today.

Companhia Vale do Rio Doce, SA (CVRD)
Valley of the Rio Doce Co, Brazil

F. 1942; originally a state corporation established to develop mining and forestry resources. Privatized in 1997, the corporation, whose personnel number some 15,500, is the largest gold producer in South America, but is principally known for its production of iron ore, aluminium and forestry products. It owns and operates the Carajás iron ore mine and railway, the port of Ponta da Madeira in the state of Tocantins, the Itabira iron ore mine, the Vitóri-Minas railway and the port of Tubarão, in the south of Brazil. Both projects have attracted criticism from environmentalists owing to the scale of their impact on the environment.

Leadership: José Luiz Perez Garrido (Chair.)
Address: Av. Graça Aranha, 60 andar, Bairro Castelo, 20005-900 Rio de Janeiro, RJ
Telephone: (21) 272-4477
Fax: (21) 272-4324
Internet: www.vale.com.br

Concertación de Partidos por la Democracia (CPD)
Concert of Parties for Democracy, Chile

First organized in 1988 as the Comando por el No, a grouping of civilian parties campaigning against the re-election of Gen. **Augusto Pinochet Ugarte** by plebiscite on 5 October 1988, it adopted its present name following the defeat of the military government in order to campaign, successfully, for the election of a civilian government.

Leadership: Ricardo Lagos Escobar (Leader, Pres. of the Republic)
Address: Londres 57, Santiago
Telephone: (2) 639-7170
Fax: (2) 639-7449
E-mail: concert@creuna.cl

Confederação Geral dos Trabalhadores (CGT)
General Confederation of Labour, Brazil

F. 1986; the Confederation represents 1,012 labour organizations with more than 6.3m. members. It is closely linked to and supports the **Partido do Movimento Democrático Brasileiro**.

> *Leadership:* Antônio Carlos dos Reis Medeiros (Pres.)
> *Address:* Rua Tomaz Gonzaga 50, 20 andar Liberdade, 01506-020 São Paulo, SP
> *Telephone and fax:* (11) 3207-6577
> *E-mail:* cgt@cgt.org.br
> *Internet:* www.cgt.org.br

Confederação Nacional do Comércio (CNC)
National Confederation of Commerce, Brazil

National confederation of 35 affiliated chambers of commerce.

> *Leadership:* Antônio José Domingues de Oliveira Santos (Pres.)
> *Address:* SCS, Edif. Presidente Dutra, 4° andar, Quadra 11, 70327 Brasília
> *Telephone:* (61) 223-6178
> *E-mail:* cncdf@cnc.com.br
> *Internet:* www.cnc.com.br

Confederação Nacional da Indústria (CNI)
National Confederation of Industry, Brazil

National confederation of industry; f. in 1938; represents 27 state industrial federations.

> *Leadership:* Armando de Queiroz Monteiro Meto (Pres.)
> *Address:* Rua Mariz e Barros 678, 2°, Maracaña, 20270-002 Rio de Janeiro, RJ
> *Telephone:* (21) 2204-9513
> *Fax:* (21) 2204-9522
> *E-mail:* sac@cni.org.br
> *Internet:* www.cni.org.br

Confederación de Cámaras Industriales de los Estados Unidos Mexicanos (COMCAMIN)
Confederation of Chambers of Industry, Mexico

National confederation f. in 1918 to represent the interests of the industrial employers; not affiliated to the **Partido Revolucionario Institucional**.

Leadership: Alejandro Martínez Gallardo (Pres.)
Address: Manuel María Contreras 133, 8°, Col. Cuauhtémoc, 06500 México, DF
Telephone: (55) 5566-7822
Fax: (55) 5535-6871
E-mail: jcbustos@concamin.org.mx
Internet: www.concamin.org.mx

Confederación de Cámaras Nacionales de Comercio, Servicios y Turismo (CONCANACO)

Confederation of National Chambers of Commerce, Mexico

National confederation f. in 1917; now links 283 regional and local chambers of commerce; not affiliated to the **Partido Revolucionario Institucional**.
Leadership: Raúl Alejandro Padilla Orozco (Pres.)
Address: Balderas 144, 3°, Col. Centro, 06079 México, DF
Telephone: (55) 5772-9300
Fax: (55) 5709-1152
E-mail: sistemas@concanacored.com
Internet: www.concanacored.com

Confederación Colombiana de Camaras de Comercio (CONFEDECAMARAS)

Colombian Confederation of Chambers of Commerce

F. 1969; 56 member organizations.
Leadership: Eugenio Marulanda Gómez (Exec. Pres.)
Address: Carrera 13, No. 27–47, Of. 502, Apdo Aéreo 29750, Santafé de Bogotá, DC
Telephone: (1) 346-7055
Fax: (1) 346-7026
E-mail: confedecamaras@inter.net.co
Internet: www.confedecamaras.org.co

Confederación General de Trabajadores del Perú (CGTP)

General Confederation of Peruvian Workers

Principal trade union organization of Peru; f. in 1968.
Leadership: Mario Huamán Rivera (Pres.)

> *Address:* Ayacucho 173, Lima
> *Telephone:* (1) 428-2253
> *E-mail:* cgtp@cgtp.org.pe
> *Internet:* www.cgtp.org.pe

Confederación General del Trabajo de la República Argentina (CGT)

General Confederation of Labour, Argentina

Peronist trade union confederation; refounded 1984; represents some 90% of the country's 1,100 labour unions, and is affiliated to the **Partido Justicialista**.
> *Leadership:* Hugo Moyano (Leader)
> *Address:* Azopardo 802, CP 1107, Buenos Aires, Argentina
> *Telephone and fax:* (11) 4343-1883, (11) 4545-4826
> *E-mail:* secgral@cgtra.org.ar
> *Internet:* www.cgtra.org.ar

Confederación General del Trabajo (CGT), El Salvador

General Confederation of Labour, El Salvador

F. 1983; has 20 affiliated unions with 85,000 members.
> *Leadership:* José Luis Grande Preza (Sec.-Gen.)
> *Address:* 2a Avda Norte 619, San Salvador
> *Telephone:* 222-5980

Confederación Paraguaya de Trabajadores (CPT)

Paraguayan Workers' Confederation

For most of the 20th century, trade union activity in Paraguay was either prohibited or severely circumscribed. The CPT was founded in 1951 and claims 43,500 members from 189 affiliated unions.
> *Leadership:* Gerónimo López (Pres.)
> *Address:* Yegros 1309-33 y Simón Bolívar, Asunción
> *Telephone:* (21) 44-3184

Confederación Revolucionaria Obrera de México (CROM)
Revolutionary Confederation of Mexican Workers

F. in 1918 as a regional organization of the Second International, the CROM formed the basis of power of Mexican governments in the 1920s and the early 1930s, but its influence waned after the election of Lázaro Cárdenas in 1934 and it was displaced by the Confederación de Trabajadores de México.

Confederación de Trabajadores de Honduras (CTH)
Workers' Confederation of Honduras

F. 1964, the CTH is the largest trade union confederation in Honduras, with some 200,000 members. It is affiliated to the Organización Regional Interamericana de Trabajadores and the International Confederation of Free Trade Unions.
   Leadership: Wilfredo Galeas Angel Meza (Pres.)
   Address: Edif. Beige 2, Avda Juan Ramón Milina, Barrio El Olvido, Apdo 720,
          Tegucigalpa
   Telephone: (504) 238-7859
   Fax: 237-8032, 238-8575
   E-mail: dinoraaceituno@yahoo.com

Confederación de Trabajadores de México (CTM)
Confederation of Mexican Workers

Since its foundation in 1936, when it displaced the **Confederación Regional Obrera Mexicana** as the favoured workers' organization, the CTM has formed an integral part of the structure of the **Partido Revolucionario Institucional**, becoming in the process the largest trade union confederation in the country, with the most privileged members in key industries. Affiliated to the International Confederation of Free Trade Unions.
   Leadership: Mario Suárez Garcia (Sec.-Gen.)
   Address: Vallarta 8, Piso 3, México, DF
   Telephone: (52) 555-350658
   Fax: (52) 555-7050966, 555-7051091
   E-mail: ctmrelaciones@netservice.com.mx

Confederación de Trabajadores de la República de Panama (CTRP)

Confederation of Workers of the Republic of Panama

F. 1956; claims 62,000 members from 62 affiliated unions or federations; affiliated to the International Confederation of Free Trade Unions and the Organización Regional Interamericana de Trabajadores.

Leadership: Guillermo Puga (Pres.)

Address: Calle 31, entre Avdas Mexico y Justo Arosemena 3–50, Apdo 8929, Panamá 9

Telephone: (507) 225-0259

Fax: (507) 221-5955

E-mail: ctrp@sinfo.net

Confederación de Trabajadores de Venezuela (CTV)

Confederation of Venezuelan Workers

Venezuela's largest trade union confederation and one of the strongest in Latin America; f. 1936, its membership includes the petroleum (Fedepetrol) and mining (Fetrametal) workers' unions, and the farm workers' union, Federación Campesina; it is currently in dispute with the Chávez administration, which is supported by its own union, the Fuerza Bolivariana de Trabajadores, over the validity of its elections; affiliated to the International Confederation of Free Trade Unions.

Leadership: Carlos Ortega (Pres.), Manuel Cova (Sec.-Gen.)

Address: Edif. José Vargas, 17°, Avda Este 2, Los Caobos, Caracas

Telephone: (58) 212 576-0022

Fax: (58) 212 574-1994

E-mail: cortega@la-ctv.com

Internet: www.ctv.org.ve

Confederation of Indigenous Nationalities of Ecuador

Confederación de Nacionalidades Indígenas de Ecuador (Conaie)

Conaie is a dissident movement founded in 1986 to give a voice to indigenous Ecuadorians, who form one-third of the population. As a pressure group in 1989 it obtained an agreement with the Ministry of Education on the establishment of bilingual, bicultural education. It adopted direct action in 1992 as part of the general increase in indigenist awareness throughout the continent of the impact of globalization. The announcement of an austerity package by the new President, Sixto Durán Ballén, on 3 September 1992 ignited a series of violent street demonstrations in Quito and Guayaquil, and, despite the mobilization of the army four days later, Conaie began a campaign of civil disobedience. Following elections in 1994, a new right-wing majority attempted to reverse 30 years of slow land reform through a Land Development Law passed on 13 June. This led to massive protests from Conaie. The Court of Constitutional Guarantees ruled the law unconstitutional on 23 June, with the result that in amended form it guaranteed the rights of those who directly worked land, whether as individuals or associations.

Conaie later joined with other Indian organizations, trade unions and grassroots activists of the Patriotic Front in protesting against the economic policies of President Jamil Mahuad Witt, elected in July 1998. In response, on 11 March 1999 the President proclaimed a state of emergency, a partial freeze on bank withdrawals and a tough austerity programme which, following the withdrawal of support from the Partido Social Cristiano on 15 March, passed Congress with only a meagre majority and in revised form. During 1999 Ecuador, which owed US $16,000m., defaulted on interest payments to its international creditors, who indicated that they would not provide further bail-outs without structural reform, and there was hyper-inflation.

On 18 January 2000 Conaie mobilized its largest demonstration against Mahuad and his neo-liberal economic policies, which included a highly controversial project to adopt the US dollar as the country's currency. This, when announced on 9 January, had instantly led to price rises of 50%–300%. With the connivance of elements in the armed forces, led by Cols Lucio Gutiérrez, Jorge Brito and Fausto Cobos, on 21 January supporters of Conaie seized the Congress and Supreme Court buildings. While President Mahuad abandoned the Palacio Carondelet and took refuge in a nearby air force base, a 'junta of national salvation' was proclaimed, consisting of the Conaie leader, Antonio Vargas, and the former president of the Supreme Court, Carlos Solórzano, as well as Col Gutiérrez, who soon ceded his role as chairman to the commander of the armed forces and acting defence minister, Gen. Carlos Mendoza. Following strong representations from the USA and other American states, however, on 26 January Congress declared that Mahuad had abandoned his post and Vice-President Gustavo Noboa Bejarano was duly sworn in as President, thus preserving constitutional forms.

The new Government decided to go ahead with both the privatization and dollarization proposals, and, after further widespread unrest, on 4 September 2000 Conaie announced an indefinite general strike. Though plans for the privatization of

Petroecuador were suspended, the dollar replaced the sucre as the national currency on 8 September. However, serious popular protests erupted again at the beginning of January 2001, starting among indigenous peasant farmers who were soon joined by public-sector workers and students. The protests, once more led by Conaie, were spurred by the sharp increases in charges for gas, electricity, petrol and public transport that had been announced by the Government of President Noboa in December 2000. Eliminating subsidies would have meant that the cost of liquid propane gas (LPG) would double, at the end of a year in which inflation had reached 91%. The increases had been made in order to reduce the budget deficit in accordance with the requirements of the **International Monetary Fund**'s structural adjustment package. The high command of the armed forces refused to intervene and hundreds of protesters were arrested. Finally the Government did negotiate an end to the 'great national mobilization', lifting the state of emergency on 2 February 2001 and restoring the subsidy on LPG.

In November 2002 Conaie's decision to support the candidature and social programme of former Col Lucio Edwin Gutiérrez Borbúa was undoubtedly a major factor in his decisive victory in the second round of the presidential elections held towards the end of that month. He thus became the first member of the indigenous community to hold the country's chief office.

Leadership: Leonidas Iza (Pres.)
Address: Avda Granados 2593 y 6 de Diciembre, Casilla 17-17-1235, Quito, Ecuador
Telephone: (2) 248930
Fax: (2) 442271
E-mail: cci@conaie.ec
Internet: www.conaie.nativeweb.org

Conselho dos Exportadores de Café Verde do Brasil (CECAFE)
Brazilian Council of Exporters of Green Coffee

Lobby group of green **coffee** exporters, formed in 1999 through the merger of the Federação Brasileira dos Exportadores do Café and the Associação Brasileira dos Exportadores do Café. Administers system of coffee quotas under the International Coffee Agreement.

Address: Av. Nove de Julho 4865, Torre A. Conj. 61, Chácara Itaim, 01407-200 São Paulo, SP
Telephone: (11) 3079-3755

Fax: (11) 3167-4060
Internet: www.cecafe.com

Consejo Superior de la Empresa Privada (COSEP)
Higher Council of Private Enterprise, Nicaragua

F. 1972, COSEP has been a powerful lobby group for free-market solutions to Nicaragua's economic problems. It includes organizations representing all the major sectors of Nicaraguan business and is a member of the Coordinadora Democrática Nicaragüense.
Leadership: Roberto Teran (Pres.)
Address: De Telcor Zacarías Guerra, 1 c. abajo, Apdo 5430, Managua
Telephone: (2) 28-2030
Fax: (2) 28-2041
E-mail: cosep@nic.gbm.net

Convergencia Nacional (CN)
National Convergence, Venezuela

Leadership: Dr Rafael Caldera Rodríguez (Leader), Juan José Caldera (Gen. Co-ordinator)
Address: Edif. Tajamar, 2° Piso, Of. 215, Parque Central, Avda Lecuna, El Conde, Caracas 1010
Telephone: (212) 578-1177
Fax: (212) 578-0363
E-mail: convergeprensa@cantv.net
Internet: www.convergencia.org.ve

Convertibility Plan

Plan introduced in Argentina in 1992 by economy minister Domingo Cavallo, the cornerstone of which was the decision to establish a new currency, the new peso, pegged at par to the US dollar. Within three months inflation had fallen to single figures and over the next two years a substantial amount of capital was repatriated.

Copper

Copper, one of the few metals to occur as such in nature, has been known since ancient times. Today, however, it is extracted from ores containing copper oxide or copper sulphide. Sulphide ores are first ground and the unwanted material settled out by flotation; the dried material is then first smelted into anode copper and then purified by electrolysis. Oxide ores are first separated in an acid bath, and the copper-containing layer purified by electrolysis. Chile contains about one-third of known copper reserves and has been the world's largest producer and exporter of copper since 1982, production rising to some 4.4m. metric tons in 2003. Leading Latin American producers in 2001 were Peru, the world's fourth largest producer after Chile, the USA and Indonesia, and Mexico. Argentina and Brazil are relatively minor producers.

Corporación Financiera de Desarrollo (COFIDE)
Financial Development Corporation, Peru

Government-owned development bank; f. 1971; 11 branches in various parts of the Republic.

> *Leadership:* Aurelio Loret de Mola Böhme (Pres.)
> *Address:* Augusto Tamayo 160, San Isidro, Lima 27
> *Telephone:* (1) 442-2550
> *Fax:* (1) 442-3374
> *E-mail:* postmaster@cofide.com.pe
> *Internet:* www.cofide.com.pe

Corporación de Fomento de la Producción (CORFO)
Corporation for the Development of Production, Chile

CORFO was founded in 1939. It forms the holding group behind the main state enterprises, and has been charged with selling off those state enterprises which are regarded as having no strategic significance. It grants loans and guarantees to firms in the private sector.

> *Leadership:* Oscar Landerretche Gacitúa (CEO and Exec. Vice-Pres.)
> *Address:* Moneda 921, Casilla 3886, Santiago
> *Telephone:* (2) 631-8200
> *Fax:* (2) 671-1058
> *E-mail:* info@corfo.cl
> *Internet:* www.corfo.cl

Corporación Nacional del Cobre de Chile (CODELCO-Chile)

The National Copper Corporation of Chile

A state-owned corporation, founded in 1976, which employs over 18,000 workers in the production of **copper** in seven operating divisions, and is the main contributor both to Chile's industrial production and to its export earnings.

Leadership: Jorge Rodríguez Grossi (Pres.)
Address: Huérfanos 1270, Casilla 150-D, Santiago
Telephone: (2) 690-3000
Fax: (2) 690-3059
E-mail: communica@stgo.codelco.cl
Internet: www.codelcochile.com

Costa Rica

República de Costa Rica

Costa Rica, the most southerly of the Central American republics, straddles the isthmus, and is bounded on the north by the San Juan river which forms its frontier with Nicaragua and on the south by Panama. It is divided into seven provinces.

Area overall: 51,060 sq km (19,730 sq miles); *capital:* San José; *population:* 4.0m. (2002 estimate), comprising mestizos 94%, Africans 3%, Amerindians 1%; *official language:* Spanish; *religion:* Roman Catholics 87%, various evangelical Protestant sects.

Constitution: The Constitution of November 1949 established a democratic, presidential republic. There is a single-chamber Legislative Assembly composed of 57 deputies elected by universal adult suffrage for a four-year term. The chief executive is a President concurrently elected for a four-year term, who may not be re-elected. Voting is compulsory. The Constitution bans the maintenance of an army.

History: Although little European settlement took place in Costa Rica until the 18th century, by then disease had devastated the indigenous population, and Costa Rica's society emerged as a relatively homogenous group of small landowners and subsistence farmers. **Coffee**, introduced in 1808, and **bananas**, introduced in 1878, became the main export crops, and when Costa Rica became independent in 1838 it was under a civilian government. However, for much the rest of the century Liberal and Conservative élites warred with one another for control until Tomás Guardia seized power in 1870 and implemented a programme of liberal reform, culminating in the introduction of free, universal primary education in 1881. In 1917 Federico Tinoco deposed the elected President and established a military dictatorship, only to be overthrown two years later by a popular revolt. The Government of Rafael Angel Calderón Guardia (1944–48) introduced a labour code and a social security system, but when it tried to nullify the victory of the opposition candidate in the 1948 presidential election, a coffee farmer, **José Figueres Ferrer**, led a successful uprising which forced the President out. Figueres' provisional Government re-wrote the Constitution, abolished the armed forces and transferred their budget to education, and transferred power peacefully to President-elect Otilio Ulate (1948–52). Finding him too conservative, however, Figueres went on to form his own party, the **Partido de Liberación National** (PLN) and was elected President in 1952. Until 1990 the PLN dominated Costa Rican politics, and though towards the end of that time there was increasing concern about the cost of the welfare state, it was only in the mid-1990s, amid social unrest and under the leadership of Figueres' son, José María Figueres Olsen (President 1994–98), that Costa Rica accepted the prevailing free-market model

Latest elections: On 7 April 2002, in the second round of voting in the presidential election, a 69-year old psychiatrist and poet, Abel Pacheco de la Espriella, of the **Partido Unidad Social Cristiana** (PUSC) won 57.96% of the votes cast, defeating Rolando Araya Monge of the Partido de Liberación Nacional (PLN), who obtained 42.04%. In the first round of voting, held on 3 February, for the first time since the present Constitution was adopted in 1949, neither of the two leading candidates had secured the necessary 40% to win outright, as a third candidate, Ottón Solís Fallas, of the Partido Acción Ciudadana (PAC), obtained a record 26.2%, two other candidates receiving less than 3% between them. In concurrent elections on 3 February for the 57-seat Legislative Assembly the results were similarly indecisive, being: PUSC 19 seats, PLN 17, PAC 14, Partido Movimiento Libertario six and Partido Renovación Costarricense one.

International relations and defence: Costa Rica is a member of the United Nations, the **Organization of American States** (OAS) and the **Central American Integration System** (*Sistema de la Integración Centroamericana—* SICA) and the **Rio Pact**. It has no armed forces, having abolished them in 1948. The country was invaded by Nicaragua on two occasions in the 1950s, when Costa Rica successfully invoked the protection of the OAS. The security forces include 2,000 rural guards, 4,400 civil guards and 2,000 border security police.

Costa Rica, economy

GNI per caput: US $4,030 (2001); *currency:* colón, plural colones; US $1 = 395.1 colones at 31 May 2003.

In 2002 agriculture accounted for 8.1% of Costa Rica's gross national income and industry for 20.7%. Some 4.4% of the land is arable, 5.9% under permanent crops and 45.8% permanent pasture. Forest and woodland has been much depleted and is now regarded as critically endangered. The main export crops are **coffee** and **bananas**; maize, beans and rice are grown for domestic consumption. Strict controls limit the exploitation of forestry products, because of serious past deforestation, and since 1996 strenuous efforts have been made to reafforest denuded areas. Cattle ranching on cleared forest land has further damaged the environment. The main mineral resources are iron ore, **bauxite**, sulphur, manganese, mercury, gold and silver. The principal industries are cement and petroleum refining. The main energy source is petroleum, and despite the discovery of significant reserves, these remain unexploited, so the state-owned refinery processes crude from Mexico and Venezuela. However, petroleum is hardly used for the generation of electric power, 99.5% of which was derived from renewable resources in 2000, using a combination of hydroelectric power, fuel wood, bagasse and industrial alcohol, and geothermal energy (which accounted for 14.1% of capacity in 2000).

Main exports are electrical components for microprocessors, products assembled in the Free Zone (the maquila sector), bananas and coffee. Principal imports are raw materials for industry and mining. In 2002 the USA was the greatest purchaser of exports, Mexico and Venezuela, the next in line, accounting for only a fraction in comparison. The USA was also the greatest purchaser of imports, followed by Guatemala. Costa Rica has a flourishing tourist industry, which accounts for some 19.5% of the country's gross domestic product (GDP).

In 1973 Costa Rica was wholly dependent on imported petroleum, so the steep rise in the cost of fuel in the 1970s had a serious impact. Heavy government expenditure, together with a weak fiscal system, had, by the early 1980s, made Costa Rica proportionately the most heavily indebted country in Latin America. Being a relatively small country, it received short shrift from the **International Monetary Fund**. A powerful, democratically elected legislature, however, strongly resisted any proposals to reduce the persistent budget deficit. Annual GDP growth averaged 4.1% in 1991–99. It declined to 1.8% in 2000 and to 1.1% in 2001, but rose to 3.0% in 2002. Inflation, however, has been a persistent problem. The rate of inflation, which reached 23.2% in 1995, remained high, at 9.2%, in 2002, when the unemployment rate stood at 6.7% and some 20.3% of the population were living in poverty.

Cotton

Commercial yarn spun from the hair-like fibres surrounding the seeds of Gossypium, a sub-tropical plant of the mallow family. At maturity the bolls within which the seeds are carried burst open and the fluffy balls are harvested by hand; separation of the fibres from the seeds is done mechanically. Assuming the availability of cheap labour, cotton is cheap to produce and capable of being made into a wide range of comfortable and hard-wearing garments, However heavy use of insecticides to protect the crop against attack from the boll weevil and other pests has adverse consequences for those who harvest it, and has been the subject of criticism in Guatemala and other Central American countries. There is no international agreement to maintain cotton prices.

Credito Hipotecario Nacional de Guatemala

State-owned mortgage bank; f. 1930; 35 agencies.

Leadership: Fabián Pira Arrivillaga (Pres.)
Address: 7a Avda 22–77, Zona 1, Apdo 242, Guatemala City
Telephone: 230-6562
Fax: 238-0744
E-mail: jpedchn@infovia.gov.gt
Internet: www.chn.net.gt

Cuba
República de Cuba

Cuba, the largest of the Greater Antilles, lies in the entrance from the Atlantic to the Gulf of Mexico, 210 km east of Mexico, 145 km (90 miles) south of Florida (USA), 80 km west of Haiti and 145 km north of Jamaica.

Area overall: 110,860 sq km (42,803 sq miles); *capital:* **Havana** (*La Habana*); *population:* 11.2m. (2001 estimate), comprising mulattos 51%, Europeans 37%, Africans 11%, Chinese 1%; *official language:* Spanish; *religion*, officially none but 55% Roman Catholic and 10% other Christian denominations.

Constitution: The present Constitution of Cuba is based on the Constitution of 24 February 1976, but was extensively revised in 1992. Legislative and constituent power is vested in the National Assembly of People's Power, which is elected by universal secret ballot for a term of five years. It elects the Council of State of 29 members, the president of which is both head of state and head of government. The president of the Council of State nominates members of the Council of Ministers, of which he is also president, subject to the approval of the Council of State. The Constitution entrenches the socialist system as the basis of government in Cuba and contains extensive provisions setting out the rights and duties of citizens.

History: Cuba was first sighted by the Spanish on **Christopher Columbus'** first voyage in 1492. As in neighbouring Santo Domingo, the docile local inhabitants were soon being worked to death and only 4,000 remained in 1550. Hence, slaves were imported from other Caribbean islands and later from Africa to work the **sugar** plantations. Havana became the key to Spanish control of the mainland, and Cuba remained Spanish after most of the rest of Spanish America had secured its independence. In the Ten Years War (1868–78) the first attempt to secure independence was defeated. However, insurrection broke out again in 1895, led by the poet and patriot José Martí, who was soon captured and executed. In 1898 the USA intervened. In the Spanish–American War Spain was defeated.

In 1902 Cuba became nominally independent, therefore, but under the terms of the **Platt Amendment** the USA maintained its tutelage over the island, and when the first President, Tomás Estrada Palma (1902–06), sought re-election, the Conservatives rose in revolt and the USA intervened again. Though in 1909 self-government was restored, resentment grew at the continued presence of US Marines, who protected Mario García Menocal (1913–21) when he sought re-election in 1917. However, when Calvin Coolidge chose not to intervene in 1925 he was blamed for the rise to power of the dictatorial Gerardo Machado y Morales, who dominated Cuban politics from 1925 to 1933, when he was overthrown in a popular revolt. This paved the way for the rise of Fulgencio Batista, who rose from the rank of sergeant to become Commander of the National Guard in 100 days. In 1934 he shunted aside the enthusiastic but ineffective Ramón Grau San Martín and nominated a more pliable President. In 1940, under a new, semi-parliamentary Constitution, with a Prime Minister as head of government, he became President himself and constitutional government was maintained until 1952. Then, although he had promised a free election, Batista seized power for himself.

In the following year a group of young men tried to seize the Moncada barracks in **Santiago de Cuba**. After Batista's troops had faithfully carried out his orders that for every soldier killed, 10 of their adversaries would die, the Archbishop of Santiago intervened to insist that the rest must at least be tried. One of them, their leader, **Fidel Castro**, was as a result imprisoned for only a year before being released, when he and his brother fled to Mexico, from where they sailed in the last days of 1956 to organize a second insurrection in Cuba.

Initially this, too, was a fiasco. Ambushed as they came ashore, only a dozen escaped to the mountains of the Sierra Maestra. In July 1957 they issued a manifesto in favour of liberal democracy, free elections, freedom of the press and peasant ownership of the land. In 1958 the regime swiftly crumbled, and at the end of the year, as a guerrilla victory coincided with a popular uprising in Havana itself,

Batista fled to the USA. Frequently, those of his supporters who did not do the same were summarily executed. Castro, as leader of the Revolution, appointed Manuel Urrutia Lleo, the judge at his trial, as interim President. In February 1959 he appointed himself Prime Minister and, not long afterwards, denounced Urrutia and replaced him with **Osvaldo Dorticós Torrado**. Within the next few months a radical programme of nationalization of foreign and domestically owned enterprises was carried out, and, after the failure of the US-sponsored Bay of Pigs expedition in 1961, Castro proclaimed his regime socialist and aligned himself closely with the Soviet Union. Meanwhile, a wave of guerrilla movements broke out in a great arc extending from Guatemala down into north-east Brazil, but most were quickly suppressed. In October 1962 US reconnaissance aircraft detected signs of preparations to locate Soviet missiles on the island, leading to a confrontation between the USA and the USSR and an agreement to dismantle the bases. A small Soviet garrison of 3,000 troops, however, remained.

In 1965 the ruling party was formally styled the Cuban Communist Party. At this stage, however, Cuba continued in some respects to act independently of the Soviet Union, and in 1965 **Che Guevara** left Cuba to try to spread the Cuban model of guerrilla warfare abroad, only to be killed in Bolivia in 1967. Cuba itself, despite a vigorous literacy and health campaign, lacked effective resources to diversify its economy, and instead, in 1970, attempted to raise a sugar harvest of 10m. metric tons, sufficient to generate a significant surplus. Though a harvest of 8.3m. tons was in fact achieved, the effort distorted the economy, which, as a consequence, became increasingly dependent on Soviet support. In 1974 elections were held in the province of Matanzas, which heralded the adoption of a Soviet-style Constitution under which the National Assembly of People's Power was inaugurated in December 1976 and Castro himself became head of state as well as head of government.

In 1975 Cuba had sent troops to Angola to aid its struggle for independence, and to Ethiopia to support the hardline Marxist government in its war against Somalia. In both theatres Cuban troops fought hard and with considerable success, winning support for the regime in the Third World. In consequence, Castro was elected president of the **Non-Aligned Movement** in 1979, only to dissipate the popularity he had won abroad by supporting the Soviet intervention in Afghanistan in December of that year. In 1980 the sudden decision to allow would-be exiles to leave the island caught the US Government unprepared, but with the inauguration of Ronald Reagan as US President in January 1981 relations took a turn for the worse. In April 1982, contrary to the trend in the rest of the hemisphere, the US authorities prohibited both trade and investment in Cuba by US citizens. US intervention in

Grenada in 1983 resulted in the death of a number of Cuban construction workers, and the clandestine US war on Nicaragua heightened tension on the island. From 1986 the government began a process of 'rectification of errors and correction of deviant trends'. The electoral defeat of the Sandinistas in Nicaragua left Cuba isolated within the hemisphere. Ironically, it was only after the collapse of the Soviet Union, which plunged Cuba into economic crisis, that the USA again tightened the economic embargo on the island by the **Cuban Democracy (Torricelli) Act, 1992**, and the **Cuban Liberty and Solidarity (Helms-Burton) Act, 1996**.

Latest elections: In elections in January 2003 more than 97% of voters were reported to have returned 609 representatives unopposed to the National Assembly of People's Power, and in March 2003 Dr Fidel Castro was unanimously re-elected President of the Council of Ministers for a sixth consecutive term.

International relations and defence: Cuba is a member of the United Nations. It was a founder member of the **Organization of American States** (OAS), from which it was excluded in 1964, and has withdrawn from the **Rio Pact**. Since the collapse of the Soviet Union and its system of alliances, Cuba has strengthened its links with Latin America and has been admitted as a full member of the **Latin American Integration Association** (LAIA—*Asociación Latinoamericana de Integración*). It remains excluded, however, from the OAS. Cuba is believed to have an army of some 35,000 regular troops, a navy of 3,000 and an air force of 8,000. Its paramilitary forces include 20,000 state security troops, 6,500 border guards and a civil defence force numbering 50,000. Defence and internal security expenditure was estimated at 692m. pesos in 2001. Three thousand troops of the former USSR were withdrawn in 1993 and Russia closed its surveillance facility on the island in 2001.

Cuba, economy

Comparable statistics are not available, but the **International Bank for Reconstruction and Development** (World Bank) estimates that Cuba is a lower middle-income country.

GNI: approximately US $2,672 (2001); *GNI per caput:* in the range of $746–$2,975 (2001); *exports:* $1,675m. (2000); *imports:* $4,829m. (2000); *currency:* peso, plural pesos; officially US $1 = 1 peso, but approximately 23 on the free market in September 1998.

In 2001 agriculture accounted for 6.5% of Cuba's gross domestic product (GDP). Some 32.7% of the land is arable, 7.5% under permanent crops and 19.8% permanent pasture. **Sugar** remains by far the most important crop; tobacco and citrus fruit are grown for export; rice, potatoes, maize and cassava are grown for domestic consumption. Cattle and poultry rearing expanded greatly before 1990, but since then the dairy industry, over-reliant on imported cheap feed from the USSR, has been hard hit and has not recovered. The main mineral resources are nickel and cobalt; gold, silver and **copper** are no longer significant and only small quantities of petroleum have so far been located. The principal industries are food processing, construction materials, chemicals, machine tools, paper and glass, and a small but highly successful pharmaceutical and biotechnology sector. Cuba is critically short of energy sources, having failed to develop the renewable resources available to it while it had time to do so.

Main exports are food and live animals, raw and processed sugar, and cobalt and nickel ores and concentrates. Principal imports are machinery and transport equipment, mineral fuels and lubricants, and petroleum and petroleum products. In 2001 Russia was the greatest purchaser of exports, followed by Canada, the Netherlands, the People's Republic of China (PRC) and Spain. Spain was the greatest supplier of imports, followed by the PRC, Italy, Canada and France.

After 1962 the economy was remodelled on Soviet lines, often unsuited to the conditions of a relatively underdeveloped country. Private employment was forbidden and the state took over all significant industry. Some liberalization in the early 1980s was reversed after 1986 and by 1989 80% of Cuban trade was with Eastern Europe. In 1990 the Soviet Union gave notice that it would no longer subsidize Cuba as it had done since the early 1960s by supplying it with oil in excess of its needs for resale on the world market. In 1990 a '**special period in time of peace**' was declared, but over the next three years the Cuban economy collapsed, reaching a nadir in 1993, when small areas of land were leased off for private cultivation, supplying most of the country's food needs. Thereafter a slow recovery was achieved by improvisation (bicycles replacing motor transport and buses being constructed on truck chassis), diversification of markets, the legalization of the dollar and the encouragement of the tourist industry. Free-market sales of agricultural produce were legalized in 1994. However, much of the economy, including the increasingly important tourist trade, continued to be controlled by powerful sectoral interests within the government. In addition to the standard Cuban peso used in internal transactions, a convertible peso, at par with the US dollar was introduced in 1994, and the dollar circulates freely in unofficial transactions and is used in special tourist facilities. Annual GDP growth has been positive since 1994, when GDP figures again became available. However, the GDP growth rate fell from 5.6% in 2000 to 3% in 2001 and 1.1% in 2002. The official unemployment rate was 3.3% at the end of 2002.

Cuban Democracy (Torricelli) Act, 1992

With the end of the Cold War US pressure on Cuba was stepped up and the embargo intensified. In 1992 President George Bush closed US ports and airports to third-country vessels suspected of carrying goods or passengers to Cuba and the US Congress passed the Cuban Democracy (Torricelli) Act. This Act reduced economic assistance to countries that traded with Cuba, increased punitive action against individuals who violated the embargo and prohibited US subsidiary companies abroad from trading with Cuba.

Members of the **Organization of American States** (OAS) generally regarded as particularly objectionable the Torricelli Act's embargo on shipments of food or medicines to Cuba. At the 25th OAS General Assembly, held on 5–7 June 1995 in Port-au-Prince, Haiti, delegates opposed the US trade embargo on Cuba, while, given the fall of communism in Eastern Europe, Brazil, Bolivia and Mexico even argued in favour of Cuba's readmission to the Organization, from which it had been excluded at the instance of the USA in 1962.

Cuban Liberty and Solidarity (Helms-Burton) Act, 1996

The longstanding US embargo, already reinforced by the **Cuban Democracy (Torricelli) Act, 1992** was greatly strengthened by the Cuban Liberty and Democratic Solidarity (LIBERTAD) Act, commonly known as the Helms-Burton Act, passed by the US Congress in February 1996. While the decision to adopt the Act was pending, Cuban MiGs shot down two aircraft piloted by Cuban refugees who had US citizenship for their alleged deliberate violation of Cuban air space. The Act was, in response, signed into law by President Bill Clinton in March 1996, reportedly with some reluctance, since it deprived him of almost all ability to conduct an independent foreign policy towards Cuba. The Act threatened to impose sanctions on all countries trading with or investing in Cuba. However, owing to strong opposition from Canada, which challenged the provisions under the **North American Free Trade Agreement**, the **European Union**, which requested the **World Trade Organization** to appoint a disputes panel to rule on the interference with the principle of free trade, and many other countries, the US President was given authority to suspend a provision of the Act that would have allowed any US citizen whose property had been confiscated after the Revolution to sue any foreign corporation that had 'benefited' from the property or from its use, even if the claimant was not a US citizen at the time of expropriation.

The 26th General Assembly of the **Organization of American States** (OAS), held in Panama City on 3–5 June 1996, was dominated by opposition to the Helms-Burton Act, a resolution condemning it being passed by 23 votes for to one (that of the USA) against after provocative remarks by the US Ambassador to the OAS, Harriet Babbitt, who had accused unspecified countries of 'collective cowardice'. In November 2002, by 173 votes to 3, the UN General Assembly condemned the US trade embargo on Cuba for the 11th time.

Curaçao

Curaçao is situated in the southern Caribbean, some 55 km north of the Venezuelan mainland. Politically it forms part of the Netherlands Antilles.

Area: 444 sq km; *capital:* Willemstad; *population:* 152,700 (1996 estimate); *official language:* Dutch.

D

da Silva, Luiz Inácio ('Lula')

'Lula' da Silva has been President of Brazil since 2002. Born in 1945 to a poor family in the drought-stricken north east of Brazil, Lula worked as a toolmaker at Villares and was recruited to the São Bernardo metalworkers' federation, of which he was elected president in 1975. As such he helped lead a series of successful strikes for better wages, which obtained a number of better deals for his members. In 1979, however, the military Government acted against the union and in the following year Lula and 14 of his colleagues were arrested. Though massive demonstrations in their favour soon secured their release, some, including Lula, were subsequently sentenced for incitement to murder and Lula was not finally acquitted until 1984. Meanwhile, he and his colleagues had founded the **Partido dos Trabalhadores** and in congressional elections held in November 1986, after the transition to democracy, Lula was elected a federal deputy from the state of São Paulo. In 1994 he ran for the presidency for the first time and at the next election, though unsuccessful, obtained more votes than any previous left-wing candidate. His success in 2002 was largely the result of patient work over many years in welding together a successful coalition between the urban poor and landless rural dwellers.

death penalty

The abolition of the death penalty was one of the objectives of liberals in Latin America from independence onwards. It was abolished in Central America in 1821, though afterwards restored in the individual states.

Debt Crisis

Term popularly given to the economic crisis afflicting many developing countries in the 1980s. It came to urgent public notice in August 1982, when Mexico, with an external debt in excess of US $90,000m., announced that it would be unable to meet its scheduled debt-service repayments. The incoming administration of President Miguel de la Madrid Hurtado was forced to make sharp cuts in government expenditure to secure the agreement of international lending agencies to reschedule the debt, a pattern which was to be repeated throughout Latin America, with the sole exception of Colombia.

Democracia Cristiana Guatemalteca (DCG)
Guatemalan Christian Democratic Party

Founded in August 1955, the DCG is a centre-right party which, despite its reformist rhetoric, has been decidedly conservative when in office. The DCG came out of an anti-Communist tradition and was founded with the help of the Roman Catholic Church in the belief that a Christian approach to politics would prevent reformist governments that held power in 1944–54, which they classified as left-wing. The DCG's policy was to oppose violence and promote social justice through direct church assistance, while, at the same time, closing ranks with the extreme right-wing **Movimiento de Liberación Nacional** in 1958. The contradictions within the DCG came to a culmination during the rule of Gen. Enrique Peralta Azurdia (1963–1966), when an anti-Communist faction accepted 10 seats in Congress while the majority of the party campaigned in opposition for basic social welfare provisions and the reform of the army. After the expulsion of the right-wing faction, the party gained considerable support from students, trade unionists and rural communities during the unrest and repression of the 1960s.

Following attacks by right-wing paramilitaries and the murder of several of its leaders, the DCG went underground in June 1980, but re-emerged for the 1982 election campaign as a partner of the Partido Nacional Renovador (PNR) in the National Opposition Union. The alliance won three seats in Congress and the PNR presidential candidate finished in third place, receiving 15.6% of the vote. The DCG initially supported the 1982 coup led by Gen. **José Efraín Ríos Montt**, who promised to put an end to violence and corruption, but distanced itself from the regime when it became an open dictatorship. The DCG gained the reputation of being the party least involved in repression and corruption and the one most likely to promote social reform. In the 1984 constituent elections it won the most seats (20 out of 88). This paved the way for the resounding victory in the November 1985 general election of the civilian DCG leader, Vinico

Cerezo Arévalo, a judo black belt who always travelled with a small arsenal of weapons.

The Cerezo Government, which took office on 14 January 1986, proved to be a conservative one. It had, nevertheless, to defend itself against three attempted coups and a number of coup plots by the extreme right wing and sections of the army in 1987–1989. The DCG attempted to recreate its progressive image by forging an alliance with the Democratic Convergence, but this could not counteract the effects of economic decline, allegations of corruption levelled against the party's leadership and general disillusionment with the DCG.

The party managed to muster only 27 seats in the November 1990 congressional elections, and Alfonso Cabrera, unable to campaign through illness, came third in the presidential contest with 17.3% of the vote. In 1994 the party's representation fell from 28 to 13 seats. After the party had joined the National Front alliance in April 1995, a number of disgruntled DCG deputies resigned their party memberships and set up a defiant independent bloc in Congress, and in the November 1995 elections the DCG's representation fell to only 3 seats. In the 1999 congressional elections it retained only 2 seats.

The party is a full member of the Christian Democrat International.

Leadership: Mario Vinicio Cerezo Arévalo, Francisco Villagran Kramer (Leader of the right-wing faction), René de León Schlotter (Leader of the left-wing faction), Alfonso Cabrera Hidalgo (Sec.-Gen.)

Address: Avda Elena 20–66, Zona 3, Guatemala

Telephone: 251-78-04

Dirty war

The term 'dirty war', *la guerra sucia,* is the term now normally used for what the 1976–83 military government of Argentina termed euphemistically the 'Process of National Reorganization'. The Process was a concerted attempt to eradicate terrorism by the use of terror. Tens of thousands of 'suspects' were arrested and, it was alleged, tortured and murdered. There were reports that people were arrested simply to fulfil the quotas imposed on government agencies. The most conservative estimates put the number of people killed, or who 'disappeared', at between 10,000 and 15,000. Such a wholesale purge inevitably included some genuine terrorists and by 1978 the capacity of the Montoneros and the Ejército Revolucionario del Pueblo for disruption had been drastically reduced by the death, exile or imprisonment of their known leaders.

Dominica

The Commonwealth of Dominica

Dominica is situated in the centre of the chain of the Lesser Antilles, and is regarded as the northernmost of the Windward Islands.

Area overall: 751 sq km (290 sq miles); *capital:* **Roseau**; *population:* 70,158 (2002 estimate), mainly black, with the only surviving population of *c*. 3,000 Caribs on the north-eastern coast; *official language:* English (a French Creole patois is also widely spoken); *religion:* 80% Roman Catholic, Protestant denominations 15%.

Constitution: The Commonwealth of Dominica is a parliamentary republic within the **Commonwealth**. The Constitution dates from independence on 3 November 1978. The head of state is a President elected by the House of Assembly for a term of five years, renewable for one further term. Parliament consists of the President and the House of Assembly of 30 members: nine Senators (who may either be elected or appointed as Parliament orders) and 21 members elected by universal adult suffrage. The President appoints the Prime Minister, who is the elected member most likely to command a majority in the House of Assembly. Other ministers are appointed by the President on the advice of the Prime Minister.

History: Dominica was given its present name by **Christopher Columbus**, who sighted it on 3 November 1493. Because of its mountainous nature, France and Britain agreed to regard it as neutral in the 17th century, but French settlers gradually began to arrive and were well established when Britain first captured the island during the Seven Years War (1759). It changed hands several times before finally being recaptured by Britain in 1805, but retains its French patois and Roman Catholic faith.

In 1833–1939 Dominica was part of the Leeward Islands Federation. Elections were first held under universal suffrage in 1951 and in 1958–1962 the island formed part of the abortive West Indies Federation. In 1967 it gained full internal self-government as a British Associated State and became independent, in 1978, under the leadership of Patrick John and the Dominica Labour Party (DLP). John's rule led to demonstrations in 1978 in which one person was killed and 10 injured, leading to the flight of the President and the formation of an interim government, which grappled unsuccessfully with the devastation caused by 'Hurricane David'. At the general election of 1980 the Dominica Freedom Party (DFP) won a decisive victory, under the leadership of Eugenia Charles, the first woman to hold the post of Prime Minister in the Caribbean. After a plot had been discovered to restore Patrick John to power by force, the Defence Force was disbanded, and in 1983 Charles argued forcefully in favour of US intervention in Grenada. When she retired in 1995 her successor, Brian Alleyne, was defeated in the general election of that year and the new Government was formed by Edison James and the Dominica United Workers Party (UWP). Meanwhile, the DLP had amalgamated in 1985 with other smaller parties to form the Labour Party of Dominica (LPD), and the poor state of the **banana** industry and concern about high government spending led to it being returned to power under the leadership of Roosevelt (Rosie) Douglas in the general election of January 2000. Douglas died suddenly in October 2000 and was succeeded as Prime Minister by his deputy, Pierre Charles, whose continued ill health gave rise to concern.

Latest elections: In the general election held on 31 January 2000, the results were: LPD 10 seats, UWP nine, DFP two. A coalition government was formed by the LPD and the DFP.

International relations and defence: Dominica is a member of the United Nations, the **Organization of American States**, the Commonwealth, and the **Caribbean Community and Common Market**. It is also a member of the **Organization of Eastern Caribbean States** and participates in the US-sponsored Regional Security System. It has no defence force but the 300-strong police force undertakes coastguard duties.

Economy: Dominica is a lower middle-income country with gross domestic product per head of US $3,696 in 2001. The economy is critically dependent on a single crop, bananas, which has been threatened by US support for the so-called 'dollar bananas' grown on the mainland. The possibilities for tourism have been limited by the need for air passengers to and from the island to change flights at larger airports on Antigua or Barbados.

Dominican Republic
República Dominicana

The modern state consists of the larger, eastern two-thirds of the island of Hispaniola (Española).

Area: 40,072 sq km (18,696 sq miles); *capital:* **Santo Domingo**; *population:* 8,230,722 (2002 census), predominantly mulatto, with some 15% African-American and 15% of European descent; *official language:* Spanish; *religion:* predominantly Roman Catholic.

Constitution: The Constitution of 1966, as amended in 1994, vests legislative power in a bicameral Congress. The Senate consists of 33 members elected for four years, one for each of the provinces and one for the National District (Distrito

Nacional). The 150 members of the Chamber of Deputies are also elected by popular vote for four years. Executive power is exercised by a President, who is elected for a four-year term by direct popular vote, and who, since 1994, has not been eligible for immediate re-election. If no candidate obtains an absolute majority in the first round of voting, a second round is held. Legislative elections are held in years that are alternate (even-numbered) to those in which presidential elections are held.

History: The port of Santo Domingo was the first Spanish capital in the Americas and, until supplanted by **Havana**, Cuba, was the main base for further exploration and settlement. The island of Hispaniola was briefly explored by **Christopher Columbus** on his first voyage in 1492–93. Ruthless exploitation of its indigenous Taino inhabitants (who called the island Quisqueya) followed, and so many of them died that after 1520 African slaves had to be imported to provide a workforce. The western part of the island was transferred to France in 1697, and was the scene of the slave revolt at the end of the 18th century which led to the independence of Haiti in 1804. Fear of a similar revolt delayed the independence of Santo Domingo until 1844, a series of invasions from Haiti having led its Spanish-speaking élite first to return to Spanish rule and later to request protection from the USA. A US protectorate was finally established after the end of the Spanish–American War (1898), when the US Government took charge of Dominican customs receipts and undertook to distribute them to the country's foreign creditors.

US marines were landed in Haiti in 1915, and, a year later, in May 1916, in the Dominican Republic also. Though, during the next eight years, direct US rule was unpopular, some useful public works were carried out, without, unlike in Haiti, resort to forced labour. As elsewhere in the Caribbean, however, the National Guard established by the occupation was to become dominant, constituting the base from which Gen. Rafael Léonidas Trujillo seized power in a military coup in 1930—in elections in which he was the only candidate he was subsequently elected as President. After 1931 Congress ceased to function. Although elections continued to be held, the country was run as a personalist dictatorship backed by the feared secret police. In 1936 the capital, Santo Domingo, was renamed Ciudad Trujillo after 'the Benefactor of the Fatherland' and in 1937 Trujillo ordered the massacre of some 15,000 Dominicans of Haitian origin.

In 1959 a small band of exiles landed on the island to try to overthrow the dictatorship. Trujillo blamed this expedition on the democratic leader of Venezuela, **Rómulo Betancourt**, and organized an unsuccessful attempt to assassinate him. The secret police, meanwhile, detained thousands of suspects, many of them key members of the élite. However, Trujillo himself was assassinated in May 1961. His compliant protégé, **Joaquín Balaguer**, was already the nominal President, and popular and US pressure drove the Trujillo family into exile. Elections in 1962 gave victory to the left-wing Partido Revolucionario Dominicano (PRD), led by Prof. Juan Bosch, who became President. He was overthrown after only seven months in office by a military coup, but when in April 1965 his supporters rose in a revolt aimed at restoring the constitutional government, US President Lyndon B. Johnson landed marines to restore order. Bosch, accused of being a Communist, was not restored to power, and because his life was under threat he was unable to campaign effectively in elections in 1966. Instead, Balaguer became President for a second term and, as unrest grew, became increasingly authoritarian. He was re-elected in 1970 and 1974 in polls boycotted by the opposition. In 1978, however, after Bosch had left the PRD to form the Partido de la Liberación Dominicana (PLD), a new PRD candidate, Silvestre Antonio Guzmán Fernández, was elected as President. Even then pressure from the US Carter Administration was required to ensure that the will of the electorate was respected by the armed forces.

Guzmán, a rich landowner, was successful in curbing the power of the military, but his rule was tainted by nepotism and the country continued to be dominated by the USA. His successor, Jorge Blanco, encountered difficult economic conditions, and in 1986 Balaguer was returned to power. In 1992, still in office though blind, he inaugurated a lighthouse erected to commemorate the 500th anniversary of the arrival of Christianity in the New World. Though re-elected in 1994, Balaguer was forced to accept a term limited to only two years and the Constitution was changed to prohibit consecutive terms. Under Leonel Fernández of the PLD, who was elected as President in 1996, efforts were made to reform public finances, tourism was expanded and the Republic was linked to both the Central American Common Market and the **Carribean Community and Common Market**.

Latest elections: Five people were killed in the run-up to presidential elections held on 16 May 2000, but it was, nevertheless, the most peaceful campaign in the history of the Republic. The candidate of the centre-left PRD, Rafael Hipólito Mejía Domínguez, obtained 49.86% of the votes cast. The two other candidates, Danilo Medina of the ruling PLD, who obtained 24.95% of the vote, and Joaquín Balaguer Ricardo, of the right-wing Christian Social Reform Party (PRSC), who received 24.64%, withdrew and Mejía was sworn in as President on 16 August.

International relations and defence: The Dominican Republic is a member of the United Nations, the **Organization of American States**, and the **Rio Pact**. It has observer membership of the **Central American Integration System** (*Sistema de la Integración Centroamericana*—SICA).

The army numbers 15,000 effectives, the navy 4,000 and the air force 5,500. There is no compulsory military service. External relations are dominated by fear of the spread of social unrest from neighbouring Haiti.

Dominican Republic, economy

GNI: US $19,000m. (2001); *GNI per caput:* $2,230 (2001); *GNI at PPP:* $57,000m. (2001); *GNI per caput at PPP:* $6,650 (2001), rank 90; *exports:* $5,253m. (2002); *imports:* $8,659m. (2002); *currency:* peso, plural pesos; US $1 = 23.50 pesos at 31 December 2002.

In 2001 agriculture accounted for 11.8% of the Dominican Republic's gross domestic product (GDP), industry for 16.1%, mining for 1.4% and services for 70%. The leading foreign-exchange earner is tourism, which is also the main object of foreign investment. Some 22.5% of the land is arable, 10.3% under permanent crops, 43.1% permanent pasture and 26.7% forest and woodland. The main crop, **sugar**, has been in decline for many years and the privatization of the state sugar corporation in 1999 has yet to prove effective. Other export crops, **coffee**, tobacco and **cocoa**, continue to do well, and have been supplemented by non-traditional items, such as cut flowers and ornamental plants. Rice, maize, beans, cassava (manioc), tomatoes, **bananas** and mangoes are grown for local consumption. The main mineral resource is ferro-nickel, the market for which fluctuates considerably; gold and silver have also been produced, in small quantities, ever since 1492. The principal industries are sugar refining, cement, textiles and clothing. All petroleum has to be imported. Other sources or energy are limited and regular power failures are blamed on an outdated and fragmented delivery regime.

Main exports are ferro-nickel ores and concentrates, petroleum products and processed food. Principal imports are petroleum and its products and consumer goods. In 2000 the USA was the greatest purchaser of exports, followed by Belgium and Luxembourg. The USA was the greatest provider of imports in that year, followed by Mexico, Japan and Spain. More than 175,000 people work in the in-bond (*maquiladora*) manufacturing sector in 513 companies (2001) in 46 free zones throughout the country.

Agriculture has been displaced from its traditional dominance of the economy by manufacturing and tourism, which, as elsewhere in the Caribbean, suffered severely as a result of the terrorist attacks on the USA in September 2001. '**Hurricane** Georges', which in September 1998 killed 300 people and caused damage to agriculture estimated at US $2,000m., was only the latest in a series of devastating hurricanes that have periodically struck the island. Since the early 1990s, however, a combination of better fiscal management and new sources of income has helped the government bring the economy under better control. In 2002 the trade deficit still stood at $3,406m. ($1,100m. if earnings from tourism and exports from the free zones were included in the calculation), but a fiscal surplus was recorded in both 2001 and 2002. GDP grew by 7.3% in 2000, but by only 3.2% in 2001. In 2002 it increased by 4.1%, while the rate of inflation averaged 5.3% in that year, compared with 8.9% in 2001. The unemployment rate was 16.1% and in 2001 one-quarter of the population was reported by the **International Bank for Reconstruction and Development** (World Bank) to be living on less than $1 a day.

Dorticós Torrado, Osvaldo

Osvaldo Dorticós was President of Cuba from 1959 until 1976. A former member of the Cuban Popular Socialist Party who had given up political life, Dorticós was unexpectedly appointed as figurehead President in July 1959 to replace Manuel Urrutia Lleo. He was regularly reappointed to that post until December 1976, when, under the new Soviet-style Constitution, he was relegated to a post on the central committee and **Fidel Castro Ruz** became executive President.

Duvalier, Dr François

Dr François Duvalier (1907–1971) was President of Haiti from 1957 until his death in 1971. He studied medicine and practised as a doctor from 1934 until he was appointed director-general of the National Public Health Service in 1946 under Pres. Dumarsais Estimé. When Estimé was overthrown, Duvalier led the opposition to his successor, Paul Magloire, and became President soon after Magloire's resignation in 1956. He reduced the size of the military, organized the Tontons Macoutes ('Uncle Bogeymen') as a private force that terrorized and assassinated alleged foes of his regime, and exploited the culture of voodoo (vaudou) to intimidate the opposition. He declared himself President for life in 1964 and despite his Government's tyranny and corruption, which condemned his people to poverty and isolation, was honoured at his death in 1971. However, on the fall of his son, in 1986, his body was exhumed and destroyed.

Duvalier, Jean-Claude

Jean-Claude Duvalier (b. 1951), President of Haiti in 1971–86, known as 'Bébé Doc', succeeded his father, on his death, at the age of only 19. A weak ruler, dominated first by his mother and later by his wife, his regime was less tyrannical than that of his father, but gathering unrest forced him to flee into exile in France in 1986. In 2004 he was living in poverty in Paris, having spent all of the immense fortune he had expatriated.

E

Earthquakes

Much of Latin America is subject to periodic earthquakes, some of devastating power, with serious political, social and economic consequences. Earthquakes result when rock strata subjected to sideways strain as a result of underlying plate movements snap, releasing the stored energy. They are therefore common in North and Central America, where the American plate meets the Cocos-Nazca plate, and in the Caribbean along the arc of the small Caribbean plate. The number of casualties is especially high among communities living in poor quality housing or shanty-towns.

The **Managua** earthquake of 1972 made one-half of the city's 300,000 inhabitants homeless. Seventy-five per cent of the city's buildings were destroyed or severely damaged. Water and electricity supplies were cut off and communications severed. President **Somoza** ordered the evacuation of the city and the summary execution of looters. After the city had been evacuated, demolition and bulldozing began. Preparations were made to dump millions of tons of debris into Lake Managua. As a result of the widespread corruption which accompanied reconstruction efforts in the succeeding years, many contracts were awarded to Somoza-owned companies and large sums of money were appropriated by the President. A decade later reconstruction had still not taken place in many areas of Managua. The failure of the Government's response to the crisis was one of the causes of the eventual fall of the Somoza Government.

The Guatemala earthquake of 1976 was one of a number of seismic shocks which struck the country in February and March. The earthquake partially destroyed the capital, most of the damage occurring in the poorer areas. In all, some 60% of the country's population were seriously affected by the destruction. In Chimaltenango 41,677 out of a total of 42,794 homes were destroyed, in Progreso 10,737 out of 15,743 and in Zacapa 14,288 of 20,989. Much of the destruction could have been avoided by better planning at the construction stage, especially in the capital, where whole shanty-towns collapsed into ravines.

On 20 June 1982 an earthquake caused the deaths of 20 people in El Salvador. Amongst all the political violence at that time the incident attracted little attention. However, the earthquake that struck the country on 10 October 1986 killed approximately 15,000 people, rendered 300,000 homeless and caused an estimated US $900m.-worth of damage. The severity of the impact was linked to increasing urbanization in the country, and to the construction of new settlements on unstable slopes.

Eastern Caribbean Central Bank, ECCB

Leadership: Sir K. Dwight Venner (Gov.)
Address: POB 89, Basseterre, St Christopher and Nevis
Telephone: 465-2537
Fax: 465-9562
E-mail: eccbinfo@caribsurf.com
Internet: www.eccb-centralbank.org

Eastern Caribbean Securities Exchange, Basseterre, St Kitts

Leadership: Balit Vohra (Gen. Man.)
Address: Bird Rock, POB 94, Basseterre
Telephone: 466-7192
Fax: 465-3738
E-mail: info@ecseonline.com
Internet: www.ecseonline.com

Economic Commission for Latin America and the Caribbean (ECLAC)
Comisión Económica por América Latina y el Caribe (CEPALC)

The Economic Commission for Latin America (ECLA, or *Comisión Económica por América Latina*—CEPAL) was established by the United Nations in 1948 to co-ordinate policies for economic development in Latin America, and remains a regional organization within the UN system. The Latin American states had wanted a Marshall Plan (i.e. one modelled on the post-Second World War European Reconstruction Program, proposed by US Secretary of State George C. Marshall) for the region; the USA wanted their agreement to a defence treaty, the **Rio Pact**. The compromise result was ECLA, which adopted its present title in 1984.

All independent Latin American and Caribbean states are members, as are Canada, France, Italy, the Netherlands, Portugal, Spain, the United Kingdom and the USA. Its funds come from two sources: the UN budget and additional voluntary contributions.

ECLAC has two stated purposes: to further the economic growth of Latin America; and to strengthen the economic relations of the region with the rest of the world. This is achieved through studies, the preparation of reports and the annual publication of the *Economic Survey of Latin America*. From the beginning its work and that of its adherents (termed *cepalistas* after the acronym of its original title in Spanish) was characterized by a distinctive viewpoint. This was first outlined by the economist Raúl Prebisch in *Economic Development of Latin America and its Principal Problems* (1949). It took as given the need for state-led economic development, but emphasized the need for the distribution of the fruits of development and the consequent need to plan for the social aspects of development, such as employment and income distribution. In 1962 it established the Latin American Institute for Social and Economic Planning (*Instituto Latinoamericano para Planificación Económica y Social*—ILPES) at Santiago, Chile, to provide training and advisory services for governments and their officials. Though it was not one of its original purposes, ECLA formed a powerful stimulus for further moves towards regional and subregional integration.

Leadership: José António Ocampo (Exec. Sec.), Colombia, until September 2003
Address: Edif. Naciones Unidas, Anda. Dag Hammarskjold, Casilla 179d, Santiago, Chile
Telephone: (2) 210-2000
Fax: (2) 208-0252
E-mail: dpisantiago@eclac.cl
Internet: www.eclac.org

Ecuador

República del Ecuador

Ecuador is situated on the west coast of South America, bisected by the Equator, from which it takes its modern name. Included in its national territory are the **Galápagos Islands** (Islas Galápagos), some 965 km (600 miles) further west.

Area: 272,045 sq km (105,037 sq miles); *capital:* Quito (population 1.4m.; the largest city is the port of Guayaquil, with some 2m. inhabitants); *population:* 12.1m. (2001 census), mostly of native American or mixed descent; *official language:* Spanish.

Constitution: In 1997 a National Constituent Assembly was elected to review and revise the 1997 Constitution; the new Constitution came into force on 10 August 1998. Legislative power is exercised by the Chamber of Representatives, elected by the people from lists drawn up by legally-recognized parties. Executive power is vested in a President elected for a four-year term by popular vote, who appoints the governors of provinces and administrative and diplomatic officials. The President may not serve more than one term of office. Voting is compulsory for all literate citizens over the age of 18 and optional for illiterates.

History: Ecuador has been dominated since independence in 1930 by a struggle between two élites. In the 19th century Conservative landowners of the sierra controlled the government, and despite a strong challenge from the Liberal coastal élite centred on Guayaquil, they were only ousted in 1932 after a four-day civil war. For a generation Ecuadorian political life was dominated by the brilliant but unstable figure of José María Velasco Ibarra, who stated that he needed only 'a balcony' in order to be elected. In 1939, however, he was exiled after manipulation of the vote on a grand scale had ensured the election of Dr Carlos Arroyo del Río. His weak Government was unable to resist Peru's incursion into lands claimed by Ecuador in the Amazon Basin, and in 1942 Ecuador was forced to accept the *fait accompli*. Velasco returned to power in 1944, and though deposed in 1947, his, civilian rule was soon restored for three consecutive terms. When Velasco's fifth and final term was ended following a further coup in 1972, a new and much more left-wing populist leader, Assad Bucaram, had already emerged, and was opposed by the armed forces.

Oil was discovered in Oriente Province in 1967 and began to flow over the Andes to Guayaquil in 1972, when the armed forces, led by Gen. Rodríguez Lara, again took power. To the surprise of the highland élite who had backed him, he took a stridently nationalist line, joining the **Organization of Petroleum Exporting Countries** in 1973 and demanding the revision of the oil contracts. By 1975 oil prices had fallen, borrowing had risen and there was economic crisis. A new military Government could not resist civilian anger, and in 1979 Ecuador became the first 'third wave' democracy in Latin America. However, the country's politics have remained volatile.

Latest elections: The first round of voting in presidential elections, held on 21 October 2002, was inconclusive. The incumbent President had decided not to contest the election and the leading candidate was former Col Lucio Edwin Gutiérrez Borbúa of the **Partido Sociedad Patriótica 21 de Enero**, who had been sentenced to six months' imprisonment in 2001 for his role in the overthrow of President **Jamil Mahuad Witt** in January 2000. His candidature and social programme were now both endorsed by the **Confederation of Indigenous Nationalities of Ecuador** and he received 20.3% of the vote. The millionaire businessman and candidate of the conservative right, Alvaro Fernando Noboa Pontón (Partido Renovador Institucional Acción Nacional) obtained 17.4%; León Roldós Aguilera (Independent) 15.43%; Rodrigo Borja Cevallos (Izquierda Democrática) 14.05%; António Xavier Neira Menendez (Partido Social Cristiano) 12.19%; Jacobo Bucaram Ortíz (Partido Roldosista Ecuatoriano) 11.85%; and five other candidates received 8.6% of the vote between them. In the run-off election on 24 November 2002 the centre-left former coup leader, who had focused his campaign on corruption in government, won 54.3% of the poll, thus achieving a decisive victory over Noboa, who received 45.7%.

International relations and defence: Ecuador is a member of the United Nations, the **Organization of American States**, the **Latin American Integration Association** (LAIA—*Asociación Latinoamericana de Integración*), the **Andean Community of Nations**, and the **Rio Pact**. Traditionally, owing to the long-lasting border conflict with Peru which was finally settled in 1998 by the Treaty of Brasília, Ecuador has maintained a substantial army. In 2002 it was some 50,000-strong. Ecuador's navy, of 5,500 men, is principally engaged in fishery protection duties (there are also 270 coastguards). The air force numbers 4,400. There is selective, compulsory military service for all male citizens from the age of 20, lasting for one year.

Ecuador, economy

GNI: US $14,000m. (2001); *GNI per caput:* $1,080 (2001); *GNI at PPP:* $38,000m. (2001); *GNI per caput at PPP:* $2,960 (2001), rank 140; *exports:* $5,030m. (2002); *imports:* $5,953m. (2002); *currency:* US dollar.

In 2002 agriculture accounted for 9.0% of Ecuador's gross domestic product (GDP), industry for 20.7% and petroleum for 12.6%. Some 5.7% of the land is arable, 4.8% under permanent crops and 18.0% permanent pasture. The main crop is **bananas**, of which Ecuador is the world's largest producer; **cocoa** and **coffee** are also grown for export, while rice, **sugar** cane, potatoes, maize, soya beans, wheat and barley are grown for local consumption. The main mineral resource is petroleum, proven reserves of which in 2002 were 3,990m. barrels. Gold, silver,

copper, lead and zinc are also found, but not much exploited. The principal industries are textiles, food and drink, tobacco, petroleum refining and construction materials. Petroleum dominates the energy market. Main exports are crude petroleum and derivatives, bananas and shrimp. Principal imports are capital goods, especially for the oil industry. In 2002 the USA was the greatest purchaser of exports, followed by the Republic of Korea and Panama. The USA was the greatest supplier of imports, followed by Colombia, Venezuela and Chile.

Ecuador's traditional agro-export economy, dominated first by cocoa and then, after 1940, by bananas, was transformed in the late 1960s by the discovery of oil by Texaco-Gulf in the Oriente region, east of the Andes. The trans-Andean pipeline was completed and exports began in 1972. Unfortunately, the military Government in power at that time was precipitate in its renegotiation of contracts with the exploration companies, with the effect of choking off further discoveries. It was not until after the country withdrew from the **Organization of Petroleum Exporting Countries** in 1992 that proven reserves were tripled and exports rose steeply.

Annual GDP growth was interrupted in 1999 by a decline of 7.3% that resulted from internal instability, the impact of the East Asia crisis and the effect of El Niño. However, GDP grew by 2.3% in 2000, by 5.6% in 2001 and by 3.3% in 2002. Dollarization in March 2000 checked inflation, which had fallen to an annual rate of 9.4% by the end of 2002. Since 2001 Ecuador has maintained a fiscal surplus. The unemployment rate was 7.7% in 2002 and some 40% of the population live below the national poverty line.

Ejército de Liberación Nacional (ELN)

National Liberation Army, Colombia

Established in January 1965, the ELN at first operated in the department of Santander (north-eastern Colombia) under the leadership of Fabio Vasquez Castaño and with the support of a (pro-Chinese) Workers' Students' and Peasants' Movement. It repudiated the pro-Soviet Communist Party on 1 August 1967, after that party had condemned guerrilla warfare as 'an erroneous form of revolution'. Earlier, on 7 January 1966, Fr Camilo Torres Restrepo, a former Dominican priest who had advocated a 'Christian revolution' to overthrow the existing social order, disclosed that he had joined the ELN, explaining that, as all lawful means of obtaining redress were barred to the people, he would pursue the armed struggle in the country until the people had gained power; however, on

15 February 1966 he was killed in a clash between guerrillas and an army unit. Torres' memory continues to provide inspiration for the movement.

In June 1975 ELN guerrillas were reported to be active in several provinces, and a major military operation was launched against them in the north, in Bolívar. Though by September 1980 the ELN was officially stated to have fewer than 40 active members, it nevertheless intensified its activities near the Venezuelan border during 1981. On 22 November 1983 ELN members kidnapped the brother of President **Betancur**, and made several demands, including an increase in the monthly minimum wage, a price freeze on consumer goods, a reduction in public service prices, the release of political prisoners, the arrest of suspected members of **Muerte a Secuestradores** and the demilitarization of rural areas. The hostage was later released unharmed.

The group rejected a cease-fire in 1984 and in 1986 was reported to be operating in several provinces. It claimed responsibility for attacks on the Caño Limón-Coveñas oil pipeline owned by the Colombian Petroleum Enterprise, and in the 1990s the oil pipeline was damaged at regular intervals, causing disruption and loss of revenue to the state oil company as well as serious environmental damage.

President Samper's peace initiative in November 1994 was greeted positively by the ELN representative, Francisco Galán. In February 1995, however, the ELN mounted a cross-border raid into Venezuela, killing eight Venezuelan marines and wounding four. The Venezuelan Government responded on 15 March by deploying 5,000 troops to round up and deport illegal Colombian immigrants in the frontier zone. The Colombian Government responded by mobilizing some 6,000 troops on the Venezuelan border; the Colombian President stated that he would gladly co-operate with the Venezuelan Government, but would not recognize its claim to a right of 'hot pursuit', which a later incident in October suggested, nevertheless, that it was exercising regardless. Finally, in talks in Spain in March 1998, a preliminary agreement was reached between the government and a new ELN leadership. Following the death on 14 February of the ELN's founding leader, the Spanish-born former priest Gregorio Manuel Pérez Martínez, a collective leadership had been formed with José Nicolás Rodríguez Bautista as political, and Antonio García as military, commander.

However, talks with the new Government headed by President Pastrana were abruptly broken off by the ELN on 16 February 1999. Then, on 12 April, activists hijacked an Avianca *Fokker 50* airliner during an internal flight from Bucaramanga to Bogotá; 15 of the 46 passengers were still being held hostage at the end of the year. The ELN's kidnapping of members of a church congregation in Cali on 30 June, however, rebounded when it was vigorously condemned by the Church. The hostages were subsequently released.

On 20 April 2000 the government agreed to create a second demilitarized zone in parts of Bolívar and Antioquia, as the location for talks with the ELN. Unlike the zone for the **Fuerzas Armadas Revolucionarias Colombianas**, this would be subject to restrictions, including international verification. The proposal was delayed by local protests, but was finally endorsed by the paramilitary Autodefensas Unidas de Colombia on 28 May, by which time peace talks with the FARC had again been suspended. Talks with the ELN took place in Geneva, Switzerland, on 24–25 July. The release of 43 prisoners on 23 December enabled government negotiators to agree terms for talks in a new demilitarized zone in the Middle Magdalena. However, these talks collapsed in mid-March 2001 following military operations in Bolívar and it was reported on 3 April that ELN and FARC commanders were conducting joint operations in the proposed zone. On 16 April 92 Colombian employees of the US corporation Occidental Petroleum were kidnapped on their way home from work on the Caño Limón-Coveñas oilfield in the Department of Arauca. Most were soon released, but in October Occidental Petroleum suspended oil drilling after the Caño Limón-Coveñas pipeline had been blown up for the 133rd time since January. Meanwhile, on 7 August, the President had suspended negotiations with the ELN when it became clear that there was no realistic possibility of a deal being concluded before the 2002 elections and, on 17 August, he signed legislation giving the armed forces increased powers to detain civilians and to give orders to the civil authorities. However, the ELN remained active, justifying its activities by a nationalist claim to be resisting the forces of globalization. In 2003 a British tourist, one of a number who had been kidnapped by the ELN, escaped from his captors; in December 2003, following negotiations, the other kidnapped tourists were released unharmed.

Leadership: José Nicolás Rodríguez Bautista (political Commander), Antonio Garcia (military Commander)

Ejército Zapatista de Liberación Nacional (EZLN)
Zapatista Army of National Liberation, Mexico

On New Year's Day 1994 the previously unknown EZLN seized control of three towns in the southern Mexican state of Chiapas: Ocosingo, Altamirano and Las Margaritas. Its agents also attacked a fourth town, the historic tourist site San Cristóbal de las Casas, where they ransacked the Palace of Justice and set fire to it before retreating into the mountains. The former Governor of Chiapas, Gen. (retd) Absalón Castellanos Domínguez, was seized at his cattle ranch and abducted as a hostage. In its manifesto, '*Today we say enough!*', the EZLN made clear the reason. The regional authorities (of whom Castellanos was the most hated representative) had, they said, stolen their lands from them. 'We possess nothing, absolutely nothing,' the EZLN went on, 'no home, no land, no work, no education.'

The Government of President **Carlos Salinas de Gortari**, which was celebrating Mexico's entry, on 1 January, into the **North American Free Trade Agreement**, was greatly embarrassed by the insurgency. Within a week, the guerrillas had extended their control to the towns of San Miguel and Guadalupe Tepayac, the country was on nation-wide alert, one-fifth of Mexico's army had been deployed to the Chiapas region and more than 145 people had been killed, some in summary executions or as the result of other atrocities. On 10 January the President reshuffled his Cabinet, dismissing the Secretary of the Interior, José Patrocinio González Garrido, a former Governor of Chiapas. Two days later, on the urgent advice of the Bishop of San Cristóbal, Mgr Samuel Ruiz, the President declared a truce, and appointed as negotiator Manuel Camacho Solís, the Secretary of External Relations, who had been passed over for the presidential nomination in 1993. Over the next few weeks, while the truce held, the negotiations continued.

The choice of the name 'Zapatista' for the new movement was significant. Though Emiliano Zapata, the celebrated Mexican revolutionary, had no connection with the state of Chiapas, his name had long been used by the ruling **Partido Revolucionario Institucional** to legitimize its virtual monopoly of political power. Chiapas was the poorest state in Mexico and the insurgents wanted investment, land reform, and the opportunity to choose their own political leaders. On his release on 16 February 1994 the former Governor agreed that the social injustice which was the root cause of the revolt really existed. One-third of the households had no electricity, while 40% had no running water. The state ranked last on major indicators of literacy (in Spanish). It was also the Mexican state where allegations of human rights violations—in particular the use by landowners of *pistoleros* to drive the Indians off their traditional lands, in conjunction with the army and the police—had most persistently been expressed.

Though the movement demanded for the native Indian population its traditional rights, however, its charismatic leader, ski-masked 'Subcomandante Marcos' (actually Rafael Sebastian Guillén Vicente, a university teacher and son of a well-to-do Tampico furniture dealer), made use of portable computers and the internet to circumvent government blocks on communications. During the summer, while the Government was preoccupied with the presidential election campaign, there was an effective stand-off between insurgents and the army and parts of Chiapas fell into near-anarchy. On 19 December 1994 the guerrillas, who by this time controlled about one-fifth of Chiapas state, demonstrated their ability peacefully to slip through the army cordon by erecting roadblocks, proclaiming 'liberated zones' and occupying the town of Simojovel and, it was claimed, 37 other municipalities.

The Government had received advance warning of this move. It tried to take advantage of it to devalue the new peso while placing the blame on the guerrillas. However, within 24 hours, while fresh troops and tanks were moved into place around the guerrilla bases, the devaluation had revealed the fundamental weakness of the Mexican economy, its dependence on short-term loans. As capital flooded out of the country, the Government lost control of the financial situation. The peso fell to unprecedented depths, precipitating a major crisis in investor confidence. By contrast, the rebels appeared to gain legitimacy. In these circumstances the new President, Ernesto Zedillo Ponce de León, prudently decided to resume negotiations over the rebel demands. Dialogue continued sporadically until the election as President in 2000 of **Vicente Fox Quesada**, who had pledged to immediately resolve the problem. In 2004 the EZLN had virtually been accepted as a legitimate interlocutor with the government, but remained on the defensive and had been marginalized.

Leadership: 'Subcomandante Marcos' (Rafael Sebastian Guillén Vicente)

Internet: www.ezln.org

El Salvador

República de El Salvador

The Republic of El Salvador is located on the Pacific side of the Central American isthmus, and has frontiers with Guatemala, Honduras and Nicaragua.

Area: 21,041 sq km (8,124 sq miles); *capital:* **San Salvador**; *population:* 6,517,800 (2002 estimate), comprising mestizos (90%), Amerindian, European (mainly Spanish); *official language:* Spanish; *religion:* Roman Catholic 78%, evangelical Protestant sects.

Constitution: The 1983 Constitution provides for a democratic, presidential republic. Legislative power is vested in a single chamber, the National Assembly (*Asamblea Nacional*), elected for three years. Executive power is vested in a President elected by the people for a five-year term. Voting is both a right and a duty of all citizens of 18 years of age and over. The country is committed to the reconstitution of the Republic of Central America.

History: Until the outbreak of civil war in 1980 El Salvador was dominated by a closed oligarchy, the so-called 'Fourteen Families'. Soon after the seizure of power by Maximiliano Hernández Martínez (President 1930–44), an outbreak of agrarian unrest in 1932, forcibly put down by the massacre known as *La Matanza*, had panicked them into accepting his dictatorship. Then, in 1944, as in neighbouring Guatemala, a popular uprising had caught the dictator unawares, and in 1948 a coup by junior officers cut short a possible transition to democracy, but installed a modernizing military regime. This was ousted in 1960, when José María Lemus attempted to prolong his rule, by another junior officers' revolt, rejected, in turn, by more conservative elements in the armed forces, fearful of a Cuban-style revolution.

Under Col Julio Adalberto Rivera (President 1962–67) and his successor, Col Fidel Sánchez Hernandez (1967–72), a new official party, the Partido de Conciliación Nacional, was able to retain power. The country benefited from US aid under the Alliance for Progress, and was the main beneficiary of the new Central American Common Market. In 1972 a civilian presidential candidate, José Napoleon Duarte, of the newly-formed Partido Demócrata Cristiano, gained so many votes that the armed forces intervened to deny him victory and to impose their own candidate. The election of Gen. Carlos Humberto Romero in 1977 was equally fraudulent. Meanwhile, however, tensions were rising over the number of Hondurans who were entering the country to take up work. In 1969 a disputed decision in the third qualifying round for the 1970 football World Cup precipitated a war, the so-called *Guerra de Fútbol*, between El Salvador and Honduras in which more than 2,000 died and thousands were made homeless.

Humberto Romero retained power until 1979, when he was overthrown in a coup. However, the armed forces were unable to agree on how to replace him and assassinations and kidnappings became routine. Though the Christian Democrats were incorporated into the ruling coalition in January 1980, it was too late to avert civil war. This erupted in March 1980, when Archbishop Oscar Romero, who had appealed to the army to cease the violence, was shot while at the altar in the act of celebrating Mass. The carnage at his funeral, when troops fired on defenceless mourners, set the countryside ablaze. By the end of 1980 13,000 had died, more than 70,000 had been made refugees and the insurgent **Frente Farabundo Martí para la Liberación Nacional** (FMLN) controlled large tracts of territory. However, the FMLN's 'final offensive' failed and, under the presidency of Ronald Reagan, massive US aid started to arrive, though it was not until 1985, at the cost of 50,000 lives, that the war was finally fought to a stalemate. In 1989 the FMLN offered to accept a constitutional role, but the offer was rejected. The extreme right-wing Alianza Republicana Nacionalista (ARENA) candidate, Alfredo Cristiani, won a substantial majority in the presidential election of 1989, inaugurating more than a decade of ARENA domination, though with UN mediation the FMLN disbanded in the early 1990s and became a legitimate political party.

Latest elections: In presidential elections held on 21 March 2004, the ruling ARENA retained power, when its candidate, Antonio ('Tony') Saca González, won 57.73% of the votes cast. Schafik Handal, of the opposition FMLN, received 35.63%.

International relations and defence: El Salvador is a member of the United Nations, the **Organization of American States**, the **Central American Integration System** (*Sistema de la Integración Centroamericana*—SICA), and the **Rio Pact**. The long-running boundary dispute with Honduras and the civil war have both taken a heavy toll on the country's military forces. Salvadorian men are liable for selective military service between the ages of 18–30, and serve for one year. In 2002 the army had a strength of 15,000, the navy 700 and the air force 1,100.

El Salvador, economy

GNI: US \$13,000m. (2001); *GNI per caput:* \$2,040 (2001); *GNI at PPP:* \$33,000m. (2001); *GNI per caput at PPP:* \$5,160 (2001), rank 107; *exports:* \$2,865m. (2001); *imports:* \$5,027m. (2001); *currency:* colon, plural colones; US \$1 = 8.750 colones since 1 January 2001.

In 2001 agriculture accounted for 9% of El Salvador's gross domestic product (GDP), mining and quarrying for 0.4% and industry for 23.7%. Some 31.3% of the land is arable, 11.9% under permanent crops and 37.3% permanent pasture. The main crops are **coffee** and **sugar** cane; maize, rice, beans and fruit are grown for local consumption and there has been some effort to encourage non-traditional exports. Climatic changes have had an adverse impact on fishing. The only mineral resources exploited are limestone, gypsum and chalk. The principal industries are textiles, food products, chemicals and petroleum refining for local consumption. The main energy source is hydroelectric power, which accounts for 50% of installed capacity, with imported petroleum accounting for 37% and geothermal generation for 13%. Main exports are coffee, metal goods, unrefined sugar, plastics and electrical machinery. Principal imports are petroleum and petroleum products and mechanical and electrical machinery. In 2000 the USA and Guatemala were the chief purchasers of exports, followed by Honduras and Nicaragua. The USA was by far the greatest supplier of imports, followed by Guatemala and Mexico.

Since the mid-19th century El Salvador has been dominated by a small oligarchy that derives its wealth from large coffee estates. A modest attempt at land reform failed to avert the outbreak of guerrilla warfare in 1980, which was accompanied by widespread sabotage. Only massive financial aid from the USA enabled the economy to survive the 1980s, despite the further blow of a massive **earthquake** in 1986. In the early 1990s the Cristiani Government reduced public spending, abandoned price controls and subsidies, and privatized the State's holdings in banks and financial institutions, sugar refining, distilling, textile production and hotels. Further measures of privatization and deregulation continued throughout the decade. However, the growth rates expected as a consequence did not materialize and in November 2000 the colón was pegged to the US dollar with the intention of attracting inward investment.

GDP grew by 2.0% in 2000, by 2.0% again in 2001 and by 2.1% in 2002. The average rate of inflation was 1.9% in 2000, while the rate of unemployment was 7.9%. At least 30% of the urban population were unemployed or underemployed in 2000.

Empresa Brasileira de Aeronáutica, SA (EMBRAER)

Brazil's leading aircraft manufacturing company, 30% government-owned.
  Leadership: Mauricio Novis Botelho (Pres. and CEO)
  Address: Av. Brig. Faria Lima 2170, 12227-901 São José dos Campos, SP
  Telephone: (12) 345-1106
  Fax: 321-1884
  E-mail: mercapit@embraer.com.br
  Internet: www.embraer.com

Empresa Nacional de Petróleo (ENAP), Chile

State oil corporation, responsible for petroleum and gas exploration and marketing.
  Leadership: Jorge Rodríguez Grossi (Pres.)
  Address: Vitacura 2736, 10°, Las Condes, Santiago
  Telephone: (2) 280-3000
  Fax: (2) 280-3199
  E-mail: webenap@enap.cl
  Internet: www.enap.cl

Empresa Nacional de Telecomunicaciones (ENTEL), Bolivia
National Telecommunications Enterprise, Bolivia

F. as state-owned telecommunications authority in 1965; privatized in 1995 and is now owned by Telecom Italia; in 2001 there were 514,800 fixed lines in use.

Leadership: Franco Bertone (CEO)
Address: Calle Federico Zuazo 1771, Casilla 4450, La Paz
Telephone: (2) 241-6641
Fax: (2) 239-1789
E-mail: rmoya@entelsa.entelnet.bo
Internet: www.entel.com.bo

Empresa Nacional de Telecomunicaciones, SA (ENTEL Chile, SA)

Leadership: Carlos Hurtado (Pres.)
Formerly state-owned telecommunications company, f. 1964; now 52%-owned by Telecom Italia; owns satellite downlink stations with connections to INTELSAT.
Address: Andrés Bello 2687, 14°, Casilla 4254, Las Condes, Santiago
Telephone: (2) 360-0123
Fax: (2) 360-2015
Internet: www.entel.cl

Encuentro Progresista-Frente Amplio (EP-FA)
Progressive Encounter-Broad Front, Uruguay

Leadership: Tabaré Vázquez Batlle (party Pres., national presidential candidate 1994 and 1999), Jorge Brovetto (party Vice-Pres.), Rodolfo Nin Noboa (national vice-presidential candidate 1994 and 1999)
Address: Colonia 1367, 2°, 11100 Montevideo
Telephone: (2) 902-2176
E-mail: presfa@adinet.com.uy
Internet: www.epfaprensa.org

The Progressive Encounter-Broad Front alliance is a broad alliance of left and left-of-centre political forces, based on the Broad Front originally formed to resist the military Government. It currently comprises 19 different political parties and movements although not all of its constituent members have congressional representation. The Front has campaigned vigorously against the government's neo-liberal policies, but has lately moderated its own political programme in order to attract voters from the centre.

Founded in 1971, the original Broad Front (Frente Amplio) came to consist of 17 parties of such diverse allegiances as the Partido Demócrata Cristiano, the Partido

Socialista del Uruguay and the Partido Comunista, in addition to various dissident Colorado and National (Blanco) factions. Internal divisions caused by political differences and by the nomination of a presidential candidate led to a serious split in March 1989 and the formation of Nuevo Espacio (New Space). The Front nevertheless scored considerable success in the November 1989 presidential election: Líber Seregni, its candidate, finished in third place having received 21% of the vote. The Front also won the municipal (departmental) election in the capital Montevideo and came third in the congressional elections, obtaining 21 seats in the Chamber and seven seats in the Senate. The Front supported a broad campaign against the Blanco Government's privatization programme and in Congress voted against proposed austerity measures.

By April 1992 the Socialists had displaced the Communists as the dominant grouping in the Frente Amplio. In parallel, the influence of the popular mayor of Montevideo, the Socialist Tabaré Vázquez, grew. In March 1994 he was declared the alliance's presidential candidate.

In 1994 the original Front fought the election in alliance with a dissident Blanco leader, Rodolfo Nin Noboa, forming the present EP-FA. The EP was formed prior to the 1994 election. It is effectively an electoral vehicle of the Broad Front with no political influence of its own. In the 1999 elections the EP-FA broke the Blancos' and Colorados' historical domination of Uruguayan politics by effectively becoming Uruguay's leading political force after it gathered 40% of the vote in the first-round presidential and congressional elections. Vázquez lost the presidential contest to Jorge Batlle of the Colorados in a run-off, but the EP-FA became Uruguay's largest formation in the 2000–05 legislature, winning 40 of the 99 Assembly seats, and 12 of the 31 Senate seats, on a share of 40.1% of the vote.

European Union (EU)

Before August 2000 the EU's system of generalized tariff preferences (General Scheme of Preferences—GSP), also known as the Lomé Convention, had grown haphazardly out of the system introduced by France and the United Kingdom to aid their former colonies in Africa, the Caribbean and the Pacific (the ACP countries). Some 90% of the countries benefiting from the regime were in sub-Saharan Africa. The Caribbean states eligible for assistance were small, island states, such as Saint Lucia and Saint Vincent and the Grenadines, both of which acceded to the General Agreement on Tariffs and Trade in 1993, in order to protect their interests against those of their much larger neighbours and the large transnational corporations.

The First Lomé Convention (Lomé I) was signed at Lomé, Togo, in February 1975. It came into effect on 1 April 1976, and was renewed and extended three times. At its core was a Stabilization of Export Earnings system ('Stabex'), under which intervention by the European Communities (EC) to maintain the producer prices of a number of specified commodities could be triggered by two 'thresholds': the degree of dependence on a particular commodity, fixed at 2.5% in the case of island states, and a reduction in export earnings of 2.5%, compared with a 'benchmark' figure calculated on the basis of average export earnings over the previous four years. Commodities covered included **bananas**, **cocoa**, **coffee** and **cotton**. Under Lomé II (effective from 1981), Sysmin, a similar but more complex facility, was added, covering mineral resources such as **bauxite**, **copper** and tin. Lomé III, signed in December 1984, came into effect on 1 March 1985, and Lomé IV, signed in December 1989, in March 1990.

Unlike its predecessors, the Fourth Lomé Convention was to remain in force for 10 years, until February 2000. A total of 71 ACP countries were parties to Lomé IV (including South Africa, which has partial membership). The agreement increased the proportion of grants to loans in EC aid, although it fell far short of the demands of ACP countries. It also contained important provisions on sustainable development, support for ACP economies experiencing short-term economic fluctuations, action on debt imbalances, technical co-operation, additional concessions on the access of ACP products to the EC, the extension of certain provisions of the Convention to include mineral and metal resources in addition to agricultural products, and the simplification of the rules of origin and improvements to Stabex. All trade concessions were to be one-way only and ACP countries were not expected to reciprocate.

Separate from the Convention, there were three Protocols which gave Caribbean countries preferential access to the European market: the **Sugar** Protocol, which guaranteed access for agreed quantities of tropical sugar at a price determined by the EC (which has, historically, been substantially greater than the world price); the Banana Protocol, which principally benefited the Windward Islands, by maintaining a price above that accorded to Latin American bananas, the access of which to France and the United Kingdom (although not to Germany) was thereby restricted; and the Rum Protocol, which was of limited value to all parties, owing to the low demand for the product in Europe. A considerable amount of EC aid was (and still is) channelled into the Caribbean states, generally in proportion to need, and both aid and trade policies appear, overall, to have benefited the recipients.

Because the GSP system had been developed over many years, it was very inconsistent in the way that it treated different countries outside the EU. For example, the import to the EC of many products from Latin American states was strictly regulated, and in the case of fresh chilled or frozen beef, formerly a major export of Argentina and Uruguay, prohibited altogether after 1975. With the accession of Spain and Portugal to the EC in 1986, however, Latin American states hoped to obtain a better trade agreement. In 1987 both the Dominican Republic and Haiti applied for admission to the Lomé Convention, but were admitted in 1989 only after it had been made clear that the decision would not set a precedent for other countries of the region.

Negotiations on the possible further renewal of the Lomé Convention commenced on 30 September 1998 and concluded in Brussels, Belgium, on 9 December 1999 when the Joint Ministerial Conference accepted the new ACP-EU Partnership Agreement, which replaced the Lomé Convention, and which came into effect in August 2000. It was essential that the new agreement be compatible with the rules of the **World Trade Organization** (WTO), which had been formed since the conclusion of Lomé IV. The ACP-EU Partnership Agreement was to remain in force for 20 years and was subject to review by a revision conference every five years. Provisions included the dismantling of Stabex and Sysmin as separate agreements, the extension of preferences to subregional free-trade areas, acceptance of the principle of performance-based aid allocation and the strengthening of existing requirements for 'good governance' and combating corruption.

The new WTO, however, had barely been established when agitation began for the US Government to use it to terminate the preferential treatment given to the ACP states. This proposal was strongly resisted by the leaders of the smaller island states and, at a meeting in Washington, DC, in September 1995, the Prime Minister of Jamaica, Percival J. Patterson, sought and received assurances that the US Government would not challenge the Lomé system. Despite this guarantee, later in the same month the US Government filed a complaint against the EU's banana regime, on behalf of Chiquita Brands. Chiquita claimed that the Lomé system favoured imports from ACP states over those from Central America and that, as a consequence, Central American exports had suffered. In May 1997 the WTO concluded that the EU's banana-import regime violated 19 free-trade regulations, although the allocation of preferential tariffs to ACP states, covered by a waiver, was upheld.

In June 1998 the EU approved a reform of the regime, to allow South and Central American producers to have greater access to the EU market from 1 January 1999. However, in March 1999 the US Government levied punitive tariffs on an apparently arbitrary selection of European products, in retaliation against the reform, which it regarded as discriminatory and incompatible with WTO provisions.

It was not until April 2001 that the trade negotiator for the US Government, Robert Zoellick, concluded an agreement to end the nine-year dispute. The agreement is not entirely beneficial to the Windward Islands, since it means both that Chiquita will gain more business and that the quotas will eventually be eliminated. However, the quotas in force at the end of 2000 will remain as set until 2006, when they will be replaced by a new system of import licences.

F

Falkland Islands
Îles Malouines, Islas Malvinas

The Falkland Islands comprise two large islands, East Falkland and West Falkland, and a number of smaller islands, situated in the South Atlantic 480 km from the mainland of South America and some 770 km (480 miles) north-east of Cape Horn. The islands are an Overseas Territory of the United Kingdom but are claimed by Argentina, where they are termed the Islas Malvinas.

Area: 12,173 sq km (4,700 sq miles); *capital:* **Stanley**, on East Falkland; *population:* 2,913 (2001 census), 96% of British descent and citizenship; *official language:* English; *religion:* Anglican, Roman Catholic, other Protestant denominations.

Constitution: The present Constitution was adopted in 1985 and amended in 1997. HM Queen Elizabeth II, the head of state, is represented by the Governor, who is advised by the six-member Executive Council (Excom). The Legislative Council is made up of eight members: six elected by the people and two ex officio, the Chief Executive and the Financial Secretary.

History: The first verifiable record of a sighting of the islands was in 1592, nearly a century before Capt. John Strong of the *Welfare* made the first recorded landing on them on 27 January 1690, and named the sound between them after the then Treasurer of the Royal Navy, Viscount Falkland. In the early 18th century sailors from St Malo in France visited the islands, which, as a result, became known as 'les îles malouines'. In 1764 Louis-Antoine de Bougainville established a settlement at Port Louis on East Falkland in the name of King Louis XV of France. A few months later, finding the islands, as he thought, still uninhabited, Commodore John Byron took formal possession of them in the name of George III of England and founded a settlement at Port Egmont, on Saunders Island off West Falkland. In 1767, however, France relinquished its claim to the islands in favour of Spain in return for an indemnity equivalent to £24,000 and in 1770 the Governor of **Buenos Aires** sent a small fleet to take Port Egmont. After a strong protest the settlers were allowed to return but the British garrison was withdrawn in 1774, ostensibly on grounds of cost.

Spain maintained a small garrison at Port Louis (renamed Soledad) until 1811, when it was withdrawn. The islands were claimed on behalf of the government of Buenos Aires in 1820, but it was not until 1826 that a Frenchman, Louis Vernet, was commissioned by that government to establish a colony. However, his right to do so was disputed by the captain of the USS *Lexington*, who, in 1831, drove out the settlers and declared the islands free of all government. Mindful of the strategic position of the islands, the new British Government sent Captain J. J. Onslow of the frigate HMS *Clio* to exercise the rights of sovereignty which they believed Britain enjoyed, and on 3 January 1833 he raised the British flag. A number of convicts who had been sent to the islands were not rounded up until the following year, and the Royal Navy administered the islands until civil administration was established in 1841, followed by a measure of self-government in 1845. Full internal self-government under adult suffrage was achieved in 1951.

British possession of the islands was regularly disputed during the 19th century, but it was not until the accession of **Juan Domingo Perón** as President of Argentina in 1946 that their recovery became an issue to be actively pursued. Although the islanders strongly resisted any attempt to compel them to become Argentine, successive governments in Buenos Aires refused to deal with them, or even to allow them to travel via Buenos Aires without the risk of being called up for military service, and argued successfully with the United Nations Committee of 24 that the islands should be 'decolonized'. In an effort to build better relations, the British Government agreed to allow Argentina to establish links with the islands under the so-called communications agreement. After 17 years of talks had failed to resolve this impasse, on 2 April 1982 an Argentine naval force occupied the islands by force, but on 14 July surrendered to a British task force. Three islanders were killed in the war.

The Argentine military Government refused to agree to a formal cessation of hostilities until Britain agreed to talks on the sovereignty of the islands. The incoming civilian Government of Raúl Alfonsín continued this policy, trying at the same time to bring pressure to bear on the British government by a series of UN General Assembly resolutions calling for talks. Meanwhile, a new airport was constructed at Mount Pleasant to enable the islands to be supplied without using Latin American airfields. In 1989, however, **Carlos Menem** took a bold and pragmatic decision to restore full diplomatic relations with Britain, while holding the issue of sovereignty 'under an umbrella'. The British government responded positively and in 1990 the protection zone around the islands was lifted while

British trade with Argentina was resumed. The islanders were at last able to control the previously unrestrained factory fishing around the islands, while generating a substantial revenue from the sale of licences. Two months later the United Kingdom announced the relaxation of its arms embargo against Argentina. However, the strain placed on bilateral relations by the presentation to Congress, in early 1998, of draft legislation on sanctions to be imposed on petroleum companies and fishing vessels operating in Falkland Islands waters without Argentine authorization, and the hostile Argentine reaction to apparent assertions of the islanders' right to self-determination made by the Prince of Wales, the heir to the British throne, during an official visit in March 1999, were reminders of the continuing political sensitivity of the issue. In July 1999, however, Argentina and the United Kingdom agreed to end the ban on Argentine citizens visiting the Falkland Islands and to re-establish direct flights there from October. An agreement previously reached about the joint exploitation of oil in the Malvinas Basin was suspended in 2000 after President de la Rúa had not only stated his intention to maintain his country's claim to the Falklands, but had also refused to talk to the representatives of the islanders. In 2003 the incoming President of Argentina, Néstor Kirchner, also reiterated his country's claim.

Latest elections: There are no political parties. In the general election of 22 November 2001 five of the eight members elected to the Legislative Council had served on the previous Council; all were strongly opposed to the Argentine claim to sovereignty over the islands.

International relations and defence: In May 2003 the new Argentine President, Néstor Kirchner, promised to maintain his country's claim to the islands by peaceful means. There are approximately 1,300 British troops stationed on the islands at an annual cost of some £68m. The Falkland Island Defence Force numbers 60 islanders.

Economy: Historically the main income of the islands came from the flocks of sheep grazed on them and the high-quality wool they produced. The belief that oil might be discovered in the Malvinas Basin was a factor leading to the increase of tensions with Argentina in the 1970s, but since exploration has become possible none has been found. The islanders have, however, benefited substantially from the award of fishing licences in the coastal zone, under an agreement with Argentina.

Falkland Islands Co Ltd (FIC)

General trading company, f. in 1851, and now part of Falkland Islands Holding PLC, a public company quoted on the London Stock Exchange. After 1851 it directed the economic development of the colony, receiving a grant-in-aid until 1880 and help with its mail service until 1886, but after that was self-funding, deriving the bulk of its revenue from the sale of wool from the islands. The company is engaged in wholesale and retail sales on the islands, operates as a shipping agent and as an agent for Lloyds of London for marine insurance, and as an agent for shipping companies, wharf owners and travel agents.

Leadership: Roger Kenneth Spink (Dir and Gen. Man.)

Address: Crozier Place, Stanley

Telephone: 27600

Fax: 27603

E-mail: fic@horizon.co.fk

Internet: www.the-falkland-islands-co.com

Federación de Cámaras de Comercio e Industrias de Honduras (FEDECAMARA)
Federation of Chambers of Commerce and Industry of Honduras

F. 1948; the national federation of Chambers of Commerce with 1,200 members.

Leadership: Ing. Javier Chacón (Pres.)

Address: Edif. Castañito, 2°, 6a Avda Col. Los Castaños, Apdo 3393, Tegucigalpa

Telephone: 232-1870

Fax: 232-6083

E-mail: fedecamara@sigmanet.hn

Federación Latinoamericana de Periodistas (FELAP)
Latin American Federation of Journalists

Leadership: Tubal Páez Hernández (Pres.), Juan Carlos Camaño (Sec.-Gen.)

Address: Avda Andrés Bello, Casa Nacional de Periodistas P-3, Maripérez, Caracas, Venezuela

Telephone: (212) 793-3380

Fax: (416) 625-1683

E-mail: cccutpba@ciudad.com.ar

Internet: www.ciap-felap.org

Federación Nacional de Cafeteros de Colombia (FEDERACAFE)
National Federation of Coffee Growers—'La Cafetera', Colombia

F. 1927 to develop and regulate the **coffee** industry, and specifically to manage the domestic quota system needed to participate in the International Coffee Agreement.
Leadership: Gabriel Silva Luján (Gen. Man.)
Address: Calle 73, No. 8–13, Apdo Aéreo 57535, Santafé de Bogotá, DC
Telephone: (1) 217-0600
Fax: (1) 217-1021
Internet: www.cafedecolombia.com

Fanmi Lavalas, La
The Lavalas Family

Personalist movement; f. 1994 as political vehicle for Jean-Bertrand Aristide, who was re-elected as President of Haiti in the 2000 elections.
Leadership: Jean-Bertrand Aristide (Pres. of the Republic)

Figueres, José

José Figueres Ferrer (1906–1990), President of Costa Rica 1948–49, 1953–58, 1970–74, was a key figure in the democratization of Latin America. In 1948 he led an uprising against the Government of Rafael Angel Calderón. As President of the provisional government he abolished the army and gave women the vote. In 1953, as a democratic socialist, he was elected President by a large majority, but unlike Jacobo Arbenz in Guatemala was careful not to alienate a strongly anti-communist US government.

financial services

The most dramatic change in the economies of the region in the last 30 years has been the growth of offshore financial services as a significant input into local economies. Panama was already well established; other important centres are the Bahamas and the Cayman Islands, and most of the smaller Caribbean island states are now trying to develop similar sectors.

Fort-de-France

Fort-de-France, the chief town and capital of Martinique, is situated on the north side of the deep bay of the same name on the west coast. It became the capital after the destruction of the former capital, St Pierre, by the eruption of Mont Pelée on 8 May 1902. At the 1999 census it had a population of 94,049.

Fox Quesada, Vicente

Vicente Fox Quesada, President of Mexico for the term 2000–06, was born in 1942 in León, Guanajuato, and pursued business studies at the Ibero-American University, Mexico City, and Harvard Business School. The son of a wealthy farmer, he managed a 450-ha ranch in Guanajuato, raising cattle and ostriches for export, before joining the Coca Cola Corpn in 1964 and rising to become its president for Mexico and Central America. In 1988 he won a seat in the Chamber of Deputies for the opposition **Partido Acción Nacional**, contested the governorship of Guanajuato in 1991 and won it with a large majority at his second attempt in 1995. Nominated by his party to contest the presidency in the 2000 elections, he defeated an undistinguished government candidate and broke the monopoly of power that the **Partido Revolucionario Institucional** had held since 1929. As President he has been handicapped by the lack of a supporting majority in Congress, but has favoured free-market solutions to Mexico's problems and was the first head of state to be invited to meet US President George W. Bush.

Free Trade Area of the Americas (FTAA)

The US Administrations of President Bill Clinton (1993–2001) revived hopes for pan-American economic integration. Leaders of 34 countries of the Americas convened in Miami, Florida, USA, in December 1994, at Clinton's invitation, to discuss a draft hemispheric free-trade agreement. They agreed to accept in principle a programme of biennial summit meetings that would lead to a convergence of existing trade blocs and to the establishment of an FTAA by 2005. In 1995 the 12 presidents of the **Rio Group** (the permanent organization which, in 1987, suc-ceeded the *ad hoc* Contadora Group), reaffirming their commitment to democracy and the elimination of corruption, asserted their support for the proposal. Elsewhere there was some concern that successful subregional co-operation might be pre-judiced. Hence formal negotiations did not begin until the Second Summit of the Americas at **Santiago de Chile** in March 1998. No agreement on the order of negotiations was reached. Nevertheless, the Third Summit of the Americas, held in Québec, Canada, in April 2001 reaffirmed the target date of 2005.

French Guiana
Guyane

The French Overseas Department of Guyana is the easternmost of the three Guianas, which form an enclave on the north-east coast of Brazil, and is bounded on the west by Suriname.

Area: 83,534 sq km (32,253 sq miles); *local capital:* Cayenne; *population*: 182,233 (2002 estimate), comprising 66% mulatto, 22% Amerindian, 'East Indian' or Chinese, 12% European; *official language:* French (Creole and various Amerindian languages are also spoken); *religion:* Roman Catholic 75%, Protestant 4%.

Constitution: The head of state is the President of France, represented locally by a Commissioner of the Republic. Both the General Council (Conseil Général) of 19 members and the Regional Council (Conseil Régional) are directly elected, and the Department is represented in the French Assemblée Nationale by two members and in the Senate by one senator. The Department sends one representative to the European Parliament at Strasbourg.

History: French settlement in the area began as early as 1604, but the present territory, formerly known as Cayenne, was finally allocated to France only in 1814, at the Treaty of Paris. Gold was discovered in small quantities in the 19th century, but until 1937 the territory was notorious as the site of a number of penal settlements, of which the best-known was Devil's Island, where Alfred Dreyfus was incarcerated. In 1946 the territory became an Overseas Department of France, with the same laws and administration as a Department of metropolitan France. However, demonstrations against French rule in the 1970s were followed by continuing pressure for greater autonomy, though only a small proportion of the electorate (some 5%) favour independence.

Latest elections: In the first round of presidential elections held on 21 April 2002, a local candidate, Christiana Taubira, of the Parti Radical de Gauche, gained 52.7% of the vote, defeating both Jacques Chirac and Lionel Jospin.

International relations and defence: There is a French garrison of some 3,000 troops in the territory.

Economy: The Department had a trade deficit of €499m. (US $541.7m.) in 2000, total exports amounting to only €121m. France is the main market for exports and the main source of imports. Shrimps are the main export product; other exports include rice, pineapples and citrus fruit. Timber products have been declining in recent years.

Frente Farabundo Martí para la Liberación Nacional (FMLN)
Farabundo Martí National Liberation Front, El Salvador

The Front was formed in 1980 in Cuba to consolidate a number of pro-Cuban guerrilla groups. It took its name from Agustín Farabundo Martí, the first leader of the Salvadoran Communist Party, who had been arrested and executed following the massacre that ended the 1932 peasant uprising. A political wing, the Frente Democrático Revolucionario, was formed at the same time. On 10 January 1981 the FMLN launched a widely heralded 'final offensive' intended to secure a decisive victory before the Reagan Administration assumed power in the USA. Within a week, however, it was clear that the nation-wide uprising that had been envisaged had not occurred, though the armed forces, having sustained heavy casualties, had failed to inflict significant losses on the guerrillas. Over the next four years the guerrillas remained in effective control of much of the countryside, including the entire Department of Chalatenango and much of Morazán (where they operated their own radio station). They repeatedly destroyed key bridges (including the bridge over the Río Lempa) on the country's sole major arterial road, the Pan American Highway. However, though they inflicted serious casualties and great economic damage, they were unable to break the army's control of key locations.

Then, in a major change of strategy in March 1985, the FMLN launched an offensive in the cities aimed at disrupting the elections. It failed, however, to halt the victory of the Partido Demócrata Cristiano. President José Napoleón Duarte opened a dialogue with the insurgents in 1986 that was to continue intermittently for seven years. The armed forces, however, which had succeeded in closing down one of the three insurgent fronts on the Volcán de Guazapa, had launched major attacks on insurgent strongholds in Morazán and Chalatenango and, increasingly confident of success, were openly criticizing the civilian government. A major attack on 31 March 1987 by the FMLN on the northern army base of El Paraíso, Chalatenango, in which at least 42 were killed, demonstrated that the dispersal of the insurgents into smaller units, a long-time objective of government tactics, had not impaired their capacity to strike.

The next crisis came with the victory of the **Alianza Republicana Nacionalista** (ARENA) candidate, Alfredo Cristiani, in the presidential elections of 1989, which, however, failed to halt the talks. A new FMLN offensive was launched in November, killing more than 1,200 in 12 days. Caught off guard, the government imposed a state of siege and a news blackout which failed, however, to conceal evidence of uniformed 'death squads' operating in both city and countryside. A year later, in mid-November 1990, FMLN guerrillas attacked military installations across half the country. In a week of fighting, which lef. 90 dead and some 300 wounded, they also shot down an air force jet with a Soviet-made SAM-7 ground-to-air missile. However, this was to be the last major offensive. In January 1991 talks resumed in Mexico City after it had become clear that neither side could obtain a significant military advantage. On 20 May the UN Security Council finally approved the creation of an observer team to monitor human rights violations. On 16 November the FMLN declared a unilateral cease-fire, and on the last day of the year, in New York, the outgoing UN Secretary-General, Javier Pérez de Cuéllar, successfully obtained agreement on a staged programme leading to a definitive peace. The peace agreement was signed at Chapúltepec Castle, Mexico, on 16 January 1992, and the demobilization of the guerrillas was achieved so swiftly that the conflict was formally declared ended on 15 December, when the FMLN registered as an official political party.

Since that time the FMLN has been the principal opposition party in El Salvador, though its effectiveness has been severely impaired by its division into three main factions. In the presidential elections of 1994 the FMLN candidate, Rubén Zamora Rivas, obtained 32% of the votes cast, and the party went on to make significant gains in the legislative elections of 1997. In 2000 and 2004, however, it failed to make much impact on ARENA's vote.

Leadership: Salvador Sánchez Cerén (Co-ordinator-Gen.)
Address: 27 Calle Poniente 1316 y 47 Avda Norte, San Salvador
Telephone: 226-5236
Internet: www.fmln.org.sv

Frente Nacional Sindical (FNS)
National Trade Union Front, Guatemala

F. 1968 to co-ordinate trade union activity; comprises two confederations, the Confederación General de Sindicatos and the Confederación Nacional de

Trabajadores, and 11 smaller federations; claims adherence of 98% of Guatemala's organized workers.

Frente Popular (FP)
Popular Front, Ecuador

Umbrella group of labour unions.
Leadership: Luis Villacis (Pres.)
Internet: www.nodo50.org/frentepopular

Frente Republicano Guatemalteco (FRG)
Guatemalan Republican Front

An authoritarian right-wing party that was formed as a vehicle for former President of the Republic Gen. (retd) **Efraín Ríos Montt**, the FRG was a key participant in the 1990 'No Sell-Out Platform' *(Plataforma No Venta*—PNV). This electoral grouping was an alliance between the FRG, the Partido Institucional Democrático and the Frente de Unidad Nacional, and was extreme right-wing and populist, standing for strict law and order. Ríos Montt was extremely unpopular, having staged a military coup in 1982, assumed dictatorial powers and fought a vicious counter-insurgency campaign which had alienated many indigenous people. The alliance was deregistered after the 1990 poll on the dubious legal grounds that heads of state who participated in coups are banned from running for the presidency. In 1993 the party again failed to regain legislative approval.

The FRG was similarly affected by this ban, but, in the 1994 legislative elections, staged an impressive recovery, winning 32 of the available seats, a result that gained Montt the presidency of Congress. The former President's wife, Teresa Sosa de Ríos, became the FRG's presidential candidate, but for the elections held in November 1995 she was replaced by Alfonso Antonio Portillo Cabrera, who received 22.1% of the vote in the first round but was defeated in the run-off election on 7 January 1996, his party winning 21 seats in the legislative elections. In 1999 he was elected President of the Republic.
Leadership: Alfonso Antonio Portillo Cabrera
Address: 3 Calle 5–50, zona 1, Guatemala
Telephone: 238-27-56
Internet: www.frg.org.gt

Frente Sandinista de Liberación Nacional (FSLN)
Sandinista National Liberation Front, Nicaragua

The FSLN was founded by Carlos Fonseca Amador in 1961 as a pro-Cuban insurgent movement. Ideologically it was Marxist-Leninist, but its title significantly included the name of Gen. **Augusto Sandino**, guerrilla hero of Nicaraguan resistance to the USA in the 1920s and 1930s. Following the withdrawal of US forces from Nicaragua in 1933, Sandino had been murdered on the orders of the commander of the National Guard, Anastasio Somoza García, who ruled Nicaragua with an iron hand from 1936 to 1956, after which, in turn, his two sons continued to rule either directly or behind the scenes. Amador and his followers planned to follow Sandino's example and to set up a rural guerrilla movement in the northern hills. However, they were badly organized, their security was inadequate and when they launched their campaign they were speedily suppressed and their student supporters arrested. Amador himself was only saved from death at the hands of his captors by the intervention of President René Schick.

In 1967 **Anastasio Somoza Debayle** succeeded Schick as President. Like his father and brother, his effective power was based on the command of the National Guard, which he retained for himself. The catalyst for the fall of the Somoza regime was the Managua **earthquake** of 23 December 1972. The earthquake showed as clearly as was needed to all concerned that no one in Nicaragua except the Somozas was going to benefit from their rule and the Sandinistas were the immediate beneficiary. In December 1974 they seized the US embassy. Though the US Ambassador had already left the country, many of the Somoza family were still there and Somoza was forced to release a number of prisoners and pay a large ransom. More than 400 'disappeared' in the reprisals that followed.

The Sandinistas were divided over how to respond. The largest faction, the *Terceristas,* led by **Daniel Ortega Saavedra**, argued for immediate insurrection in alliance with a broad front comprising other disenchanted elements, and the bulk of the combatants sided with this faction. On 13 October 1977 they launched a national offensive against the Government. Important elements in the Church, notably the Cardenal brothers, already supported the FSLN. The signal for a general insurrection came in January 1978 when the editor of *La Prensa*, Pedro Joaquín Chamorro, whose editorials had been increasingly critical of the regime, was shot down in the street by an unknown gunman. This action, which was almost universally believed to be the work of the National Guard, brought about the unity that had up to that time been lacking. In August 1978 25 Sandinistas captured the National Palace, taking 1,500 hostages. A general strike was called. Attacks were launched simultaneously from the north, by the FSLN, and from the south by a democratic opposition front sponsored by Costa Rica and Panama. By mid-September a full-scale civil war was being waged. The National Guard fought fiercely to retain its power and privileges, but the Somozas lacked broad-based support, and when the President finally fled the country on 17 July 1979, members of the Junta of National Reconstruction and its Provisional Governing Council left Costa Rica to take charge of the devastated country. Over 50,000 people are believed to have died in the 18 months of fighting.

After taking over power in Nicaragua in 1979, the Provisional Government headed by the FSLN embarked on a series of reforms, including a literacy campaign, the provision of free medical care and the abolition of the death penalty. However, the US Reagan Administration believed that the insurrection in neighboring El Salvador formed part of a world-wide Communist conspiracy, supported by the Soviet Union through **Havana** and **Managua**, and sponsored a clandestine insurgent movement to overthrow the Nicaraguan government—see **Fuerzas Democráticas Nicaragüenses**. When free elections in 1985 gave the Sandinista leader, Daniel Ortega Saavedra, a sizeable majority, the US government still refused to recognize it. After the disclosure of the 'Iran-Contra' scandal in 1986, the US Congress refused to fund further action against Nicaragua, but kept the *contras* in being, and in the 1990 elections the Sandinistas were defeated by a 14-member coalition led by **Violeta Barrios de Chamorro**. Since then the Sandinistas have continued in existence as Nicaragua's leading opposition party. It is run by a 15-member directorate, the leading faction in which is Daniel Ortega's Izquierda Democrática. In the November 2001 elections Ortega received 42.3% of the votes cast, compared with 56.3% cast for Enrique Bolaños of the **Partido Liberal Constitucionalista**, and his party won 42 of the 90 seats in the Legislative Assembly.

Leadership: Daniel Ortega Saavedra (Sec.-Gen.)
Address: Costado Oeste Parque El Carmen, Managua
Telephone: (2) 66-0845
Fax: (2) 66-1560
Internet: www.fsln-nicaragua.com

Frente Unitario de Trabajadores (FUT)
United Workers' Front, Ecuador

F. 1971; umbrella organization linking three major trade union organizations, the Confederación Ecuatoriana de Organizaciones Clasistas (CEDOC), the

Confederación Ecuatoriana de Organizaciones Sindicales Librea (CEOSL) and the Confederación de Trabajadores del Ecuador (CTE).
Leadership: Edgar Ponce

Front Révolutionnaire pour l'Avancement et le Progrès d'Haïti
Revolutionary Front for the Advancement and Progress of Haiti

Army-sponsored paramilitary group which is estimated to have killed some 4,000 supporters of President **Jean-Bertrand Aristide** during his first term of office.

Fuerzas Armadas Revolucionarias (FAR)
Revolutionary Armed Forces, Guatemala

On 13 November 1960 Col Rafael Sessan Pereira of the Guatemalan army led an unsuccessful military coup against the government. His troops were angry at the presence on Guatemalan soil of Cuban exiles being trained, as it transpired, for the unsuccessful Bay of Pigs expedition. When the coup failed, Pereira fled to Mexico, but two junior officers who had supported him, Lt Marco Antonio Yon Sosa (1938–1970) and Ensign Luís Turcios Lima (1941–1966), returned to Guatemala. Both had been trained at the Guatemalan military college and in the USA. A third colleague, Alejandro de León, was murdered by the political police in Guatemala City in 1961, while they were trying to negotiate with the **Partido Guatemalteco del Trabajo** (PGT). At this time they were surprised to discover the extent of peasant support available to them. With the help of the PGT, they began guerrilla operations in the countryside in February 1962.

Key ideological differences, however, resulted in the lack of a unified strategy for their operations. Turcios Lima, who, despite his initial ignorance of guerrilla warfare, successfully established a rural insurgency in the Eastern Mountains in the Department of Zacapa, was closely aligned with the PGT and, as a result, obtained support from left-wing middle-class intellectuals. His young second-in-command, César Montes, was also close to the PGT and was able to ensure its continuing support when, in December 1962, after a series of defeats, the remaining guerrillas regrouped under the umbrella title of the FAR. A second front, led by Col Paz Tejada, that had meanwhile been established by the PGT itself, failed to survive, though the PGT remained committed to the idea of insurrection. The third front in the Department of Izábal was led by Yon Sosa. Influenced by Mao Zedong (he himself was partly of Chinese descent) and by the Fourth International, Yon

Sosa rejected the political line of the PGT and sought to establish 'liberated areas'; in March 1965 his Revolutionary Movement of the 13 November (MR-13), named after the date of the abortive 1960 coup, broke with both the FAR and with the PGT.

Neither of the two movements received any external support. Most of their weapons were seized from the Guatemalan army (which, as a result of Guatemala's nominal participation in the Second World War, had far more than it needed), and the remainder were purchased with the funds generated by bank raids. Both movements, despite their ideological differences, were essentially rural guerrilla movements, inspired by the Cuban Revolution and following the strategy advocated by **Che Guevara** and Régis Debray. Hence they were relatively small movements centred on a few hundred dedicated activists, maintaining their core support and bases in the countryside well away from major population centres.

In 1966 the armed forces reluctantly accepted the accession of a civilian government under Julio César Méndez Montenegro. Effective power, however, resided in the military commander, Col Carlos Arana Osorio, who, with the aid of 'death squads', waged a savage counter-insurgency campaign against both the FAR and MR-13. In 1970 Arana himself became President, initiating 22 years of military rule. Though the Constitution remained in place and elections took place regularly, in practice none but military candidates, or those approved by the military, stood any chance of success.

During the temporary absence of Turcios Lima in **Havana** in 1966, the PGT had, just before the elections, issued a declaration of support for Méndez Montenegro. Though on his return he did not reverse this decision, the FAR did reject the amnesty offered by the government and vowed to fight on. Meanwhile, on 5 March 1966, police had captured the entire leadership of the PGT, including its Secretary-General, Víctor Manuel Gutiérrez, in Guatemala City. The guerrillas kidnapped two key government figures in order to force an exchange, only for it to be confirmed that all 28 PGT detainees had been summarily shot. As a result even the PGT rejected the amnesty. Soon afterwards Turcios Lima was killed in a car accident.

He was succeeded as commander of the FAR by César Montes (b. 1942). A civilian, who lacked the military contacts of his predecessor, he had to face a renewed onslaught from the armed forces, this time backed by a number of 'death squads'. Though few of the 6,000-10,000 Guatemalans who died in 1966–68 were members of any guerrilla organization, the 300-strong FAR suffered significant losses and the gradual erosion of its support in the countryside. In response, MR-13 joined the FAR, with Yon Sosa as leader and César Montes as his second-in-command. In January 1968 the FAR broke with the increasingly hesitant PGT. Meanwhile, in order to protect its captured members, it had increasingly had to switch its focus to the capital, and to adapt its tactics to urban guerrilla warfare. In fact, the attempted kidnapping and killing of US Ambassador Gordon Mein in 1967 was the first case of its kind in Latin America and prompted a wave of similiar attacks on diplomatic personnel and leading figures in business and industry throughout the hemisphere.

What had been the MR-13 continued to wage its campaign in the countryside. Like the rest of the FAR, however, it discovered that the native population was reluctant to accept the good faith of *ladinos* (people of Spanish or part-Spanish extraction). In 1970 Yon Sosa himself was killed and his group, which had removed its base to the north of the Department of El Quiché, barely survived. In 1982 it linked up with other groups in **Unidad Revolucionaria Nacional Guatemalteca**.

Fuerzas Armadas Revolucionarias de Colombia (FARC)
Colombian Revolutionary Armed Forces

Among several independent 'republics' set up in Colombia during the period of 'La Violencia' (1946–53) was that of Gaitania (later called Marquetalia), in the department of Tolima. It was founded in 1949 by Fermín Charry Rincón (a member of the central committee of the Communist Party, also known as Jacobo Frias Alape). He was killed in January 1960 and was succeeded by Manuel Marulanda Vélez (also called Pedro Antonio Marín or 'Tirofijo'—'Sure Shot'). Marquetalia was occupied by the Colombian army in May 1964, but its guerrillas decided to continue their struggle and in April 1966 set up the FARC under the leadership of Marulanda and other members of the Communist Party's central committee.

Between 1976 and 1980 FARC members were involved in a number of armed attacks and in clashes with army units. An amnesty offer made by President Turbay Ayala was rejected by the FARC on 17 June 1980. However, although it continued its attacks, the FARC showed interest in an amnesty offer of President **Belisario Betancur**, which came into force in November 1982, and early in 1983 FARC delegates had talks with a presidential armistice commission. Nevertheless, the FARC commenced insurgency activities together with the Movimiento 19 de Abril (M-19) in June 1983, and in November it reached agreement on the formation of a political alliance with the M-19 and the (pro-Castro) **Ejército de Liberación Nacional** (ELN).

In October 1983 the FARC proposed that a cease-fire should take effect from 20 January 1984, and a truce from 20 January 1985 (which would give it time to demobilize its forces and to form a political party). Agreement was reached with the peace commission on 28 March 1984 for a cease-fire to take effect on 28 May of that year, on terms including the demilitarization of rural areas. A process of reintegrating guerrillas into civilian life began on 1 December 1984, and on 28 May 1985 the FARC founded a political party, the Unión Patriótica (UP). It also agreed to hand over to the authorities a list of those who had deserted after the truce to a splinter group, the Ricardo Franco Front. In September 1985 the FARC requested that the cease-fire be extended until September 1986, and it agreed not to engage in armed campaigning during the forthcoming elections in which the UP was taking part. However, progress towards a final peace settlement, which the FARC had supported since 1982, appeared to falter shortly after the new Liberal administration took over in 1986. Some 300 UP members had died in the 30 months of the cease-fire and it was clear that extreme right-wing groups were trying to provoke the FARC into renewed fighting.

In June 1987 fighting resumed when a 200-strong force of suspected FARC guerrillas ambushed and killed 27 soldiers, wounding 42 others, in the south-eastern jungles of Caquetá. This began a long period in which intermittent guerrilla activity alternated with tortuous peace negotiations with each new government. When Ernesto Samper Pizano became President in August 1994 the usual indications came from both the FARC and the ELN that they were prepared to enter into dialogue. The President announced on 17 November that his Government was prepared to enter into peace talks without preconditions. On 18–19 May 1995 the President made a series of offers to guerrilla groups for their integration into mainstream political life, with representation in a new, single-chamber Congress. The FARC accepted the proposals in principle, but continued its attacks in the La Uribe region; later attacks on anti-drugs headquarters in Cali and Bogotá confirmed suspicions that they were collaborating with the Cali drugs cartel. Meanwhile, massive popular protests at the effects of the **coca** eradication programme had spread across the southern Departments of Guaviare, Putumayo, Caquetá, Meta and Cauca, leading to the deaths of at least 18 in clashes with police and troops. Though agreement was reached with the Putumayo growers, the President insisted that violence in Caquetá was fuelled by 'hidden interests' and talks were suspended on 23 August. Both protests and guerrilla violence continued at a high level

Following mediation by the Church, the International Red Cross and former US President Jimmy Carter, President Samper ordered the evacuation of troops, for a period of one month, from a large part of the Department of Caquetá and military hostages were released on 15 June 1997. Though senior officers denounced the move and accused the President of acceding to the demands of the USA, the President then proposed the establishment of a Peace Commission to negotiate terms with both the FARC and the ELN. On 21 August the FARC command agreed to enter into talks. However, following the assassination, on 8 August, of the Liberal Senator Jorge Cristo, the army launched a major offensive against the FARC, this claiming the deaths of more than 600 guerrillas and effectively ending the peace process.

In an unprecedented move, the President-elect, Andrés Pastrana Arango, met personally with Manuel Marulanda on 9 July 1998 and agreed a timetable and conditions for peace negotiations with the FARC. Once in office, his Government proceeded to evacuate a large area in which to hold talks with the FARC, much to the fury of the armed forces. The President even travelled in person to an agreed jungle location on 7 January 1999. The FARC leader, however, did not keep the appointment. By September the conflict had spread into Venezuela, Ecuador, Peru, Brazil and Panama, all of which mobilized forces to contain it. The new factor was the emergence of a right-wing 'death squad' organization, the **Autodefensas Unidas de Colombia**, that threatened reprisals. On 24 October, as massive demonstrations for peace took place, the Government recommenced negotiations with the FARC. A third round of negotiations began in November and the FARC called a Christmas truce, though this followed an attack, on 12 December, on a naval base at Jurado in which some 50 marines were killed.

On 30 April 2000 the FARC made a second attempt to relaunch itself as a political party, the Bolivarian Movement for a New Colombia. Talks resumed with the government but were suspended by the FARC on 18 November in protest at the US-backed 'Plan Colombia'. Later, on 29 December, Diego Turbay, president of the Congressional peace commission, and six of his colleagues died in an ambush in the FARC zone. Negotiations continued throughout 2001, without success. However, at Los Pozos on 9 February 2001, following 15 hours of face-to-face talks, President Pastrana and Marulanda apparently reached an agreement on new 'confidence-building measures'. The FARC agreed to cease kidnappings for ransom and to exchange prisoners, beginning with the surrender to the authorities of 62 child soldiers, and on 13 March it was reported that agreement had been reached on the composition of an international facilitating commission to oversee the implementation of the Los Pozos agreements. However, the FARC did not discontinue the kidnappings that had in recent years become an important source of income for this well-resourced movement, together with the drugs trade. Following a new agreement with the FARC on 5 October the President announced the extension of the FARC demilitarized zone, to the great annoyance of the security forces. On 18 October, however, the FARC responded by demanding that troops be withdrawn from the area around the zone, following this with other new demands, which were also rejected.

After three years of negligible progress, the peace talks finally collapsed on 13 January 2002, when the FARC refused to agree to a cease-fire. On 20 February troops entered the demilitarized zone. They quickly seized the town of San Vicente del Caguán, meeting no resistance from the retreating guerrillas, who had precipitated the breakdown by hijacking a civil airliner and kidnapping Senator Jorge Eduardo Gechem Turbay, president of the Senate peace commission. However, they were not able to command the whole of the zone, whose area totalled some 16,000 square miles and was populated by about 100,000 people. While the Colombian military gained control of the principal towns of the demilitarized zone, the FARC remained in control of wide areas of the mostly mountainous and jungle area, as well as of some other parts of the country. In February 2003 the FARC kidnapped three US citizens, described by the US Department of State as specialist contractors, when their plane crashed in FARC-controlled territory on an intelligence-gathering mission. This was reportedly the first time the FARC had captured US citizens working for the US government. Former defence minister, Gilberto Echeverri Mejía, was kidnapped by the FARC while taking part in a peace march in April 2002 and was held hostage for more than a year before he was killed, on 5 May 2003, during an attempt to rescue him by army special forces in which nine other hostages also died. The army stated that the hostages had been executed before the arrival of government forces and that all of the rebels had escaped. In the aftermath of this incident, President Uribe stated that he would release FARC prisoners in exchange for other hostages only if they were sent abroad.

Though still theoretically left-wing, observers generally agree that since 1997 the FARC has in practice lost any claim to political motivation and has degenerated into a terrorist movement dedicated solely to its own enrichment through kidnapping for profit and dealing in narcotics. It is estimated to have an annual income of US \$200m.–\$300m. from drugs-trafficking, 'taxation', protection rackets and kidnapping. Its armed fighters are estimated to number 6,000–17,000.

Leadership: Manuel Marulanda Vélez ('Tirofijo')

Fuerzas Democráticas Nicaragüenses (FDN)
Nicaraguan Democratic Forces

In November 1981 US President Reagan authorized National Security Decision Directive 17 which allowed for a clandestine force to be formed for the purpose of launching a counter-revolutionary guerrilla campaign in Nicaragua from bases in Honduras. This force soon became known to its opponents as *contras* (short for counter-revolutionaries) and the name endured, though the anodyne title chosen by the US Central Intelligence Agency (CIA) was Nicaraguan Democratic Forces.

In its initial stages the covert war against the Sandinistas did not go well. Focusing on so-called economic targets in the northern half of the country, the insurgents gained little popular support and were unable to establish bases within the country. When the movement seemed on the point of stalling, however, the Reagan Administration intensified its campaign. On 3 January 1984 irregular forces co-ordinated by a US warship attacked oil facilities at Puerto Sandino. On 25 February similar attacks on the Atlantic port of El Bluff and the Pacific harbour of Corinto were accompanied by the laying of mines which damaged four freighters, one of Soviet registration. On 5 April the USA vetoed a UN Security Council resolution condemning the mining of the ports. Meanwhile, at a press conference, President Reagan had complained that the Nicaraguans were 'exporting revolution' and stated openly, 'We are going to try and inconvenience the government of Nicaragua until they quit that kind of action'.

The failure of the FDN to make headway against the Provisional Government stemmed from three causes. First, the personnel of the FDN, mostly former members of **Somoza**'s National Guard, were chosen largely for their opposition to communism. They were not particularly competent and, after the assassination of Somoza himself in Paraguay in 1980, lacked leadership. Hence, the CIA sponsored a second opposition movement in the south of the country, the Alianza Revolucionaria Democrática (ARDE). ARDE, led by a disaffected ex-Sandinista, Edén Pastora ('Comandante Cero'), began operations in September 1982. Pastora had the popular appeal that the members of the FDN lacked. However, he refused to accept Somocista leadership. In May 1984 he was seriously injured by a bomb explosion which destroyed his headquarters and killed four people, including a visiting US journalist. On 31 May 1985 the killing of two Costa Rican border guards called into question Costa Rican support for ARDE, which, after a major government offensive at the end of the month, sued for peace.

In June 1984, following the bomb incident, the US Congress, by the Boland Amendment, voted to sever financial assistance to the insurgents. In November 1984 a free election was held in which **Daniel Ortega Saavedra** was elected President by a substantial majority, despite US attempts to provoke abstentions. Meanwhile, members of the US National Security Council (NSC) attempted to continue the war by transferring funds from the sale of arms to Iran to the *contras*, but they were unable to do more than to keep the *contras* in their camps across Nicaragua's border with Honduras. At the opening of the UN General Assembly in December 1985 President Ortega rejected US demands for his Government to negotiate with the *contras*, whose activity had declined to such an extent that the **coffee** harvest was completed without casualties. The hostility of the US Administration had succeeded in bringing to the fore elements that favoured a more militant response, accompanied by a curtailment of civil liberties. US troops were deployed in Honduras and US helicopters were used to transport *contra* forces. In late March 1986 an incursion by Nicaraguan troops into Honduras was used by the USA as a pretext to inflame opinion against the Sandinista Government. Continuing Sandinista confidence in ultimate victory made it easy for the US Administration to gain support in the US House of Representatives in June 1986 for a vote to transfer $100m. in economic and military aid to the *contras*. In Nicaragua this was regarded as a declaration of war and was followed by the closure of the opposition newspaper, *La Prensa*, and the expulsion of the conservative Bishop Pablo Antonio Vega, who had argued in favour of aid for the *contras*.

Nevertheless, when the disclosure of the Iran-*Contra* affair caused a scandal in the USA in November 1986, the most acute danger to Nicaragua had in fact already passed. Thereafter the *contra* forces were held in their camps in Honduras while US forces conducted a series of exercises on Honduran soil that were intended to impress the Sandinistas. The final phase of the insurgency, in 1986–1990, consisted of a series of negotiations between Nicaragua, the USA and other interested parties. A final resolution of the conflict came in 1990 as a result of the election victory of **Violeta Barrios de Chamorro** and the formal demobilization of the *contras* under UN auspices.

Fujimori, Alberto Keinya

Alberto Keinya Fujimori , b. 1938 in Lima, President of Peru 1990–2000, the son of Japanese immigrant parents, studied in the USA and became a successful business-man. He was the unexpected winner of the Peruvian presidential elections in 1990, but his populist supporters, in the form of **Cambio-90** (C-90), did not obtain a majority in Congress. In 1992, with military support, he carried out a 'self-coup' (*autogolpe*) against his own Government, dissolved Congress and ruled by decree. The capture of Abimael Guzmán, leader of the formidable guerrilla movement **Sendero Luminoso**, in September 1992 seemed to vindicate him. Forced to yield to external pressure to restore democratic government, he did so by calling a Constitutional Convention, in which he could command a majority, and writing a new Constitution, under which he was elected to a second term in 1995. In his second term his Government became increasingly unpopular and, amid accusations of corruption, he persuaded Congress to reinterpret the Constitution and allow him to run for a further term in 2000. Though he was the leading candidate in the first round of voting, before the second round could be held a video was circulated which appeared to show his chief henchman, **Vladimiro Montesinos**, head of the much-feared secret police, the Servicio Nacional de Inteligencia, bribing a congressman. While on a visit to Japan, Fujimori resigned the presidency, taking advantage of the fact that, as a registered Japanese citizen, he could not be extradited.

G

Galápagos Islands

Islas Galápagos

Group of islands, also known as the *Archipiélago Colón*, some 965 km (600 miles) west of the mainland of Ecuador, celebrated both for their giant turtles and other unusual species, but also for having inspired Charles Darwin to formulate his theory of natural selection.

Granma

Granma is the official daily newspaper of the **Partido Comunista de Cuba**. It is named after the motor launch which carried **Fidel Castro** and his comrades from Mexico to Cuba in December 1956–January 1957.

Grenada

The island of Grenada is the most southerly of the Windward Islands, in the Lesser Antilles, and lies some 145 km (90 miles) north of Trinidad. With Carriacou, the largest island of the Grenadines, and Petit Martinique, the country is the second smallest in the western hemisphere.

Area: 344.5 sq km (133 sq miles); *capital:* **St George's** (on Grenada); *population:* 100,895 (2001 census), comprising 85% of African descent, 11% of mixed African descent, the rest mainly European and East Indian, though some claim descent from the indigenous Caribs; *official language:* English; *religion:* over 50% Roman Catholic, 11% Anglican, 33% various Protestant denominations.

Constitution: Grenada is a constitutional monarchy within the **Commonwealth**. Under the 1974 Constitution the sovereign, HM Queen Elizabeth II, is represented by a Governor-General, who chooses the Prime Minister from the majority party in the House of Representatives, which has 15 popularly-elected members. There is also an appointed Senate of 13 members. The Constitution was suspended after the revolution of 1979, which established a provisional government, but restored after the overthrow of the Revolutionary Military Council in 1983.

History: **Christopher Columbus** landed on Grenada in 1498 and named it Concepción. It was taken over in 1650 by the French, who encountered stiff resistance from the Carib inhabitants, and ceded to Great Britain in 1763. It was recaptured by France in 1779, but returned in 1783. A slave revolt led by Julian Fedon in 1795–96 succeeded initially in gaining almost complete control of the island, but was afterwards harshly suppressed. The slave trade was ended in 1808 and slavery itself abolished in 1834.

Grenada joined the Federation of the West Indies in 1958. When it collapsed four years later attempts to link up with other islands were unsuccessful. Under the leadership of Sir Eric Gairy and his Grenada United Labour Party (GULP), which had won the first election held under universal suffrage in 1950, Grenada obtained internal self-government as a British Associated State in 1967. Gairy, however, was feared and distrusted by many people on the islands, though the opposition National Party (NP), led by Herbert Blaize, was unable to muster enough votes to defeat him. Independence in 1974, therefore, was opposed by the New Jewel Movement (NJM), founded in 1973 by young left-wingers led by the charismatic Maurice Bishop (whose father had been shot dead by the police during a demonstration). In 1976 the NJM gained 48% of the votes cast in the first post-independence elections, but Gairy retained power until 13 March 1979, when, while on a visit to New York to advise the UN and the world of the danger posed by extraterrestrials, he was overthrown.

After the overthrow of Gairy, a provisional revolutionary government (PRG) was formed, led by Bishop as Prime Minister, but retaining the Queen as head of state. The USA was suspicious of the PRG's desire for closer ties with Cuba and the USSR. Though the USSR remained aloof, Cuba sent a construction batallion to help British contractors to build an international airport at Pointe Salines. In 1983, however, it was the militant wing of the NJM, in alliance with the army, led by Gen. Hudson Austin, which organized a coup to depose Bishop, who was summarily shot, together with some of his ministers. The US Administration of Ronald Reagan used this as a pretext to intervene militarily, with the support of seven Eastern Caribbean states, and installed an interim government led by Nicholas Braithwaite of the New Democratic Party (NDP). In elections in December 1984, however, Herbert Blaize and the NP were victorious. . Blaize died in December 1989, and in elections held in 1990 the NP, under his successor, Ben Jones, was narrowly defeated by Braithwaite's NDP, which won seven seats in the House of

Representatives. In elections held in 1995 the New National Party (NNP), led by Keith Mitchell, was victorious. In 1999 the NNP won all 15 seats in the House of Representatives, but disbanded soon afterwards.

Latest elections: Following the general election held in 2003, at which it won 49.8% of the vote and eight of the 15 seats in the House of Representatives, the NNP again formed the government. The National Democratic Congress received 45.1% of the vote and won the remaining seven seats. Neither GULP, which obtained 3.2% of the vote, nor the People's Labour Movement, which received 2.3% of the vote, won any seats.

International relations and defence: Grenada is a member of the United Nations, the **Organization of American States**, the Commonwealth, and the **Caribbean Community and Common Market**, as well as of the **Organization of Eastern Caribbean States**. A regional security unit was formed in 1983 and trained by British officers; a paramilitary section, the Special Services Unit, participates in the US-sponsored Regional Security System.

Economy: The economy recovered partially in 2002 following a sharp decline in tourism in the previous year. World prices for nutmeg, Grenada's main export crop, fell further from their 1999 peak.

GNI: US $363m. (2001); *GNI per caput:* $3,610 (2001); *GNI at PPP:* $632m. (2001); *GNI per caput at PPP:* $6,290 (2001); *exports:* $59.7m. (2002); *imports:* $233.2m. (2002); *currency:* Eastern Caribbean dollar (EC$), plural dollars; US $1 = EC$2.70 since July 1976.

Grenada United Labour Party (GULP)

F. 1950 by Eric Gairy, who had made his name as leader of the Grenada Manual and Metal Workers' Union, organizing a series of strikes in which four people were killed. At the first elections held under universal suffrage the party (then called the Grenada People's Party) won 71% of the vote and Gairy became Chief Minister. When Grenada gained full responsibility for its internal affairs in 1967, Sir Eric Gairy became Prime Minister, presiding over such an arbitrary and repressive regime that his opponents rightly feared the approach of independence, which came in 1974. Though GULP was able to regroup after the restoration of electoral democracy in 1984, it was unsuccessful until Gairy died in 1997 and since then has been weak and divided. Despite linking up with the United Labour Congress in 2001 it was unsuccessful in the 2003 elections.

Leadership: Wilfred Hayes (Pres.), Gloria Payne-Banfield (Leader)
Address: St George's

Guadeloupe

Guadeloupe is an Overseas Department of the French Republic, consisting of the island of Guadeloupe and some smaller islands (La Désirade, Iles des Saintes, Marie Galante) in the Windward Islands, and St-Barthélemy and the northern (French) part of St-Martin/St Maarten in the Leeward Islands.

Area overall: 1,705 sq km; *capital:* **Basse-Terre** (on Guadeloupe); *population:* 435,739 (2002 estimate), comprising 90% African or mulatto, 5% European; *official language:* French; *religion:* Roman Catholic 84%, Protestant 1%, others, including Hinduism and various African religions.

Constitution: The head of state is the President of France, represented locally by a Commissioner of the Republic. In June 2001 it was agreed to merge the directly elected 42-seat General Council (Conseil Général), elected for a six-year term, with the Regional Council (Conseil Régional) of 41 members in a new 'collectivité territoriale' and to establish an independent Executive Council. In 2003 the French National Assembly (Assemblée Nationale) approved these constitutional changes for submission to referendum. Guadeloupe is represented in the Assembly by four members and in the Senate by two senators, all of whom are also members of the Regional Council. It sends one representative to the European Parliament at Strasbourg.

History: The island of Guadeloupe was named by **Christopher Columbus** on his first voyage in 1493. French settlement began in 1635. In 1946 the territory became an Overseas Department of France, with the same laws and administration as a Department of metropolitan France. However, pressure for greater autonomy began to build up in the 1980s and was only defused by the success of the moderate Left in France in 1988.

Latest elections: In the first round of presidential elections held on 21 April 2002, Christiana Taubira, of the Parti Radical de Gauche, gained 37.1% of the vote, defeating both Jacques Chirac and Lionel Jospin. In elections to the National Assembly held on 9 and 16 June the results were: Objectif Guadeloupe two seats, Parti Communiste Guadeloupéen one seat, Gauche Plurielle one seat.

International relations and defence: In mid-2001 President Chirac rejected a joint proposal from the French overseas departments in the region that they be allowed to join the **Association of Caribbean States** as associate members. There is a French garrison of some 4,000 troops in the Caribbean, with its headquarters on Martinique.

Economy: French aid and subsidies ensure that Guadeloupe has one of the highest standards of living in the Caribbean, gross domestic product per head being estimated at €13,071 in 2001. The traditional export crops of **sugar** and **bananas** both fared badly in the 1990s and early 2000s, the former because of low world prices and **hurricane** damage, and the latter because of hurricane damage and US pressure on the **European Union** to end import quotas. Tourism, which became the Department's principal source of income in 1988, expanded rapidly, but remained critically dependent on French visitors. Virtually the sole industrial activity is the refining of sugar and the distillation of rum.

Guatemala
República de Guatemala

Guatemala is the northernmost of the Central American states, bordered on the north and north-west by Mexico, on the north-east by Belize, and on the south-east by Honduras and El Salvador. It is divided into 22 Departments.

Area overall: 108,889 sq km (42,042 sq miles); *capital:* **Guatemala City**; *population:* 11,240,000 (2002 census, provisional), comprising 55% mestizo (known as ladinos), and 43% Amerindian; *official language:* Spanish; *religion:* over 66% Roman Catholic, more than 20% evangelical Protestant.

Constitution: The present Constitution was drawn up by a Constituent Assembly in 1984 and came into effect in 1986; it was amended in 1994 to enhance the scope of constitutional guarantees and, in 1996, to transfer responsibility for national security from the army to the police. Legislative power is vested in a Congress of 113 members, 91 of whom are elected by the Departments and 22 returned by means of a national list. They serve for four years and can be re-elected only once for a further, non-consecutive term. There is universal suffrage but voting is compulsory only for literate citizens. The President is elected for a four-year term, by absolute majority, and may not be re-elected.

History: Present-day Guatemala was formerly, in colonial times, a province of the Captaincy-General of Guatemala, which covered most of contemporary Central America. It became independent as part of Mexico in 1821, and as part of the Central American Republic in 1824. In 1838 a popular revolt led by an illiterate muleteer led to the break-up of the Republic and the emergence of an independent Guatemala. For the next century Guatemala was ruled by successive dictators. In 1944 a popular revolt overthrew Jorge Ubico and, for the first time, a serious attempt was made to create a civilian government, led by the moderate left-winger, Juan José Arévalo. In 1950, however, democratic presidential elections resulted in the victory of Col Jacobo Arbenz, who had been a key figure in the 1944 revolt. Arbenz tried to continue the policy of social reform already established, but when he proposed the nationalization of the unused lands of the United Fruit Co he was deposed in a revolt engineered by the US government. The land programme was reversed, but the new dictator was assassinated in 1957 and power reverted to the senior members of the army, while junior officers were among those who established a pro-Cuban guerrilla movement in 1960.

In 1966–1970 a civilian President, Julio César Méndez Montenegro, held office, but, though fairly elected, he was only allowed to do so after he had agreed to allow the army a free hand in a counter-insurgency campaign being planned by its commander, Gen. Arana. Key figures were killed by both urban and rural guerrillas, while government-backed 'death squads' killed anyone whose education or background made them a possible left-wing sympathizer. In 1970 Arana himself became President, inaugurating 16 years of military rule under five Presidents. At first the guerrillas appeared to have been quelled. In 1976, however, a devastating **earthquake** struck Guatemala City and left hundreds of thousands homeless. Then, in 1978, at Panzós, in Alta Verapaz, soldiers brought in by local landowners fired on a gathering of Kekchi Indians who were demonstrating peacefully for land rights. The 140 who died were only the first in a panicky onslaught on the indigenous peoples who made up the majority of Guatemala's population. Led by Gen. Romeo Lucas García, a large landowner himself, the armed forces behaved as if every Indian was an enemy and the country was in a state of civil war. This policy was continued by Gen. **Ríos Montt**. Only in 1985 did Guatemala's pariah status in the international community persuade the armed forces to allow the election of a civilian, Vinicio Cerezo Arévalo. Though he was succeeded by another civilian, the human rights situation in the country remained so grim that it was only after the failure of an attempted coup in 1993 that it became possible for the United Nations to broker a peace agreement with the various insurgent movements. The agreement came into effect in 1996, but it has proved almost impossible to persuade the Congress to implement its undertakings in respect of it.

Latest elections: In the first round of presidential elections held on 7 November 1999, Alvaro Colom Caballeros, of the Alianza Nueva Nación (incorporating the former guerrilla organization, **Unidad Revolucionaria Nacional Guatemalteca**), finished in third place with only 12.3% of the vote. In the run-off election held on 26 December, on the other hand, Alfonso Antonio Portillo Cabrera of the ruling **Frente Republicano Guatemalteco**, a populist who admitted having killed two men allegedly in self-defence in 1982, won a decisive victory, receiving 68.3% of the vote, compared with the 31.7% obtained by the former mayor of Guatemala City, Oscar Berger Perdomo of the **Partido de Avanzada Nacional**.

International relations and defence: Guatemala is a member of the United Nations, the **Organization of American States**, the **Central American Integration System** (*Sistema de la Integración Centroamericana*—SICA) and the **Rio Pact**. As a result of its history of insurgency, Guatemala has traditionally maintained a large army. Under the 1996 accords, however, the army's strength was to be reduced by one-third. The regular army numbered more than 29,000 in 2002, comprising mainly conscripts. Conscription similarly forms the basis of paramilitary forces with a strength in excess of 19,000. There is a small navy of coastal patrol vessels with a strength of 1,500 and an air force of 700.

Guatemala, economy

The spread of civil war within the country in the late 1970s ended 20 years of economic growth and development, though this was resumed in the 1990s. Guatemala is one of the poorest countries on the American mainland.

GNI: US $19,600m. (2001); *GNI per caput:* $1,680 (2001); *GNI at PPP:* $51,000 (2001); *GNI per caput at PPP:* $4,380 (2001), rank 120; *exports:* $2,864.6m. (2001); *imports:* $5,142.1m. (2001); *currency:* quetzal, plural quetzales; US $1 = 7.905 quetzales at 31 May 2003.

In 2002 agriculture accounted for 22.5% of Guatemala's gross domestic product (GDP), industry for 19.3% and mining and quarrying for 0.5%. Some 12.5% of the land is arable, 5.0% under permanent crops, 23.9% permanent pasture and more than 33% forest and woodland. The main export crops are **coffee**, **sugar**, **bananas**, oil palm and cardamom; maize, beans and vegetables are grown and cattle and pigs are reared for local consumption. The main mineral resources are **copper**, lead and zinc; a project to mine nickel was abandoned in the 1980s because of low world prices and local unrest. The principal industries are food, beverages and tobacco, building materials and textiles. There is a significant *maquiladora* sector employing some 80,000 workers in bond in the production of clothing for re-export. The main energy source is petroleum, proven reserves of which were estimated at 526m. barrels in 2000. Hydroelectric power is generated on the Usumacinta and Chixoy.

Main exports are coffee, raw and processed sugar, bananas and basic manufactures. Principal imports are machinery and transport equipment and petroleum and petroleum products. In 2002 the USA was the greatest purchaser of exports, followed by El Salvador, Honduras, Costa Rica, Germany and Mexico. The USA was the greatest supplier of imports, followed by Mexico, Japan and El Salvador.

Powerful vested interests have repeatedly frustrated tax reform, and despite the damage done by 36 years of civil war the government has not been allowed to honour its pledge to increase revenues to the levels required to stabilize the economy. Social welfare spending is minimal and two-thirds of the population (mainly the indigenous population) live in poverty. In 1990–2001 GDP grew at an average annual rate of 3.9%, but in 2001 declined by 2.1%. The rate of inflation, which averaged 11.5% in the 1990s, was 7.6% in 2001.

Guatemala City
Santiago de Guatemala

A new city, founded after the destruction of Antigua Guatemala by an **earthquake** in 1774 to serve as the capital of the former Captaincy-General. Today it is a seriously overcrowded city, with a population estimated in 2001 at 1,022,000, many of whom live in shanty-towns. The usual English form is used to distinguish it from the name of the country of which it is the capital.

Guevara, Che

Guevara de la Serna, Dr Ernesto, known to history by the Latin American nickname for Argentines, 'Che', was born in Rosario, Argentina, in 1928. He was the son of a well-to-do family of part-Irish extraction. From infancy he suffered from asthma, and was declared unfit for military service at the age of 18, despite being a keen sportsman. As a medical student, he travelled extensively in South America, and when he qualified in 1953 travelled to Bolivia, and then to Guatemala, where he witnessed the fall of the Arbenz Government. In Mexico City in 1955 he was introduced to **Fidel Castro** and his brother, who were looking for a doctor to accompany their expedition to Cuba.

After the initial ambush and escape to the Sierra Maestra, Guevara soon found himself in charge of a column and later became Castro's second-in-command. In 1959 he was placed in charge of the National Bank and later given the task of trying to industrialize the country of which he had by now become a citizen. During this time he published his widely-influential *Reminiscences of the Cuban Revolutionary War* and a textbook, *La guerra de guerrillas* (Guerrilla Warfare), which taught that a revolution could create its own conditions for success and inspired a wave of guerrilla movements in the region. After a brief and unsuccessful attempt to help the Marxist government of Congo-Brazzaville, he returned to Bolivia in 1956 to establish a guerrilla *foco* near Camiri in the Department of Chuquisaca. Wounded and captured in a battle with Bolivian rangers at Quebrada del Yuro, he was taken to the town of Higueras and shot on the morning of 9 October 1967, on the orders of the Bolivian high command.

Guyana

The Co-operative Republic of Guyana

Guyana is the westernmost and largest the three Guianas, which form an enclave on the north-east coast of Brazil, and is bounded on the east by Suriname and on the west by Venezuela, which claims two-thirds of its national territory. It is divided into 10 Regions.

Area: 214,969 sq km (83,000 sq miles); *capital:* Georgetown; *population:* 763,000 (2001 estimate), comprising 51% 'East Indian', 41% black, 12% mulatto and 6% Amerindian, mainly Carib; *official language:* English (Creole, Hindi, Urdu and Chinese are also spoken); *religion:* Christian (Anglican and Roman Catholic) 50%, Hindu 33%, Muslim 10%.

Constitution: Guyana became an independent republic within the **Commonwealth** on 23 February 1970. The 1980 Constitution established a semi-presidential republic. The President, who is the supreme executive authority, is the nominee of the party with the largest number of votes in the legislative elections, serves for up to five years and may be re-elected. The unicameral National Assembly, the legislature, is elected by universal adult suffrage by proportional representation. The President appoints the Prime Minister and the Cabinet, which may include non-elected members. The Cabinet is collectively responsible to the legislature.

History: The first European settlement in what is now Guyana was made on an island in the Essequibo river in 1616 by the Dutch, who introduced slaves to work the **sugar** plantations. The settlements changed hands on a number of occasions in the 18th century before being assigned to Britain in 1814 by the Treaty of Paris. Following the abolition of slavery in 1834, indentured labourers were brought in to ensure that no shortage of labour occurred. It was not until 1928, after persistent overspending by the colony's government and the collapse of sugar prices, that a Legislative Council was established, which was given a majority of elected members in 1945.

Latest elections: At the general election held on 19 March 2001, the People's Progressive Party/CIVIC (PPP/CIVIC) won 34 seats, the People's National Congress Reform 27 seats, the Guyana Action Party/Working People's Alliance two seats and two minor parties one seat each. The PPP/CIVIC leader, Bharrat Jagdeo, was re-elected as President.

International relations and defence: As Venezuela claims some two-thirds of Guyana's national territory, and has done so since independence, the country relies heavily for its security on the guarantees of the **Organization of American States** and the support of other Caribbean states that are members of the Commonwealth. There is a full-time Combined Guyana Defence Force of 1,600 troops (including 100 on naval and 100 on air force duties), and a 1,500-strong Guyana People's Militia. The country is a member of the **Caribbean Community and Common Market**.

Guyana, economy

Guyana is classified by the **International Bank for Reconstruction and Development** (World Bank) as a heavily-indebted low-income country. Its economy is dominated by agriculture, forestry and mining, but only about one-fifth of the potential arable land is utilized. Much that was low-lying coastal land was reclaimed by the Dutch during the colonial period.

GNI: US $641m. (2001); *GNI per caput:* $840 (2001); *GNI at PPP:* $3,280m. (2001); *GNI per caput at PPP:* $4,280 (2001); *imports:* $563.1m. (2001); *currency:* Guyana dollar ($G), plural dollars; US $1 = $G193.80 at 30 April 2003.

Some 2.2% of the land is farmed as arable, 0.1% is under permanent crops and 5.7% under permanent pasture. **Sugar** and rice are the main export crops, the former accounting for some 16.1% of gross domestic product (GDP) in 2001. Mining accounted for 15.4% of GDP in 2001, but demand has been falling for **bauxite**, of which the country has extensive deposits, though gold and diamond production has been rising. The principal industries are aluminium, sugar refining and food processing and timber. The main energy source is petroleum, most of which is imported from Trinidad and Tobago. Main exports are sugar, gold and bauxite. Principal imports are consumer goods, capital goods and fuel and lubricants. In 2002 Canada was the greatest purchaser of exports, followed by the United Kingdom. The USA was the greatest supplier of imports, followed by Trinidad and Tobago.

In the period that followed independence Guyana adopted a socialist-style economy, nationalizing 32 companies and establishing a state holding company, the Guyana State Corpn, to manage the key export sectors. It borrowed heavily to do so and by 1985 its credit was exhausted. In 1983 inflation had reached 400%. The Hoyte Government's Emergency Recovery Programme (ERP), adopted in 1987, involved wholesale privatization, a Social Impact Amelioration Programme (SIMAP) being introduced in 1990 to offset some of the ERP's harsher conse-quences. Thereafter, GDP began to increase steadily, though there was a brief recession in 1998 owing to the combined effects of the East Asia crisis and El Niño.

GDP in 2000–01 grew by 1.5% (0.8% per caput). In 2001 the rate of inflation averaged 2.6%.

H

Haiti

République d'Haïti

Haiti consists of the Western third of the island of Hispaniola in the Greater Antilles (see also Dominican Republic).

Area: 27,750 sq km (10,714 sq miles); *capital:* **Port-au-Prince**; *population:* 8.1m. (2001 estimate), 95% of whom are of African descent; the small mulatto minority, however, remains disproportionately wealthy and powerful; *official languages:* French and, since 1987, the Creole patois spoken by 85% of the population; *religion:* Voodoo (vaudou) is an officially recognized religion, overlapping with adherence to the Roman Catholic Church (66%).

Constitution: The Constitution of March 1987 established a semi-presidential system. Executive power is divided between a President directly elected by the people for a five-year term and a Prime Minister responsible to the bicameral legislature, consisting of a Senate (Sénat) whose 27 members sit for six years, one-third retiring every two years, and a Chamber of Deputies (Chambre des Députés) elected for four years.

History: The western half of the island was first settled by the French in the 17th century, and was the wealthiest part of the French empire when the slave revolt began in 1792, leading, ultimately, to Haiti's independence, under Jean-Jacques Dessalines, in 1804. The payment of a vast indemnity to French slaveowners left Haiti bankrupt and the former estates were divided into holdings that were too small to be worked profitably. Periods of dictatorship were interspersed with a series of weak and unstable governments. In 1915 the US government intervened militarily to restore order. However, US military rule, which lasted until 1934, was unpopular and racial discrimination and forced labour exacerbated hostility towards the still powerful mulatto élite. Military intervention in 1950 was followed by the election of **Dr François Duvalier**, who, once in power, established a dictatorship supported by a black militia, the notorious 'Tontons Macoutes'. Though thousands died and thousands more fled abroad, the regime was tolerated by successive US governments, though aid was formally withdrawn. Duvalier died of natural causes and was succeeded by his son, **Jean-Claude Duvalier** (President 1971–85), who was eventually overthrown by a mass revolt. There were enough Duvalierists left, however, to frustrate the first attempt to hold free elections in 1987, and it was not until 1990 that presidential elections were successfully held. The popular choice, **Fr Jean-Bertrand Aristide**, widely known for his work with the poor, was viewed with great distrust by the traditional élite. Within months the army had stepped in to forestall social change, and after increasing pressure from the US government and the **Organization of American States** (OAS) for his restoration, killings again escalated and US troops were landed to maintain order. Aristide returned in October 1994 and received a massive legislative majority in the following year, though the need for continuing austerity precluded any very substantial reform. Re-elected in December 2000 in an election marred by violence and accusations of fraud, Aristide proved unable to contain increasing violence by both opponents and supporters of the Government. On 29 February 2004 he escaped from the country with US assistance and an interim President, Boniface Alexandre, took office, appointing Gérard Latortue as Prime Minister in March.

Latest elections: In the presidential election held on 28 November 2000 Jean-Bertrand Aristide of the **Fanmi Lavalas** (FL) won 91.7% of the votes cast. The FL retained 26 of the 27 seats in the Senate and won 73 of the 83 seats in the Chamber of Deputies.

International relations and defence: Haiti is a member of the United Nations, the OAS, the **Caribbean Community and Common Market** and the **Rio Pact**. Relations with the Dominican Republic have traditionally been bad and the frontier has been closed for long periods. Haiti's armed forces were dissolved by the Aristide Government in 2001.

Haiti, economy

Once some of the richest territory in the Caribbean, Haiti's agricultural land has been stripped bare by bad management and corrupt government. More than one million Haitians live and work in the Dominican Republic, and thousands more try to leave the country every year for the prospect of a better life elsewhere.

GNI: US $3,900m. (2001); *GNI per caput:* $480 (2001); *GNI at PPP:* $15,000m. (2001); *GNI per caput at PPP:* $1,870 (2001), rank 166; *exports:* $327.1m. (2000);

imports: $1,090.7m. (2000); *currency:* gourde, plural gourdes; US $1 = 40.54 gourdes at 31 May 2003.

In 2002 agriculture accounted for 24.7% of Haiti's gross domestic product (GDP) and industry for 7.6%. Some 28.1% of the land is arable, 11.5% under permanent crops and 17.7% permanent pasture. The main cash crop is **coffee**; rice, maize, **bananas**, avocados, vegetables and fruit are grown for local consumption, but the main staple, rice, much of it smuggled, is imported. Cattle, pigs, goats and poultry are reared for food. The main mineral resource is **bauxite**, but the one mine closed in 1983 owing to low world prices. The principal industries are the manufacture of clothing and toys and the assembly of electronic components. Haiti was the major producer of baseballs until production was switched to the People's Republic of China. Many of the local inhabitants are so poor that they have to sell their blood for plasma, much of which is exported to the USA. The main energy source is hydroelectricity, which, even when supplemented by thermal generation, is inadequate to supply local needs.

Main exports are light manufactures, coffee and **cocoa**. Principal imports are food and live animals, manufactured goods and fuel. In 2001 the USA was the greatest purchaser of exports, followed by the **European Union** (EU), the Dominican Republic and Japan. The USA was the greatest supplier of imports, followed by the EU and Canada. The country consistently runs a massive deficit on visible trade. The USA has been unable to stop the use of Haiti as a transhipment area for cocaine smuggled from Colombia.

Haiti's GNI declined by 0.9% in 2002. More than 80% of the population are estimated by the **International Bank for Reconstruction and Development** (World Bank) to be living in extreme poverty and 62% are malnourished, according to the FAO. Unemployment and underemployment affect 85% of the population. The wealthiest 4% of the population account for almost two-thirds of Haiti's GNI.

Hamilton

Hamilton, capital of Bermuda, is situated on Great Bermuda, and had an estimated population of 1,100 in 2001. An excellent deep-water port, its main revenue comes from visiting cruise liners.

Havana

La Habana

Chief city and capital of Cuba, La Habana ('the harbour') is situated on its north coast. The strategically important harbour is sheltered from the dangerous 'northers' by a high bluff. With a population estimated in 1999 at 2,189,716, the city is overcrowded and basic services are decaying so that, though it has been declared a World Heritage Site, much of the old quarter is in a poor state of repair.

Haya de la Torre, Víctor Raúl

Víctor Raúl Haya de la Torre (1895–1979), politician, founder and leader of the **Alianza Popular Revolucionaria Americana** (APRA) of Peru, was born in Trujillo, Peru. Of middle-class origin, he was studying at San Marcos University, Lima, when he became president of the student union and leader of the student strike of 1919 which helped end the dictatorship of Augusto Leguía. Exiled in 1923, he visited the Soviet Union, but decided that its model was inappropriate for what he preferred to term 'Indoamerica'. He found the *indigenista* movement in Mexico more appropriate and it was in Mexico in the following year that he founded APRA. This he intended to be a continental movement opposing the US domination of the hemisphere. However, what he created instead when he returned to Peru in 1930 was the country's first fully-organized political party with a popular base. After he had unsuccessfully contested the presidency in 1931, his followers rose in revolt. The uprising failed, however, Haya was imprisoned and the armed forces became implacably hostile to APRA's political ambitions. Under the dictatorship of Gen. Odría, (1948–56) Haya spent five years in an annexe to the Colombian embassy before again being exiled. By this time he had abandoned his hostility to the USA and his political position had moved far to the right. However, when in 1962 he secured the largest share of the vote in the presidential elections the armed forces intervened to annul the result and in 1963 he was defeated. In 1979, although by then frail and ill, he was elected president of the constitutional convention that wrote the 1980 Constitution.

Honduras
República de Honduras

Honduras is situated in the heartland of Central America, with its main sea coast, on the Caribbean Sea, facing north, towards the Bay Islands, which are part of its national territory. Its longest land frontier is to the south-east, with Nicaragua. It has access to the Pacific Ocean through the Gulf of Fonseca, which is effectively controlled by both Nicaragua and El Salvador, which forms an enclave to the south-west. The country is divided into 18 Departments.

Area: 112,492 sq km (43,433 sq miles); *capital:* **Tegucigalpa**; *population:* 6,535,344 (2001 census), 90% mestizo (ladino), 7% Amerindian, 2% black and 1% white; *official language:* English (Garifuna is also spoken); *religion:* Roman Catholic 86%, Protestant 10%.

Constitution: The 1982 Constitution (amended in 1995) provides for a demo-cratic, presidential republic. Legislative power is vested in a single chamber, the National Assembly (*Asamblea Nacional*), currently of 128 members. Executive power is vested in a President elected for four years by a simple majority vote. All adults over the age of 18 are citizens. The army is declared professional and non-political; the right to life is inviolable and there is no death penalty.

History: From 1932 until 1948 Honduras, formerly the poorest of the Central American states, was ruled by the relatively benign dictatorship of Tiburcio Carías Andino. After he retired constitutional government was repeatedly interrupted by military coups, until in 1966 the ruling junta chose Gen. Osvaldo López Arellano as President. He was still in power when in 1969 a disputed decision in the third qualifying round of the 1970 World Cup football competition triggered a 13-day war with neighbouring El Salvador. Two thousand people were killed and serious damage was inflicted on both sides before the conflict was brought to an end by the mediation of the **Organization of American States** (OAS). Honduras withdrew from the Central American Common Market, rendering it almost completely useless, and over the next 11 years it stagnated.

In 1975, as a result of the suicide of Eli Black, head of United Brands (successor to the United Fruit Co), it was revealed that López Arellano had been paid US $500,000 to break ranks with the leaders of other **banana**-producing countries and stop asking for more money. Within a week he had been deposed. With the outbreak of insurgency in El Salvador in 1980, Honduras was inevitably drawn into the conflict.

Latest elections: On 12 March 2001 the National Elections Tribunal accepted as valid the candidature for the presidency of Roberto Maduro of the opposition **Partido Nacional** (PN). It had been opposed by the ruling **Partido Liberal** (PL) on the grounds that he had been born in Panama, but the PL candidate, Rafael Pineda Ponce, the current president of the National Congress, had proposed a compromise which enabled his rival's candidature to be accepted. At the elections held on 25 November Maduro won the presidency decisively and in elections to the National Congress the PN secured 52.21% of the vote and 61 seats. The PL received 44.26% of the vote and 55 seats, with the balance being shared between the Partido de Unificación Democrática—1.11% of the vote, five seats—, the Partido Innovación y Unidad—Social Democracia—1.45% of the vote, four seats—and the Partido Demócrata Cristiano de Honduras—0.97% of the vote, three seats.

International relations and defence: Honduras is a member of the United Nations, the OAS, the **Central American Integration System** (*Sistema de la Integración Centroamericana*—SICA) and the **Rio Pact**. Much of the frontier with El Salvador, determined by the International Court of Justice in 1992, has yet to be demarcated. Compulsory military service was ended in 1995 and the full-time armed forces totalled 8,300 in 2002, including a naval contingent of 1,000 and an air force contingent of 1,800. A paramilitary Public Security and Defence Force numbers 6,000. The USA maintains some 350 troops in Honduras.

Honduras, economy

Honduras is the archetypical '**banana** republic', the north coast being geared to the growing and transport of the fruit for export principally to the USA. Adverse weather conditions, however, especially the devastating '**Hurricane** Mitch' in 1998 and 'Hurricane Michelle' in 2001, have been the cause of widespread flooding

GNI: US \$5,900m. (2001); *GNI per caput:* \$900 (2001); *GNI at PPP:* \$18,000m. (2001); *GNI per caput at PPP:* \$2,760 (2001), rank 144; *exports:* \$1,330.9m. (2002); *imports:* \$2,976.3m. (2002); *currency:* lempira, plural lempiras; US \$1 = 17.208 lempiras at 30 April 2003.

In 2002 agriculture accounted for 13.5% of Honduras' gross domestic product (GDP) and industry for 20.4%. Some 9.5% of the land is arable, 3.2% under permanent crops and 13.5% permanent pasture. The main cash crops are **coffee** and bananas; a wide range of staples are grown mainly by peasant farmers for domestic consumption. Pine and other softwoods are exploited for export. Fisheries are an important resource. The main mineral resources exploited are lead, zinc, silver and gold, but tin, iron ore, coal, uranium and antimony deposits have also been identified. The principal industries are food processing, brewing, textile manufacture and **sugar** refining. The main energy source is hydroelectricity which has suffered in recent years from mismanagement and lack of investment.

Main exports are shellfish, bananas and coffee. Principal imports are machinery and electrical appliances, chemicals and chemical products and petroleum and petroleum products. In 2002 the USA was the greatest purchaser of exports, followed by Guatemala and El Salvador. The USA was the greatest supplier of imports, followed by El Salvador, Germany and Guatemala.

Honduras has long been one of the poorest and least-developed countries in Latin America, despite a relatively prosperous enclave on the north coast. World recession, falling commodity prices and civil war in neighbouring states in the 1980s resulted in stagnation. In 1989 the country defaulted on its debt, but policies sponsored by the **International Monetary Fund**, beginning with a massive devaluation of the lempira in 1990 and 1991, initiated a period of modest growth, though the fiscal gap remained a problem. 'Hurricane Mitch' and the crisis of 1999 brought some relief from international lending agencies, but it also focused attention on the poor infrastructure, serious damage to the environment and high level of corruption. GDP grew by an annual average rate of 3.1% in 1990–2001. In 1999 it declined by 1.9%, but grew by 4.9% in 2000 and by 2.6% in 2001. An inflation rate of 6.0% was recorded in 2000; the rate rose to 9.6% in 2001. Officially, the rate of unemployment stood at 4.2% in 2001, but in reality at least one-third of the population were either unemployed or seriously underemployed.

Hurricanes

The Greater and Lesser Antilles, together with Central America and coastal regions of Mexico and the USA, lie within the hurricane belt: the region of the Atlantic in which tropical storms can reach windspeeds in excess of 320 kph (200 mph) over water. The relatively high levels of death and damage these cause in Latin America are mainly due to a lack of adequate preparation for evacuation or safe refuge, unstable buildings, and wind-damage to **banana** and other large plantations. In September 1974 'Hurricane Fifi' struck the northern coast of Honduras, killing some 8,000 people, most of them poor peasants. The northern coast was the location of most of the country's agriculture and industry: three-quarters of the banana harvest was lost as a result of flooding and land-slips. In the affected areas 75% of homes and 90% of roads were destroyed or seriously damaged. Coastal areas of Nicaragua, Belize, El Salvador and Guatemala were also seriously damaged.

In 1988 'Hurricane Joan' compounded Nicaragua's economic crisis, leaving some 300,000 people homeless. The cost of structural damage was estimated at US \$828m. **Coffee** production fell by 12% and that of bananas by 8% as a direct result of the hurricane and huge tracts of forest were levelled. The effects of 'Hurricane Joan', the worst hurricane of the 20th century, contributed significantly to the defeat of the Sandinista Government in 1990.

I

Inforpress Centroamericano

Guatemalan news agency, the leading agency in Central America, f. 1972. Politically independent, it publishes weekly news bulletins in both Spanish and English.

Address: Calle Mariscal 6–58, Zona 11, 0100 Guatemala City
Telephone and fax: 473-1704/2242
E-mail: inforpre@guate.net
Internet: www.inforpressa.com/inforpress/

Instituto Colombiano de la Reforma Agraria (INCORA)

Colombian Institute of Agrarian Reform

Public agency f. 1962 to administer public lands and to acquire further lands, to reclaim land by irrigation and other projects and to increase productivity in agriculture and stock-rearing.

Leadership: Jorge Cardoso (Dir)
Address: Centro Administrativo Nacional (CAN), Avda El Dorado, Apdo Aéreo 151046, Santafé de Bogotá, DC
Telephone: (1) 222-0963
Fax: (1) 222-1536
E-mail: atenusuario@incora.gov.co
Internet: www.incora.gov.co

Instituto Costarricense de Turismo

Costa Rican Institute of Tourism

F. 1955 to promote tourism in Costa Rica, which has become a leading destination for 'ecotourism'. In 2001 1,131,406 visitors were recorded, while receipts from tourism in that year totalled US $1.14m.

Leadership: Ing. Carlos Roesch Carranza (Pres.)
Address: Edif. Genaro Valverde, Calles 5 y 7, Avda 4, Apdo 777, 1000 San José
Telephone: 223-3254
Fax: 223-3254
Internet: www.tourism-costarica.com

Instituto Nacional de Radio y Televisión (INRAVISION)
National Institute of Radio and Television, Colombia

F. 1964 to provide a government-run service of radio and television broadcasting.
Leadership: Gustavo Samper Rodríguez (Dir)
Address: Centro Administrativo Nacional (CAN), Avda El Dorado, Santafé de
   Bogotá, DC
Telephone: (1) 222-0700
Fax: (1) 222-0080
E-mail: inras@col1.telecom.com.co

Instituto Nacional de Transformación Agraria (INTA)
National Institute of Agrarian Transformation, Guatemala

F. in 1962 as a gesture towards the demand for land reform. An earlier land reform programme under President Jacobo Arbenz (1950–54) had been terminated after he was overthrown in 1954 by a US-sponsored coup; the new organization initiated only a modest programme of land colonization which avoided expropriation. In the 1980s, however, the development of the *Franja Transversal del Norte*, or Northern Development Zone, a broad strip located to the south of Guatemala's northern frontier and incorporating valuable lands in El Quiché, Alta Verapaz and El Petén, was strongly criticized for benefiting the small military élite at the expense of its indigenous inhabitants.
Leadership: Ing. Nery Orlando Samayoa (Pres.)
Address: 14a Calle 7–14, Zona 1, Guatemala City
Telephone: 28-0975

Inter-American Bar Association (IABA)

F. 1940 to promote the rule of law by establishing and maintaining relations between associations of lawyers in the Americas; now claims to have 90 associations and 3,500 individual members in 27 countries.

Leadership: Raúl Lozano Merino (Pres., Peru); Dr Louis G. Ferranti (Sec.-Gen., USA)
Address: 1211 Connecticut Ave NW, Suite 202, Washington, DC 20036, USA
Telephone: (212) 466-5944
Fax: (212) 466-9546
E-mail: iaba@iaba.org
Internet: www.iaba.org

Inter-American Commission on Human Rights (IACHR)

The Inter-American Commission on Human Rights is an organ of the **Organization of American States** (OAS), created to promote the observance and defence of human rights and to serve as consultative organ of the organization. It derives its powers from the Statute of the IACHR approved by the OAS General Assembly at its ninth regular session, held in La Paz, Bolivia, in October 1979. These powers include the right and, indeed, the duty to bring cases before the **Inter-American Court of Human Rights**.

Leadership: Santiago A. Canton (Exec. Sec.)
Address: 1889 F Street, NW, Washington, DC 20006, USA
Telephone: (202) 458-6002
Fax: (202) 458-3992
E-mail: cidhoea@oas.org
Internet: www.iachr.org

Inter-American Convention on Human Rights

This Convention, drawn up in 1969, forbade torture and maltreatment of prisoners, guaranteed freedom of expression and of religion, and provided for the creation of an **Inter-American Court of Human Rights**. It entered into force on 18 July 1978, upon its ratification by Grenada (the others parties are Colombia, Costa Rica, Dominican Republic, Ecuador, El Salvador, Guatemala, Haiti, Honduras, Panama and Venezuela.) Nicaragua ratified the Convention in September 1979.

Inter-American Court of Human Rights

The Inter-American Court of Human Rights was created in 1978 to apply and interpret the **Inter-American Convention on Human Rights** which came into force in that year. It met for the first time in San José, Costa Rica, on 3 September 1979, with a membership of seven judges. Its mandate was to deal with violations of civil and political rights, but its decisions would not be legally binding and states which had not ratified the 1969 convention would be able to ask the court for an advisory opinion but not to have cases tried by it. By 1998 the Convention had been ratified by 25 member states of the **Organization of American States** (OAS), of which 18 had accepted the competence of the Court. The seven judges are drawn from leading jurists of the member states.

On 7 July 1999 Peru withdrew from the Convention following the Court's ruling that four Chileans, who had been sentenced to life imprisonment by military courts in which they could not contest or even examine the evidence against them, should receive new trials. The Court ruled on 27 September that the Peruvian decision to withdraw without giving one year's notice as required, was 'inadmissible', giving rise to the possibility that sanctions might be imposed against Peru by the OAS General Assembly in June 2000. However, Peru decided in January 2000 to accept the jurisdiction of the Court in the case of a retired army officer, Gustavo Cesti Hurtado, who had been sentenced to three years' imprisonment after denouncing high-level corruption in the armed forces.

Leadership: Manuel E. Ventura Robles (Sec.)

Address: Apdo Postal 6906-1000, San José, Costa Rica

Tel: (506) 234 0581

Fax: (506) 234 0584

E-mail: corteidh@corteidh.or.cr

Internet: www.corteidh.or.cr

Inter-American Development Bank (IDB)

The Bank was founded in April 1959, under the Agreement Establishing the Inter-American Development Bank, to finance economic and social development projects and to provide technical assistance in member countries. It initially had an authorized capital stock of US $850m. The present financial resources of the Bank consist of the ordinary capital (which includes subscribed capital, paid-in capital and reserves), funds raised in capital markets through bond issues, the Fund for Special Operations, and trust funds. The powers of the IDB are vested in a Board of Governors, on which each member country is represented by one Governor and one alternate. Executive powers are delegated to an Executive Board of 12 Directors, eight of whom are elected by regional member countries, two by member countries not in the region, one by Canada and one by the USA. Voting is on a weighted basis, the USA holding 30% of the votes in respect of its capital contribution. The IDB's ordinary capital totalled $101,000m. in 2001. The paid-in portion of subscriptions accounts for 4.3% of the total. The remainder is callable capital, which, together with the preferred creditor status afforded the IDB by its borrowing member countries, serves as backing for the Bank's borrowings in the world's financial markets. The Bank has an annual lending capacity of about $8,500m. to finance public- and private-sector projects, sector and policy reform programmes, emergency operations for natural disasters and financial crises, credit guarantees, and reimbursable technical co-operation. The Bank is owned by its 46 member countries. In the Americas there are 26 borrowing member countries (Argentina, Bahamas, Barbados, Belize, Bolivia, Brazil, Chile, Colombia, Costa Rica, Dominican Republic, Ecuador, El Salvador, Guatemala, Guyana, Haiti, Honduras, Jamaica, Mexico, Nicaragua, Panama, Paraguay, Peru, Suriname, Trinidad and Tobago, Uruguay, and Venezuela) and two non-borrowing countries (Canada and the USA). There are a further 18 non-borrowing member countries from outside the region: Austria, Belgium, Croatia, Denmark, Finland, France, Germany, Israel, Italy, Japan, Netherlands, Norway, Portugal, Slovenia, Spain, Sweden, Switzerland, United Kingdom.

Leadership: Enrique V. Iglesias (Pres.)

Address: 1300 New York Ave, NW, Washington, DC 20577, USA

Telephone: (202) 623-1000

Fax: (202) 623-3096

Internet: www.iadb.org

Inter-American Press Association (IAPA)
Sociedad Interamericana de Prensa

F. 1942 in an attempt to protect the freedom of the press in the Americas and to promote and maintain the dignity, rights and responsibilities of journalists.

Leadership: Julio E. Munoz (Exec. Dir)

Address: Jules Dubois Bldg, 1810 SW 3rd Ave, Miami, F. 33129, USA

Telephone: (305) 634-2465

Fax: (305) 635-2272

E-mail: info@sipiapa.org

Internet: www.sipiapa.com

Inter-American Regional Organization of Workers
Organización Regional Interamericana de Trabajadores (ORIT)

Trade union international; f. 1951 under US auspices to combat the influence of international communism; regional branch of the International Confederation of Free Trade Unions (ICFTU). Though it withdrew from ICFTU in 1969, the AFofL-CIO remained the most powerful member of ORIT; the organization has been accused of supporting coups against left-wing governments in the region.

> *Leadership:* Luis A. Anderson (Gen. Sec.)
> *Address:* Edif. José Vargas, Avda Andrés Eloy Blanco No 2, 15°, Los Caobos,
>   Caracas, Venezuela
> *Telephone:* (212) 578-3538
> *Fax:* (212) 578-1702
> *E-mail:* secgenorit@cantv.net
> *Internet:* www.chiosorit.org

Inter-American Treaty of Reciprocal Assistance – *see* Rio Pact

International Bank for Reconstruction and Development (IBRD—World Bank)

The IBRD was established in 1945, originally to fund the reconstruction of war-devastated Europe; more recently it has funded major development projects in countries that do not possess the funds to do so themselves. Its capital comes from members' subscriptions which are fixed in proportion to their quotas with the **International Monetary Fund**. The Board of Governors consists of one representative from each member state, usually either its finance minister or central bank president. The board of 24 executive directors is responsible for day-to-day operations; five of the directors are appointed from the five states with the largest shares of capital stock and the rest are elected by the remaining states. The board is chaired by the Bank's president.

> *Leadership:* James D. Wolfensohn (Pres. and Chair. of Exec. Board); David de
>   Ferranti (Vice-Pres., Latin America and the Caribbean Regional
>   Office)
> *Address:* 1818 H St NW, Washington, DC 20433, USA
> *Telephone:* (202) 477-1234
> *Fax:* (202) 477-6391

E-mail: pic@worldbank.org
Internet: www.worldbank.org

International Monetary Fund (IMF)

The IMF was founded in 1945 to promote international monetary co-operation by maintaining a stable system of exchange rates. Its working capital comes from the member states according to quotas fixed broadly in proportion to the size of their economies. They may call on those funds, within certain limits, in order to stabilize their currencies, or request additional funds if required. The Board of Governors consists of one representative and one alternate from each member state. The USA, the United Kingdom, Germany, France and Japan appoint one Executive Director each; the remaining member states elect one each from the People's Republic of China, Russia and Saudi Arabia and 17 others from the other states according to groups.

Requests for additional loans from the IMF are subject to certain requirements ('conditionality') which the Fund believes will enable the country concerned to achieve stability in the shortest possible time. These requirements have historically been much resented in Latin America and have led to serious unrest on occasions— a recent example is the fall of the de la Rúa administration in Argentina in 2001. However, finance ministers have frequently found it convenient to blame the Fund for measures that they themselves found politically too difficult to impose, and in March 2004 the Fund advanced the Kirchner Government in Argentina a substantial loan despite its evident failure to meet its obligations.

Leadership: Horst Kohler (Man. Dir, Germany)
Address: 700 19th St NW, Washington, DC 20431, USA
Telephone: (202) 623-7300
Fax: (202) 623-6220
E-mail: public affairs@imf.org
Internet: www.imf.org

Izquierda Democrática (ID)
Democratic Left, Ecuador

Left-of-centre movement, f. 1977; in 1991 absorbed the Fuerzas Armadas Populares Eloy Alfaro-¡Alfaro Vive! ¡Carajo! (*Eloy Alfaro Popular Armed Forces-Alfaro Lives! Damn it!*). Gen. José Eloy Alfaro Delgado founded the Partido Liberal Radical (PLR) in 1895. Under its banner a close oligarchy of coastal landowners and bankers controlled the country until 1925; the PLR, however, also curtailed the privileges of the Church and embarked on a measure of social reform.

Leadership: Rodrigo Borja Cevallos (Leader)

Address: Polonia 161, entre Vancouver y Eloy Alfaro, Quito

Telephone: (2) 256-4436

Fax: (2) 256-9295

J

Jagan, Cheddi

Dr Cheddi Bharat Jagan (1919–97), was born in Port Mourant, British Guiana, the son of an 'East Indian' sugar plantation foreman. He trained in the USA and qualified as a dentist. Together with **Forbes Burnham** he founded the **People's Progressive Party** (PPP) in 1950 and in the first elections held under universal suffrage, in 1953, the PPP won 51% of the vote and 18 of the 24 seats and Jagan became Chief Minister. After only six months, however, in October 1953, the Governor, acting on the orders of the Conservative Government in Britain, suspended the Constitution and dismissed Jagan. His pretext for doing so was that the colony was threatened by Communist subversion. However, after a new Constitution had been introduced in 1956 Jagan and the PPP won the elections of 1957 and were still in power when full internal self-government was introduced in 1961. Not until the election of 1964, held under new rules, were the PPP defeated by Forbes Burnham and the People's National Congress he had formed in 1957. Jagan continued to lead the party after the adoption of the executive presidency in 1980 and the succession of Desmond Hoyte in 1985, but boycotted the elections until the reforms of 1991, brought about by domestic and international pressure. In 1992 Jagan, as candidate of the PPP in alliance with CIVIC, was elected as President, appointing the CIVIC leader, Samuel Hinds, as Prime Minister. He was unsuccessful, however, in persuading the political parties to rewrite the Constitution, and much of his programme of social reform was incomplete when he died in March 1997 of a heart attack at the age of 78.

Jamaica

Jamaica is the third largest island of the Greater Antilles, situated in the Caribbean Sea, 145 km (90 miles) south of Cuba and 160 km (100 miles) west of Haiti. The island is divided into 14 parishes.

Area: 10,991 sq km (4,244 sq miles); *capital:* **Kingston**; *population:* 2,624,700 (2002 estimate), of which 90% are of African descent, just over 1% 'East Indian' and fewer than 1% of European or Chinese origin; *official language:* English; *religion:* 47% Christian (Church of God 21%, Adventist 9%, Pentecostalists 8%), 53% other, including Rastafarians.

Constitution: Jamaica is a constitutional monarchy within the **Commonwealth**, the present Constitution dating from independence on 6 August 1962. The head of state is HM Queen Elizabeth II, who is represented by a Governor-General. There is a bicameral legislature consisting of a Senate of 21 appointed members (13 appointed on the advice of the Prime Minister, 8 on the advice of the leader of the opposition), and a House of Representatives of 60 Members of Parliament elected by universal adult suffrage. The Prime Minister is appointed by the Governor-General as the leader of the largest party in the House of Representatives and the other 11 members of the Cabinet, which is accountable to the House, are appointed from among its members on the advice of the Prime Minister.

History: Jamaica was first sighted by Europeans led by **Christopher Columbus** in 1494. The Spanish soon depopulated the island of its indigenous Taino people to work as slaves in Hispaniola, later introducing slaves from Africa to work the local plantations. In 1655 the island was captured by Britain and became a major **sugar** producer through the labour of a greatly increased number of slaves. After the abolition of slavery in 1834, tension between the rich planters and the poor workers remained, and direct rule was imposed after the 1865 Morant Bay Rebellion.

In the 1930s a greater measure of self-rule was gradually introduced, leading to the formation of the **People's National Party** (PNP) in 1938. Under Norman Manley, Jamaica became one of the two main members of the West Indies Federation in 1958; the leader of the opposition **Jamaica Labour Party** (JLP), Alexander Bustamante, however, successfully called for a referendum on withdrawal, which led to the collapse of the Federation. Bustamante led the island to independence on 6 August 1962, since when power has alternated between the two parties. The oil crisis of 1973 began a difficult period for the economy, and in 1980 the democratic socialist government of **Michael Manley** was defeated. His successor, Edward Seaga, espoused free-market reforms, which have become a permanent feature.

Latest elections: At the general elections held on 16 October 2002, the PNP, led by P. J. Patterson, won 52.2% of the votes cast and 34 seats, and the JLP 47.2% of the votes and 26 seats.

International relations and defence: Jamaica is a member of the United Nations, the **Organization of American States**, the Commonwealth and the **Caribbean**

Community and Common Market. In 2002 the Jamaica Defence Force comprised an army of 2,500, a coastguard of 190 and an air wing with a strength of 140. In addition there were some 950 reservists.

Jamaica, economy

Jamaica has a relatively diversified economy by Caribbean standards, but it has had to depend on external support since the 1970s and remains vulnerable to external factors.

GNI: US $7,300m. (2001); *GNI per caput:* $2,800 (2001); *GNI at PPP:* $9,000m. (2001); *GNI per caput at PPP:* $3,490 (2001), rank 133; *currency:* Jamaican dollar (J$), plural dollars; US $1 = J$59.25 at 31 May 2003.

In 2002 agriculture accounted for 6.5% of Jamaica's gross domestic product (GDP), mining and quarrying for 4.2% and industry for 13.2%. Some 15.8% of the land is arable, 10.0% under permanent crops and 20.8% permanent pasture. The main cash crops are **sugar**, **bananas** and **coffee**; sweet potatoes, yams and other vegetables are grown, and goats, cattle and pigs raised for local consumption. The main mineral resource is **bauxite**: Jamaica is the world's third largest producer of bauxite, alumina and bauxite accounting for 60% of export earnings in 2001 (US $737m.). The principal industrial products are food, drink and tobacco, cement, chemicals, fertilizers and alumina. The main energy source is imported petroleum, one-third of which is required for alumina production.

Main exports are alumina, sugar and bananas. Principal imports are machinery, petroleum and other manufactured goods. In 2002 the USA was the greatest purchaser of exports, followed by the United Kingdom, Canada and Norway. The USA was the greatest supplier of imports, followed by Trinidad and Tobago, Japan and Venezuela.

Since 1989 the government has pursued a policy of financial deregulation, first devaluing the Jamaican dollar and then, in 1990, allowing it to float. The endemic fiscal deficit was attributed in part to inefficient tax collection. GDP per head rose steadily in the 1990s and unemployment had fallen in 2002 to 15% of the workforce. Much of this was the result of the growth of tourism which, however, has not generally been sufficient to offset the deficit on visible trade. The number of visitors (not including cruise passengers) was 1,276,516 in 2001. Annual GDP growth in 1990–2001 averaged only 1.2%. GDP grew by 1.7% in 2001 and by only 0.4% in 2002. Despite a recorded unemployment rate in 2002 of 15%, however, the proportion of the population living in poverty had fallen from 44.5% in 1991 to 17% in 2001.

Jamaica Chamber of Commerce

F. 1779; has 400 members and is linked with 11 other chambers in the Associated Chambers of Commerce of Jamaica (f. 1974).

Address: 7–8 East Parade, POB 172, Kingston
Telephone: 922-0150
Fax: 924-9056
E-mail: jamcham@cwjamaica.com
Internet: www.jcc.org.jm

Jamaica Commodity Trading Co Ltd.

Government agency, f. 1981 (as successor to State Trading Corpn) to oversee all importing.

Leadership: David Gaynair (Chair.)

Jamaica Labour Party (JLP)

Right-wing libertarian party, f. 1943 by Alexander Bustamante in alliance with the affiliate, the Bustamante Industrial Trade Union. The JLP won a majority of seats in parliament in the first elections held under full adult suffrage in 1944 and was in power at independence in 1962. It is committed to free enterprise in a mixed economy and to close co-operation with the USA.

Leadership: Edward Seaga (Leader)
Address: 20 Belmont Rd, Kingston 5
Telephone: 929-1183
Fax: 968-0873
E-mail: info@thejlp.com
Internet: www.thejlp.com

Jamaica Tourist Board (JTB)

F. 1955, the JTB is a statutory body charged with promoting the tourist industry. In 2001 there were an estimated 1,276,516 visitors to the country, exclusive of cruise passengers, from whom receipts totalled some US $1,300m.

Leadership: Adrian Robinson (Dir of Tourism)
Address: ICWI Bldg, 2 St Lucia Ave, Kingston 5
Telephone: 929-9200
Fax: 929-9375

E-mail: info@visitjamaica.com
Internet: www.jamaicatravel.com

John Paul II

John Paul II, the first non-Italian to be elected Pope for more than 400 years, was born Karol Wojtyła in Kraków, Poland, in 1920. He studied theology in an underground seminary during the Second World War and was ordained in 1946, when Poland was already under Communist rule. He was appointed Archbishop of Kraków in 1967 and made a Cardinal in 1967. After the premature death of John Paul I in 1978, he was elected as his successor. In Latin America his pontificate has been noted for its consistent opposition to Marxism in any form and particularly to the fusion of Christian and Marxist ideas known as 'Liberation Theology', as well as to priests (e.g. the Cardenal brothers in Nicaragua and Jean-Paul Aristide in Haiti) taking an active role in politics.

K

Kingston, Jamaica

Kingston is the capital and principal port of Jamaica. At the census of 2001 the parish of St Andrew, which includes Kingston, had a population of 651,880.

Kingstown, St Vincent

The main town and capital of St Vincent and the Grenadines, with a population of 13,526 at the 2001 census.

Kourou, French Guiana

Situated some 70 km to the west of the Departmental capital, Cayenne, Kourou, which had a population at the 1999 census of 19,107, is better known as the location of the launch-site for the European Space Agency, whose 'Mars Express' successfully entered orbit in December 2003.

L

Lacalle, Luís Alberto

Luís Alberto Lacalle de Herrera, President of Uruguay 1990–95, was born in **Montevideo** in 1941 and qualified as a lawyer in 1964. The grandson of the former leader of the **Partido Nacional**, Luís Alberto de Herrera Quevedo, he gained a seat in the Chamber of Deputies for the party in 1971. During the military take-over in 1973 he was arrested but quickly released and spent the next 12 years working as a lawyer and engaged in clandestine agitation against the dictatorship. He survived an assassination attempt in 1978. Elected as a Senator on the return of democracy in 1984, he was chosen by his party to contest the 1989 elections, which he unexpectedly won, becoming only the third member of his party to hold the office since 1836. Though his advocacy of free-market reforms divided his party, under his leadership Uruguay entered the **Southern Common Market** and benefited considerably as a result.

La Paz

Administrative capital of Bolivia, La Paz had a population of 793,293 at the 2001 census, making it the second largest city in the country or, if its suburbs are included, the largest. Situated close to Lake Titicaca at the northern end of the Bolivian altiplano at an altitude of 3,640 m, it is the highest capital city in the world.

Latin American Economic System
Sistema Ecónomico Latinoamericano (SELA)

F. 18 October 1975 with the aim of counterbalancing US economic influence in the hemisphere, SELA is an intergovernmental organization working to promote intra-regional co-operation in order to accelerate the economic and social development of its 27 member states, which include Cuba but not the USA. It aims to provide a permanent system of consultation and co-ordination for the adoption of common positions and strategies on economic and social matters in international bodies and forums and *vis-à-vis* third countries. Its supreme body is the Latin American Council, which consists of one representative from each member country and holds ordinary sessions once a year. It elects the organization's permanent secretary, but it has no powers to make decisions affecting the national policies of member states. SELA has contributed to the search for common regional positions in respect of the critical problems facing Latin America and the Caribbean in the fields of debt, external financing, trading relations, services, the industrialization process, commodities, intellectual property and the region's role in the international economy. It supported the member states in the execution of the results of the **Uruguay Round** of the General Agreement on Tariffs and Trade, provided technical support to the **Rio Group** and serves as the regional focal point for the System for Technical Co-operation Among Developing Countries.

Leadership: Salvador Arriola (Permanent Sec.)

Address: Avda Francisco de Miranda, Torre Europa, Piso 4, Urb. Campo Alegre,
　　　　　Caracas 1060, Venezuela

Telephone: (212) 955-71-11

Fax: (212) 951-52-92

E-mail: difusion@sela.org

Internet: www.sela.org

Latin American Integration Association (LAIA)
Asociación Latinoamericana de Integración (ALADI)

A Latin American Free Trade Area (LAFTA), consisting of Mexico and all the states of South America except for Panama, was created by the Treaty of **Montevideo** of 1960 that came into effect on 1 June 1961. However, because of the very different levels of economic growth of the member states, it failed to achieve its objective of promoting intra-regional trade and, by 1980, only 3% of all trade concessions had been made since the Treaty came into effect. Therefore, by the second Treaty of Montevideo, on 12 August 1980, LAFTA was reconstituted as LAIA. The new organization had the more limited purpose of protecting existing trade arrangements. Its 12 members—10 South American states, Cuba and Mexico—are divided into three tiers: most developed (Argentina, Brazil, Mexico); intermediate (Chile, Colombia, Cuba, Peru, Uruguay, Venezuela); and least developed (Bolivia, Ecuador, Paraguay). The main organ of the Association is the Council of Ministers, which meets when summoned by the Committee of Representatives. The Committee is the main permanent body of the Association and is responsible for implementing its decisions. It consists of one representative and a deputy representative from each state. A number of other countries and organizations have observer status.

Leadership: Juan Francisco Rojas Penso (Sec.-Gen.), Venezuela
Address: Cebollati 1461, Casilla 577, 11200 Montevideo, Uruguay
Telephone: (2) 410-1121
Fax: (2) 419-0649
E-mail: sgaladi@aladi.org
Internet: www.aladi.org

Latin American Parliament
Parlamento Latinoamericano

The Latin American Parliament was established to promote contacts between national legislative bodies, to further Latin American integration in all fields, to oppose any form of colonialism and to defend peace. It consists of delegations of members of the parliaments of Argentina, Bolivia, Brazil, Chile, Colombia, Costa Rica, Cuba, Ecuador, El Salvador, Guatemala, Honduras, Mexico, Nicaragua, Panama, Paraguay, Peru, Uruguay and Venezuela. The decision to set up such an organization was taken at a meeting of representatives of Latin American countries and institutions held in Lima, Peru, on 6–11 December 1964. The first session of the Parliament was held on 17–18 July 1965. At its 17th meeting, held on 19 June 1985, it decided *inter alia* to admit a delegation from Cuba (by 145 votes to 25) and to readmit Nicaragua (whose membership had been suspended in 1979), despite some opposition from Costa Rica and Paraguay.

Leadership: Andres Townsend Ezcurra (Sec.-Gen.)
Address: Av. Auro Soares de Maoura Andrade 564, São Paulo, Brazil
Telephone: (11) 3824-6835
Fax: (11) 3824-6324
Internet: www.parlatino.org.br

Liberalism

Liberalism originated in Spain as a term to designate the complex of ideas associated with the French Revolution. In 19th century Latin America, Liberals opposed dictatorship, legislated where possible for decentralized or federal government, established systems of lay education, ended religious exemptions from government authority and supported the disestablishment of the Church.

Lima

Lima, chief city and capital of Peru, lies on a plateau above the Pacific port of Callao, and its greater metropolitan area had a population estimated in 2001 at 7,060,600. It was founded by Francisco Pizarro (who is buried in the Cathedral) in 1535 but the present name, a Spanish corruption of the native name Rimac, was preferred to his title of the City of the Kings (Ciudad de los Reyes), and as the colonial capital of all of Spanish South America it was rebuilt after a disastrous **earthquake** in 1746. It has been the seat of the National University of San Marcos since 1551.

M

Mahuad Witt, Jamil

Jorge Jamil Mahuad Witt, President of Ecuador in 1998–2000, was born in Loja, province of Loja, in 1949. He obtained his doctorate in law in the Pontifical Catholic University of Ecuador, Quito, in 1979 and an MBA from the John F. Kennedy School of Government at Harvard in 1989. He was given his first government post under Jaime Roldós Aguilera in 1983, and served as a deputy in the 1986–88 and 1990–92 legislatures. Having campaigned unsuccessfully for the presidency in 1988, he was elected mayor of Quito in 1992 and re-elected in 1996. In 1998, in the second round of voting in the presidential election, he defeated the rich businessman Alvaro Noboa and became President. He immediately implemented a drastic programme of free-market reforms, so that although he was successful abroad in settling by the Treaty of **Brasília** the country's long-running boundary dispute with Peru, he became so unpopular at home that, as the economic situation worsened, he proposed the adoption of the dollar as the national currency. The resulting uproar was so great that he fled the country in January 2000 and was deemed to have resigned.

Managua

Managua, previously a minor town lying on the shore of Lake Managua, was chosen in 1857 as capital of Nicaragua as a compromise between the two political power centres of León and Granada. Unfortunately it lies in an **earthquake** zone and was severely damaged in 1931 and almost destroyed in 1972, after which much of it lay in ruins until **Anastasio Somoza Debayle** ordered it to be bombed in a vain attempt to stop the Sandinista Revolution in 1979. The metropolitan area, much of which is still ruined, was estimated to have a population of 1,039,000 in 2001.

Manley, Michael

Michael Norman Manley (1924–1997), Prime Minister of Jamaica 1972–80 and 1989–92, was the son of Norman Manley, Prime Minister 1955–62, and became leader of the **People's National Party** on his father's death in 1969. In 1972 he achieved an emphatic electoral victory and until 1980 led a Government committed to democratic socialism. Though it was unable to nationalize the **bauxite** industry owing to a combination of US pressure and the 1973 economic crisis, Manley took a leading role in rallying the Third World countries to non-alignment and established close relations with neighbouring Cuba. A major achievement was the formation of the **Caribbean Community and Common Market** in 1973. However, the economic crisis persisted and he was forced to return to the **International Monetary Fund** for support in 1978. Defeated by Edward Seaga in 1980, Manley returned to power as leader of a much more moderate Government in 1989, but resigned owing to ill health only three years later.

Martinique

The island of Martinique is situated in the Lesser Antilles, 25 km to the south of Dominica and 37 km to the north of St Lucia.

Area (including islets): 1,100 sq km (425 sq miles); *capital:* **Fort-de-France**; *population:* 422,277 (2002 estimate), 95% of African descent and 5% European; *official language:* French (a Creole patois is also widely spoken); *religion:* Roman Catholic 95%.

Constitution: Martinique became an Overseas Department of France in 1946. It elects four deputies to the National Assembly and two to the Senate. Members of the Conseil Régional and the Conseil Général agreed proposals for greater autonomy in June 2001 which would lead to the creation of a collectivité territoriale governed by a single 41-member Assembly elected for a five-year term. In March 2003 the French parliament agreed to submit these proposals to a referendum.

History: French settlement in the island began in 1635 and was initially strongly resisted by the indigenous Caribs. The Carib name for the island, Madinina, may have suggested the dedication to St-Martin. The island was soon covered with **sugar** plantations worked by slaves imported from Africa. Slavery was abolished at the time of the French Revolution, but restored by Napoleon, whose first wife, Joséphine (Marie-Josèphe Tascher de la Pagerie), came from Martinique. The sugar economy was devastated by the catastrophic eruption of Mont Pelée in 1902, which destroyed the former capital, St-Pierre, and all but one of its inhabitants. It recovered to some extent in the aftermath, but **bananas** became a more important source of revenue. In 1946 the Governor was replaced by a Prefect and an elected Conseil Général, which was given enhanced powers in 1960. In 1974 the island was granted regional status, the Conseil Régional having additional powers on economic matters. The socialist poet and politician, Aimé Césaire, leader of the Parti Progressiste Martiniquais (PPM), and his successors successfully argued for greater autonomy, effectively defusing much of the pressure for independence.

Latest elections: In elections to the Conseil Régional in March 1998, the Mouvement Indépendantiste Martiniquais won 13 of the 41 seats, the rest being divided among the PPM (seven), the Rassemblement pour la République (six), the Union pour la Démocratie Française (five), the Parti Martiniquais Socialiste and other groups (seven).

International relations and defence: In mid-2001 President Chirac rejected a joint proposal from the French overseas departments in the region that they be allowed to join the **Association of Caribbean States** as associate members. There is a French garrison of some 4,000 troops in the Caribbean, with its headquarters on Martinique.

Economy: In recent years bananas have accounted for some 40% of export revenues. The production of rum, the island's most celebrated export, utilized about one-third of the sugar harvested, and accounted for a further 10% of exports by value. Since the 1980s efforts have been made to diversify crops, with some success in the case of melons and pineapples, and to increase local processing of agricultural products. The main industrial activity on the island, however, is the refining of imported crude petroleum, the finished product accounting for a further 16% of exports. Until 2001 there had been a steady growth in the number of tourists, the overwhelming majority of them French, visiting the island.

Menem, Carlos Saúl

Carlos Saúl Menem, President of Argentina 1989–99, was born in the inland province of La Rioja in 1935, to a Syrian family which had converted to Catholicism. A lawyer by profession, he joined the Peronist Youth at an early age and in 1973 was elected Governor of La Rioja. During the 1976 military coup he was one of the first to be arrested and was held in prison until 1978 and under house arrest until 1982. With the return of democracy in 1983 he was re-elected Governor of La Rioja and was again re-elected in 1987, by which time he had clearly emerged as a charismatic vote-winner, with a populist style which earned him the nomination for the presidency of the **Partido Justicialista**. He achieved a decisive victory in the 1989 presidential election.

Mercosur – *see* Southern Common Market

Mercado de Valores de Buenos Aires, SA (Merval)
Buenos Aires Stock Exchange, Argentina

The leading stock exchange in Argentina and one of the most important in Latin America. The Merval index of share prices is internationally cited as an indicator of the health of the Argentine economy.
  Leadership: Eugenio de Bary (Pres.)
  Address: 25 de Mayo 175, 8°–10°, 1002 Buenos Aires
  Telephone: (11) 4342-4607
  Fax: (11) 4313-0639
  E-mail: merval@merval.sba.com.ar
  Internet: www.merval.sba.com.ar

Mexico
Estados Unidos Mexicanos—The United Mexican States

Mexico is the southernmost of the three large countries that make up the political map of North America. It is bounded on the north by the USA, on the east by the Gulf of Mexico, on the south-east by Belize and Guatemala and on the west by the Pacific Ocean. Cuba lies some 210 km to the east of the Yucatán Peninsula.
  Area: 1,964,375 sq km (758,449 sq miles); *capital:* **Mexico City** (*México, DF*); *population:* 103.4m. (2002 estimate), the majority of mixed Spanish and Amerindian descent, at least 15% Amerindian and 9% European (mostly Spanish); *official language:* Spanish (at least 62 indigenous languages were still spoken in 2003); *religion:* 90% Roman Catholic, 7% Protestant.
  Constitution: Like the first republican constitution of the United Mexican States (1824), the 1917 Constitution established a federal, presidential republic, but with a distinctive feature. The principle of 'no re-election' means that the President, who has extensive powers, serves one six-year term only and cannot serve again. The federal legislature consists of a Senate, with two representatives from each of the 31 states, and a Chamber of Deputies, chosen by single-member, single-ballot by

199

districts. States have a common model constitution but hold their elections at various times. They elect a governor, as chief executive, and a state legislature.

History: The history of advanced civilizations in Mexico begins some 2,500 years ago. Tenochtitlán, in the Valley of Mexico, was founded by the Aztecs in 1325, and in less than 200 years they had established an empire trading as far south as modern Costa Rica. The conquest of Mexico in 1519 by Hernán Cortés and his followers led to a catastrophic fall in population over the next 80 years, largely as a result of European diseases such as measles and smallpox. By the 18th century Spanish settlement had spread as far north as California and as far east as Florida, and at independence in 1821 Mexico was the largest self-governing country in the world.

Unfortunately a series of incompetent leaders left the new republic very vulnerable. Central America seceded in 1824. Then, in the so-called Mexican War (1846–48), Mexico lost more than half of its territory to the USA. During the American Civil War Napoleon III of France tried to establish a puppet Empire in Mexico. Mexican resistance, led by Benito Juárez (President 1858–72) was successful and the Emperor Maximilian was shot at Querétaro in 1867. The restored republic did not last, however; in 1876 the military hero of the war against the French, Porfirio Díaz, rose in revolt against the civilian government, and, once President (1877–80, 1884–1911), established a dictatorship which was to last for some 30 years. During this period the country was linked, internally and to the USA, by railways, and efforts were made to encourage economic development. By the early 1900s Mexico's traditional mining sector had been supplemented by iron and coal mines and transformed by the discovery of petroleum, which by 1918 was to make the country the second largest oil producer in the world.

In 1910, however, Díaz's attempt to achieve re-election, for an unprecedented eighth term, triggered a revolt led by Francisco I. Madero, the hitherto unregarded younger son of a wealthy northern family, whose slogan was '*sufragio efectiva, no re-elección*' ('a free vote and no re-election'). In 1911 Díaz fled and Madero was elected as President, only to be overthrown by a military coup in February 1913. For the next four years the country was torn apart by a civil war fuelled by widespread desire for social change. The Revolution, as the period after 1910 soon became known, produced two famous figures: Emiliano Zapata, leader of agrarian forces in the south, and Francisco ('Pancho') Villa, commander of the Constitutionalist Army of the north and *de facto* ruler of much of the country. The followers of both contributed to the radicalism of the Constitution of 1917, which established the principle of no re-election. However, it was many years before the violence subsided; both Zapata (in 1919) and Villa (in 1923) were assassinated and the leader of the Constitutionalists, Venustiano Carranza, was himself overthrown and killed in 1920.

Power passed into the hands of leaders from the northern state of Coahuila: Alvaro Obregón (1920–24) and Plutarco Elías Calles (1924–28). However, when the Constitution was changed to allow Obregón to be re-elected in 1928, he was assassinated at his victory banquet. With re-election out of the question, Calles chose instead to create an official party through which he could continue to control matters, and the Partido Nacional Revolucionario (PNR) came into existence in 1929. Under **Lázaro Cárdenas** (1934–40), however, the PNR instead became the vehicle for the President of the day to rule, to carry out far-reaching social change and even to nominate his successor. Cárdenas immediately began a major pro-gramme of land reform and in 1938 nationalized Mexico's oil industry. Despite his immense and genuine popularity, as late as 1938 Cárdenas was challenged by a military revolt in the north. The revolt was premature, however, and was easily dispersed. In 1940 the election of Cárdenas's chosen candidate, Gen. Manuel Avila Camacho (President 1940–46), induced the supporters of his rival, Gen. Almazán, to riot. In 1942, however, the sinking of the oil tanker *Potrero del Llano* brought Mexico into the Second World War as an ally of the USA. At the end of the war, a civilian, Miguel Alemán Valdes, was elected as President (1946–52) and the armed forces lost their special position within the ruling party, renamed the **Partido Revolucionario Institutional** (PRI).

The new administration was business-oriented and dedicated to economic growth, leading to the choice in 1952 of a President committed to eliminating the corruption and waste that had inevitably resulted. Then, in 1958, the PRI turned to the Left with the choice of Adolfo López Mateos (1958–64) who, as Secretary of Labour, had won the confidence of the trade unions. In his six-year term he distributed more than 17m. ha of land, boosting the myth of the Revolution just at the moment when it might have been vulnerable to the challenge from Cuba. However, his successor, Gustavo Díaz Ordaz, was a colourless bureaucrat, who, when faced in 1968 with massive student demon-strations on the eve of the Olympic Games, failed to control those who wanted to use force. Troops fired without warning on a peaceful gathering in the Plaza de las Tres Culturas at Tlatelolco, killed at least 217 and apprehended many others. Mexico should have gained from the first so-called 'oil shock' of 1973. Instead, however, by the end of the term of office of Luis Echeverría (1970–76) the country was in crisis and had been forced to devalue the peso. The discovery in the Gulf of unexpectedly large oil reserves inspired Gustavo López Portillo (1976–82) to spend even more and by 1982 Mexico was bankrupt, with a foreign debt of more than US $100m. which it could no longer afford to service.

Miguel de la Madrid Hurtado (1982–88) tried to tackle the **Debt Crisis** by a conventional strategy of reining in public spending, but by the end of his term he was already facing a challenge from within his Party for democratic elections and a better deal for the masses. The results of the 1988 elections showed a narrow majority for the official candidate, the Harvard-trained economist, **Carlos Salinas de Gortari** (1988–94). Salinas embarked on a dramatic programme of privatization and in 1992 ended more than 70 years of land reform. His chosen successor was assassinated before he could contest an election and Ernesto Zedillo, who replaced him (1994–2000), wisely kept his promise to ensure a free election in 2000.

Latest elections: In presidential elections held on 2 July 2000, **Vicente Fox Quesada** of the Alianza por el Cambio, comprising his own centre-right **Partido Acción Nacional** (PAN) and the small Partido Verde Ecologista de México (PVEM), was victorious, obtaining 43.4% of the votes cast. He defeated Francisco Labastida Ochoa of the PRI, who received 36.9% of the vote, following the decision on 14 June of Porfirio Muñoz Ledo of the Partido Auténtico de la Revolución Mexicana to withdraw from the contest and endorse the candidacy of Fox. **Cuauhtémoc Cárdenas Solórzano** of the Alianza por México, led by his centre-left Partido de la Revolución Democrática (PRD), received only 17% of the vote. This result ended the monopoly of power that the PRI, under various names, had held since its formation in 1929.

The Alianza por el Cambio did not obtain an overall majority in either House of Congress. In the elections to the Chamber of Deputies the results were: Alianza por el Cambio 223 seats (PAN 208, PVEM 15), PRI 209, PRD 52, others 16; and in the elections to the Senate: PRI 60 seats, Alianza por el Cambio 51 (PAN 46, PVEM 5), PRD 15, others two. The chairs of committees were subsequently allocated proportionately, though it was noted that the PRI retained control of finance and foreign affairs in the Chamber and of defence in both houses.

International relations and defence: Mexico's foreign policy is based on the 1932 Estrada Doctrine, which rejects all forms of intervention and seeks to maintain diplomatic relations with all other states regardless of their views. It is a member of the United Nations, the **Organization of American States**, the **North American Free Trade Agreement**, the **Latin American Integration Association** and the **Rio Pact**. It has a regular army of 144,000, a navy, principally involved in coastal protection, of 37,000, and an air force with a strength of 11,770. A part-time compulsory selective service system operates and there is a 14,000-strong rural militia.

Mexico, economy

GNI: US $550.2m. (2001); *GNI per caput:* $5,530 (2001); *GNI at PPP:* $820m. (2001); *GNI per caput at PPP:* $8,240 (2001), rank 80; *exports:* $160,682m. (2002); *imports:* $168,677m. (2002); *currency:* nuevo peso, plural nuevos pesos; US $1 = 10.30 nuevos pesos at 31 May 2003.

In 2002 agriculture accounted for 4% of Mexico's gross domestic product (GDP), mining and manufacturing for 18.6% and construction for 4.8%. Some 12.7% of the land is arable, 1.3% under permanent crops, 40.9% permanent pasture and 17% forest and woodland. The main export crops are **sugar** cane and maize; tomatoes, **coffee** and fruit and vegetables are also important export crops. Sorghum, wheat, barley and rice are also grown for local consumption. Cattle-ranching is a major economic activity, mainly in the dry north. The main mineral resource is petroleum, of which Mexico was the world's fourth largest producer in 2003. Mexico is the world's largest silver producer; iron ore, zinc, lead, coal, sulphur, bismuth, graphite, antimony and other minerals are also exploited. The principal industries are metal products, machinery and tools, food, drink and tobacco manufacture, and iron and steel production. In 2001 54% of export revenues came from manufacturing products in bond (*maquiladoras*) for re-export to the USA. The main energy sources are petroleum and natural gas, though exports of these have declined steeply.

Main exports are electrical machinery, road vehicles and parts, telecommunications and sound equipment and petroleum and petroleum products. Principal imports are electrical equipment, industrial machinery and parts and road vehicles. In 2002 the USA was by far the greatest purchaser of exports. The USA was also by far the greatest supplier of imports, with small quantities also coming from Japan, the People's Republic of China and Germany.

In the 1970s the government spent well rather than wisely, and the threat of default in 1982 gave the world the term **Debt Crisis**. Over the next six years the **Partido Revolucionario Institucional** Government pursued a series of austerity plans, with limited success, and under **Carlos Salinas de Gortari** (1988–94) embarked on a substantial programme of selling state enterprises (the petroleum and petroleum derivatives sectors were excluded, however), which gave it enough leeway to continue to subsidize basic foodstuffs. However, this was achieved by maintaining an unsustainable exchange rate which led to the so-called 'tequila crisis' of 1994 and to a forced devaluation. Though the economy recovered in 1996, the Government had to resume borrowing, and the country remained very vulnerable to external shocks such as the East Asian Crisis of 1997 and the Russian devaluation of 1999. Annual GDP growth rose in the late 1990s and reached 6.6%

in 2000. In 2001, however, GDP declined by 0.2% owing to a fall in demand from the USA. Growth of 0.7% was recorded in 2002. The annual rate of inflation in 2002 was 4.2% and the official unemployment rate 2.8%, though this concealed a very high rate of underemployment, much of it in the informal sector.

Mexico City
Ciudad de México, DF

Mexico City, chief city and capital of the United Mexican States, is located in the Valley of Mexico, in an intermontane valley. The city proper is that area that lies within the Federal District (*Distrito Federal*), which has its own elected Mayor and which at the 2000 census had a population of 8,605,239. However, a large part of its conurbation now extends into the State of Mexico and the combined population of these two areas is estimated at some 23m., making it the largest city in the world.

Montesinos, Vladimiro

Vladimiro Montesinos Torres, former head of Peru's intelligence service, began his career in the army in the early 1970s, but in 1977 was imprisoned for a year and dismissed. He then worked as a lawyer in the capital, Lima, until he met **Alberto Fujimori** during his 1989–90 election campaign. Fujimori put him in charge of anti-drugs operations sponsored by the USA and after the closure of Congress in 1992 Montesinos became increasingly important as an adviser to the President. He was secretly appointed head of the National Intelligence Service (*Servicio de Inteligencia Nacional*), which was criticized at home and abroad for alleged human rights abuses, and played a key role in the bloody end to the siege of the Japanese embassy in 1997. Soon afterwards videos shot with one of his own hidden cameras showed him allegedly bribing a congressman. In 2000 Montesinos, who had taken refuge in Panama after the flight of Fujimori, was extradited back to Peru to stand trial.

Montevideo

Montevideo, port, principal city and capital of Uruguay, is situated on a low eminence on the north bank of the Río de la Plata estuary, downstream from **Buenos Aires**. It was founded by Spanish settlers in 1726 to block the southward movement of Portuguese settlers from Brazil, and changed hands frequently between 1807 and 1830, when it became the capital of independent Uruguay and centre of its national life. There are no fewer than nine beaches within the city limits. In mid-2001 Montevideo had a population estimated at 1,381,541.

Montserrat

A British Overseas Territory in the Caribbean in the Lesser Antilles, located 47 km (27 miles) south-west of the island of Antigua. After lying dormant for 350 years, the Soufrière Hills volcano began to erupt on 18 July 1995. In April 1996 the southern half of the island, including the capital, Plymouth, became uninhabitable as a consequence of the eruption and was evacuated. A series of pyroclastic flows followed and an Exclusion Zone was extended to two-thirds of the island, including virtually all of the best agricultural land. Eruptions reached a new degree of intensity in March and April 1997. The remaining inhabitants were evacuated from the Zone, though some returned to tend crops or livestock, resulting in the loss of 19 lives on 25 June. At one point, with two-thirds of the population already in either the United Kingdom or neighbouring Antigua and Barbuda, the port destroyed and the airport in the danger zone, it looked as if the island would have to be abandoned altogether. Fuelled by periodic dome collapses, eruptions from the now seven active craters continue at a reduced level, though a massive eruption in September 2003 caused significant damage near Salem, close to the edge of the 'safe' zone.

Area: 102 sq km (39 sq miles); *capital:* Plymouth, uninhabitable; government centre temporarily at Carr's Bay on the north-west coast; *population:* 4,482 (at 2001 census; 10,639 in 1991), mainly of mixed African and Irish descent; *official language:* English; *religion:* Roman Catholic, Anglican (Episcopalian).

Constitution: Under the Constitution of 1989, the Governor is Chief Executive and chairs the Executive Council, comprising the Chief Minister, three other ministers, the Attorney-General and the Financial Secretary. The Legislative Council has a Speaker, nine elected, two official and two nominated members.

History: Montserrat is the only territory in the world settled predominantly by Irish Catholics from 1632. Slaves were imported to cultivate **sugar** and **cotton**, and limes for the Royal Navy. The island was governed as part of the Leeward Islands Federation from 1871 to 1956. Universal suffrage was introduced in 1952. In 1978 the Montserrat Labour Party was displaced by the People's Liberation Movement (PLM) led by John Osborne. However, in 1987 the UK government intervened to close a number of offshore banks and impose regulation on the financial services sector. In September 1989 UK assistance was needed when the island was devastated by '**Hurricane** Hugo' and in September 1991 the PLM was defeated by the National Progressive Party (NPP) led by Reuben Meade.

In elections held in November 1996 no party gained a majority and a coalition government was formed under Bertrand Osborne, who, however, resigned in August 1997 after public protests at the standard of emergency accommodation provided by the British Government. His successor, David Brandt, found the new

British Secretary of State, Clare Short, no more helpful and took offence at an insensitive comment by her that the Montserratians wanted 'golden elephants'.

Latest elections: In the elections of April 2001, held on a single constituency basis, the New People's Liberation Movement (NPLM), led by John A. Osborne, won seven seats and the NPP two. The new Government was formed by the NPLM.

International relations and defence: The United Kingdom is responsible for both. Montserrat is a member of the **Caribbean Community and Common Market** and of the **Organization of Eastern Caribbean States**.

Economy: Despite the destruction of its infrastructure and all of its main economic resources, with the exception of offshore financial services, the remaining territory has a middle-income economy, as defined by the **International Bank for Reconstruction and Development** (World Bank). Gross domestic product per head in 2001 was US $8,063. There is no significant commercial agriculture, but crops are grown and stock reared for local consumption. New facilities have been constructed in the north of the island with the aid of substantial British government and **European Union** grants; they include a new port and regional airport that are due to open in 2004. The intention is to base a new tourist industry on the attraction of the volcano. More than 9,000 people visited the island in 2002. *Currency:* Eastern Caribbean dollar, pegged to the US dollar at US $1 = EC$2.70.

Moscoso, Mireya Elisa

Mireya Elisa Moscoso Rodríguez, President of Panama in 1999 when it gained the Panama Canal under the Panama Canal Treaties of 1977, was born in Panama City in 1946. Her father, head of the village school of Pedasí, Los Santos, died when she was only nine years old and she was educated in the Convent of María Inmaculada in Panama City before going to work in the directorate-general of the Social Security Fund. In 1964 she took part in the presidential campaign of Arnulfo Arias Madrid, the veteran politician who had twice already, in 1940 and 1949, been elected as President, but had not been allowed to complete either term. In 1968 she was at his side in his third successful campaign. Arias took office on 1 October, but on 11 October he was deposed by a coup led by Col **Omar Torrijos Herrera**, and when he went into exile in Miami, Florida, she went with him. They were married in 1969. In 1972 she returned briefly to Panama to visit her sick mother, but was arrested and threatened with torture before being released. However, in 1978 they were both able to return, and, after the accidental death of Torrijos in 1981, Arias contested the 1984 elections as candidate of the Authentic Panamanian Party (PPA), only narrowly losing to Torrijos' chosen successor.

Arias died in Miami in 1988 and Moscoso took over the reins both of his estates and of the PPA. In 1989 the PPA led a coalition supporting Guillermo Endara, one of Arias' closest colleagues, but **Gen. Manuel Antonio Noriega Morena**, the commander of the defence forces, cancelled the election and imposed his own candidate. After the US intervention in December, however, Endara was declared the winner, and in 1991 Moscoso became president of the Partido Arnulfista (PA), a moderate nationalist and conservative party. She had married for the second time in 1991 and bore her second husband's surname, Gruber, from 1991 until their divorce in 1997. Meanwhile, in 1993 the PA became the second largest party in the National Assembly and Moscoso the effective leader of the opposition. At the 1998 elections, making a positive virtue of her lack of higher education and extensive experience of business and farming, she was elected as President, although her **Nueva Nación** coalition failed to gain a majority in the legislature.

Movimiento de la Izquierda Revolucionaria (MIR)
Movement of the Revolutionary Left, Bolivia

Founded in 1971, the MIR professes to be left-wing but in power has usually proved to be conservative. Having its main power base in the liberal urban middle class, the party was formed in opposition to the 1971 military coup as a merger of small left-wing groups and young Christian democrats. It drew considerable support from the radical student movement and was linked to the insurgent Ejército de Liberación Nacional in the early years of the military dictatorship of Gen. **Hugo Bánzer Suárez** (1971–78).

The MIR gradually moved away from its Marxist roots but nevertheless remained in strong opposition to the military regime, which continued to persecute and imprison members of the party, among them Bánzer's future political ally, Jaime Paz Zamora. The party contested the elections of 1978, 1979 and 1980 as part of an alliance led by the Movimiento Nacionalista Revolucionario de Izquierda (MNRI), with Paz Zamora as running-mate of the victorious but ill-fated MNRI leader, **Hernán Siles Zuazo**, in 1979 and 1980. Paz Zamora came third with 8.8% of the vote in the July 1985 presidential contest and in the simultaneous congressional elections the depleted MIR won 16 seats. When Congress had to vote in the second round of the presidential elections, the MIR joined with other centre-left parties in electing the presidential runner-up, **Víctor Paz Estenssoro** of the **Movimiento Nacionalista Revolucionario** in preference to ex-dictator Bánzer.

Having failed to form an alliance with the Partido Demócrata Cristiano, the MIR contested the May 1989 elections alone, winning 41 congressional seats. In the presidential election Paz Zamora was placed a close third with 19.6% of the vote. In the absence of a conclusive winner, the runner-up, Gen. Bánzer, withdrew and switched the 46 congressional votes of the **Acción Democrática Nacionalista** (ADN) to Paz Zamora, who in August was duly elected as President by Congress. The price exacted for this support was the necessity for the MIR to share power with the ADN in the Acuerdo Patriótico (AP). In August 1991, in a major cabinet reshuffle, three MIR ministerial posts were allocated to members of the MIR-Nueva Mayoría (MIR-NM) faction, which, due to the domination of the ADN, had previously been circumspect in its support for the MIR's involvement in the AP coalition. In March 1992, however, the MIR-NM confirmed its support for Bánzer as AP candidate in the 1993 presidential elections.

After persistent criticism of his presidency, Paz Zamora entered into 'permanent' retirement in March 1994, but returned less than eight months later following the arrest on drugs charges of the party's secretary-general, Oscar Eid Franco. In the June 1997 presidential elections Paz Zamora came third with 16.7% of the votes cast and his party won 25 seats in the Chamber and six in the Senate. The party was included in the resultant ruling coalition Government headed by the ADN. The MIR candidate, Jorge Torres, obtained 15.9% of the votes in municipal elections in La Paz in 1999, by which time the party officially styled itself the MIR-NM.

The party is a member of the Socialist International.

Leadership: Jaime Paz Zamora (Pres.), Oscar Eid Franco (Sec.-Gen.)

Address: Calle Ingavi 600, Casilla de Correo 7397, La Paz

Telephone: (2) 31-0416

Fax: (2) 40-6455

E-mail: mir@ceibo.entelnet.bo

Internet: www.cibergallo.com

Movimiento de Liberación Nacional (MLN)

National Liberation Movement, Guatemala

Founded in 1960, the MLN is an extreme right-wing party that traditionally has represented agrarian (especially **coffee** growers) and industrial élites.

The Movement, a self-proclaimed 'party of organized violence', was founded by Mario Sandoval Alarcón as the successor of the Movimiento Democrático Nacional of Col Castillo Armas, who, with US backing, overthrew the reformist Arbenz

Government in 1954. The MLN staged the 1963 coup led by Col Peralta Azurdia and formed a government with the Partido Revolucionario until it was itself overthrown in 1964. The MLN's presidential candidate came third in the 1966 elections, but from 1970 the party was in government for eight years, its leader Col Carlos Arana Osorio was President in 1970–74, and in 1974–1978 Gen. Kjell Laugerud presided over an MLN-Partido Institucional Democrático (PID) Government, with Sandoval as acting Vice-President. It was in the 1970s that 'death squads' linked to the MLN were most active. For the July 1984 constituent elections the MLN entered into a coalition with the Central Auténtica Nacionalista (CAN) and won most of the coalition's 23 seats, becoming the largest bloc in the Constituent Assembly. It entered into another coalition with the PID before the November 1985 general elections, but strongly opposed the policies of the new Partido Democracia Cristiana Guatemalteca Government—in particular its support for the Central American peace process—which it accused of being Marxist.

By early 1990 opposition to the peace process had mellowed. In response to the opening of peace talks with the **Unidad Revolucionaria Nacional Guatemalteca** (URNG) guerrillas in Oslo, Norway, the MLN supported the eventual incorporation of the URNG into the political mainstream. In the November 1990 general election, the MLN, in coalition with the Frente de Avance Nacional (FAN), won a mere four seats in the Congress and its presidential candidate, Col Luis Ernesto Sosa, came fifth in the first round of the presidential contest, receiving 17.3% of the vote. The party secured two seats in its own right in 1994, but gained only 2.3% of the votes in the presidential contest in 1995 and retained only one seat in Congress. It lost its Congressional representation in 1999, when its presidential candidate, Carlos Humberto Pérez Rodríguez, obtained only 0.55% of the vote.

Leadership: Carlos Humberto Pérez Rodríguez (former presidential candidate)
Address: 2–32, Zona 10, Guatemala City
Telephone: (502) 332-0420, 332-0130
Fax: (502) 331-0130
E-mail: mln@wepa.com.gt

Movimiento de Liberación Nacional—Tupamaros (MLN—T)
National Liberation Movement-Tupamaros, Uruguay

The left-wing MLN—T has its roots in the guerrilla movement of the same name of the 1960s and 1970s. Although it is now committed to democratic politics, the movement has never renounced its past. It campaigns for radical economic reforms and represents the more left-wing faction within the Frente Amplio (FA) as part of an alliance known as the Movimiento de Participación Popular (MPP).

The MLN was founded in 1962 by Raúl Sendic Antonaccio as the political wing of the Tupamaros guerrilla group (named in honour of the 18th century Peruvian Indian leader Tupac Amaru). It was originally concentrated in rural areas, motivated by the plight of the **sugar** cane cutters (whom Sendic had helped to organize in strikes in 1961–62), and fought for agrarian reform and rural workers' rights. The group switched its attention to the cities in 1966 and became engaged in armed struggle. Between 1966 and 1972 the Tupamaros became one of Latin America's most successful urban guerrilla groups.

Following the army offensive launched against them in 1972, and the ensuing military dictatorship, the MLN was virtually annihilated. On the return to civilian rule, all guerrillas were released in an amnesty in 1985, Sendic announcing that the MLN would now be working within the democratic political system. While piloting MLN-T towards parliamentary involvement, Sendic founded a movement to promote rural reform but he died shortly afterwards. Although at first excluded from the FA, the MLN—T was finally permitted to join it in late 1988. In May 1989 it obtained legal recognition as a political party.

The MLN—T has become an influential although minority faction of the Encuentro Progresista—FA alliance. As part of the umbrella MPP, the MLN—T has two senators and five deputies in the legislature elected in October 1999.

Leadership: José Mujica (Sec.-Gen.)

Address: Tristan Navaja 1578, CP 11.200, Montevideo

Telephone: (2) 409 22 98

Fax: (2) 409 99 57

E-mail: mln@chasque.apc.org

Internet:. www.chasquenet/mlnweb

Movimiento Nacionalista Revolucionario (MNR)

Nationalist Revolutionary Movement, Bolivia

The MNR was founded in 1941 and over the decades has spawned various factions with suffixes in their title, reflecting internal party divisions. Most recently, the main party current was known as the MNR (Histórico—MNRH). The MNR's founders included the social reformer, **Víctor Paz Estenssoro**, the left-wing **Hernán Siles Zuazo** and the fascist sympathizer, Carlos Montenegro. The party's original policies reflected Paz Estenssoro's attempt, during the Second World War, to combine the nationalist developmentalist ideas of the **Alianza Popular Revolucionaria Americana** of Peru with those of European fascism, as enunciated by Italian dictator Benito Mussolini. The MNR first participated in government in 1943–46 under President Gualberto Villaroel.

When the military overthrew Villaroel in 1946, numerous MNR leaders were killed or exiled. Paz Estenssoro fought the 1951 elections from exile as the MNR's presidential candidate and won the highest vote, although not an outright majority. The incumbent President handed power to a military junta which, less than a year later, was toppled by an MNR-led popular uprising, known thereafter as the 1952 Revolution, assisted by the police and tin miners. Paz Estenssoro was allowed to return from Argentina and was appointed as President in April 1952.

Paz Estenssoro's coalition government with the Labour Party introduced a number of progressive reforms, including the nationalization of the mines, agrarian reform and the enfranchisement of illiterates. The MNR remained in power for two more terms, with Siles Zuazo taking the presidency in 1956 and Paz Estenssoro being elected President again in 1960. In November 1964, following widespread strikes and disorder, Paz Estenssoro was overthrown and forced into exile by the Vice-President, Air Force Gen. René Barrientos Ortuño, who took power with the assistance of the army. The MNR was thrown into disarray and only re-emerged on the political scene in 1971 as supporters of the military coup of Gen. **Hugo Bánzer Suárez (Acción Democrática Nacionalista**—ADN). Since then its main tendency has been centre-right.

The MNR participated in Bánzer's government until 1974, when it was expelled for protesting that the promised process of democratization had not begun. By then, the left wing of the party, led by Siles Zuazo, had broken away and formed the Movimiento Nacionalista Revolucionario de Izquierda (MNRI), to which Paz Estenssoro's faction, the MNRH, came second in the 1979 and 1980 presidential elections. Paz Estenssoro was beaten by Siles in both elections, winning 35.9% and 20.1% of the vote respectively in the two campaigns. The MNRH, however, won 44 seats in the Congress in 1979.

Following another period of military government (1980–82) and three years of opposition to an MNRI government, Paz Estenssoro once again contested the presidency. In the elections held in June 1985 he obtained 26.4% of the vote, 2.2% less than Bánzer of the ADN. However, in a run-off congressional vote in August 1985, the centre-left parties added their votes to those of the 59 MNRH congressmen and brought Paz Estenssoro to power again. He quickly introduced a strict austerity programme to reduce rampant inflation, a policy in which he persisted despite the collapse of the international tin market in late 1985.

Faced with general labour unrest, Paz Estenssoro found greater common ground with the right-wing ADN than with his erstwhile supporters of the centre-left. A 'pact for democracy' between the MNRH and the ADN was duly signed in October 1985. In the municipal elections of December 1987 the MNRH polled poorly, amid widespread discontent with the Government. This was further fuelled by the US-assisted anti-drugs programme, which threatened the livelihood of many peasant **coca** growers, whose numbers had been swollen by unemployed miners. Nevertheless, in the May 1989 general elections the MNRH presidential candidate, Gonzalo Sánchez de Lozada (former Minister of Planning), headed the popular poll with 23.1% of the vote. A run-off election in the newly elected Congress, in which the MNRH had 49 seats, did not produce a renewal of the pact with the ADN. Personal animosity between Sánchez de Lozada and ADN leader Bánzer resulted in the ADN transferring its support to Jaime Paz Zamora of the **Movimiento de la Izquierda Revolucionaria**, who was elected President.

Three months after the election of Paz Zamora as President, the 84-year-old Paz Estenssoro announced his desire to resign the MNR leadership. At the next party congress in mid-1990 the decision was formalized and Sánchez de Lozada was elected as his successor, although in 1992 he briefly stood down following a death threat from an MNR congressional deputy. In the June 1993 elections Sánchez de Lozada again defeated Bánzer, winning 33.8% of the popular vote and this time obtained congressional endorsement as President, with Víctor Hugo Cárdenas Conde of the Movimiento Revolucionario Túpaq Katarí de Liberacíon (MRTKL) becoming Vice-President. In the simultaneous legislative balloting the MNR/MRTKL alliance raised its representation to 69 out of 157 seats, thus confirming the MNR's status as the dominant ruling party.

In the June 1997 presidential elections, the MNR candidate, Juan Carlos Durán Saucedo, came a poor second, winning only 17.7% of the vote, while in the concurrent congressional elections the party's representation was reduced to 26 seats in the Chamber of Deputies and three in the Senate. The MNR's Guido Capra came second with 16% of the votes cast for the mayoralty of **La Paz** in 1999, whereas Percy Fernandez of the MNR was an easy winner in Santa Cruz de la Sierra. Paz Estenssoro died in June 2001 at the age of 93. In the presidential election of June 2003, the MNR candidate, Gonzalo Sánchez de Lozada, gained the largest percentage of the vote (22.5%) and was later chosen by Congress to serve as President. In the concurrent legislative elections the party won 11 seats in the Senate and 36 seats in the Chamber of Deputies, making it the largest party in each house.

Leadership: Gonzalo Sánchez de Lozada (former President of the Republic), Carlos Sánchez Berzain (Sec.-Gen.)

Address: Calle Nicolás Acosta 574, La Paz
Telephone: (2) 249-0748
Fax: (2) 249-0009
E-mail: mnr2002@ceibo.entelnet.bo
Internet: www.bolivian.com/mnr

Movimiento Nuevo País-Pachakútik (MNPP)
New Country Movement-Pachakútik, Ecuador

The most important of the new wave of *indigenista* movements in Ecuador, appealing to a combination of indigenous, environmental and related social groups. It supported the successful candidature of Col Lucio Edwin Gutiérrez Borbua for the presidency in October–November 2000 and won eight seats in the National House of Representatives.
Leadership: Freddy Ehlers Zurita (Leader)

Movimiento Revolucionario Túpac Amaru (MRTA)
Túpac Amaru Revolutionary Movement, Peru

The MRTA is a pro-Cuban Marxist-Leninist guerrilla group founded by Luis Varese Scoto. It commenced an armed campaign in 1984 with the seizure of a radio station, but until 1994 its activities, though troublesome, were overshadowed by those of **Sendero Luminoso**. On 18 April 1989 the army successfully ambushed an MRTA column near the village of Molinos in the Department of Junin, killing 62. In July 1990, the MRTA leader, Víctor Polay Campos ('Comandante Rolando'), was arrested but escaped from custody, only to be arrested again in San Borja in June 1992.

In 1995 arrests of alleged MRTA insurgents included that of Cistero García Torres ('Comandante Ricardo'). Responsibility for the detonation of two bombs near a police station on 26 July 1996 was attributed to the MRTA and one man was arrested. However, the well-planned seizure by 17 MRTA guerrillas of the Japanese embassy, in which 490 were taken hostage, including the President's own brother, on the night of the Emperor's birthday (17 December) came as a complete surprise to President **Fujimori**. The President refused to either negotiate or admit any degree of responsibility for the welfare of the hostages, some of whom were released over the following two weeks. At year end only 81 of those most closely connected with the government, the security forces and the President himself, remained in the heavily armed compound and the guerrilla leader, Nestor Cerpa Cartolini ('Comandante Huerta'), held a press conference inside the compound to reiterate his refusal to yield his central demand, the release of all MRTA prisoners, currently held in sub-human conditions.

The 126-day embassy siege ended abruptly on 22 April 1997 in a bloodbath. On 31 January President Fujimori had met the Japanese Prime Minister, Ryutaro Hashimoto, in Toronto, Canada, after further negotiated hostage releases had raised hopes of a peaceful resolution. Nestor Cerpa Cartolini continued to demand the release of some 400 imprisoned guerrillas and safe passage out of the country, and five rounds of talks were held between him and a government negotiator between 11–24 February. The talks were broken off on 7 March when the guerrillas detected tunnelling activity and, despite successful efforts by the Japanese government to find a country willing to accept the guerrillas, both they and the government refused to agree to a deal. On 19 March both the interior minister and the national police chief resigned. Their respective successors, Gens César Saucedo Sánchez and Fernando Diaderas, took the decision to launch a carefully planned attack. Lulled into over-confidence, four of the guerrillas were killed outright when a mine was exploded under the basement where they were playing football; commandos then burst into the building from all sides. Two soldiers were also killed and one of the 72 hostages, Supreme Court judge Carlos Giusti, died shortly afterwards of a heart attack. However, all of the guerrillas were killed, including those who offered to surrender and those who had been wounded. President Fujimori, however, was triumphant, and the MRTA were unable to carry out their threat of reprisals. Five generals were among the 19 immediately charged by the military authorities for the security lapse.

Following the shooting of mine owner Luis Hochschild Pflaud, Congress, on 12 May 1998, granted the President exceptional powers to legislate by decree, and on 21 May, in a draconian so-called 'law against aggravated terrorism', President Fujimori redefined all organized crime as a form of terrorism. Not only would it be subject to military law, but would also be liable to the same drastic penalties first imposed for terrorism in 1992. On 2 November he was able to report the capture of 'Yoel', the new MRTA leader, and despite their hunger strike some 600 of his comrades remained in prison.

Movimiento V República (MVR)
Fifth Republic Movement, Venezuela

Movement f. 1998 to promote the presidential candidature of Lt-Col (retd) **Hugo Chávez Frías**; stands for nationalism and a 'Bolivarian revolution' in Venezuela.

Leadership: Lt-Col (retd) Hugo Chávez Frias
Address: Calle Lima, cruce con Avda Libertador, Los Caobos, Caracas
Telephone:(212) 782-3808
Fax: (212) 782-9720

Muerte a Secuestradores (MAS)
Death to Kidnappers, Colombia

Extreme right-wing paramilitary organization dedicated to rooting out guerrilla groups in Colombia; operates in 'death squads', generally believed to consist of off-duty members of the police and armed services.

N

Nacional Financiera, SNC

National Finance, Mexico

Parastatal development bank and finance company f. 1943 to fund industrial development in Mexico; has 37 branches throughout the Republic.

Leadership: Mario Laborin Gómez (Dir-Gen.)
Address: Insurgentes Sur 1971, Torre IV, 13°, Col. Guadalupe Inn, 01020
México, DF
Telephone: (55) 5325-6700
Fax: (55) 5661-8418
Internet: www.nafin.com.mx

Nassau

Principal town and capital of The Bahamas, situated on the island of New Providence. Population 210,832 (2000 estimate).

National Alliance for Reconstruction (NAR)

F. 1983 as a coalition of moderate opposition parties at a time when petroleum prices were falling and the Government in Trinidad and Tobago was deeply unpopular. At the general election of December 1986, the coalition, under the leadership of A. N. R. Robinson, took 33 of the 36 seats in the House of Representatives with just 67% of the vote, and the coalition was reorganized as a single party. Following the incident in July 1990 when a group of Islamist radicals took over the parliament building and held a number of hostages, the party was overwhelmingly defeated in the December 1991 elections, gaining only 24% of the vote and retaining only the two seats it held on Tobago.

Leadership: Nizam Mohammed (Leader)
Address: 71 Dundonald St, Port of Spain
Telephone: 627-6163
E-mail: ttnar@yahoo.com
Internet: www.geocities.com/ttnar/website/main.html

National Trade Union Centre (NATUC)

F. 1991 to unify the trade union movement in Trinidad and Tobago by bringing together the Trinidad and Tobago Labour Union Congress and Council of Progressive Trade Unions.
Leadership: Errol K. McLeod (Pres.)
Address: c/o NUGFW Complex, 145–147 Henry St, Port of Spain
Telephone: 623-4591
Fax: 625-7756

National Workers' Union of Jamaica (NWU)

F. 1952; the NWU is affiliated to the International Confederation of Free Trade Unions and has 10,000 members.
Leadership: Clive Dobson (Pres.)
Address: 130–132 East St, POB 344, Kingston 16
Telephone: 922-1150
Fax: (876) 922-6608
E-mail: nwyou@cwjamaica.com

Nationale Democratische Partij (NDP)
National Democratic Party, Suriname

F. 1987 by Standvaste, the 25 February Movement; the NDP is supported by the armed forces.
Leadership: Lt-Col Desiré (Desi) Bouterse
Address: Benjaminstraat 17, Paramaribo
Telephone: 49-9183
Fax: 43-2174
E-mail: ndpsur@sr.net
Internet: www.sr.net/users/ndp.sur

Nationale Partij Suriname (NPS)
Suriname National Party

F. 1946; the NPS is the leading party in the Niew Front coalition, which has held power since 1989.

Leadership: Otmar Roel Rogers
Address: Wanicastraat 71, Paramaribo
Telephone: 47-7302
Fax: 47-5796
E-mail: nps@sr.net
Internet: www.nps.sr

Netherlands Antilles

The Netherlands Antilles consist of the islands of Curaçao and Bonaire in the southern Caribbean, close to the coast of Venezuela, and two and a half smaller islands in the Lesser Antilles—St Eustatius (20 km north-east of St Christopher), Saba (27 km to the north-east of St Eustatius) and St Maarten (56 km north of Saba).

Area overall: 800 sq km (309 sq miles); *capital:* **Willemstad**; *population:* 175,653 (2001 census), 85% of African or mixed descent; *official language:* Dutch; *religion:* Christian (Roman Catholics predominate).

Constitution: The Netherlands Antilles are part of the Kingdom of the Netherlands together with Aruba, which was separated in 1986. They enjoy full autonomy in domestic and internal affairs. The Queen of the Netherlands is represented by the Governor, who is appointed for a term of six years. The government of the Netherlands Antilles appoints a Minister Plenipotentiary who represents the Antilles in the government and, where appropriate, in the Council of Ministers of the Kingdom. The Governor is assisted by a Council of Ministers, responsible to the *Staten* (States) of the Antilles, which consists of 22 representatives elected for four years by universal suffrage, and divided thus: Curaçao 14, Bonaire three, St Maarten three, Saba one, St Eustatius one.

History: A Spanish expedition located Bonaire and Curaçao in 1499, but the Spaniards regarded the islands as useless. Dutch settlement began with the capture of St Maarten in 1630. Curaçao was taken in 1634, St Eustatius in 1635, Bonaire in 1636 and Saba in 1640, but all the islands changed hands several times before 1648, and in the case of St Eustatius Dutch sovereignty was not finally recognized until 1816. In 1648 Curaçao became the centre of the slave trade for the Dutch West India Co, that trade reaching its peak on the island in 1685–1713. Slaves imported to the

Guianas in the 18th century passed instead through St Eustatius, whose support for the insurgents in the American War of Independence precipitated war between Britain and the Netherlands. **Sugar** cultivation began in the islands in 1650 but was not very successful, though sufficient to help support the 'plantocracy'. Though the slave trade was abolished in 1818, slavery itself continued until 1863. Meanwhile, in 1845 the islands had, together with Aruba, for the first time been placed under a single Governor, based on Curaçao. The building of an oil refinery by Royal Dutch Shell in 1915 brought a new prosperity to the islands, and in 1936 the first steps were taken towards self-government.

Latest elections: Following the general election of 18 January 2002, the composition of the Staaten was: Frente Obrero i Liberashon 30 di mei 5, Partido Antía Restrukturá 4, Partido Nashonal di Pueblo 3, Partido Laboral Krusado Popular 2, Unión Patriótico Bonairiano 2, Democratic Party—St Maarten 1, Democratische Partij—Bonaire 1, National Alliance 1, Democratic Party—Statia 1, Windward Islands People's Movement 1.

International relations and defence: The Governor has executive power in external affairs, which are the responsibility of the Kingdom as a whole. The Governor is Commander in Chief of the armed forces. A small contingent of Dutch troops is stationed in Willemstad and a coast guard force operates from St Maarten and Aruba. Military service is compulsory. The US navy and air force have a base on Curaçao to patrol for illicit drugs.

Economy: Three main activities dominate the economy of the islands: tourism, 'offshore' financial services and petroleum refining.

Nevis

The smaller of the two islands making up the federated state of St Christopher (St Kitts) and Nevis. Nevis lies just 3 km south-east of St Kitts and is 93.3 sq km in area. The principal town is Charlestown, on the west coast.

New National Party (NNP), Grenada

F.1984; the NNP is a centre party formed following the US intervention in Grenada by a merger between three former opposition parties: the Grenada Democratic Movement, the Grenada National Party and the National Democratic Party. In 1995 it gained office, winning eight of the 15 seats in parliament with only 32.7% of the vote. In the 1999 elections it won all of the seats in the legislature, though one member subsequently resigned and became Leader of the Opposition.

Leadership: Dr Keith Mitchell (Leader), Lawrence Joseph (Chair.)
Address: St George's
E-mail: nnpnews@caribsurf.com
Internet: www.nnpnews.com

Nicaragua
República de Nicaragua

Nicaragua is the largest of the Central American states and is situated in the centre of the Central American isthmus. It is bounded on the north-west by the Gulf of Fonseca and by El Salvador, on the north and north-east by Honduras, on the east by the Caribbean Sea, to the south by Costa Rica and to the west by the Pacific Ocean. Included in its national territory are the Corn Islands off Bluefields and various islands and cays off the Miskito (Mosquito) Coast of the Caribbean.

Area: 120,254 sq km; *capital:* **Managua**; *population:* 5,482,340 (2003 estimate), 77% mestizo, 10% European, 9% of African and 4% of native American descent; *official language:* Spanish (Garifuna, Creole and English are also spoken); *religion:* predominantly Roman Catholic.

Constitution: The 1986 Constitution, which came into effect on 9 January 1987, vests legislative power in a single-chamber National Assembly of 90 representatives elected by all citizens over the age of 16 in accordance with a system of proportional representation. The Chief Executive, the President of the republic, is also directly elected; if the leading candidate fails to achieve 35% of the votes cast in a presidential election, the issue is decided by a second round of voting. The President serves for 5 years and may be re-elected for one consecutive term.

History: In 1911 the USA dispatched marines to Nicaragua to forestall the possibility of European intervention. By the Bryan-Chamorro Treaty of 1913 Nicaragua then agreed to sign over to the USA all rights to build an interoceanic canal through its territory. The withdrawal of US forces in 1934 left the commander of the US-trained National Guard, Anastasio Somoza García, with unrivalled power. With Sandino out of the way, in 1936 he seized power and thereafter ruled either in his own name or through puppet Presidents until he was assassinated in León in 1956. Power then passed to his eldest son, Luís Somoza Debayle (1956–63), who held the first elections under secret ballot in 1963 and handed over power to his nominee, René Schick. Luís Somoza died soon afterwards and his role as commander of the National Guard passed to his younger brother, **Anastasio Somoza Debayle**, who held power through various ruses until 1979. When Managua was devastated by an **earthquake** in 1972 the funds donated in aid were not used to rebuild it and during Somoza's rule some 43% of the country's economy passed into his family's hands.

In January 1978 the assassination of the editor of *La Prensa*, Pedro Joaquín Chamorro, triggered a massive uprising led by the **Frente Sandinista de Liberación Nacional** (FSLN), which, when Somoza finally fled, led a five-member ruling junta of national reconstruction. The provisional government lost no time in confiscating the wealth of the Somozas and their chief supporters, revoking the 1974 Constitution, dissolving the puppet Congress and sweeping away the National Guard. A Statute on Rights and Guarantees for the Citizens of Nicaragua, decreed in August 1979, established freedom of the individual, of speech and of the press, organized a successful literacy campaign, set up free education and abolished the death penalty. However, from 1981 onwards the provisional government was subjected to constant attacks by anti-Sandinista forces, popularly known as the '*contras*' (short for 'counter-revolutionaries'). These forces were raised and armed by the USA and the combination of their attacks on soft ('economic') targets and US financial pressure disrupted the recovering economy. In 1984 free elections were held, but at the last moment the opposition parties which had been campaigning freely withdrew on US instructions and then denounced the elections as fraudulent. **Daniel Ortega**, the FSLN candidate, was elected as President with 66.9% of the votes cast.

In 1986 the 'Iran-Contra' scandal emerged in the USA, revealing that funds for the *contras* had been raised, in part, by the sale of arms to Iran. However, though the *contra* campaign soon diminished, their forces remained a considerable nuisance, and the economy continued to decline. In a free election in 1990 Ortega was defeated by **Violeta Barrios de Chamorro** (President 1990–96). Attempts were made to reconstruct the economy on free-market lines and the United Nations was brought in to oversee the demobilization of the *contras*. The FSLN nominated Ortega unsuccessfully for the presidency in 1996 and again in 2001, when he was at some pains to distance himself from his guerrilla past, campaigning in a pink shirt and making it clear he accepted the mixed economy. He even stated that, if elected, he would order the return of US property confiscated by the former Sandinista government from US citizens. However, the Bush Administration made its hostility to a Sandinista victory very clear, issuing a series of economic threats which eroded Ortega's initial lead. The US Ambassador, wearing a **Partido Liberal Constitucionalista** (PLC) baseball cap, even distributed emergency food aid at the side of Ortega's Liberal rival, Enrique Bolaños.

Latest elections: In presidential elections held on 4 November 2001, Enrique Bolaños Geyer of the ruling PLC received 56.3% of the votes cast, compared with

42.3% cast for former President Ortega and 1.4% for Alberto Saborio of the Partido Conservador de Nicaragua (PCN). In concurrent elections for the 93-member National Assembly, the PLC won 47 seats (53.2%), the FSLN 43 (42.1%) and the PCN two (2.1%).

International relations and defence: Nicaragua is a member of the United Nations, the **Organization of American States**, the **Central American Integration System**, and the **Rio Pact**. In 2002 the armed forces had a total strength of some 14,000. Conscription, introduced in 1983, was abolished in 1990.

Nicaragua, economy

Nicaragua's typical export economy has been devastated by the combined effects of the US-sponsored insurgency, economic sanctions and mismanagement. In 1996 its debt was equivalent to some 800% of GNI and, despite some recent improvement, Nicaragua remains a heavily indebted poor country, the second poorest in the Americas.

GNI at PPP: US $12,500m. (1999); *GNI per caput at PPP:* $2,650 (1999); *exports:* $596.3m. (2002); *imports:* $1,795.5m. (2002); *currency:* (gold) córdoba, plural córdobas; US $1 = 15.03 córdobas at 31 May 2003.

In 1998 agriculture accounted for 34% of Nicaragua's gross domestic product (GDP), industry for 22% and services for 44%. Some 14.9% of the land is arable, 1.8% under permanent crops and 37.0% permanent pasture. Forestry had been so heavily exploited by 1996 that further logging concessions were banned. The main cash crops are **coffee**, **cotton**, **sugar**, **bananas** and sesame. Beef and veal production, formerly a significant source of export revenue, has yet to recover. The main mineral resources are gold, silver, salt and marble. The principal industries are food processing, cement manufacture and construction. The main energy source is imported petroleum; hydroelectricity supplied 9% of production in 2001 and the Momontombo geothermal plant had been shut down.

Main exports are coffee, meat, lobsters, shrimp and gold. Principal imports are machinery, petroleum and petroleum products and road vehicles and parts. In 2002 the USA was the greatest purchaser of exports, followed by El Salvador and Honduras. The USA was the greatest supplier of imports in that year, followed by Venezuela, Costa Rica, Guatemala and Mexico.

The Sandinista Government of 1979–90 nationalized a number of industries and carried out a substantial land-reform programme, but maintained a mixed economy of which the private sector accounted for more than 50%. The government of **Violeta Barrios de Chamorro** (1990–97) left the land reform substantially intact, but privatized a number of large state farms, settling former *contras* on the land. However, the country remained heavily indebted and compensation was not forthcoming from the USA. The export-oriented economy remained vulnerable to low world prices, labour shortages and crop diseases.

In 1985–1994 GDP declined in real terms by an average of 6.1% per year. Despite the devastation caused by '**Hurricane** Mitch' in October 1998, GDP grew by 4.1% in that year, and by 7.4% in 1999, 5.5% in 2000, and 3.2% in 2001. Growth slowed to 1.1% in 2002. The rate of inflation fell to 7.4% in 2001, when unemployment was officially estimated at 10.7%, though at least one-quarter of the population were either unemployed or underemployed.

Nicaragua, Lake

Lake Nicaragua, from which the country takes its name, is the larger of two lakes on the Pacific side of Nicaragua, the waters of which discharge via the San Juan river into the Caribbean. Covering an area of 8,157 sq km, it is one of the largest freshwater lakes in the world. Since the late 19th century the lake and its river system have been of interest as a possible alternative route to Panama for an interoceanic canal.

Nieuw Front (NF)
New Front, Suriname

Political alliance, f. 1987 as Front voor Demokratie en Ontwikkeling (*Front for Democracy and Development*); adopted present name for the 1991 elections; now includes the Nationale Partij Suriname, the largest party in the coalition, Pertaja Luhur, Surinaamse Partij van de Arbeid and Verenigde Hervormings Partij; it won 33 seats in the National Assembly in the general election of 25 May 2000, and elected Runaldo Ronald Venetiaan as President.

Non-Aligned Movement (NAM)

Movement f. 1961 by a meeting of 25 heads of state and government to link countries wishing to distance themselves from the contemporary East–West divide. Currently has 113 members, whose representatives meet every three years. The 13th triennial conference was held in 2003 in Kuala Lumpur, Malaysia. There is no permanent secretariat.

Address: c/o Permanent Representative of South Africa to the UN, 333 East
Street, 9th Floor, New York, NY 10016, USA
Telephone: (212) 213-5583
Fax: (212) 692-2498
E-mail: webmaster@foreign.gov.za
Internet: www.nam.gov.za

Noriega, Gen. Manuel

Manuel Antonio Noriega Morena, b. 1938, came from a poor Panamanian family.
After training in the Colegio Militar in Peru he entered the Panamanian National
Guard (later the Panamanian Defence Forces) and rose to become chief of national
intelligence, in which capacity he worked closely with the US Central Intelligence
Agency. After the death of Gen. **Omar Torrijos** he succeeded him as commander of
the Defence Forces and, as such, the power behind successive puppet Presidents. On
15 December 1989 he was himself appointed President by Congress, but on
20 December US President George Bush ordered a US intervention force into
Panama. Persuaded to surrender, Noriega was placed on trial in the USA, convicted
of racketeering, drugs-trafficking and money-laundering, and sentenced to 40 years
in prison.

North American Free Trade Agreement (NAFTA)

In January 1988 the USA and Canada signed a Free Trade Agreement. Soon after
the accession of **Carlos Salinas de Gortari** to the presidency of Mexico, in
December of the same year, negotiations were opened for Mexico to join the
Agreement. Negotiations were held between Canada, Mexico and the USA in
February 1992, at which the US and Mexican delegations announced an Integrated
Border Plan, whereby the two Governments would work to clear environmental
damage along their common frontier. These negotiations resulted in the completion
of a draft treaty for a NAFTA. Mexico initialled the Agreement on 12 August 1993
and it was signed on 17 December, coming into effect on 1 January 1994.

There is no central secretariat, the administration of the agreement being shared
between national sections with offices in Ottawa, Washington, DC, and Mexico
City.

Address: Blvd Adolfo López Mateos 3025, 2°, Col. Héroes de Padierna, 10700
México, DF
Telephone: (5) 629-9630

Fax: (5) 629-9637
E-mail: canada/mexico/usa@nafta-sec-alena.org
Internet: www.nafta-sec-alena.org

Nueva Nación (NN)
New Nation, Panama

Political alliance between the Partido Revolucionario Democrático (PRD), Partido Solidaridad, the Partido Liberal Nacional and the Movimiento Papa Egoró, supporting the presidential candidature of Martín Torrijos of the PRD.

O

O Globo

Daily morning newspaper founded in **Rio de Janeiro**, Brazil, in 1925; circulation *c*. 325,000 weekdays, 600,000 Sundays. Now the centrepiece of a vast and influential media empire which includes the popular *Diário de São Paulo* and *TV Rede Globo*.

Leadership: Francisco Graell (Dir)
Address: Rua Irineu Marinho 35, CP 1090, 20233-020 Rio de Janeiro, RJ
Telephone: (21) 2534-5000
Fax: (21) 2534-5510
Internet: oglobo.globo.com

Oranjestad

Oranjestad is the chief town of Aruba, one of the islands of the Netherlands Antilles. It is a port, situated on the west coast of the island, and had a population of 20,700 in mid-2002. It is an important petroleum processing centre, but its main income, and that of the island, comes from tourism.

Organization of American States (OAS)
Organización de los Estados Americanos (OEA)

The Organization of American States is a multi-functional regional organization within the United Nations. Although it originated in a series of meetings to discuss commerce and trade, its purpose is to further peace, security, mutual understanding and co-operation among the states of the western hemisphere. With the belated accession of Canada in 1990 and Belize and Guyana in 1992, it had 35 member states, although Cuba, one of the founder members, is excluded and its membership has remained in suspension since 1964.

The OAS is the successor organization to the old Pan American Union. Established by Charter at the Ninth Inter-American Conference held at Bogotá (now **Santafé de Bogotá**, Colombia) in 1948, in 1970 the organization was reconstituted on its present basis by the Protocol of **Buenos Aires**. The General Assembly, which met for its first regular session at **San José**, Costa Rica, in 1971, replaced the Inter-American Conferences and various councils for specific purposes. The annual meeting of the General Assembly, a full-scale conference of foreign ministers, is held in different capitals in rotation, but the headquarters, where the Permanent Council sits and where Meetings of Consultation of Ministers of Foreign Affairs are normally held, is in Washington, DC, USA. The Permanent Council consists of representatives of each of the member states with the rank of Ambassador, the chairmanship rotating among the representatives in alphabetical order every three months. Although the OAS Charter does allow for a role in international peace-keeping in certain circumstances, the countries of the region were also linked by a separate defence treaty, the Inter-American Treaty for Reciprocal Assistance, commonly known as the **Rio Pact**, concluded in 1947 as a continuation of wartime co-operation against the Axis Powers and inevitably dominated by the USA.

For many years the OAS fulfilled a useful role in airing current political issues and, through the work of its related agencies, achieving important, though less specta-cular, gains for Latin American co-operation. Although derided in some quarters at the time, the pressure by the Administration of US President Jimmy Carter (1977–81) for the improvement of human rights had a dramatic effect. It was ultimately to contribute significantly to the restoration of democracy throughout the hemisphere. In 1979 the **Inter-American Court of Human Rights** was established, with its seat in San José. Then, after the Falklands hostilities of 1982, open conflict between the USA and the majority of the Latin American states, both over this issue and over US policy towards Central America, effectively stultified the political work of the OAS.

After the collapse of the USSR and the end of the Cold War, there was a noticeable *rapprochement* between Latin America and the USA, which was increasingly seen as a model both of democratic government and economic liberal-ism. This was accompanied by dramatic moves towards closer economic integration in the region. Upon taking office in September 1994, the newly elected Secretary-General of the OAS, former President César Gaviria Trujillo of Colombia (who was re-elected for a second term in 1999), immediately announced his support for the creation of a single free-trade zone in the Americas (see **Free Trade Area of the Americas**). The Organization's special role in regional peace-keeping remained primary and, from the end of the 1980s, the notion of collective intervention to maintain democracy was slowly, if reluctantly, accepted.

However, after the US intervention in Panama in 1989, other states were noticeably less willing to accept US action unchallenged. The 26th General Assembly, held in **Panama City** in June 1996, was dominated by opposition to the US Helms-Burton Act, which reinforced the economic blockade of Cuba. A resolution condemning the act was voted against only by the USA. Despite the tensions that remained between the USA and the other states, it was clear that in practice there was a very high level of political co-operation between them, though their opinion of Cuba varied widely. The Inter-American Democratic Charter, adopted at a special session in **Lima**, Peru, on 11–12 September, allowed the Organization, by a vote of two-thirds of the 34 active member states, to exclude from membership any country experiencing 'an unconstitutional interruption of the democratic order or an unconstitutional alteration of the constitutional regime that seriously impairs the democratic order'. The OAS has also been very active in trying to avert potential conflicts in Central America. The main problem in recent years has been that on the undelimited border between Belize and Guatemala, which in 2000 had revived its claims to 12,272 sq km or about one-half of Belize's territory. Tensions between Nicaragua and Honduras also increased after the Nicaraguan government had accused Honduras of breaking the agreement mediated by the OAS in March 2000 to demilitarize their mutual land border. However, a confidence-building agreement was reached and signed in Washington, DC, on 7 June.

At an emergency meeting held in Washington, DC, on 19 September 2001, the Permanent Council of the Organization for the first time invoked the mutual assistance clause of the 1947 Inter-American Treaty of Reciprocal Assistance, the Rio Pact, to form the legal basis for co-operation against the threat posed to one of its members, the USA, as a result of the terrorist attacks carried out on 11 September.

Leadership: César Gaviria Trujillo (Sec.-Gen.), Colombia
Address: 17th St and Constitution Ave, NW, Washington, DC 20006, USA
Telephone: (202) 458-3000
Fax: (202) 458-6319
E-mail: pi@oas.org
Internet: www.oas.org

Organization of Eastern Caribbean States (OECS)

The OECS was founded on 2 July 1981, with the encouragement of the USA, to meet concerns that with apparent Soviet and Cuban interest in the revolution in

Grenada other states in the Lesser Antilles might be threatened. Its membership consists of Antigua and Barbuda, Dominica, Grenada, Montserrat, St Christopher and Nevis, St Lucia, and St Vincent and the Grenadines. In October 1982 a regional defence agreement was concluded by Antigua and Barbuda, Barbados, Dominica, St Lucia and St Vincent and the Grenadines, and this agreement was adhered to by St Christopher and Nevis on 8 February 1984. The British Overseas Territories of Anguilla and the British Virgin Islands are associate members. Its objectives are to promote unity and solidarity among its members, the defence of their sovereignty, the harmonization of their foreign policies, and their economic integration. The supreme organ is the Authority of Heads of Government

Following an appeal for help made on 21 October 1983 by the Governor-General of Grenada, the Prime Minister of which had been killed in a coup, armed contingents from Antigua and Barbuda, Dominica, St Lucia and St Vincent and the Grenadines took part in the military intervention by US and Caribbean combat forces which began on 25 October and eventually resulted in the installation of a new government in Grenada. The last US and Caribbean forces had been withdrawn from Grenada by September 1985.

Leadership: Dr Vaughan Lewis (Dir-Gen.)
Address: POB 179, The Morne, Castries, St Lucia
Telephone: (758) 452-2537
Fax: (758) 453-1628
E-mail: oesec@oecs.org
Internet: www.oecs.org

Organization of Petroleum Exporting Countries (OPEC)

F. 1960 to defend the interests of petroleum exporting nations and to co-ordinate and unify their policies, OPEC seeks to get the best possible return for its members by a system of production quotas. As this inevitably has negative consequences for non-oil developing countries, it also makes loans and grants from the OPEC Fund for International Development to selected developing countries. Member states are Algeria, Indonesia, Iran, Iraq, Kuwait, Libya, Nigeria, Qatar, Saudi Arabia, United Arab Emirates and Venezuela. Since 1998, when prices fell until they were lower, in real terms, than before the first 'oil shock' of 1973, President **Hugo Chávez Frías** of Venezuela has played a leading role in seeking to revive OPEC, with the result that by the beginning of 2004 the guide price for crude had risen above the US $22–$28 per barrel range informally agreed as the norm.

Leadership: Dr Alvaro Silva Calderón (Sec.-Gen.), Venezuela

Address: Obere Donaustrasse 93, 1020 Vienna, Austria
Telephone: (1) 211-12
Fax: (1) 214-98-27
E-mail: prid@opec.org
Internet: www.opec.org
Organization for the Prohibition of Nuclear Weapons in Latin America and the Caribbean
Organismo para la Proscripción de las Armas Nucleares en América Latina (OPANAL)

The Organization was founded in 1967 to oversee the implementation of the 1967 Treaty for the Prohibition of Nuclear Weapons in Latin America (known as the Treaty of Tlatelolco), establishing a nuclear weapon-free zone intended to cover the whole of the western hemisphere south of the USA. At a Conference of the Organization held in August 1992 agreement was reached on terms on which Argentina, Brazil and Chile would accede to the Treaty, which they signed in 1993. All 33 Latin American and Caribbean states have signed the treaty, i.e. Antigua and Barbuda, Argentina, Bahamas, Barbados, Belize, Bolivia, Brazil, Chile, Colombia, Costa Rica, Cuba (in 1995), Dominica, Dominican Republic, Ecuador, El Salvador, Grenada, Guatemala, Guyana, Haiti, Honduras, Jamaica, Mexico, Nicaragua, Panama, Paraguay, Peru, St Christopher and Nevis, St Lucia, St Vincent and the Grenadines, Suriname, Trinidad and Tobago, Uruguay, Venezuela. All have also ratified it with the exception of Cuba.

Leadership: Ambassador Edmundo Vargas Carreño (Sec.-Gen., Chile)
Address: Schiller 326, Piso 5, Col. Chapultepec Morales, Mexico, DF 11570,
          Mexico
Telephone: (55) 5255-2914
Fax: (55) 5255-3748
Internet: www.opanal.org

Organization of Solidarity of the Peoples of Africa, Asia and Latin America (OSPAAAL)
Organización de Solidaridad con los Pueblos de Africa, Asia y América Latina

Organization, f. 1966 at the first Conference of Solidarity of the Peoples of Africa, Asia and Latin America in **Havana**, to co-ordinate movements of national liberation across the three continents; hence its more popular name, the Tricontinental. Claims membership of 56 organizations in 46 countries, but has been largely inactive and isolated since the assertion of Soviet influence in Cuba in 1970. Publishes a quarterly magazine, *Tricontinental.*

Leadership: Juan Carretero Ibáñez (Sec.-Gen.)

Address: Apdo 4224, Calle C No. 670 esq. 29, Vedado, Havana 10400, Cuba

Telephone: (7) 34 915 231 829

Fax: (7) 34 915 211 1736

E-mail: osp@urbs.org

Internet: www.ospaal.org

Ortega, Daniel

José Daniel Ortega Saavedra, b. 1945, La Libertad, Chontales. Ortega was educated in **Managua**, but soon abandoned the law course he had begun in 1962, and was one of the first to join the **Frente Sandinista de Liberación Nacional** (FSLN) which had been formed the previous year. By 1965 he was already one of its leaders. In 1967, when **Anastasio Somoza Debayle** seized power, he was arrested and imprisoned for some seven years. Freed in 1974, he escaped to Cuba but returned to Nicaragua in the following year, arguing successfully for a strategy of insurrection. When the pretext presented itself in 1978, he led the Sandinista uprising against the dictatorship and, once successful, served as head of the provisional government in 1979–84 before being elected as President, in which office he served in 1984–90. The provisional government distributed much of the land that had been taken over by the Somozas and their cronies, and instituted a literacy programme, but was denied funds to rebuild by the USA, which in 1981 sponsored a clandestine insurgent movement against it, the so-called *contras*, which inflicted serious damage on commercial targets. In 1990 Ortega was defeated in his bid for re-election by a conservative coalition led by **Violeta Barrios de Chamorro**. He was renominated in 1996 and fought a third campaign as a moderate in 2001, when, though handicapped by allegations that he had sexually abused his step-daughter, Zoilamérica Narvaez, he defeated two rivals to gain the FSLN presidential nomination for the fourth time. The US Government made its hostility to his election very clear and he was again defeated.

Oviedo, Gen. (retd) Lino César

Lino César Oviedo Silva was appointed Commander-in-Chief of the Paraguayan army by President Juan Carlos Wasmosy in 1993 in return for his political support.

On 22 April 1996, however, the President requested his resignation on account of his open campaign for the leadership of the ruling **Asociación Nacional Republicana—Partido Colorado** (ANR—PC). Oviedo, who had hopes of becoming President in 1998, refused to resign and, with the support of some 5,000 troops, in turn demanded the resignation of the President, who sought asylum in the US embassy. Strengthened by popular demonstrations in his favour and by the support of other regional powers, Wasmosy agreed to a compromise on 24 April, whereby Oviedo would resign his commission in order to be appointed as defence minister. This having been done, however, Congress refused to ratify the appointment, which was withdrawn. The new army commander, Gen. Oscar Díaz Delmas, did not intervene and three days later the President's former rival, Luís María Argaña, was elected leader of the ANR—PC. A vigorous purge of senior military commanders followed. On 13 June Gen. Oviedo was arrested and imprisoned on the orders of the Attorney-General, Aníbal Babrera. The order aroused unrest in the army and Oviedo was subsequently cleared of charges of insurrection by the appeals court on 7 August and freed.

It was Oviedo who won the presidential nomination of the ANR—PC in a primary election, held in September 1997, in which he obtained 36.75% of the vote compared with the 34.97% cast in favour of Argaña. Gen. Oviedo lost no time in attacking President Wasmosy for alleged corruption and, having eluded capture when the President ordered him to be placed under 'disciplinary arrest', continued to denounce the President while in hiding. On 9 March 1998 the Special Military Court found Oviedo guilty of rebellion and sentenced him to 10 years' imprisonment and dishonourable discharge. The Supreme Court confirmed the decision on 17 April. On the following day Oviedo's candidature was declared void by the Supreme Electoral Tribunal and he was replaced by Raúl Cubas Grau as the ANR—PC's presidential candidate, with Argaña as vice-presidential candidate. Despite protests, the elections were held as planned, and on 10 May Cubas was victorious, receiving 54% of the votes cast. Having taken office, Cubas appointed two Oviedista generals to his Cabinet and commuted Oviedo's sentence to time already served. The new Congress immediately voted to condemn the pardon, and to institute impeachment proceedings against President Cubas. On 2 December, however, the Supreme Court ruled the vote to be unconstitutional.

On 23 March 1999 Vice-President Luís María Argaña Ferraro was assassinated in the streets of the capital, **Asunción**, when three men in military uniform opened fire on the car in which he was travelling. Tensions had been running high and the 66-year old Argaña and his supporters had just succeeded in regaining control of the headquarters of the PC, from which they had been expelled on 14 March by supporters of Gen. Oviedo and Cubas. The latter were immediately accused by Argañistas of being at least the 'moral instigators' of the crime and large crowds filled the streets demanding the President's resignation. The President responded by detaining Oviedo, having earlier refused to obey an order of the Supreme Court to do so. On 26 March four people were killed and 60 were injured when snipers fired on crowds holding a vigil outside Congress. Congress had, by then, already initiated impeachment proceedings, and on 28 March, hours before it was due to vote on the critical resolution, President Cubas resigned and fled to Brazil, where he was granted political asylum, while Gen. Oviedo simultaneously sought and was granted asylum in Argentina. Oviedo was subsequently dishonourably discharged from the army.

On 18 May 2000 three people were wounded in an attempted coup staged by Oviedo's supporters within the First Cavalry Division. The coup failed as, under pressure from Brazil and the USA, the command of the armed forces resumed control. Oviedo himself was arrested in Brazil on 11 June but was not extradited.

In March 2002 a faction of the ANC—PC seceded to form a new organization to support Oviedo's candidature for the 2003 presidential elections and his supporters were responsible for the second of several attempts to impeach the President in the following month. They failed, however, to gain the necessary two-thirds' majority in the Chamber of Deputies. Meanwhile, pressure from supporters of both Vice-President Franco and Gen. Oviedo continued, forcing the President to proclaim a state of emergency in July 2002 after two people had been killed in clashes with police in Ciudad del Este. A final Oviedista-backed attempt to impeach the President failed on 11 February 2003. The resolution to approve the charges was carried by 25 votes to 18 in the Senate, with one abstention and one absence, thus falling short of the two-thirds' majority constitutionally required. After that, elections took place without incident on 27 April 2003, in which the ruling ANR—PC retained power.

P

Panama
República de Panamá

Panama is situated at the narrowest point of the Central American isthmus. It is bounded on the north by the Caribbean Sea, on the west by Costa Rica, on the south by the Pacific Ocean and on the south-east by Colombia, from which it is separated by the low-lying marshy territory of Darién, which covers about one-third of the Republic.

Area: 75,517 sq km; *capital:* **Panama City**; *population:* 2,897,000 (2001 estimate), mainly mestizo with significant proportions of African (*c.* 15%) and European (*c.* 10%) descent; *official language:* Spanish; *religion:* Christian (Roman Catholic 80%, Protestant 15%), Muslim 5%.

Constitution: Panama is a presidential republic. The President is chief executive and is elected by direct popular vote for a five-year term. An appointed Cabinet assists the President. The legislature, the National Assembly, is also popularly elected for a five-year term.

History: Before 1903 Panama was a province of Colombia. However, the USA wished to construct an inter-oceanic canal across its territory and in 1903 a spontaneous revolution broke out in the territory. While US warships prevented Colombia from reinforcing its troops, independence was proclaimed and within days the provisional government had signed away the rights to the canal route. Construction began in 1904, the year in which Constitutional rule was established in Panama under Manuel Amador Guerrero. However, the USA intervened in 1908, 1912 and 1916 to guarantee the outcome of the presidential elections held in those years. Meanwhile, the choice of Pablo Arosemena (President 1910–12) established a tradition of dynastic succession which has lasted ever since.

In the 1920s there was a massive influx of US investment into Panama. Growing unrest led to the defeat of the Conservatives in 1928 by a rival sector of the élite, the Liberals, led by Florencio Harmodio Arosemena. After 1941, when Arnulfo Arias was deposed by a military coup, Panama remained closely aligned with the USA, and its small élite became extremely rich. Not only was it able to negotiate better terms for the use of the Canal, but it also came, on paper, to have the largest merchant navy in the world. Arias was re-elected in 1949, but was deposed in 1953 by the commander of the police, José Antonio Remón, who in 1953 renamed the police the National Guard.

In 1968 the usual pattern of political affairs was interrupted when Brig.-Gen. **Omar Torrijos Herrera** ousted Arias, who had just been elected for the fourth time. Torrijos closed the National Assembly and banned all political parties, after which he ruled Panama from behind the scenes through a succession of puppet Presidents. The Banking Act of 1970 established the country's pre-eminent position as an offshore banking centre. In 1975 Panama joined the **Non-Aligned Movement** and in 1977 successfully negotiated the Panama Canal Treaties with the Carter Administration of the USA. After the death of Torrijos in 1981, Gen. **Manuel Antonio Noriega Morena** emerged as the most powerful figure in the country, making and unmaking Presidents until the US intervention in 1989.

Latest elections: In presidential elections held on 2 May 2004 Martín Torrijos (Patria Nueva), son of **Omar Torrijos Herrera**, was elected with 47.44% of the votes cast. Former President Guillermo Endara Gallimany (Solidaridad) came second with 30.86% of the vote, and the candidate of the ruling party, José Miguel Alemán (Visión de País), third with 16.39% of the vote.

International relations and defence: Panama is a member of the United Nations, the **Organization of American States**, the **Central American Integration System**, the **Caribbean Community and Common Market** and the **Rio Pact**. In 1990 the armed forces were disbanded and replaced by a Public Force, essentially the 11,000-strong national police force with naval and air units. The USA continues to maintain a garrison of some 14,000 troops in the Canal area (part of the former Canal Zone) at the invitation of the Panamanian government.

Panama, economy

GNI: US $9.5m. (2001); *GNI per caput:* $3,260 (2001); *GNI at PPP:* $16m. (2001); *GNI per caput at PPP:* $5,440 (2001), rank 104; *exports:* $809.5m. (2001); *imports:* $2,964m. (2001); *currency:* balboa, plural balboas; US $1 = B1.

In 2001 agriculture accounted for 6.8% of Panama's gross domestic product (GDP), mining for 0.2% and industry for 7.5%. Some 7.2% of the land is arable, 1.9% under permanent crops and 20.3% permanent pasture. The main export crops are **bananas**, **sugar** cane and **coffee**. The small livestock sector was expanded in the

1990s as part of a diversification programme. Fish resources are extensively exploited, Pamana being the world's third largest exporter of shrimp. Despite substantial known reserves of **copper**, plans to develop them were postponed in 1997 owing to low world prices. Deposits of gold, silver and coal have not been developed. The principal industries are agricultural processing, food and beverages, clothing and household materials. The main energy source is hydroelectric power. Panama is wholly dependent on imported petroleum.

Main exports are bananas, fish and shrimp. Principal imports are petroleum and petroleum products, electric and electronic equipment, road vehicles and transport equipment. In 2000 the USA was the greatest purchaser of exports, followed by Sweden, Costa Rica and Honduras. The USA was the greatest supplier of imports in that year, followed by Ecuador, Venezuela and Japan.

Since 1985 the Panamanian economy has been continually monitored by the **International Monetary Fund**. In 1987 it lost a major source of income when the transit of Alaskan crude oil ceased after the completion of a pipeline across the USA. Panama has the largest ship register in the world, but earnings have not recovered fully from the US boycott of the late 1980s. In order to balance its trading account, the country remains heavily dependent on offshore banking, ship registration, canal fees and the profits from the **Colón Free Zone**, the second largest free zone in the world. However, the fiscal deficit has constantly exceeded expectations. Annual GDP growth declined sharply in the early 1990s, but recovered somewhat towards the end of that decade. Growth in 2001, however, was only 0.3% and in 2002 1.5%. Officially unemployment in August 2001 stood at 15.9%.

Panama Canal

The former Canal Zone was incorporated into Panama on 1 October 1979. Since 31 December 1999, the Canal has been administered by an 11-member Panama Canal Authority (*Autoridad del Canal de Panamá*) as a commercial enterprise, and in 2000 a five-year programme of modernization was announced, including widening the Culebra Cut and dredging certain other sections. A number of countries protested at the decision to raise tolls substantially in October 2002.

Panama City
Panamá

Principal town and capital of the Republic of Panama, with a population of 463,093 at the 2000 census

Paraguay
República del Paraguay

Paraguay is one of only two landlocked countries in South America and the only one that has been landlocked since independence. Forty per cent of its territory, where the majority of the population lives, lies on the east bank of the Paraguay River, which gives it access to the sea by way of the Paraná river and the Río de la Plata estuary. Sixty per cent, the semi-arid, infertile and sparsely populated Chaco Boreal (Northern Chaco), stretches westwards from the west bank of the Paraguay to the foothills of the Andes. It is bordered on the north-west by Bolivia, on the north-east and east by Brazil, and on the east, south and south-west by Argentina.

Area: 406,752 sq km (157,048 sq miles); *capital:* **Asunción**; *population:* 5,206,101 (2002 census), 95% of mestizo descent; *official languages:* Guaraní, Spanish; *religion:* preponderantly Roman Catholic, Mennonite in the Chaco.

Constitution: Under the 1992 Constitution, which curtailed his previously extensive powers, executive power is vested in the President, who is directly elected by simple plurality for a non-renewable five-year term and who governs with the assistance of the Council of Ministers, which he appoints. Legislative authority is vested in the bicameral National Congress, consisting of a 45-member Senate and an 80-member Chamber of Deputies, directly elected by proportional representation for five-year terms. Voting is compulsory for all men and women of 18 years of age and older. Women have been able to vote since 1958.

History: Paraguay was one of the last parts of South America to come under Spanish control. Early settlers from the Río de la Plata found no gold or silver there and it was left to Jesuit missionaries to explore it and to convert the Guaraní inhabitants to Christianity. It was the first country in Spanish America successfully to declare independence in 1811, and by 1813 it had come under the paternalist rule of Dr José Rodríguez de Francia, who cut off the country from the outside world until his death in 1842. His successor, Carlos Antonio López, opened it up again. His son, Francisco Solano López succeeded him, only to lead his country to disaster. By insisting in leading his forces across Argentine territory to attack Brazil, he found himself at war simultaneously with Argentina, Brazil and Uruguay. In the six years of war known in Paraguay as the 'National Epic' and more widely as the War of the Triple Alliance (1865–70), Paraguay lost 90% of its male population and was forced to cede large tracts of territory to Argentina and Brazil.

In the wake of the defeat the Liberals came to power and wrote a Constitution, but this was soon swept aside by the armed forces. In 1904, after a series of military coups and a brief civil war the Liberals returned to power. The army, however, continued to intervene regularly to displace governments, until the election, in 1920, of the first of the two Ayala brothers who were to dominate Paraguayan politics for more than a decade, and to nominate their successor, José Guggiari (President 1938–31). It was in his time that Paraguayan forces first came into contact with Bolivian troops in the disputed area of the Chaco Boreal. In the war that followed, Paraguayan forces successfully drove Bolivian troops back to the foothills of the Andes, but were unable to capture the oilfields that lay beyond. A three-year period of military rule, albeit by reformist officers, followed the 1932–37 Chaco War with Bolivia. A new Constitution introduced in 1940 failed to bring about needed changes and, after a succession of unstable governments, **Gen. Alfredo Stroessner Mattiauda** took power in a military coup in 1954.

During Stroessner's 35-year rule (the *stronato*) Paraguay was under a permanent state of siege and all constitutional rights and civil liberties were suspended. The country's economic and political structure was nonetheless stabilized and its infrastructure greatly modernized. Stroessner was declared the winner of all eight elections, which were held at five-year intervals. He was overthrown on 3 February 1989, in a 'palace coup' led by his son-in-law, Gen. Andrés Rodríguez, who was sworn in immediately as interim President. The subsequent presidential and congressional elections on 1 May 1989, in which Rodríguez and the **Asociación Nacional Republicana—Partido Colorado** (ANR—PC) won a sweeping victory, were considered to have been relatively free and open by international observers. Election to membership of the Group of Rio in October 1990 and entry in March 1991 into the **Southern Common Market** (Mercosur), with Argentina, Brazil and Uruguay, did much to restore the country's international credibility. The ANR—PC has remained the leading party since the restoration of democratic institutions, with the **Partido Liberal Radical Auténtico** (PLRA), the principal party of opposition.

Latest elections: Presidential and legislative elections were held in May 1998, with the PLRA and Encuentro Nacional (EN, now Partido Encuentro Nacional) contesting them as the Alianza Democrática. The contest for the Chamber of Deputies resulted in the ANR—PC taking 45 seats, the PLRA 27 and EN 8. In the Senate contest the ANR—PC took 24 seats, the PLRA 13, the EN seven and the Partido Blanco one. In the concurrent presidential elections Raúl Alberto Cubas Grau (ANR—PC) received 55.4% of the votes cast, defeating Domingo Laíno (PLRA-EN) who obtained 43.9%. Following the assassination of his Vice-President, Luís María Argaña, however, in which he was widely regarded as having been implicated, Cubas fled the country in March 1999. He was succeeded as President by the President of the Senate, Luís González Macchi, and a special election was held on 13 August 2000 in order to choose a new Vice-President. In elections held on 27 April 2003 Óscar Nicanor Duarte Frutos (ANR—PC) obtained 37.1% of the vote and was elected President for the term 2003–08. In concurrent congressional elections the ANR—PC remained the largest party with 16 seats (out of 45) in the Senate and 37 (out of 80) in the Chamber of Deputies.

International relations and defence: Paraguay is a member of the United Nations, the **Organization of American States**, the **Latin American Integration Association**, the Mercosur, and the **Rio Pact**. In 2002 the army numbered 14,900 of which the great majority were conscripts. The navy numbered 2,000 and the air force 1,700. Military service, for one year in the army or two in the navy, is compulsory for all adult males.

Paraguay, economy

GNI: US \$7.6m. (2001); *GNI per caput:* \$1,350 (2001); *GNI at PPP:* \$29m. (2001); *GNI per caput at PPP:* \$5,180 (2001), rank 106; *exports:* \$870.9m. (2000); *imports:* \$2,193.0m. (2000); *currency:* guaraní (G), plural guaranies; US \$1 = G6,373.8 at 31 May 2003.

In 2001 agriculture accounted for 23.6% of Paraguay's gross domestic product (GDP), industry (including mining, manufacture, construction and power) for 25.6% and services for 50.8%. Some 7.4% of the land is arable, 0.2% under permanent crops and 53.3% permanent pasture. The main crops are soya beans, **cotton** and **sugar** cane. Cattle (9.9m. head in 2002) are raised for export, but beef exports were disrupted in 2000 by local outbreaks of foot-and-mouth disease. Mineral resources are limited; limestone is exploited (for local use), but deposits of **bauxite**, **copper**, iron ore and manganese are not. The principal industry is agricultural reprocessing, including the manufacture of food and beverages. Paraguay has abundant hydroelectric power and sells the surplus output of the Itaipú Dam to Brazil. All petroleum has to be imported.

Main exports are soya beans, food and live animals, basic manufactures and raw cotton. Principal imports are foodstuffs, raw materials, fuels and lubricants and tobacco. In 2002 Brazil was the greatest purchaser of exports, followed by Uruguay, Argentina, the Netherlands and Chile. Argentina and Brazil were the greatest suppliers of imports in that year, followed by the USA.

Paraguay is still a predominantly agricultural country, but no attempt at land reform has taken place and much is inefficiently exploited. The country's position means that smuggling is a major economic activity and Paraguay's informal economy is believed to be as extensive as its formal one. In 1995 a major banking scandal occurred which had a negative impact on the economy, and from 1997 the economy was in recession from which it is now only slowly recovering. With a low tax take and widespread tax evasion the fiscal deficit was expected to exceed 3% in 2003, but Paraguay is not heavily indebted, debt standing at 39.2% of GNI in 2001. After the 1997 crisis, GDP contracted slightly each year from 1998 to 2000. The 2001 GDP growth rate was 2.7%, but the inflation rate of 10.5% in 2002 was only slightly lower than in previous years.

Paramaribo

Port city and capital of Suriname, situated on a shingle bank on the edge of the Caribbean. Originally founded by the French, it was captured by Britain and transferred to Dutch rule in 1667. It retains much of its old Dutch colonial architecture. In January 2000 the city's inhabitants numbered 224,218.

Partido Acción Ciudadana (PAC)
Citizen Action Party, Costa Rica

Centre party f. 2000 as vehicle for the election of its leader.
Leadership: Otton Solís (Leader)
Address: Sede San José en San Pedro de Montes de Oca, de ferreterias el Mar 200
m Sur 25 m Este y 350 m Sur
Telephone: 281-2727
Fax: 280-6640
E-mail: accionciudadana@amnet.co.cr
Internet: www.pac.or.cr

Partido Acción Nacional (PAN)
National Action Party, Mexico

F. 1939 as a right-wing Catholic party. Having repositioned itself as a Christian Democratic party, after the introduction of a degree of proportional representation in the 1960s the PAN began to gain enough votes nationally to win seats in the Chamber of Deputies. It was not until the 1980s, however, that it won control of a state for the first time and emerged as the only effective opposition to the ruling **Partido Revolucionario Institucional**.
Leadership: **Vicente Fox Quesada** (Leader, President of the Republic); Luis Felipe Bravo Mena (Pres.); Manuel Espino Barrientos (Sec.-Gen.)

Address: Avda Coyocán 1546, Col. del Valle, México, DF
Telephone: (55) 5200-4000
E-mail: correo@cen.pan.org.mx
Internet: www.pan.org.mx

Partido de Avanzada Nacional (PAN)
Party of National Advancement, Guatemala

Party dedicated to advancing the interests of private enterprise, the PAN won the presidency in 1995/96 under the leadership of a businessman, Alvaro Enrique Arzú Irigoyen, who had previously served as mayor of the national capital and presided successfully over the conclusion of the peace agreement which ended more than 30 years of armed conflict. Oscar Berger Perdomo, the party's presidential candidate in 1999, however, was decisively beaten and subsequently left the party.

Leadership: Alvaro Enrique Arzú Irigoyen (Leader)
Address: 7a Avda 10–38, Zona 9, Guatemala City
Telephone: 334-1702
Fax: 331-9906
Internet: www.pan.org.gt

Partido Colorado (PC)
Colorado (Red) Party, Uruguay

The PC has dominated Uruguayan politics throughout most of the country's history. One of Uruguay's two traditional parties, it is a broad-based, inclusive, centrist political force. It is composed of different organized factions with their own leaders, which compete among themselves. The Colorados emerged from the 1836–48 civil war and were named after the red flag of one of the warring factions. The party first came to power in 1865 and governed Uruguay uninterruptedly for 93 years. In the early 20th century its leader and two-term President, **José Batlle y Ordóñez** (1903–07 and 1911–15), introduced a wide-ranging social welfare system. Thereafter, *Batllismo,* as the party's dominant strand came to be known, became associated with welfarism and industrial development. Having lost a national election for the first time in the 20th century in 1958, the Colorados regained power in the 1966 elections and won again in 1971. In 1973, however, the constitutional government was deposed by the military, which then ruled the country for over a decade.

The November 1984 election, which marked the end of military rule, was won by the PC and the leader of its largest faction 'Unity and Reform', Julio María Sanguinetti, became the country's President. Sanguinetti's most controversial policy was the *caducidad* ('no punishment') law, granting immunity from prosecution to military and police officers accused of gross human rights violations during the period of military rule in 1973–85. Although widely opposed, mollification of the military was uppermost in the government's mind and the amnesty law was passed by Congress in December 1986 with the assistance of the **Partido Nacional (Blancos)**.

The Colorados lost the November 1989 elections to the Blancos but won the subsequent 1994 (Sanguinetti) and 1999 (**Jorge Batlle Ibáñez**) presidental elections. However, the party failed to gain a congressional majority of its own in both elections, forcing it to forge a coalition with the Blancos. The party is divided between a neo-liberal faction headed by President Batlle and a social-democratic one, led by former President Sanguinetti. The party has 10 senators (plus the Vice-President) and 33 deputies in the 2000–2005 legislature.

Leadership: Julio María Sanguinetti Cairolo *(Foro Batllista* faction, President 1985–90 and 1995–2000); Jorge Batlle Ibáñez (*1999 Battlismo Radical* faction, President of the Republic 2000–2005)

Address: Andrés Martínez Trueba 1271, Montevideo

Telephone: (2) 4090180

Internet: www.partido-colorado.org

Partido Comunista de Chile (PCCh)
Chilean Communist Party

Legalized in 1990.

Leadership: Gladys Marín Millie (Leader)

Address: Avda Vicuña Mackenna 31, Santiago

Telephone and fax: (2) 695-4791

Fax: (2) 695-1150

E-mail: www@pcchile.cl

Internet: www.pcchile.cl

Partido Comunista de Cuba (PCC)
Cuban Communist Party

Before the Revolution of 1959 the Cuban Communist Party operated legally and had representation in Batista's Congress as the Partido Socialista Popular (PSP).

The present party was founded in 1961 through the amalgamation of the PSP with **Fidel Castro**'s Movimiento 26 de Julio and the Directorio Revolucionario 13 de Marzo as the Organizaciones Revolucionarias Integradas (ORI). In 1962 ORI was renamed the Partido Unido de la Revolución Socialista Cubana, which assumed its present title in 1965. In the mid-1970s locally elected People's Power committees were constituted, electing representatives to the National Assembly of People's Power inaugurated in December 1976. Only candidates approved by the Party may stand though competition between approved candidates is permitted. The Party, which has more than 700,000 members, is directed by a Political Bureau of 24 members and a Central Committee of 150 members.

Leadership: Dr Fidel Castro Ruz
E-mail: root@epol.cipcc.inf.cu
Internet: www.pcc.cu

Partido Conservador Colombiano (PCC)
Colombian Conservative Party

Founded in 1849, the Conservatives dominated 19th century Colombian politics, until their hold was broken in the War of a Thousand Days. Unlike most other parties of the period, it is still one of the two main parties in Colombia and claims nearly three million members. Though the rival **Partido Liberal Colombiano** (PL) has dominated politics since 1958, for 16 years, from 1958 to 1974, the two parties shared power, alternating in the presidency. In 1982 a Liberal split enabled the moderate wing of the party under **Belisario Betancur Cuartas** (President 1982–86) to gain power. The alleged association between later Liberal presidents and drugs interests enabled Alvaro Uribe Velez, running as candidate of the right-wing Colombia First coalition, to secure an unprecedented outright win in the first round of the presidential elections of 2002.

Leadership: Humberto Zululaga Monedero (Sec.-Gen.)
Address: Avda 22, No. 37–09, Santafé de Bogotá
Telephone: (1) 369-0011
Fax: (1) 369-0187
Internet: www.conservatismocolombiano.org

Partido Demócrata Cristiano (PDC)
Christian Democratic Party, Chile

Leadership: Adolfo Zaldívar (Pres.)

Address: Alameda B. O'Higgins 1460, 2°, Santiago
Telephone: (2) 757-4400
Fax: (2) 757-4400
E-mail: info@pdc.cl
Internet: www.pdc.cl

Partido da Frente Liberal (PFL)
Liberal Front Party, Brazil

F. 1984 by moderate members of the PDS and the **Partido do Movimento Democrático Brasileiro**.

Leadership: Jorge Bornhausen (Pres.)
Address: Câmara dos Deputados, 70160-900, Brasília, DF
Telephone: 311-4305
Fax: 224-1912
E-mail: pfl25@pfl.org.br
Internet: www.pfl.org.br

Partido Guatemalteco del Trabajo (PGT)
Guatemalan Workers Party

Originated as the Partido Comunista Guatemalteco, f. 1923 and banned until after the Second World War. The party was revived in 1949 by José Manuel Fortuny and was legalized in 1951, under the presidency of Jacobo Arbenz, assuming its present name in 1952. At the fall of Arbenz it was immediately banned. In 1962 a section took up armed struggle in alliance with the **Fuerzas Armadas Revolucionarias**, led by Víctor Manuel Gutiérrez, who disappeared in 1966 after he and some 20 others had been arrested. However, several groups survived and in 1981 the largest joined **Unidad Nacional Revolucionaria Guatemalteca**; this faction now known as PGT-Camarilla. The other factions are PGT-Núcleo de Conducción y Dirección and PGT-Comisión Nuclear.

Leadership: Ricardo Rosales (also known as 'Carlos González')

Partido Justicialista (PJ-Peronist)
Justicialist Party, Argentina (Peronists)

Founded in 1945, the PJ is populist in outlook, encompassing groups from the far right to the far left. Formerly the Movimiento Nacionalista Justicialista, the PJ grew out of the nationalist *Peronista* movement led by Lt-Gen. **Juan Domingo Perón Sosa** during his 1946–55 presidency. Perón returned to power in 1973 after he was deposed by a military coup in 1955, but died in the following year and was succeeded by the Vice-President, his wife María Estela ('Isabel') Martínez de Perón, whose Government was overthrown by the armed forces in March 1976.

In the October 1983 elections which followed the Falklands/Malvinas war and the collapse of the military regime, the Peronists lost to the **Unión Cívica Radical** (UCR) in both the presidential and congressional elections, but beat the UCR in the provincial governorship elections. The party, with Isabel Perón as its figurehead, obtained 40.5% of the vote, which translated into 111 seats in Congress, while its presidential candidate—Italo Luder—came second (with 40.2% of the vote) to Raul Alfonsín Foulkes of the UCR. This defeat resulted in a long period of internal turmoil which split the Peronist movement into two main rival factions with parallel leaderships: the right-wing *oficialistas* (official wing) and the *renovadores* (reno-vator wing). A party congress in July 1985, intended to reunite the party, resulted in an *oficialista* takeover of the party machinery. All *oficialista* candidates were confirmed for the forthcoming congressional elections because of a boycott by the left wing, which subsequently put forward alternative candidates under the name of the *Frente Renovador* (Renovation Front), led by Antonio Cafiero. Neither the official PJ, which fought the election as the leading party in the FREJULI alliance, nor the Renovation Front did well, overall PJ representation in the congress being reduced by 10 seats.

Despite further splits within the two factions in 1986, which produced four distinct PJ blocs in Congress, the Peronists began to gain in popularity. Benefiting from widespread discontent with the UCR Government's austerity measures and its lenient treatment of the army, the PJ won the highest number of votes (41.5%) in the September 1987 congressional elections and narrowed the gap between the PJ and UCR representation in Congress. As well as increasing their congressional seats to 105, the PJ won 16 provincial governorships, including that of the crucial province of **Buenos Aires**. With the general election of 1989 in view, the PJ regrouped. Isabel Perón was finally replaced as the party's president and a leadership comprising *oficialistas, renovadores* and the Federalism and Liberation faction, linked to **Carlos Saúl Menem**, was elected. Small left-wing and right-wing factions were ignored and Herminio Iglesias' right-wing group, which had contested the elections separately as the October 17 Party, was expelled in December 1987.

The modern PJ emerged from 1989 when Menem gained the leadership of the party and the nation. The dominant *menemista* faction, promoting a free-market economy and privatization, moved the party sharply to the right. Menem took office in July 1989 and struggled with a fundamentally destabilized economy with policies as diverse as rationing, an expansion of the state privatization programme, and large reductions in the workforce of the state iron and steel plants. Although Menem largely continued his UCR predecessor's policy of leniency towards the military, measures such as an amnesty for crimes perpetrated during the so-called '**Dirty war**' of 1976–83 could not prevent increasingly vocal discontent over army low pay and lack of status.

The PJ's electoral performance between 1989 and 1997 was a strong one, and Menem himself overcame a long period of unpopularity in his party for his perceived abandonment of Peronism. In congressional and gubernatorial elections held in August, September, October and December 1991, the PJ increased the number of seats it held in the Chamber of Deputies from 112 to 119, and won the governorships of 14 provinces. The Peronists won the Chamber elections (for 127 seats) in October 1993, increasing their total number of seats to 125; this total was further raised, to 137 seats, in the elections (for 130 seats) of May 1995, when they also took nine of the 14 provincial governorships at stake. The Peronists had won 136 seats in the elections held in April 1994 to the new 305-member Constituent Assembly, which was responsible for drawing up a new constitution.

Menem was re-elected President in May 1995 with 49.8% of the vote and was sworn into office on 8 July together with the majority of the previous Cabinet. In a Senate election for the federal district of Buenos Aires in October 1995, the PJ won only 22.6% of the vote, compared with 45.7% for the centre-left Front for a Country in Solidarity (FREPASO) coalition and 24.3% for the UCR. Nevertheless, the Peronists held power in 14 of the 23 provinces following provincial elections held between July and October 1995.

The party's electoral success came to an end in the October 1997 congressional elections, in which 127 of the 257 seats in the Chamber of Deputies were contested. The PJ secured 36.1% of the popular vote compared with the 45.6% won by the Radical (UCR)-led *Alianza*. The PJ's representation in the Chamber was reduced to 118 seats, compared with the *Alianza*'s 110, leaving the balance of power in the hands of the *Alianza* and smaller parties which collectively held 29 seats. The defeat was ascribed to public concern at rising unemployment and the imposition of orthodox economic policies.

In the presidential election held on 24 October 1999, a decade of Peronist rule was ended when Eduardo Duhalde, the PJ candidate, was defeated by Fernando de la Rúa of the opposition *Alianza*. De la Rúa and his FREPASO running-mate, Carlos 'Chacho' Alvarez, secured 48.5% of the popular vote compared with Duhalde's 38.1%. In simultaneous legislative elections, in which 127 of the 257 seats in the

Chamber of Deputies were at stake, the PJ won 50 seats (with 33.7% of the vote), so that its representation overall declined to 101 seats.

In opposition, the PJ experienced the familiar problem of internal dissension, much of it generated by the wish of former President Menem, whom many blamed for the state of the economy, to justify his past record by securing re-election to a third term. The party's difficulties increased in May 2001 when Menem was subpoenaed by a federal judge to testify in an investigation into the illegal supply of arms to Croatia and Ecuador during his presidency. However, by August the country was in a state of economic crisis so serious that the electorate gave the PJ a working majority in Congress. Consequently, when in December rioting forced President de la Rúa to resign, it was former Vice-President Eduardo Duhalde who was chosen by Congress to serve as interim President. Three factions within the party contested the presidential elections held on 27 April 2003, in which Nestor Carlos Kirchner Ostoic, of the Frente para la Victoria, supported by President Duhalde, narrowly defeated Menem, of the Frente por la Libertad, supported by the libertarian **Unión del Centro Democrático**. A second round of voting was scheduled to be held on 18 May, but when on 14 May polls showed that Kirchner was set to gain some 63% of the expected vote, Menem withdrew, successfully denying his rival the legitimacy of a popular mandate.

The PJ is a member of the International Democrat Union, the Christian Democrat International and the Christian Democrat Organization of America.

Address: Matheu 128, 1082 Buenos Aires

Telephone: (11) 4952-4555

Fax: (11) 4954-2421

E-mail: bpj@hcdn.gov.ar

Internet: www.pj.org.ar

Leadership: Carlos Saúl Menem (Pres.), Rubén Marín (first Vice-Pres.), Carlos Reutemann (second Vice-Pres.), Eduardo Duhalde (President of Argentina 2001–03), Humberto Jesús Roggero (congressional Pres.), Eduardo Bauza (Sec.-Gen.)

Partido de la Liberación Dominicana (PLD)

Party of Dominican Liberation

Moderate left-wing party, f. 1973 by Prof. Juan Bosch when he resigned the leadership of and left the Partido Revolucionario Dominicana. After Bosch's retirement, the PLD candidate, Leonel Fernández, won the presidency in 1996, but lacked a congressional majority.

Leadership: Leonel Fernández Reyna (Leader)
Address: Avda Independencia 401, Santo Domingo, DN
Telephone: 685-3540
Fax: 687-5569
E-mail: pldorg@pld.org.do
Internet: www.pld.org.do

Partido de Liberación Nacional (PLN)
Party of National Liberation, Costa Rica

F. by **José Figueres Ferrer** in 1952, the PLN is a social-democratic party pledged to ongoing social reform. It currently claims to have 500,000 members. It is affiliated to the Socialist International.

Address: Mata Redonda, 125 m Oeste del Ministerio de Agricultura y Ganadería,
      Casa Liberacionista José Figueres Ferrer, Apdo 10.051, 1000 San José
Telephone: 232-5033
Fax: 231-4097
E-mail: palina@sol.racasa.co.cr
Internet: www.pln.org

Partido Liberal de Honduras (PLH)
Liberal Party, Honduras

One of the few 19th-century Liberal parties remaining in Latin America, the PLH was founded in 1891. It dominated politics in Honduras until the rise of Tiburcio Carias Andino (President 1933–1949) and returned to power at the end of military government in 1980 under the presidencies of Roberto Suazo Córdova (1982–86) and José Simón Azcona del Hoyo (1986–90). Since then the **Partido Nacional** (PN) has won four successive elections, though in the congressional elections of 2002 the PLH won 40.8% of the vote and 55 seats, compared with the ruling PN's 46.5% share of the vote and and 61 seats.

Leadership: Carlos Roberto Flores Facussé (Pres.)
Address: Col. Miramonte atrás del Supermercado La Colonia, No. 1, Tegucigalpa
Telephone: 232-0520
Fax: 232-0797

Partido Liberal Colombiano (PL)
Colombian Liberal Party

Colombia's oldest political party, its origins stem from 1815, in the era of independence. Since the Pact of Sitges (1958) the Liberals have dominated Colombian politics. However, under the presidencies of Ernesto Samper Pizano (1994–98) and Andrés Pastrana Arango (1998–2002) civil unrest and poverty reached epidemic proportions and successive rounds of peace talks with guerrilla groups were a total failure. At the 2002 elections the official PL presidential candidate, Horacio Serpa Uribe, received only 31.72% of the vote, and the congressional party subsequently pledged its support to the incoming Conservative President.

Leadership: Luis Fernando Jaramillo (Pres.)
Address: Avda Caracas, No. 36–01, Santafé de Bogotá, DC
Telephone: (1) 287-9311
Fax: (1) 287-9540
Internet: www.partidoliberal.org.co

Partido Liberal Constitucionalista (PLC)
Constitutionalist Liberal Party, Nicaragua

F. 1967, the PLC is the main element in the Alianza Liberal electoral alliance. At the elections of 2001 its candidate, Enrique Bolaños Geyer, won the presidency and the party won 47 of the 90 seats in the single-chamber National Assembly.

Leadership: Dr Leopoldo Navarro Bermúdez (Pres.), Enrique Bolaños Geyer
(Pres. of the Republic).
Address: Semáforos Country Club 100 m al Este, Apdo 4569, Managua
Telephone: (2) 78-8705
Fax: (2) 78-1800
E-mail: plc@ibw.com.ni
Internet: www.plc.org.ni

Partido Liberal Radical (PLR)
Radical Liberal Party, Ecuador

The PLR was founded in 1895 as the Partido Liberal, and was the ruling party in Ecuador until 1944. The present PLR regards itself as the direct heir of the 19th century liberal tradition, but support for it is negligible.

Leadership: Carlos Julio Plaza A.

Partido Liberal Radical Auténtico (PLRA)
Authentic Radical Liberal Party, Paraguay

This centrist party is the descendant of the Partido Liberal (PL), founded in 1887, which dominated Paraguayan politics from 1904 until 1936. It was founded in 1978 by Domingo Laíno, and has been the second party in Paraguayan politics since that time. The party was a founder member of the Acuerdo Nacional, a coalition of four opposition parties which pressed for democratization and respect for human rights under the **Stroessner** regime. The PLRA was denied legal status, boycotted all elections and organized anti-government rallies.

The PLRA was legalized on 8 March 1989, one month after the military coup that overthrew Stroessner. In elections held in May 1989 Laíno stood as the PLRA presidential candidate and the party came second in both the presidential and the congressional polls, although its share of the vote was far smaller than that of the ruling **Asociación Nacional Republicana—Partido Colorado** (ANR—PC). This pattern was repeated in the 1991 Constituent Assembly elections and the 1993 and 1998 elections. In 1998, the party, running in alliance with Encuentro Nacional (EN), won 27 seats in the Chamber of Deputies and 13 in the Senate, while Laíno came second, with 43.9% of the vote, in the presidential contest. In the 2000 special vice-presidential election the PLRA candidate, Julio César Franco, won a narrow victory, taking 49.64% of the votes cast to 48.82% for the ANR—PC candidate, Félix Argaña, brother of the assassinated Vice-President. In the 2003 presidential election Franco ran second to the ANR—PC candidate, Oscar Nicanor Duarte Frutos, but remained Vice-President, while the PRLA won 12 seats in the Senate and 21 in the Chamber of Deputies.

The PLRA is a member of the Liberal International.

Leadership: Julio César Ramón ('Yoyito') Franco Gómez (Vice-Pres. of the Republic and party Pres.), Domingo Isabelino Laíno Figueredo (founder and 1998 presidential candidate)

Address: Mariscal López 435, 1750 Asunción
Telephone: (21) 24-4867
Fax: (21) 20-4867
E-mail: plra@quanta.com.py
Internet: www.plra.org.py

Partido do Movimento Democrático Brasileiro (PMDB)
Party of the Brazilian Democratic Movement

The Movimento Democrático Brasileiro (MDB) was originally established by the armed forces in 1965 and was intended to act as a safe official opposition to the ruling Aliança Renovadora Nacional which maintained its majority in Congress until 1979. In that year MDB victories in the local elections obliged the armed forces to accept a more rapid transition to democracy and the MDB assumed its present name. In February 1982 elements of the former MDB led by Dr Tancredo Neves formed the Partido Popular, but rejoined the PMDB when the armed forces prohibited electoral alliances. Neves was elected governor of Minas Gerais and was a major figure in the campaign for direct elections (*diretas-já*), but resigned in 1984 to campaign successfully for the presidency under the indirect system. After his untimely death the PMDB remained a member of the Aliança Democrática under **José Sarney**.

Leadership: Michel Temer (Pres.)
Address: Câmara dos Deputados, Edif. Principal, 70160-900 Brasília, DF
Telephone: (610) 318-5120
E-mail: pmdb@pmdb.org.br
Internet: www.pmdb.org.br

Partido Nacional (PN)
National Party, Honduras

The PN was founded in 1902 as a conservative party to oppose the previously dominant Liberals. They came to power for the first time with the election of Gen. Tiburcio Carías Andino in 1932 and held on to it by irregular methods until displaced in 1957. A further brief period of rule in 1971–72 was terminated by military intervention. Though the PN remains predominantly conservative, there are a variety of tendencies within it. In the 2001 elections its presidential candidate, Ricardo Maduro, was successful and in concurrent elections to the National Assembly it won 61 of the 128 seats, the first time that it had obtained a plurality since the restoration of civil government in 1980.

Leadership: Carlos Urbizo (Pres.)
Address: Paseo el Obelisco, Comayagüela, Tegucigalpa
Telephone: 237-7310
Fax: 232-0797

Partido Nacional (Blanco)
National Party (*Whites*), Uruguay

Like Uruguay's other traditional party, the **Partido Colorado**, the Partido Nacional is an inclusive, centrist party composed of several organized factions. Deriving their name from the white flag of one of the factions in the 1836–48 civil war, the Blancos were founded by an alliance of rural chieftains (*caudillos*) and urban élites. With a mainly rural base of support, the Partido Nacional was for a long time the permanent opposition party to the ruling Colorados and only fully turned to parliamentary politics after an unsuccessful uprising in 1904. The party did not win national power in the 20th century until 1958, when it obtained six of the nine seats on the then collective executive, the National Governing Council. It retained a majority in this collective executive in the elections of 1962. However, in 1966, when the presidential system was reinstated, the party lost the elections to the Colorados. In the 1970s the Partido Nacional began a process of renewal and adopted a left-of-centre programme that appealed to a more modern, urban constituency. Its leader, Wilson Ferreira Aldunate, won the most votes of any single candidate in the 1971 presidential elections, but lost the election under the aggregate party vote system. He was forced into exile after the 1973 military coup. Other reformist party members who remained in the country suffered persecution and imprisonment. Ferreira Aldunate was imprisoned by the military for six months to prevent him from contesting the presidency in the 1984 elections, but he none-theless acknowledged the legitimacy of the victory of the Colorado candidate, Julio María Sanguinetti, and gave congressional support to his administration. He seemed certain to be the party's presidential candidate in 1989, but died of cancer before the election took place.

For the presidential elections of November 1989, the party selected **Luís Alberto Lacalle Herrera**, representing the neo-liberal right wing, as its candidate. Lacalle won the election, though he received only 37% of the vote. The Lacalle Government's programme of economic liberalization and austerity measures met with sustained opposition not only from the Inter-Union Workers' Assembly-Workers' National Convention labour confederation, which staged numerous general strikes between 1990 and 1992, but also from sections of the Partido Colorado and even a faction of the Blancos.

In the 1994 elections the Blancos lost power to the Colorados. Lacalle was again the party's presidential candidate in 1999, but he fared poorly, coming a distant third to the Frente Amplio (FA) and Colorado candidates. He supported the Partido Colorado candidate Jorge Batlle in the run-off presidential election. In 1999 the party's electoral performance was its worst ever: it received only 22% of the national vote and, as a result, held only 22 seats in the Chamber and seven in the Senate, fewer than both the Encuentro Progresista-FA alliance and the Colorados. Since 1995 the Blancos have served in governing coalitions with the ruling Colorados.

Leadership: Luis Alberto Lacalle Herrera (*Herrerista* faction; Pres. of the party's directorate, Pres. of the Republic 1990–95, presidential candidate 1999), Juan Andrés Ramírez (Leader, *Desafío Nacional* faction), Alberto Zumarán (Sec.-Gen.)
Address: Juan Carlos Gómez 1384, Montevideo
Telephone: (2) 916–3831
E-mail: partidonacional@partidonacional.com.uy
Internet: www.partidonacional.com.uy

Partido Nuevo Progresista (PNP)
New Progressive Party, Puerto Rico

F. 1987, the PNP favours statehood and has a membership of some 225,000.
Leadership: Leo Díaz Urbino (Pres.), Hugo Pérez (Sec.-Gen.)
Address: POB 1992, Fernández Zuncos Station, San Juan, PR 00910-1992
Telephone: (787) 289-2000
E-mail: susanag@coqui.net
Internet: www.pnp.org

Partido Popular Democrático (PPD)
Popular Democratic Party, Puerto Rico

F. 1938, the PPD is the dominant party in Puerto Rican politics. It has approximately 660,000 registered members and favours maintenance of the territory's present status as a Commonwealth within the American union. In the 2000 territorial elections it won 19 of the Senate's 28 seats and 27 of the 51 seats in the House of Representatives.
Leadership: Sila María Calderon (Pres. and Leader)
Address: 403 Ponce de León Av., POB 5788, Puerta de Tierra, San Juan, PR 00906
E-mail: juanluis@pavanet.net
Internet: www.geocities.com/~ela2000

Partido Renovador Institucional de Acción Nacional (PRIAN)
Institutional Renewal Party of National Action, Ecuador

Right-wing populist party created to support the candidature of Alvaro Noboa Pontón, a wealthy **banana** grower, in the October 2002 presidential elections in

Ecuador. Noboa ran second to Col Lucio Edwin Gutiérrez Borbua in the first round of balloting for the presidency, but was defeated in the second ballot, when he obtained 41.3% of the votes cast.

Leadership: Alvaro Fernando Noboa Pontón (Leader)

Internet: www.prian.org.ec

Partido de la Revolución Democrática (PRD)
Party of the Democratic Revolution, Mexico

Democratic socialist party; f. 1989 by a merger between the Corriente Democrática, formerly a progressive bloc within the **Partido Revolucionario Institucional**, and the Partido Mexicano Socialista. The PRD presented **Cuauhtémoc Cárdenas** (son of former President **Lázaro Cárdenas**) as its candidate at the 1994 and 2000 presidential elections. The party remains strong in the national capital, where Cárdenas was successful in winning the mayoralty at the first direct elections for the post.

Leadership: Leonel Godoy (acting Pres.)

Address: Monterrey 50, Col. Roma, 06700 México, DF

Telephone: (55) 5525-6059

Fax: (55) 5208-7833

Internet: www.prd.org.mx

Partido Revolucionario Dominicano (PRD)
Dominican Revolutionary Party

The Dominican Revolutionary Party, a democratic socialist party affiliated to the Socialist International, was founded covertly in 1939 under the leadership of Juan Bosch to organize opposition to the dictatorship of Rafael Trujillo. After the assassination of Trujillo in 1961, unrest prevailed until elections in December 1962 gave a clear victory to the PRD, and Bosch became President in February 1963. However, accused falsely of being a Communist, he was overthrown in a military coup after only seven months in office. PRD supporters, in alliance with junior military officers, launched a counter-coup on 24 April 1965. Fierce fighting ensued, leading, on the orders of US President Lyndon B. Johnson, to the dispatch of 23,000 US marines to restore order. This intervention had the additional effect, however, of ensuring that the PRD did not return to power, and after the 1966 elections had resulted in the re-election of **Joaquín Balaguer**, the PRD boycotted the elections of 1970 and 1974. Bosch had, however, left the PRD in 1973 and at the 1978 elections the PRD candidate, Silvestre Antonio Guzmán Fernández was elected President. Since that time the PRD has been one of the two majority parties in the Dominican Republic, regaining the presidency most recently in the 2000 elections.

Leadership: Hatuey Decamps (Chair.)
Address: Espaillat 118, Santo Domingo, DN
Telephone: 687-2193
E-mail: prd@partidos.com
Internet: www.prd.partidos.com

Partido Revolucionario Febrerista (PRF)
Febrerista Revolutionary Party, Paraguay

The origins of the Febreristas lie in the military coup of February 1937, led by junior officers keen to bring about reform in Paraguay. The present party, founded in 1951 to advance these reformist ideas, is a social-democratic party and is affiliated to the Socialist International. It failed to secure representation in the April 2003 elections.

Leadership: Carlos María Liubetic (Pres.)
Address: Casa del Pueblo, Manduvira 552, Asunción
Telephone: (21) 49-041
E-mail: partyce@mixmail.com

Partido Revolucionario Institucional (PRI)
Institutional Revolutionary Party, Mexico

F. 1929 by Plutarco Elías Calles as the Partido Nacional Revolucionario (PNR) and funded initially by a precept on the salaries of all government servants, the PNR was an avowedly socialist party dedicated to carrying through the promises of the Mexican Revolution embodied in the Constitution of 1917. In 1933 it enacted a Labour Code which embodied the best practice of its time. **Lázaro Cárdenas** (President 1934–40) wrested control of the party from Calles in 1935 and consolidated its control of the political process. It was reorganized in 1938 as the Partido de la Revolución Mexicana with four sectors: labour, represented by the Confederación de Trabajadores de México, the agrarian sector, represented by the Confederación Nacional de Campesinos, the armed forces, and an amorphous grouping of organizations termed the Popular Sector, dominated by the teachers union and formally organized in 1943 as the Confederación Nacional de Organizaciones Populares (CNOP). In 1945 the party was again reorganized, adopting its present name for the 1946 elections. The armed forces were then absorbed into the CNOP and the new tripartite sectoral structure was established all the way down to district level.

The PRI continued to dominate Mexican politics until the 2000 elections, when **Vicente Fox Quesada** was elected as President, but the PRI remained the largest party in the Chamber of Deputies and retained its pre-eminence in the Senate.

Leadership: Roberto Madrazo Pintado (Pres.)

Address: Insurgentes Norte 59, Edif. 2, subsótano, Col. Buenavista, 06359 México, DF

Telephone: (55) 5591-1595

Fax: (55) 5546-3452

E-mail: miusuario@pri.org.mx

Internet: www.pri.org.mx

Partido Revolucionario Social Cristiano (PRSC)
Social Christian Revolutionary Party, Dominican Republic

Centre-right Christian Democratic party; f. 1964 as a vehicle for the election to the presidency in 1966 of **Joaquín Balaguer**, who had previously served as titular President under the dictatorship of Rafael Trujillo. Balaguer remained President until 1978, pursuing a policy of close alignment and economic links with the USA. Following unrest in 1984 the rival **Partido Revolucionario Dominicano** split, and in 1986 Balaguer was returned for a fifth term, in 1990 for a sixth, and, amid serious dissension, in 1994 for a seventh. This final term, however, he was persuaded to curtail and allow fresh elections to be held in 1996. In the 1998 congressional elections the PRSC won only two seats in the Senate and 17 in the Chamber of Deputies.

Leadership: (vacant)

Address: Avda San Cristóbal, Ensanche La Fe, Apdo. 1332, Santo Domingo, DN

Telephone: 566-7089

Partido Roldosista Ecuatoriano (PRE)
Ecuadorian Roldosista Party

Personalist party founded in 1982 to serve as a vehicle for the presidential campaign of Abdalá Bucaram Ortiz. It took its name from that of the reforming President

Jaime Roldós Aguilera, who was killed in a plane crash in May 1981 after only two years in office. Bucaram, however, was not successful in presidential elections until 1996, when he received 54.5% of the vote in the second ballot, in what was generally regarded as a rejection by the electorate of the 'free-market' policies pursued by his predecessor, Sixto Durán Ballén of the Partido Unitario Republicano. However, he was soon criticized for his eccentricity and unpredictability and in February 1997 Congress voted in favour of his dismissal on the grounds of mental incapacity. In the elections of 2002 the PRE won 14 of the 100 seats in Congress, making it the third largest party.

Leadership: Abdalá Bucaram Ortiz

Partido da Social Democracia Brasileira (PSDB)
Party of Brazilian Social Democracy

Centre-left party founded by dissident members of the **Partido do Movimento Democrático Brasileiro**, the **Partido da Frente Liberal**, Partido Democrático Social, Partido Democrático Trabalhista, Partido Socialista Brasileiro and Partido Trabalhista Brasileiro. Supported candidature of **Fernando Henrique Cardoso** for President.

Leadership: José Aníbal Pontes (Pres.)
Address: SCN, Quadro 04, Bloco B, Torre C, Sala 303/B, Centro Empresarial Varig, 70710-500, Brasília, DF
Telephone: (61) 424-0500
Fax: (61) 424-0519
E-mail: tucano@psdb.org.br
Internet: www.psdb.org.br

Partido Socialista de Chile (PS)
Socialist Party of Chile

The first Partido Socialista de Chile was formed in 1933 by the amalgamation of other smaller parties around the New Public Action (APN) of Col Marmaduque Grove, leader of the short-lived Socialist Republic of 1932, with the backing of the National Confederation of Legal Trade Unions. In 1936 it joined with the Partido Comunista de Chile (PCCh) and Radicals to form the Popular Front. Grove was blocked by the PCCh from the presidential nomination in 1938, which went instead to the Radicals' Pedro Aguirre Cerda (President 1938–41), and the PS subsequently left the front when the PCCh supported Hitler. With the election of another Radical, Juan Antonio Ríos Morales, the PS rejoined the governing coalition, though Grove himself broke away in 1943 to align himself and his faction with the PCCh. An even more serious split occurred in 1948 after two PS deputies voted for the ban on the Communists, the so-called *Ley Maldita.* They later both joined the Popular Action Front (FRAP) and merged again in 1957.

In 1958 the FRAP nominated Dr **Salvador Allende** for the presidency. In the elections held in 1958 and 1964 he came second. In 1970, as the candidate of a wider coalition, Unidad Popular, he was successful, but when his Government was overthrown by the armed forces in 1973 many PS members were imprisoned, tortured and either exiled or killed. What was left of the party split into two main factions, one of which signed the National Agreement in 1985 but refused to join the United Left (IU) in 1987. The other faction, led by Dr Clodomiro Almeyda, Allende's foreign minister, refused to sign the National Agreement, but under the old name of the Socialist Party of Chile was a founder member of the IU.

Leadership: Gonzalo Martner (Pres.)
Address: Paris 873, Santiago
Telephone: 630-6900
E-mail: pschile@terra.cl
Internet: www.pschile.cl

Partido Sociedad Patriótica 21 de Enero (PSP)
Patriotic Society of 21 January, Ecuador

Ad hoc party created to support the campaign of Col Edwin Gutiérrez for the presidency, consisting of his former army colleagues and the left-wing Movimiento Popular Democrático in alliance with the *indigenista* **Movimiento Nuevo País-Pachakútik**. It takes its name from the date of the coup in 2000 which resulted in the fall of President **Jamil Mahuad Witt** and in which Col Gutiérrez took part.

Leadership: Col Lucio Edwin Gutiérrez Borbua (Leader, Pres. of the Republic)
Internet: www.sociedadpatriotica.com

Partido dos Trabalhadores (PT)
Workers' Party, Brazil

F. 1980; an independent labour party associated with the authentic branch of the trade union movement; claims 350,000 members.

Leadership: José Dirceu de Oliveira e Silva (Pres.)
Address: Congresso Nacional, 70160 Brasília, DF
Telephone: (61) 224-1699
E-mail: infopt@pt.org.br
Internet: www.pt.org.br

Partido Unidad Social Cristiana (PUSC)
Social Christian Unity Party, Costa Rica

Christian Democratic party, f. 1983. In 2002 its candidate, Abel Pacheco de la Espriella, won the presidency with 58% of the votes cast in the second round, and the party won 19 seats in the Legislative Assembly.
Leadership: Lorena Vasquez Badilla (Pres.)
Address: 100 m norte y 25 m este del costado este de Plaza de Sol, Apdo. 10.095,
            1000 San José
Telephone: 248-2470
Fax: 248-2179
Internet: www.pusc.or.cr

Paul VI

Paul VI (1963–78) became the first reigning Pope to visit Latin America when he presided over the Second General Conference of Latin American Bishops (CELAM) at Medellín, Colombia, in 1968. The Conference, the first to be held since the Second Vatican Council (Vatican II, 1962–65), rejected violence as un-Christian, but gave a significant boost to the emerging doctrine of Liberation Theology by criticizing the sin inherent in the maintenance of unjust political and social structures. Its main practical effect was to endorse the formation of Christian 'base communities' (*comunidades de base*), which was to be of particular importance in strengthening the social impact of the Church in Brazil, Chile, Paraguay and the Central American republics.

Paz Estenssoro, Víctor

Víctor Paz Estenssoro, President of Bolivia 1952–56, 1960–64 and 1985–89, was born in Tarija, Bolivia, in 1907. He studied law and economics at the Universidad Mayor de San Andrés (UMSA) before joining the Ministry of Finance in 1932; his time there, however, was interrupted by his service in the army in the Chaco War

(1933–36). In 1939 he was appointed professor of economic history at UMSA. In June 1942 he, **Hernán Siles Zuazo** and Walter Guevara Arce together founded the **Movimiento Nacionalista Revolucionario** (MNR), of which he became leader, and, as such, served as Minister of Finance in the Government of Gualberto Villarroel (1943–46). When it was overthrown he went into exile in Argentina. In the 1951 presidential election he obtained the most votes, but the result was annulled by the armed forces. In the following year his supporters deposed the military junta and seized power in the Bolivian Revolution of April 1952, and he returned to become President for the first time. His Government nationalized the tin mines and carried out a significant programme of agrarian reform. However, it was soon under serious economic pressure and in his second term, after a three-year spell as Ambassador to the United Kingdom, his Government had to contend with bitter labour disputes and serious social unrest.

In 1964 Paz was re-elected, only to be deposed six months later in a coup led by air force Col René Barrientos, with the support of Hernán Siles' faction of the MNR. He lived in Peru from 1965 until 1971, but though he backed the coup that brought Gen. **Hugo Bánzer** to power in 1971, his party was expelled from government in 1974 and he was exiled again, this time to Argentina. As candidate of the main faction of the MNR, the MNR (Histórico—MNR-H), he led a left-wing coalition in the elections of 1979 and 1980, both annulled by the armed forces, but in 1985, though he ran second in the poll, Congress chose him in preference to Bánzer and his party and he became President for the third time. He died in 2001.

People's National Congress/Reform (PNC/Reform)

The People's National Congress was founded in former British Guiana in 1955 by **Forbes Burnham** when he split from the People's Progressive Party. In 1964 Burnham led the party to victory and was in office when Guyana attained independence, becoming President under the new Constitution. After the PNC was defeated in 1992, its then leader, former President Desmond Hoyte, became leader of the opposition, and after Janet Jagan was elected President in 1997, encouraged widespread and at times serious unrest in an attempt to oust her. Following Jagan's resignation in 1999, however, the party split in 2000 and the Reform wing became dominant.

Leadership: Robert Corbin (Leader), Stanley Ming (Reform Leader)
Address: Congress Place, Sophia, POB 10330, Georgetown
Telephone: 225-7852
Fax: 225-6055

E-mail: pnc@guyana-pnc.org
Internet: www.guyanapnc.org

People's National Movement (PNM)

A moderate nationalist party; f. 1956; now one of the two main political parties in Trinidad and Tobago. In the October 2002 elections, the PNM secured 50.7% of the votes cast and 20 seats in the 36-member House of Representatives.
   Leadership: Patrick Manning (Leader), Dr Linda Baboolai (Chair.)
   Address: 1 Tranquillity St, Port of Spain
   Telephone: 625-1533
   E-mail: pnm@cariblink.net
   Internet: www.pnm.org.tt

People's National Party (PNP)

F. 1938, the PNP was the first mass party to be formed in Jamaica. It retains its socialist principles and is affiliated to the **National Workers' Union of Jamaica**.
   Leadership: Percival J. Patterson (Leader, Prime Minister)
   Address: 89 Old Hope Road, Kingston 5
   Telephone: 929-1183
   Fax: 927-4389
   E-mail: information@pnpjamaica.com
   Internet: www.pnpjamaica.com

People's Progressive Party-CIVIC (PPP-CIVIC)

The first mass political party in former British Guiana, the PPP was founded in 1950 by Dr **Cheddi Jagan**. As a Marxist-Leninist party, unaffiliated to the Communist movement, it won the 1957 elections and held office until 1964. The PPP won the 1992 elections in coalition with CIVIC, when Dr Jagan was elected as President and appointed the leader of CIVIC, Samuel Hinds, as Prime Minister. Hinds was briefly to succeed Jagan as interim President on his death in March 1997. Jagan's widow, Janet, assumed the leadership of the PPP. PPP/CIVIC won a renewed mandate in November 1997 and Janet Jagan became President. The US-born President was soon subjected to a concerted attack that included racist slurs, however, and after intervention by the **Caribbean Community and Common Market**, an inter-party agreement was concluded. However, peace was not restored until Jagan resigned the presidency following a mild heart attack in August 1999. She was succeeded as President by Bharrat Jagdeo, but remained leader of the PPP.

Leadership: Janet Jagan (Leader), Donald Remotar (Gen. Sec.)
Address: Freedom House, 41 Robb Street, Lacytown, Georgetown
Telephone: 227-2095
Fax: 225-6055
E-mail: pr@ppp-civic.org or ppp@guyana.net.gy
Internet: www.ppp-civic.org

People's United Party (PUP)

Labour party founded by George Price in 1950 to seek Belize's independence from Great Britain. It won eight of the nine seats in the Legislative Assembly at the first election held under universal suffrage, and formed the Government which, under Price's leadership, achieved independence in 1981. Merged with the Christian Democratic Party in 1988. In the general election of 5 March 2003, the PUP won 53.2% of the vote and 22 of the 29 seats in the House of Representatives.

Leadership: Said Musa (Leader), Jorge Espat (Chair.)
Address: 3 Queen Street, Belize City
Telephone: 223-2428
Fax: 223-3476
Internet: www.pupbelize.org

Perón, Juan Domingo

Juan Domingo Perón Sosa (1895–1974), was President of Argentina in 1946–55 and 1973–74. In 1943 he was a key member of the secret lodge, the United Officers Group, that overthrew the President. As Minister of Labour and, later, Vice-President (1944–45), he forged a political alliance with the main trade unions. Hence, when in October 1945 the navy forced him to resign the vice-presidency, massive demonstrations ensured his release from imprisonment on the island of Martín García and he returned in triumph. Nominated for the presidency, the open opposition of the US government ensured him a massive majority and, once in power, he showed little regard for legitimate opposition, which by 1948 had virtually ceased to exist. Meanwhile, his popularity had reached unprecedented levels, owing to the support of his wife Evita (Eva Duarte de Perón), who distributed apartments, jobs and other benefits to needy supplicants from a desk in the Minsitry of Social Welfare. Though under a new Constitution (1949) he was re-elected to a second term of office in 1951, Evita was by that time terminally ill and after her death in July 1952 he seemed to lose interest in power. He was overthrown by a revolt in the Córdoba garrison in September 1955 and escaped first to Paraguay and then to Spain, where he lived in exile outside Madrid.

Though the armed forces were unsuccessful in stamping out Peronism, they were able to keep Perón himself out of office until 1973, when the way was opened for him to return. By then, however, the left and right in Argentine politics were polarized to such an extent that Perón satisfied neither. He died of natural causes in 1974. The **Partido Justicialista**, which he founded, remains the dominant Argentine political party.

Peru

República de Perú

Peru, the third largest country in South America, is situated on the west of the continent, bounded on the north-west by Ecuador, on the north-east by Colombia, on the east by Brazil and Bolivia, on the coast to the south by Chile, and on the west by the Pacific Ocean.

Area: 1,285,216 sq km (496,225 sq miles); *capital:* **Lima**; *population:* 26,749,947 (2002 estimate), 45% native Peruvian, 37% mestizo, 15% of European descent: *official languages:* Spanish, Quechua, Aymará; *religion:* Roman Catholic 90%, Protestant 6%.

Constitution: The 1993 Constitution, which revised and updated earlier documents, provided for a modified presidential republic. Executive power is vested in a President directly elected by popular vote for a five-year term and eligible for re-election once. The President appoints the Council of Ministers, which is answerable to the legislature and may be censured by it; its President is often referred to as the Prime Minister. The legislature is a single-chamber Congress chosen by the direct popular vote of all citizens over the age of 18. Voting is compulsory for those aged 18–70. There is an independent Constitutional Court which has the power to interpret the Constitution.

History: Peru, the centre of Spanish rule in South America, was the last of the South American states to be liberated; the decisive victory being obtained in the Battle of Ayacucho (1825). From the beginning it was under strong centralized rule and under Gen. Ramón Castilla (President 1845–67) was able to achieve a measure of economic growth; in 1872 a civilian government was established. However, Peru's defeat by Chile in the War of the Pacific (1879), and its consequent loss of the coastal provinces of Tacna, Arica and Tarapacá, was a serious setback. The victory of the Civilista Party in the elections of 1904 seemed to indicate the emergence of a stable oligarchic government, first under José Pardo (President 1904–08, 1915–19) and Augusto Leguía (1908–12). However, when Guillermo Billinghurst was swept to power in 1912 on a platform of social reform and public welfare, the armed forces stepped in and, by deposing him, regained the veto power which had characterized 19th century Peru. The armed forces restored Leguía to power in 1919 and supported him when he established a personalist dictatorship (1919–30) which put an end to the Civilista dream.

Leguía's position seemed secure at the time of the conclusion of a peace treaty with Chile, the second Treaty of Ancón, by which Peru regained Tacna (though not the other provinces). In the following year, however, he was overthrown by a revolt of junior officers. From then until 1985 the armed forces repeatedly intervened in Peru, often to forestall the election of the **Alianza Popular Revolucionaria Americana** (APRA). APRA, with its radical nationalism, *indigenista* flavour and grandiose, if vague, ambitions, appealed to a new and wider constituency than any of the traditional parties, and a clash between its supporters and soldiers in 1932 left a legacy of suspicion. In 1948 Gen. Manuel Odría seized power to prevent an Aprista victory, and the party's leader, **Víctor Raúl Haya de la Torre**, spent eight years in the Colombian embassy. Civilian government was restored in 1952, but was almost immediately interrupted again by the armed forces. The elections of 1963 re-established civilian government under **Fernando Belaúnde Terry**, a moderate Catholic. However, when he appeared to be insufficiently bold in maintaining Peru's interests in the long-running dispute between the government and the International Petroleum Corpn, he was deposed by the army and a military government under **Gen. Juan Velasco Alvarado** took power. In a unique experiment, discussed beforehand in the school for senior staff officers, the *Centro de Altos Estudios Militares*, the armed forces attempted to carry out a controlled social revolution, taking over the big estates of the coastal zone, nationalizing the principal industries and engaging in ambitious development projects. Ultimately, the land reform was only partially successful owing to structural inefficiencies compounded by an increasingly unreliable climate.

The pace of reform slowed and was partially reversed after Velasco Alvarado was deposed by Gen. Francisco Morales Bermúdez in 1975. In 1979 a convention was elected to write a new Constitution. Haya de la Torre, who had served as its president, died soon after and the Aprista candidate was defeated by Belaúnde (1980–85). In his second term Belaúnde seems to have had no policy except drift. He was the first civilian in 40 years to complete his term of office, but by the time he was succeeded by the Aprista Alan García Pérez (1985–90) a formidable Maoist guerrilla movement, **Sendero Luminoso** (SL), had made much of the country ungovernable. In 1990 the electorate chose a political unknown, a businessman of Japanese descent, **Alberto Keinya Fujimori**. Fujimori, who promised a totally new approach, led in effect a coup against his own Government in 1992 and established an emergency dictatorship. When the SL leader was captured and the movement defeated, he was re-elected, but unrest grew at his authoritarian style and strenuous efforts to bend the Constitution to secure a second re-election. Accusations of corruption against the head of the secret police, **Vladimiro Montesinos**, were strengthened by the publication of secret videos (the 'Vladivideos') that showed money actually changing hands. Fujimori resigned and fresh elections were held in 2001.

Latest elections: In the first round of the elections held on 8 April 2001 Alejandro Toledo of the centre-left **Perú Posible** led the field with 36.6% of the vote, compared with 26% for Alan García of the APRA and 24% for Lourdes Flores Nano. In the run-off election, held on 3 June, Toledo won outright, obtaining 51.9% of the vote compared with 48.1% for García, with 13% of the votes blank. **Perú Posible** won 45 seats in the new 120-seat Congress. The 55-year-old Toledo, the first person of indigenous ancestry to be elected as President in a free vote, was sworn in on 28 July after negotiations with the 11-member Independent Moralizing Front had given the government additional support—though not a working majority.

International relations and defence: Peru retains compulsory selective military service for a period of two years. The army has a strength of 70,000, the navy 25,000 and the air force 15,000. There are 188,000 army reservists and paramilitary forces totalling some 77,000.

Peru, economy

GNI: US $52.2m. (2001); *GNI per caput:* $1,980 (2001); *GNI at PPP:* $118m. (2001); *GNI per caput at PPP:* $4,470 (2001), rank 117; *exports:* $7,688m. (2002); *imports:* $7,426.5m. (2002); *currency:* nuevo sol, plural nuevos soles; US $1 = 3.495 soles at 31 May 2003.

In 2002 agriculture accounted for 9.1% of Peru's gross domestic product (GDP), mining for 6.4% and manufacturing industry for 14.7%. Some 2.9% of the land is arable, 0.2% under permanent crops and 21.1% permanent pasture. The main crops are rice, **sugar** and **cotton**; maize, wheat, potatoes and barley are grown for local consumption. The El Niño current of 1997–98 damaged the traditionally important fishing industry, which accounted for only 0.5% of GDP in 2003. The main mineral resources exploited are gold, **copper**, zinc and petroleum. The principal industries are food processing, metalworking, textiles, cement, road vehicle assembly, fishmeal manufacture and petroleum refining. The main energy source is petroleum, though Peru has substantial unexploited hydroelectric power resources.

Main exports are gold, copper and copper alloys, other metalliferous ores and fishmeal. Principal imports are petroleum and petroleum products, road vehicles and parts and various forms of machinery. In 2001 the USA was the greatest purchaser of exports, followed by Switzerland, the People's Republic of China and Japan. The USA was the greatest supplier of imports, followed by Chile, Colombia and Venezuela.

Mining has been the foundation of Peru's export economy since colonial times and Peru remains highly sensitive to fluctuations in world prices for primary products. From the 1950s successive governments pursued policies of state-led industrial development, sheltered behind high tariffs, but with limited success. In 1991, according to President **Fujimori**, the mining sector was severely under-capitalized, but, with new investment earnings from exports of copper, zinc, lead and gold, grew significantly in the late 1990s while the fishmeal industry was devastated by the combined effects of over-exploitation and El Niño. After 1980 the country was plunged into recession and by 1988 was heavily indebted and suffering from an acute balance-of-payments crisis. An austerity package and stabilization programme introduced in 1990 made industry more competitive but at a high cost. Annual GDP growth in 2000 was 3.1%, declining to 0.2% in 2001 and rising again, to 5.2%, in 2002 when there was a strong recovery in the mining sector. Inflation hit a low of 0.2% in 2002 but the unemployment rate of 8.9% of the workforce and underemployment affecting perhaps 40% fuelled continuing social unrest.

Perú Posible (PP)
Possible Peru

Centre-left party, f. 1994 as a vehicle for the presidential candidacy of Alejandro Toledo. PP contested the 1995 elections in coalition with Coordinación Democrática, but ran on its own in 2000.

Leadership: Alejandro Toledo (Leader), Luis Solari (Sec.-Gen.)
Address: Avda Faustino Sánchez Carrión, Lima
Telephone: (1) 423-8723

Petróleo Brasileiro, SA (PETROBRÁS)

State-owned corporation, f. 1953 to control the production of petroleum in Brazil. It controls distribution of all petroleum products through its subsidiary, Petrobrás Distribuidora, SA, and controls 27 affiliated companies and four subsidiaries engaged in the manufacture of petrochemicals though another subsidiary, Petrobrás Química, SA (PETROQUISA).

Leadership: Dilma Vana Roussef (Chair.)
Address: Av. República de Chile 65, 20035-900 Rio de Janeiro, RJ
Telephone: (21) 534-4477
Fax: (21) 230-5052
Internet: www.br-petrobras.com.br

Petróleos Mexicanos (PEMEX)

State corporation, f. 1938 to exploit all aspects of Mexico's oil and gas resources, following the nationalization of all foreign oil companies operating in Mexico by the Government of President **Lázaro Cárdenas** on 18 March 1938, a day that is still celebrated in Mexico as a public holiday. In 2002 it had some 107,000 employees.

Leadership: Raúl Muñoz Leos (Dir-Gen.)
Address: Avda Marina Nacional 329, 44°, Col. Huasteca, 11300 México, DF
Telephone: (55) 5254-2044
Fax: (55) 5531-6354
Internet: www.pemex.com

Petróleos de Venezuela, SA (PDVSA)

Following the nationalization of Venezuela's hydrocarbon industry in 1975, PDVSA was created as the state corporation with overall reponsibility for all aspects of oil and gas exploration, production, refining and marketing within Venezuela. It was given additional responsibilities for the development of petro-chemicals in 1978 and of coal in 1985. It has nine subsidiaries, each individually responsible for production within a specific sector or region.

Leadership: Ali Rodríguez Araque (Pres.)
Address: Edif. Petróleos de Venezuela, Torre Este, Avda Libertador, La Campiña,
Apdo 169, Caracas 1010-A
Telephone: (212) 708-4743
Fax: (212) 708-4661

E-mail: saladeprensa@pdvsa.com.ve
Internet: www.pdvsa.com.ve

Petroleum Co of Trinidad and Tobago Ltd (Petrotrin)

State petroleum company created in 1993 by the merger of Trinidad and Tobago Oil Co Ltd and Trinidad and Tobago Petroleum Co Ltd. Activities cover petroleum and gas exploration, production and refining as well as a variety of downstream operations in the manufacture of petroleum products.

Leadership: Rodney Jagai (Pres.)

Address: Petrotrin Administration Bldg, Cnr Queen's Park West and Cipriani Blvd, Port of Spain

Telephone: 625-5240

Fax: 624-4661

E-mail: connect@petrotrin.com

Internet: www.petrotrin.com

Pinochet Ugarte, Augusto

Augusto Pinochet Ugarte, *de facto* President of Chile 1973–1989, was born in Valparaíso in 1915. The son of a dock clerk, he was twice rejected for admission to the military academy, but was eventually accepted and graduated in 1936, becoming for a time an instructor at the academy. After three years at the Army War College (1949–52) he became a staff officer. Between 1961 and 1964 he commanded the 7th Infantry Regiment in Antofagasta, before returning to the Army War College as assistant director and professor of geopolitics, a subject on which he wrote a standard text-book. Promoted to the rank of colonel in 1966, he attended training courses at the School of the Americas in Panama in 1965 and 1968. He was armed forces chief-of-staff when Gen. Carlos Prats González was forced out in 1973. Believing him to be a constitutionalist, President **Salvador Allende** appointed Pinochet commander of the army, but it was he who within days led the coup that deposed Allende on 11 September 1973, and became president of the four-man junta which replaced him.

At least 9,000 people, mainly middle-ranking political leaders and trade union-ists, were killed during the first few months of the junta's rule. Meanwhile Pinochet had successfully persuaded his colleagues to appoint him as President. In 1978 he successfully ousted Air Force Gen. Gustavo Leigh, the only junta member opposed to him who remained in power, and in 1980 forced the adoption by means of a referendum (held on 11 September) of a Constitution which extended his presidential term by eight years, at the end of which a further referendum was to decide, by a simple majority, whether he should serve a further eight-year term. However, after an attempt was made to assassinate Pinochet in September 1986, it became clear that even moderate conservatives were becoming disillusioned with a regime which, under the influence of the so-called 'Chicago Boys', had opened up the economy to the outside world, drastically widened the gap between rich and poor and left both open to the effects of a deep recession in 1980–83. In 1988, to his obvious surprise, Pinochet was defeated and forced to give way to a civilian government in 1989. However, he retained the post of commander-in-chief of the armed forces and remained a threat to his successors until he was arrested in London, United Kingdom, and charged with crimes against humanity. Legal proceedings against Pinochet were ultimately abandoned, however, on the grounds of his mental incapacity.

Platt Amendment

Amendment to the Act of the US Congress granting independence to Cuba in 1902, by which the USA reserved the right to intervene in Cuba to maintain democratic government and to maintain a military base on the island. It was invoked for the first time in 1906, when unrest erupted after Tomás Estrada Palma, Cuba's first President, sought re-election, and Cuba was again occupied and governed by the USA in 1906–1909. The Amendment was abrogated in 1934, when the two countries signed a Reciprocity Treaty.

Plenario Intersindical de Trabajadores-Convención Nacional de Trabajadores (PIT-CNT)

Inter-Union Workers' Plenary-National Workers' Convention, Uruguay

Following the military coup in Uruguay in 1983 trade union activity was quickly suppressed. However, in 1981 the government enacted the *Ley de Asociaciones Profesionales* which permitted a limited degree of non-political union activity and allowed a mass meeting to take place on 1 May, which resulted in a peaceful mass demonstration attended by some 100,000 people. The PIT, which was formed as a result, then led a series of strikes and demonstrations against the crumbling regime, mobilizing by the end of 1983 as much as 15% of the population and bringing much of the country to a halt in January 1984. The PIT-CNT remained active independently of the talks that resulted in the return of democratic government in March 1985, and continued to be a radical force opposing the conservative labour policies of the incoming Colorado Government.

E-mail: pitcnt@adinet.com.uy

Internet: www.chasque.apc.org/icudu/

Port-au-Prince

Port-au-Prince, port, chief town and capital of Haiti, is situated on the coast of the Gulf of Gonâve, on the edge of the coastal plain stretching inland to Lake Saumâtre, on the west side of the island of Hispaniola. In mid-1997 it had an estimated population of 917,112.

Port of Spain

The principal town on the island of Trinidad and the capital of the Republic of Trinidad and Tobago, Port of Spain was estimated by the UN to have a population of 54,000 in 2001. Its elected Borough Council dates from 1914.

Prensa Latina (Agencia Informativa Latinoamericana, SA)

Cuban news agency, f. 1959 to disseminate news about Latin America and its relations with Cuba and the Cuban Revolution.

Leadership: Pedro Margolles Villanueva (Dir)

Address: Calle 17, No. 354, esq. I. Vedado, Havana

Telephone: (7) 32-5561

Fax: (7) 33-3069

E-mail: difusion@prensa-latina.cu

Internet: www.prensa-latina.cu

Privatization

Privatization, the transfer of public assets to private ownership, became fashionable in the region after 1983, inspired by the emerging **Washington Consensus** and the example of Margaret Thatcher in the United Kingdom. The Government of Gen. **Augusto Pinochet** in Chile, while encouraging private enterprise, had retained control of key industries. Similarly, earlier Argentine governments had legislated for the return of nationalized industries to private hands, but it was left to the

Government of **Carlos Saúl Menem** to make this a key feature of economic policy after 1991, after which other governments rapidly followed suit. Privatization was generally by a process of public tender rather than by stock market flotation, and a curious feature was the participation of European state-owned companies, as in, for example, the purchase of Aerolíneas Argentinas by a consortium led by Iberia, part of which had subsequently to be bought back by the Argentine government. A general problem was that governments highly sensitive to the political cost of rising utility prices would continue to intervene to keep them down; where they did not, as in Ecuador and Peru, political violence ensued. The receipts were intended to be used as a 'one-off' to pay off the public debt, but in practice they were often used in a short-term fashion to bridge fiscal deficits.

Puerto Rico
Commonwealth of Puerto Rico/Estado Asociado Libre de Puerto Rico

Puerto Rico is the smallest of the islands of the Greater Antilles and is situated some 120 km east of the island of Hispaniola and 64 km west of the nearest point in the US Virgin Islands. *Total area:* 8,959 sq km (3,459 sq miles); *capital:* **San Juan**; *official languages:* Spanish, English; *population:* 3,839,810 (2001 estimate), comprising white 80.5%, black 8.0%, Amerindian 0.4% and Asian 0.1%; *religion:* about 75% Roman Catholic.

Constitution: By Public Law 600 of 3 July 1950 the US Congress granted Puerto Rico full internal self-government. Its Constitution as a state in free association with the USA came into effect on 25 July 1952. The island is represented in the US House of Representatives by a non-voting Resident Commissioner, who is directly elected for a four-year term. The legislature consists of a 27-member Senate and a House of Representatives of 51 members. The chief executive is a Governor directly elected for a four-year term. Puerto Ricans are full citizens of the USA. US tax laws do not apply to Puerto Rico, but Puerto Rican customs duties are the same as those of the USA with the exception of that for **coffee**, which is taxed in Puerto Rico.

History: Puerto Rico, known to its indigenous inhabitants as Boriquén, was first explored by the Spanish in 1493, on Columbus' first voyage, and subsequently settled by them. **Sugar** and coffee became the main export crops. It was captured from Spain in the Spanish–American War of 1898 and ceded to the USA by the Treaty of Paris. In 1900 a civil administration was established and in 1917 Congress granted US citizenship to the islanders, though the island continued to be administered as a Territory until 1948, when Luis Muñoz Marín was chosen as the first elected Governor.

Latest elections: In the gubernatorial election of 7 November 2000 Sila María Calderón of the **Partido Popular Democrático** (PPD) was elected with 48.65% of the votes cast, defeating Carlos I. Pezquera of the **Partido Nuevo Progresista** (PNP), who received 45.68% of the vote, and Rubén Berríos Martínez of the Partido Independentista Puertorriqueño (PIP) who received 5.20%. In the concurrent legislative elections the results were: for the Senate PPD 19 seats, PNP eight, PIP one; for the House of Representatives PPD 27 seats, PNP 23, PIP one.

International relations and defence: Puerto Rico commands the strategically important Mona Passage, named after the now uninhabited island of Mona, 80 km West of Mayagüez. The US Government maintains a key naval base at Roosevelt Roads in the east of the island. Areas of the neighbouring island of Vieques formed part of this base until May 2003, when longstanding protests at the damage done to the island by military exercises led to its abandonment. The Commonwealth's National Guard of 11,000 troops forms part of the local US military presence.

Puerto Rico, economy

GNI: US \$42,100m. (2001); *GNI per caput:* \$10,950 (2001); *GNI at PPP:* \$69m. (2001); *GNI per caput at PPP:* \$18,090 (2001); *exports:* \$34,900m. (1999); *imports:* \$25,300m. (1999); *currency:* US dollar.

In 2000–01 agriculture accounted for 0.7% of Puerto Rico's gross domestic product (GDP), industry for 43.3%, wholesale and retail trade for 13.3%, finance, insurance and real estate for 14.1% and tourism for 6.2%. Some 3.9% of the land is arable, 5.5% under permanent crops, and 23.5% permanent pasture. The main crops are **coffee**, **sugar** and tobacco. Mineral resources are limited. The principal industries are pharmaceuticals, scientific instruments, computers and microprocessors and other electrical goods. The island is heavily dependent on imported oil and gas to meet its energy needs.

Puerto Rico has operated an annual trade surplus since 1982. Main exports are drugs and pharmaceuticals, food products and electronic computers. Principal imports are drugs, pharmaceuticals and other chemical products, electrical machinery and transport equipment. In 1997 the USA was the greatest purchaser of exports, followed by the Dominican Republic, Japan, Germany, Belgium and the Netherlands. The USA was the main source of imports, followed by Japan, the Dominican Republic, Venezuela, the United Kingdom and Ireland.

Puerto Rico's prosperity is based on a combination of substantial federal and local tax exemptions and a low wage economy, which began with 'Operation Bootstrap' in the late 1940s. The first 'oil shock' impacted sharply on growth, but in the early 1980s a further infusion of federal funds brought recovery. Puerto Rico benefited from the sustained growth of the US economy after 1990, recording average annual GDP growth of 4.5% in 1990–2000, though the ending of the possession's tax credit in 1996 hit the economy hard. High spending on public works accounts for the fact that the government sector is the second largest in terms of employment. GDP grew by 1.7% in 2001 and by 2.0% in 2002. The consumer price index rose by only 2.8% in 2001, but the unemployment rate stood at 11.4%. Significant under-employment helps keep wages low relative to the continental USA.

Puerto Rico Industrial Development Corpn (PRIDCO)

Public agency appointed to administer the government-sponsored industrial development programme.

Leadership: William Riefkohl (Exec. Dir)

Addresses: 355 Roosevelt Ave, Hato Rey, San Juan, PR 00918 and POB 362350, San Juan, PR 00936-2350

Telephone: (787) 758-4747

Fax: (787) 754-1415

E-mail: publicaffairs@pridco.com

Internet: www.pridco.com

R

Real Plan

The Real Plan, introduced by Brazil's finance minister, **Fernando Henrique Cardoso**, in three stages between March and July 1994, was a systematic attempt to end the country's persistent inflation and stabilize the currency. It took its name from the new currency, the real, which replaced the cruzado, and whose exchange rate was initially pegged to the US dollar at 2 to 1. At the same time elaborate rules were introduced to maintain price stability, the banks were required to maintain enhanced reserves and treasury guarantees for state expenditure were ended. Between June and September the monthly rate of inflation fell from more than 50% to 2%. Unfortunately, the government was not as successful at eliminating the persistent public-sector deficit, and had from the beginning to borrow heavily to avoid uncontrolled devaluation. Hence, though this was also partly a consequence of the 1994 'tequila' crisis, the 1997 East Asian crisis and the Russian devaluation in 1998, the total public debt more than doubled as a proportion of gross domestic product between 1994 and 2002.

Rio de Janeiro

Rio de Janeiro, in the state of Rio de Janeiro, Brazil's second largest city and principal port, is situated on Guanabara Bay, one of the largest natural harbours in the world. Discovered in the early 16th century, it was at first mistaken for the estuary of a river, hence the name which in Portuguese means 'River of January'. Between 1822 and 1960 it was Brazil's capital and still retains many of the fine buildings and amenities of that period. Its fine beaches and dynamic social life make it one of the world's major tourist destinations, particularly during February, the month of Carnival. At the 2001 census it had a population of 5,857,904.

Rio Group

The Rio Group was established at a meeting of the heads of state of eight Latin American countries (Argentina, Brazil, Colombia, Mexico, Panama, Peru, Uruguay and Venezuela) in Rio de Janeiro on 18 December 1986, by the Declaration of Rio de Janeiro, which established a Permanent Mechanism for Consultation and Co-operation (*Mecanismo Permanente de Consulta y Cooperación*). It was formed to provide a forum for discussion of regional issues, including the civil wars then under way in Central America, regional security arrangements, the problems of debt and development and Cuba's role in Latin America, and was initially commonly referred to as the 'Group of Eight'. There is no permanent secretariat, its location rotating instead between the member countries according to the venue of the current summit.

A third summit meeting, excluding Panama, whose indefinite suspension for 'increasing violations of political and human rights' was agreed at the meeting, took place in the Peruvian town of Ica, on 11–12 October 1988. The resulting joint communiqué stressed the Group's important role in strengthening 'the institutional development' of democracy in Latin America by its promotion of peace and regional economic integration. In this vein it welcomed democratic developments in Paraguay and Chile, and stated that it would initiate the investigation of human rights abuses in Panama. The communiqué went on to condemn terrorism and promised new policies and methods, subject to respect for national sovereignties, to combat drugs-trafficking. It also expressed concern for the 'world-wide' deterioration of the environment, stating that the region's own environmental problems were closely linked to poverty and underdevelopment. Increased multilateral and bilateral support for Latin America was therefore needed to promote increased trade, economic restructuring and the reduction of debt burden. The Group promised 'innovative mechanisms' to deal with intra-Latin American debt commitments.

At a meeting in **Buenos Aires** on 4–5 December 1989, the Group issued the *Declaration of Buenos Aires*, under which foreign affairs and economic and planning ministers agreed to meet every six months with a view to establishing a Latin American common market by 1992. They also agreed to adopt measures to reduce intra-regional trade tariffs, to eliminate other non-tariff barriers and a pledge to 'begin a progressive co-ordination of macroeconomic policies' to facilitate Latin American integration. At the fourth summit, held at Caracas, Venezuela, in October 1990, Bolivia, Chile, Ecuador and Paraguay joined the Group, which became generally known as the Rio Group from then on.

At the ninth presidential summit, held in Quito, Ecuador, in September 1995, member states committed themselves to the creation of a Free Trade Area of the

Americas by 2005 and in 2000 the five Central American states and the Dominican Republic were admitted as full members of the Group. The Group has also held a series of ministerial conferences with representatives of the **European Union**, with a view to negotiating a free-trade agreement for the region.

Rio Pact

A formal alliance system for the Western hemisphere, established by a treaty signed on 2 September 1947 at an Inter-American Defence Conference held at Petrópolis near **Rio de Janeiro**, Brazil, by 19 of the 21 American republics. Its formal title in English is the Inter-American Treaty of Reciprocal Assistance and, in Spanish, Tratado Interamericano de Asistencia Recíproca. Since then, Ecuador, Nicaragua, Trinidad and Tobago and the Bahamas have adhered to the Treaty, but Cuba withdrew on 29 March 1960, and Mexico gave notice in 2002 of its intention to do so also. By Article 3 of the Treaty the signatories 'agree that an armed attack by any states against an American state shall be considered as an attack against all the American states', and consequently 'undertake to assist in meeting the attack in exercise of the inherent right of individual or collective self-defence recognized by Article 51 of the UN Charter'. The procedure for doing so is that 'on the request of the state or states directly attacked and until the decision of the organ of consultation of the inter-American system', each of the signatories 'may determine immediate measure which it may individually adopt in fulfilment of the obligation contained in the preceding paragraph and in accordance with the principle of continental solidarity. The organ of consultation shall meet without delay for the purpose of examining these measures and agreeing upon measures of a collective character that should be adopted'. The Treaty was invoked on 14 occasions between 1948 and 1962; it has only been invoked once since, by the USA in 2001.

Ríos Montt, Gen. Efraín

José Efraín Ríos Montt, *de facto* ruler of Guatemala in 1982–83, was born in 1926 in Huehuetenango, Department of Huehuetenango. He entered the Academia Militar in 1943 and in 1973, with the rank of general, returned from his post as military attaché in Washington, DC, USA, to contest the 1974 presidential election as the candidate of the Christian Democrats. Defeated, he spent the next three years at the Madrid embassy. When he returned to Guatemala he was unexpectedly converted to evangelical Christianity in the form of the Church of the Word, a branch of Gospel Outreach of California. He was engaged in Bible study when in

March 1982 soldiers entered the church to tell him that President Romeo Lucas García had been overthrown and to invite him to assume the presidency of the ruling junta. Within three months he had forced the resignation of the other two members and made himself dictator, preaching evangelical messages weekly to the people by radio and TV. His predecessor had launched a veritable onslaught on the indigenous population in 1978, and Ríos Montt, who had taken a leading role in it, was now free to wage his version of a counter-insurgency campaign, in which, it is estimated by Human Rights Watch, some 10,000 Guatemalans were killed, many of them after torture, either by the armed forces or by the so-called Civil Defence Patrols (*Patrullas de Autodefensa Civil*). Established by giving the villagers the choice of 'beans or bullets' , many of these were simply paramilitary 'death squads'. In addition, some 100,000 were made homeless, many of whom crossed the frontier into Mexico to escape persecution. The situation was so bad that Ríos was overthrown in August 1983 by the country's Minister of Defence with, it was believed, the covert support of the USA, which had earlier lifted the embargo on the supply of arms to Guatemala originally imposed by President Jimmy Carter. Though constitutionally banned from contesting the presidency, he was elected to Congress and was elected president of Congress in 1994. Following attempts to have him extradited to Spain, Congress lifted his immunity from prosecution in 2001.

Roseau

Roseau, chief port and capital of Dominica, is situated on the south-western coast of the island. Its population in 2001 was estimated by the UN at 26,000, including the outlying suburbs. Cruise ships call regularly at the port but have brought only limited economic benefits to the town.

S

Saba

Saba, the smallest island of the Netherlands Antilles, measuring only 13 sq km, is the peak of a single, dormant volcano which rises from the sea bed to a height of 866 m (2,842 ft), the highest point in the Kingdom of the Netherlands, known as Mt Scenery. It is situated some 27 km to the north-east of St Eustatius and 45 km to the south-west of St Maarten/St-Martin. It had a population of 1,466 in 1996.

St-Barthélemy

Island dependency of the French Overseas Department of Guadeloupe. Situated some 230 km to the north-west of the main island, it is 21 sq km in area

St Eustatius

St Eustatius, otherwise known as Statia, one of the smaller islands of the Netherlands Antilles, is some 21 sq km in area and rises to a height of some 600 m at its zenith, Mazinga, the crater of an extinct volcano. Though much of its original forest was felled to make way for **sugar** plantations, it is noteworthy for its wildlife. It had a population of 2,609 in 1996.

St Christopher (St Kitts) and Nevis

St Christopher and Nevis is the smallest country in the western hemisphere in both area and population. It is situated in the Lesser Antilles to the west of Antigua.

Area: 269.4 sq km; *capital:* **Basseterre**, on St Kitts; *language:* English; *population:* 45,841 (2001 census), 90% of African descent; *religion:* mainly Anglican.

Constitution: A constitutional monarchy within the **Commonwealth**. The National Assembly has 11 elected members, three nominated members and one ex officio member. There is a separate Nevis Island Assembly.

History: The islands were visited and named by **Christopher Columbus** in 1493. British settlement on St Kitts began in 1623, but the island was shared with France until 1713. Independence was delayed by disagreements between the islands but finally achieved in 1983.

Latest elections: In the general election of 6 March 2000, the St Kitts-Nevis Labour Party (SKNLP) won eight seats, the Concerned Citizens' Movement two and the Nevis Reformation Party one. The Government was formed by the SKNLP, led by Dr Denzil Douglas.

International relations and defence: St Christopher and Nevis is a member of the United Nations, the **Organization of American States**, the **Commonwealth,** the **Caribbean Community and Common Market**, and the **Organization of Eastern Caribbean States**. There is a volunteer defence force and a police tactical unit. St Christopher and Nevis participates in the US-sponsored Regional Security System.

St Christopher (St Kitts) and Nevis, economy

GNI: US \$299m. (2001); *GNI per caput:* \$6,630 (2001); *GNI at PPP:* \$459m. (2001); *GNI per caput at PPP:* \$10,190 (2001); *exports:* \$55.04m. (2001); *imports:* \$166.67m. (2001); *currency:* Eastern Caribbean dollar (EC\$), plural dollars; US \$1 = EC\$2.70 since July 1976.

In 2002 agriculture accounted for 3.3% of gross domestic product (GDP) and industry for 8.7%. Some 19.4% of the land is arable, 2.8% under permanent crops and 5.6% permanent pasture. The main export crop is **sugar**. The main economic activity is tourism. The principal export industry is the assembly of electronic components.

Main exports are machinery and components and sugar preparations. Principal imports are machinery and transport equipment, basic manufactures and fuels. In 2001 the USA was the greatest purchaser of exports, followed by the United Kingdom. The USA was the greatest supplier of imports in that year, followed by Canada and the United Kingdom.

Sugar, despite heavy subsidization by the **European Union**, is in decline, and government expectations are focused on the development of telemarketing and similar services. Regulation of the small offshore sector has been criticized by OECD, but since 2002 the country has no longer been regarded as uncooperative.

Sales of citizenship rights have also been heavily criticized but continue never-theless. Annual average GDP growth in 1990–2001 was 4.2%. The GDP growth rate declined to 2.4% in 2001 and to 1.5% in 2002, as demand slackened for tourism.

St George's

St George's, chief town and capital of Grenada, is situated at the south end of the island's west coast. At the 2001 census it had a population of 3,908

St John's

St John's, situated on an inlet on the north-west corner of Antigua, is the main port, chief town and capital of the state of Antigua and Barbuda. The UN estimated its population at 24,000 in mid-2001.

St Lucia

St Lucia is situated in the lesser Antilles, 34 km south of Martinique and 42 km north of St Vincent.

Area: 616 sq km (238 sq miles); *capital:* **Castries**; *language:* English (Kweyol, a French patois, is also widely spoken); *population:* 160,145 (2002 estimate), 90% of African descent; *religion:* Roman Catholic 64%, Anglican 3%, other Protestant denominations 7%.

Constitution: St Lucia is a constitutional monarchy within the **Commonwealth**. There is an 11-member Senate and a directly elected 17-member House of Assembly.

History: Tradition has it that **Christopher Columbus** visited and named the island on 13 December 1502. The first settlers were French and the island changed hands 14 times until confirmed as British in 1814. It became an Associated State in 1967 and gained independence in 1979.

Latest elections: In the general election of 3 December 2001 the St Lucia Labour Party (SLP) received 54.2% of the vote and won 14 seats, while the United Workers' Party obtained 36.6% of the vote and three seats. The Government was formed by the SLP led by Dr Kenny Anthony.

International relations and defence: St Lucia is a member of the United Nations, the **Organization of American States**, the Commonwealth, the **Caribbean Community and Common Market**, and the **Organization of Eastern Caribbean States**. The Royal Saint Lucia Police Force of 300 has a Special

Service Unit for defence purposes. St Lucia participates in the US-sponsored Regional Security System.

St Lucia, economy

GNI: US \$619m. (2001); *GNI per caput:* \$3,950 (2001); *GNI at PPP:* \$778m. (2001); *GNI per caput at PPP:* \$4,960 (2001); *exports:* \$51.81m. (2001); *imports:* \$258.74m. (2001); *currency:* Eastern Caribbean dollar (EC\$), plural dollars; US \$1 = EC\$2.70 since July 1976.

In 2001 agriculture accounted for 5.8% of St Lucia's gross domestic product (GDP) and industry for 4.5%. Some 6.5% of the land is arable, 22.6% under permanent crops and 3.2% permanent pasture. The main crop is **bananas**; vegetables and fruit are grown and livestock reared for local consumption. The principal foreign exchange earner is tourism. The main industry is brewing.

Main exports are bananas, beverages and tobacco. Principal imports are food, fuels and machinery and transport equipment. In 2000 the United Kingdom was the greatest purchaser of exports, followed by Barbados and the USA. The USA was the main supplier of imports in that year, followed by the United Kingdom and Japan.

The banana industry has been hard hit by the US-led erosion of **European Union** trade preferences in the 1990s. Public-sector debt was equivalent to 56% of GDP in September 2002. Average annual growth in GDP in 1990–2001 was 0.5%; in 2001 GDP declined by 5.4%, but growth of 0.2% was recorded in 2002. The rate of unemployment was 18.9% in 2001.

St-Martin/Sint Maarten

St-Martin/Sint Maarten is situated in the lesser Antilles to the north-west of St Kitts. It was named by **Christopher Columbus**, but divided between France and the Netherlands in 1648. The 10.2 km frontier is the only land frontier in the Lesser Antilles.

St-Martin. *Area:* 52 sq km (20 sq miles); *capital:* Marigot; *language:* French; *population:* 30,000. A dependency of the French Overseas Department of Guadeloupe.

Sint Maarten. *Area*: 34 sq km (13 sq miles); *capital:* Philipsburg; *language:* Dutch; *population:* 36,231 (1996 estimate). Part of the Netherlands Antilles.

Economy: The introduction of the euro on 1 January 2002 gave the two parts of the island a single currency for the first time. The principal economic activity of the island is tourism. English is widely spoken.

St Vincent and the Grenadines

St Vincent and the Grenadines, the third smallest state in the western hemisphere, consists of the island of St Vincent itself and 32 small islands and keys to the south of the main island, the southernmost of which, Petit St Vincent, directly adjoins Petit Martinique, the nearest island in Grenada.

Area: 389 sq km (150 sq miles); *capital:* **Kingstown**; *language:* English (Creole is also spoken); *population:* 109,022 (2001 census), 66% Afro-Caribbean, 19% of African descent, 6% 'East Indian', 4% white, 2% Carib Amerindian; *religion:* more than 33% Anglican, 25% Methodist, 10% Roman Catholic.

Constitution: A constitutional monarchy within the **Commonwealth**. The House of Assembly has 15 elected members and six nominated Senators.

History: St Vincent was named by **Christopher Columbus** in 1498, but fierce Carib resistance precluded its colonization. In 1675 a Dutch ship was wrecked on the island with its cargo of African slaves who joined with the Caribs in resisting French and British colonization. Though the island finally passed to Great Britain in 1783, a revolt by the Black Caribs in 1795–96 gained control of most of the island; the descendants of those who were deported to Roatan, off the coast of British Honduras, now form the Garifuna community of Belize.

Latest elections: At a general election held on 28 March 2001, the Unity Labour Party (ULP) won 57% of the vote and 12 seats and the New Democratic Party 40.9% of the vote and three seats. The government was formed by the ULP led by Dr Ralph Gonsalves.

International relations and defence: St Vincent and the Grenadines is a member of the United Nations, the **Organization of American States**, the Commonwealth, the **Caribbean Community and Common Market**, and the **Organization of Eastern Caribbean States**. The islands participate in the US-sponsored Regional Security System.

St Vincent and the Grenadines, economy

GNI: US $317m. (2001); *GNI per caput:* $2,740 (2001); *GNI at PPP:* $577m. (2001); *GNI per caput at PPP:* $4,980 (2001); *exports:* $42.2m. (2001); *imports:* $181.9m. (2001); *currency:* Eastern Caribbean dollar (EC$), plural dollars; US $1 = EC$2.70 since July 1976.

In 2002 agriculture accounted for 9.9% of St Vincent and the Grenadines' gross domestic product (GDP) and industry for 4.9%. Some 17.9% of the land is arable, 17.9% under permanent crops and 5.1% permanent pasture. The main legal export crop is **bananas**; other fruit and vegetables are produced for local consumption, and marijuana is illegally cultivated for trade to other islands. Tourism has been handicapped by the need for passengers to transfer flights in Barbados or St Lucia. The largest industry is the milling of flour; rice is also milled and animal feed produced for the Eastern Caribbean market; electronic components are also assembled on the island. There is a small 'offshore' financial sector. The main energy source is imported petroleum.

Main exports are bananas, flour and rice. Principal imports are food, basic manufactures, machinery, road vehicles and fuels and lubricants. In 2002 the United Kingdom was the greatest purchaser of exports, followed by Trinidad and Tobago and Barbados. The USA was the greatest supplier of imports, followed by the United Kingdom and Barbados.

The traditional mainstay of the economy, bananas, was adversely affected during the 1990s by the US-led campaign against **European Union** trade preferences. The current account deficit on the balance of payments widened in 2001 to 18.6%. Annual GDP growth in 1995–99 averaged 4.4%; after a brief recession in 2000–01 GDP growth of 0.8% was recorded in 2002.

Salinas de Gortari, Carlos

Carlos Salinas de Gortari studied in Mexico and at Harvard Business School before entering government service. Chosen by the ruling **Partido Revolucionario Institucional** as President of Mexico, 1988–94, with no previous experience of elective office, he was elected with the slenderest of majorities in a hotly contested election. He went on to reverse more than 70 years of government policy and to emerge as a leading proponent of the free market. Key policies included the privatization of some 400 state-owned enterprises, ending the land reform pro-gramme by allowing *ejidatarios* (workers on government co-operative farms) to buy their lands, and negotiating successfully for a **North American Free Trade Agreement** which ended Mexico's traditional protectionist polices. However, his six-year term ended in economic crisis, since when his unpopularity in Mexico has been so great that he has chosen to live in Ireland.

San José, Costa Rica

San José, the chief city and capital of Costa Rica, is situated on the central plateau of Costa Rica. The population of the city in 2002 was officially estimated at 328,293 and that of the metropolitan area at 1,425,484, but one-quarter of the country's population lives in or around the capital. The city was founded as Villa Nueva in the 1730s and became the capital in 1823, growing substantially in the 19th century as the **coffee** industry developed.

San Juan, Puerto Rico

San Juan, the chief town and capital of the Commonwealth of Puerto Rico, is situated on the north coast of the island, on one of the best harbours in the Caribbean. It was first explored by the Spanish in 1508 and soon became the site of a substantial fortified base, which was attacked by Sir Francis Drake in 1595. It was captured by US forces in 1898 during the Spanish–American War. At the 2000 census it had a population of 421,958.

San Salvador

San Salvador, chief town and capital of the Republic of El Salvador, was founded in 1528 and became the capital at the dissolution of the Central American Republic in 1839. It is also the country's financial, commercial and industrial centre. Situated in a seismically active zone at the edge of the central highlands of the country, it was devastated by **earthquakes** in 1854, 1873, 1917 and 1986, when more than 900 people died in the ruins. The municipal area had a population of 485,847 in mid-2001.

Sandino, Gen. Augusto César

Augusto César Sandino, 1895–1934, was a Nicaraguan farmer and mining engineer. After the second US intervention in Nicaragua in 1926, he took up arms as a commander of guerrillas against the occupation forces, and continued to fight the occupation until the US marines were withdrawn in 1933, when Gen. Anastasio Somoza García emerged as commander of the US-trained National Guard. In 1934 he was invited to dine at the presidential palace, seized on leaving by Somoza's men, and murdered. His body was secretly buried under the main runway at **Managua** airport. His name was subsequently adopted by the **Frente Sandinista de Liberación Nacional** as a symbol of heroic and successful resistance to foreign rule.

Santiago de Chile

Santiago, chief city and capital of Chile, is situated in the central valley on the River Mapocho, a short journey from Chile's main port, Valparaíso, and principal seaside resort, Viña del Mar. It was founded by Spanish settlers who came overland from Peru in 1541, became the capital at independence in 1818 and is today a busy industrial city as well as the centre of the country's political and cultural life. The population of the metropolitan region in 2000 was 6,061,200.

Santiago de Cuba

Santiago, called 'de Cuba' to distinguish it from the capital of Chile, is a port at the eastern end of the south coast of Cuba, and an important outlet for Cuba's agricultural exports. Founded on its present site in 1522, it served as the capital of the island until 1589, and is now Cuba's second largest city, with an estimated population of some 441,524 (1999). The Moncada Barracks, in the city, is celebrated for the doomed attempt of **Fidel Castro** and his companions to capture it in 1953.

Santo Domingo

Santo Domingo, chief city and capital of the Dominican Republic, is a port situated at the mouth of the River Ozama, on the south coast of the island of Hispaniola, and the country's chief industrial centre. It was founded in 1496 by Bartolomeo Colón to replace his brother's unsuccessful settlement at Isabella on the north coast, and is the oldest continuously inhabited European town in the western hemisphere. The Cathedral houses the remains of **Christopher Columbus**. Between 1936 and 1961 the city was known as Ciudad Trujillo, after the dictator, Rafael Trujillo.

Sarney, José

José Sarney, President of Brazil 1985–1990, was a member of the pro-military Aliança Renovadora Nacional party under the military government and subsequently leader of its conservative splinter-group, the Partido Democrático Social. Chosen as vice-presidential candidate in a bargain with the more liberal opposition **Partido do Movimento Democrático Brasileiro**, he became acting President of Brazil on 15 March 1985 when Tancredo Neves, the first civilian to be elected President after the long period of military rule, was taken ill on the morning of his inauguration. One month later Neves died. Sarney tried to implement the programme Neves had proposed, introduced the Cruzado Plan of 1986 in an effort to stabilize the economy and summoned a National Constituent Assembly to produce a more democratic Constitution, which it did in 1988. However, he remained distrusted for his military connections and his failure to maintain the Cruzado Plan. His period of office was marked by bitter political infighting and continued economic crisis.

Sendero Luminoso (SL)
Shining Path, Peru

The Partido Comunista del Perú-Sendero Luminoso (PCP-SL), not to be confused with the Partido Comunista Peruano, and better known simply as Sendero Luminoso (SL), was unusual in a number of respects. It was founded in 1970 by a former professor of philosophy, Abimael Guzmán Renoso (b. 1935), alias 'Presidente Gonzalo', who recruited a considerable number of his students at San Cristóbal de Huamanga University in Ayacucho as 'weekend guerrillas'. Its name, which in Spanish means 'the shining path', refers to Marxism and is taken from a phrase of the Peruvian Marxist writer, José Carlos Mariátegui (1895–1930). Philosophically the movement has taken a very hard line and rejected all forms of collaboration. Strategically it has pursued the Maoist path of 'prolonged popular warfare', laying great emphasis both on secrecy and on building a secure base among the Andean peasantry of the Department of Ayacucho and surrounding areas.

It opened its campaign on 17 May 1980, the day when Peru returned to civilian government after 12 years of military rule. In what became a trademark operation, electricity pylons were blown up, plunging **Lima** into darkness. Initially care was taken to avoid open confrontation, with efforts focused instead on building up a 'people's revolutionary army', estimated to number up to 3,000 activists, and on sabotage, kidnapping and the assassination of local officials.

In 1985 SL marked the New Year with an attack on a Lima army club. A major attack on Cerro de Pasco on 28 January paralysed **copper** production, and the visit of Pope **John Paul II** in February was marked by a daring attack which again blacked out the capital. The second phase of the SL's campaign began when the new President, Alan García of the **Alianza Popular Revolucionaria Americana** (APRA), offered SL an amnesty, which was not reciprocated. An attack by the SL on APRA headquarters on 7 October in which three died, was followed by a new state of emergency in six Departments, but SL stepped up its guerrilla attacks. On

9 February 1986, President García proclaimed a national state of emergency and decreed a curfew in Lima, blacked out when guerrillas simultaneously attacked seven offices of the ruling APRA, six banks and the San Jorge prison. Sporadic violence continued until on 18 June rebel-inspired mutinies in three prisons, Lurigancho in the suburbs of Lima, and El Frontón and Santa Bárbara at Callao, were met by troops using tanks, heavy weapons and explosives which killed more than 250 inmates, 'at least' 100 of them, according to the President, massacred at Lurigancho after they has surrendered. He promised to arrest those responsible, but, after appeals to other Latin American states, and, through Argentina, to the USA, to help avert a possible coup, his weak position became clear. Despite a Lima court detaining Gen. Jorge Rabanal, commander of the armoured division at Lurigancho, the President conspicuously laid the blame for the massacres on the police, who acted throughout under military orders.

Though the loss of key elements in SL's command structure and the fear of a new military government seemed at first to have resulted in a substantial reduction in the scale if not the number of its attacks, a reprisal attack on a tourist train at Cuzco, which killed seven and wounded at least 28, was a reminder of the movement's continued strength in the provinces. In October 1986 39 insurgents were killed, including the reputed third highest ranking member in the SL hierarchy, but the assassination of Adm. Geronimo Cafferata confirmed its continuing power and the state of emergency in Lima was renewed.

In 1987, having established control of the Upper Huallaga Valley, SL began to benefit from the huge profits of Peru's illegal narcotics trade. Despite the creation by the government of a unified military command structure in April, the movement's strategy continued to be directed at either dividing the armed forces or provoking a military coup, but this did not happen. Instead police captured Guzmán's deputy and military commander, Osman Morote, in early June 1988. The previous month the discovery of five bodies in an unmarked grave confirmed the reported massacre by soldiers of 28 peasants in Cayará. President García, who had initially been critical of such excesses, indirectly defended the armed forces, who had been increasingly insistent that he should do so. Amnesty International confirmed that there had been a sharp increase in reported cases of torture and unlawful killing in the Andean emergency zone since 1987. The government, which had extended the state of emergency to cover six provinces and Lima itself, was also thought to be behind the emergence of a right-wing counter-terrorist group, the so-called Commando Rodrigo Franco.

On 26 July 1988, Abimael Guzmán, the 53-year-old revolutionary leader, called for a new, third stage in the struggle. 'Our process of the people's war has led us towards the apex', he claimed. 'We have to prepare for insurrection, which will be the taking of the cities.' By November, when the power lines between Lima and the Mantaro hydroelectric plant in the central Sierra were severed and a state of emergency was declared in Junín, seven Departments were under martial law and the insurgents seemed well on their way to their objective. On 10 May 1989 SL declared an 'armed strike' in the Central Andean Departments of Junín, Pasco and Huancano, and both the violence and criticism of President García spread rapidly. An 'armed strike' in Lima in July was successful in keeping the buses off the streets and closed many shops in the shanty towns, but had little effect on industry. Later in the year SL tactics focused on the disruption of the municipal elections held on 12 November. A daring demonstration in the heart of Lima became a one-hour gun battle in which several passers-by were casualties, and led President García to place the capital under martial law. In the countryside, where more than 50 mayors had been killed and many candidates had in consequence withdrawn, it proved impossible to hold elections in some sparsely populated areas. According to a Senate committee report, 3,198 people had died violently as a result of insurgent and 'death squad' activity in 1989, compared with 1,986 in 1988, making a total of some 15,800 since 1980.

Despite all efforts to prevent them, however, presidential elections were held in 1990, resulting in the unexpected election of a political unknown, the businessman **Alberto Keinya Fujimori**. Aiming to break the alliance of drugs-trafficking and insurgency, President Fujimori's Government soon reversed its initial refusal to accept US money for crop substitution. A fresh onslaught by SL had already blacked out Lima, Trujillo and Ica on 6 April, and, under cover of darkness, bomb and grenade attacks caused extensive damage to property. Twelve days later the Government extended the state of emergency to a further eight provinces, suspending constitutional guarantees over some two-thirds of the country. Despite this, incidents continued, while further evidence emerged of the involvement of military personnel in 'death squad' activity. Amnesty International claimed that under the Fujimori Government 120 people had already 'disappeared', making a total of some 3,700 since 1980. Congress eventually granted the President emergency legislative powers for 150 days from 18 June to deal with both the military emergency and the economic crisis that existed.

On 5 April 1992, with the aid of a well-executed military coup, President Fujimori suspended the Constitution and dissolved Congress and the judiciary. However, the results were not at all in accordance with SL's strategy of 'the intensification of contradictions'. In response to the coup fresh attacks on targets in Lima and Callao killed 10 and caused numerous other casualties. But on 28 April, acting under their new powers, the Government sent troops into the shanty town of Raucana on the edge of Lima. On 5 May a decree increased penalties for terrorist offences and eliminated restraints on 'disappearances'. The following day paramilitary police led a four-day assault on the high security Miguel Castro prison in Lima, parts of which were said to be controlled by SL. After fierce resistance it was reported that, at the cost of 35 prisoners and two police killed and 20 wounded, 451 prisoners had been forced to surrender. On the night of 4–5 June a bomb attack, apparently by SL, on the studios of TV Channel 2 in Lima killed five. On 16 July a new 'urban militia' was instituted. On the same night a large car bomb had killed 20 and injured more than 250 in the Miraflores district, and there were widespread attacks on police posts. On 25 July President Fujimori decreed that in future 'terrorist criminals' would be tried by military courts.

In September 1992, after 12 years of conflict which cost some 23,000 lives and had led President Fujimori to abandon constitutional government, Guzmán himself was arrested. Though the President immediately claimed this justified his dictatorial measures, Guzmán was not captured by the army but was discovered as a result of efficient police work in a 'safe house' in Lima, where he was captured together with his alleged 'No. 2', Elena Reboredo Iparaguirre, and 19 other members of the Central Committee. In a series of searches carried out on 17 October more SL leaders were reportedly captured. After Guzmán had been exhibited in a steel cage to the press on 24 September he was returned to custody at La Punta naval base at Callao. At his trial, which, though it lasted 10 days, was held in secret and allowed for no defence witnesses, as President Fujimori had predicted, he was sentenced to life imprisonment, the highest penalty then available, though the death penalty was subsequently reintroduced.

In the months that followed many of Guzmán's key followers were also captured, though violence continued in the rural areas and much of the country continued to be under martial law. On 1 October the President claimed before the United Nations that Guzmán had made a formal offer of peace from the naval prison at Callao. Subsequently a major split was reported in the movement between its imprisoned leader and armed militants led by Oscar Ramírez Durand ('Feliciano'). Casualties had fallen to some 300 in 1993 and 6,000 former guerrillas surrendered under the government's 'Law of Repentance' before it expired on 31 October 1994. On 28 July the President had claimed that terrorism had been defeated. However, on 13 November the Government extended the existing state of emergency in Lima and Callao for a further 90 days, citing continuing terrorist activity as its excuse. This activity has since continued, though at a comparatively low level.

Siles Zuazo, Hernán

Hernán Siles Zuazo, President of Bolivia 9–16 April 1952, 1956–60, 1982–85, was born in **La Paz** in 1914. The son of President Hernando Siles (1930–36), he served in the Chaco War and was decorated, before qualifying as a lawyer at the Universidad Mayor de San Andrés in 1939. Elected a deputy in 1940, he, **Víctor Paz Estenssoro** and Walter Guevara Arce together founded the **Movimiento Nacionalista Revolucionario** (MNR), which seized power in the Bolivian Revolution of April 1952. As Vice-President in 1952–56 he became increasingly disillusioned with Paz Estenssoro's leadership, and in 1954 split the party, assuming the leadership of the more radical faction within it and being himself elected President in 1956. However, in 1964 he was expelled from the MNR and from exile encouraged the coup that overthrew Paz. Exiled from 1966 to 1973, he joined the left-wing fraction of the MNR, the MNR de Izquierda (MNRI), which was opposed to the dictatorship of Gen. **Hugo Bánzer** (1971–78). After the fall of Bánzer, Siles was elected President in 1979 and 1980, but was kept out of power by the armed forces until 1982, when the economy was already collapsing, and his MNRI disintegrated. Persuaded to cut short his term peacefully in 1985, he died in 1996.

Sistema de la Integración Centroamericana (SICA)
Central American Integration System

SICA is an international organization established by the member states to carry out and co-ordinate the decisions of the Presidential Summits and the decisions of the Council of Foreign Ministers of the Central American states to further the political and economic integration of the region. It was established by the Protocol of Tegucigalpa, signed on 13 December 1991, by Guatemala, El Salvador, Honduras, Nicaragua, Costa Rica and Panama. The Protocol, which established the system's juridical standing and institutional structure, came into force on 1 February 1993. The Dominican Republic has observer status.

> *Address:* Secretaría General del SICA, Blvd Orden de Malta No. 470, Urb. Sta Elena, San Salvador, El Salvador
> *Telephone:* (503) 289-6131
> *Fax:* (503) 289-6124
> *E-mail:* info@sgsica.org
> *Internet:* www.sgsica.org

Socialism

In 1900 workers' movements in Latin America were still very weak, the main influences on them being those of anarchism and anarcho-syndicalism, brought from Spain and Italy by the migrant workers who worked in the southern hemisphere during the northern winter. In Mexico the strikes at the Cananea **copper** mine in 1906 and the Río Blanco textile factory in 1907 were followed only in 1913 by the formation of Mexico's first labour central, the Casa de Obrero Mundial. Its members supported the Constitutionalists during the Revolution. Socialist ideas became mainstream in 1924 under the 1920s governments supported by the **Confederación Revolucionaria Obrera de México** and constituted the ideology of what was to become the **Partido Revolucionario Institucional** (PRI). Consolidated under **Lázaro Cárdenas** (1934–40), the party was to remain officially socialist until the late 1980s.

In other countries socialist ideas were taken up by the ruling liberals, leading to the social reformism of the Governments of Alfonso López Pumarejo (1934–38, 1942–45) in Colombia and Ramón Grau San Martín in Cuba (1933–34). With the rapid spread of Marxist ideas after the First World War, Luis Emilio Recabarren was the founder of both the Chilean Communist and Socialist parties. In 1932 a socialist republic was proclaimed by a group of junior officers and between 1937 and 1941 the Socialists formed the main contingent of the Popular Front Government of Pedro Aguirre Cerda. Socialist influence reached a peak during the Second World War, strengthened by a significant influx of Republican exiles from Spain. However, though Marxist ideas and concepts became mainstream among Latin American intellectuals after 1945, for many others they were too closely associated with Communist influence and discouraged as such by the Catholic Church. Though democratic socialist parties existed in almost all Latin American states, few achieved any significant level of power comparable with the Labour parties of the former British and Dutch Caribbean states, as under Norman and **Michael Manley** in Jamaica. The major exception, the Chilean **Partido Socialista**, was banned after the fall of **Salvador Allende** in 1973, but returned to power with the election of Ricardo Lagos Escobar in 2000.

Sociedad Nacional de Industrias (SNI)
National Industrial Association, Peru

F. 1896 to foster industrial development. It includes 90 directors representing major companies, and some 2,500 members, and is organized in a series of committees, each representing a specific industrial sector.

Leadership: Roberto Nesta Brero (Pres.)
Address: Los Laureles 365, San Isidro, Apdo 632, Lima 27

Telephone: (1) 421-8830
Fax: (1) 442-4573
E-mail: sni@sni.org.pe
Internet: www.sni.org.pe

Sociedad Rural Argentina (SRA)
Argentine Rural Society

A private society of landowners, f. 1866 to promote agricultural development. The SRA's annual Show at Palermo, **Buenos Aires**, remains the centrepiece of the annual social calendar. It has more than 9,000 members, including many of the most politically influential in the country.

Leadership: Enrique C. Crotto (Pres.)
Address: Florida 460, 1001 Buenos Aires
Telephone: (11) 4324-4700
Fax: (11) 4324-4774
E-mail: prensa@ruralorg.com.ar
Internet: www.ruralorg.ar

Somoza Debayle, Anastasio

Anastasio Somoza Debayle (1925–1980) succeeded his brother Luís as commander of the Nicaraguan National Guard in 1963, and, as effective ruler of Nicaragua until his overthrow by the Sandinistas in 1979, continued a family tradition of dictatorship and corruption established by his father, Anastasio Somoza García (1896–1956) in 1936. He was assassinated by Argentine guerrillas in **Asunción**, Paraguay, in 1980.

South Georgia
Las Georgias del Sur

Despite the Spanish form of its name, South Georgia, a dependency of the Falkland Islands situated 1,300 km (800 miles) to the east of them in the South Atlantic, is a single, mountainous island, three-quarters of which is permanently covered by snow. It has no permanent inhabitants. It was discovered by Capt. James Cook in 1775 and claimed for Britain, which maintains an Antarctic research station on the island. It was first crossed in 1916 by Ernest Shackleton, at the end of his successful voyage from Antarctica in an open boat in search of aid. In 1927 it was claimed by Argentina and in 1955 the United Kingdom submitted the dispute over its sovereignty unilaterally to the International Court of Justice, which, however, declined to hear the case on the grounds that Argentina had refused to accept its jurisdiction. In the sequence of events leading up to the Falklands War, in March 1982 a team of scrap merchants were landed on the island and were subsequently revealed to have been Argentine naval personnel; they were ejected from the island six weeks later. Britain withdrew its military detachment from the island in 2001 but maintains a scientific research station there.

South Sandwich Islands

The South Sandwich Islands, an uninhabited island group in the South Atlantic with a total area of 311 sq km (120 sq miles), are situated 750 km (470 miles) south-east of South Georgia. They were discovered by Capt. James Cook and claimed for Britain in 1775. In 1948 they were claimed by Argentina and in 1955 the United Kingdom submitted the dispute over their sovereignty unilaterally to the International Court of Justice, which, however, refused to hear the case on the grounds that Argentina had refused to accept its authority. In December 1976 some 50 Argentines set up a scientific base on Southern Thule. They were removed by British forces in June 1982.

Southern Common Market

Mercado Común del Sur/Mercado Comum do Sul (Mercosur/Mercosul)

On 26 March 1991 the Presidents of Argentina, Brazil, Paraguay and Uruguay, meeting at **Asunción**, Paraguay, signed an agreement, the Treaty of Asunción, to create a new common market in the Southern Cone, with its headquarters at **Montevideo**, Uruguay. This was followed by a 47% reduction in tariffs in June of the same year and the signature of a framework free-trade agreement with the USA. The new grouping, the Southern Common Market (*Mercado Común del Sur*—Mercosur or, in Portuguese, *Mercado Comum do Sul*—Mercosul), represented a natural development in view of the geographical unity of the Paraguay-Paraná Basin and a long series of bilateral accords, but its targets were exceptionally ambitious. With an estimated population in 1991 of more than 190m. and a combined gross national product of some US $550,000m., from the beginning it aimed to achieve free movement of goods and services by 31 December 1994. Despite all difficulties, agreement was reached on the twin problems of the common external tariff and trade imbalances. The Ouro Prêto Protocol, signed in December 1994, gave Mercosur international legal status and the power to sign agreements with other such entities. The customs union came into existence on schedule on 1 January 1995. From then on, there was a marked increase in intra-regional trade. Though Argentina and Brazil continued to have sharp differences on trade in motor vehicles, these were resolved at a presidential summit in March 2000, where they also agreed to defer longstanding disputes on footwear, pigs, poultry, steel, **sugar** and textiles, thus opening the way for enlargement.

From the beginning both Bolivia and Chile made it clear that they did not want to be excluded from Mercosur. At the ninth summit at Punta del Este, Uruguay, on 7 December it was agreed to establish a free-trade zone with Bolivia and extend current bilateral agreements with Chile until March 1996. Following expiry of this deadline, agreement was reached on both Chile's physical integration (to provide a number of specified points of access) and its initial tariff regime, under which it could enter into associate status. At the 10th summit meeting, held in San Luís, Argentina, on 25 June 1996, Chile was admitted as an associate member with effect from 1 October. A framework free-trade agreement was also approved for Bolivia which would provide it with guaranteed access to both Atlantic and Pacific ports from 1997, and in June 2000 Chile announced its decision to seek full membership of Mercosur.

The other major issue facing Mercosur was relations with other groups and with the USA. In January 1995 foreign ministers of the Andean countries, meeting at Santa Cruz de la Sierra, Bolivia, agreed to seek a free-trade agreement with Mercosur by 30 June. At the Seventh Ibero-American Summit, held on 8–9 November 1997, in Venezuela, representatives of the **Andean Community of Nations** and Mercosur agreed in principle to form a single trading bloc. In September 1996, at a meeting in Montevideo, the Mercosur countries concluded a co-operation agreement with the **European Union** (EU), signed in Madrid on 20 December 1996, which envisaged a future free-trade zone incorporating both blocs. Furthermore, in 1999 the EU and Mercosur agreed to initiate discussions with a view to forming an integrated trading bloc some time after 2001.

The chief organ of decision-making is the Common Market Council, the presidential summit, which meets twice a year.

Leadership: Reginaldo Braga Arcuri (Dir), Brazil
Address: Edif. Mercosur, Luis Piera 1992, 1°, 11200 Montevideo, Uruguay
Telephone: (2) 412-9024
Fax: (2) 418-0557
E-mail: sam@mercosur.org.uy
Internet: www.mercosur.org.uy

special period in time of peace

The 'special period in time of peace' is the name given to the period in Cuba following the collapse of the Soviet Union in 1991. The ending of the substantial subsidy previously given to the Cuban government both directly and indirectly through the supply of substantial quantities of oil which Cuba could sell on the world market for hard currency plunged the economy into serious crisis. In 1992, for the first time since the Revolution, it was made legal for Cubans to own US dollars, enabling a widespread black market to grow up. Bicycles and even tricycle rickshaws were introduced as part of an effort to conserve scarce resources. However, every effort was made to develop an alternative source of revenue in the form of tourism, and since 1993 the economy has slowly recovered.

Stanley

Originally Stanley Harbour, Port William, f. 1833, Stanley is now the principal settlement and capital of the Falkland Islands. Its population in 1996 was 1,636. During the Argentine occupation in 1982 it was renamed Puerto Argentino, a name that the Argentine government has since agreed to drop.

Stroessner, Gen. Alfredo

Alfredo Stroessner Mattiauda (1912–), President of Paraguay 1954–89, was the son of a German immigrant family. He entered the army in 1932, won the Silver Star on active service in the Chaco War, and rose to become commander-in-chief in 1951. In 1954 he deposed President Federico Chávez and assumed the presidency. He was re-elected, initially by plebiscite and later in a series of rigged elections, for eight successive terms every four years up to and including 1986, maintaining control over the country through a strong military establishment, the detention and torture of political opponents and his control over the **Partido Colorado**. In 1989 he was deposed by his son-in-law and went into exile in Brazil.

Sucre

Sucre, which shares the status of capital of Bolivia with **La Paz**, is the seat of the Supreme Court, of an archbishopric and of the ancient University of San Francisco Xavier (1624). It is situated in the south-centre of the Bolivian highlands. It was founded in 1539, became the capital of the Charcas presidency of Upper Peru in 1561 and was the scene of Bolivia's declaration of independence in 1825. In 1839 it became the capital, and when in 1898 it was proposed to move the capital to La Paz, civil war broke out, resulting in the present compromise. Its population at the 2001 census was 215,778.

Sugar

In Latin America sugar is generally produced by extraction from the sap of sugar cane. A large perennial tropical grass of the genus *Saccharum,* sugar cane grows to a height of some 5 m. Mechanical harvesting has proved so wasteful that much is still cut by hand, a most exhausting task. It is then processed on site to extract and purify the juice, which is evaporated to separate the crystals of raw sugar (sucrose) from the concentrated syrup (molasses or treacle). This is the form in which it is exported, for further refining in the countries where it is to be consumed. Molasses is fermented and distilled to make rum, the staple spirit of the Caribbean Basin, and the raw juice of sugar cane can be and is used to produce ethanol, which may either be added in limited quantities to motor spirit to make it go further or used to fuel specially-adapted engines. By 1992 ethanol accounted for about one-half of the fuel used by Brazilian motorists. Brazil is the world's largest producer of sugar cane, producing 360.6m. metric tons in 2002. Second in Latin America was Mexico (46m. tons), followed by Colombia, Cuba, Guatemala and Argentina. In Cuba sugar remains the essential basis of the export economy, although production has fallen sharply and exports had to be suspended briefly in 1993. Sugar also remains a major export commodity in Belize, Barbados, the Dominican Republic, Guyana and St Christopher and Nevis.

Suriname

Suriname is the central one of the three Guianas, which form an enclave on the north-east coast of Brazil, and is bounded on the east by French Guiana and on the west by Guyana, with which it has a boundary dispute.

Area: 163,820 sq km (63,251 sq miles); *capital:* **Paramaribo**; *language:* Dutch (Sranan, English and Hindi are also spoken); *population:* 440,000, the majority of 'East Indian' descent, the rest mainly Afro-Caribbean; *religion:* Christian, Hindu, Muslim.

Constitution: Legislative power is vested in a directly elected National Assembly, which elects a President as head of state and of government for a five-year term.

History: Dutch settlement began in 1602, and an English settlement established in 1651 was ceded to the Dutch in 1667. In 1682 the Dutch West India Co introduced **coffee** and **sugar** cane and began to import African slaves to work on the plantations. When slavery was abolished in 1863, indentured labourers were brought from China, Java, and India to work on the plantations, adding to the population mix. During the Napoleonic Wars, when the Netherlands were occupied by France, Suriname briefly came under British rule: 1799–1802, 1804–15. It gained internal autonomy in 1954 and independence in 1975. The armed forces took over government in 1980, led by Sgt-Maj. Désiré ('Desi') Bouterse, who pursued a policy of non-alignment and established relations with Cuba. The Netherlands, however, refused to agree to US plans to overthrow him and in 1987 elections were held for a new civilian government. After a further brief military interlude in 1990–91 civilian government was again restored, but Bouterse's influence continued to be disruptive and Suriname's role as a transhipment point for illegal drugs caused tension abroad.

Latest elections: In elections held on 25 May 2000 the Niewe Front (NF) alliance, led by **Runaldo Ronald Venetiaan**, won 33 seats in the 51-member National Assembly, which in August 2000 elected Venetiaan as President.

International relations and defence: Suriname is a member of the United Nations, the **Organization of American States**, the **Commonwealth**, and the **Caribbean Community and Common Market**. At independence Suriname inherited an unresolved boundary dispute on the headwaters of the Corantijn river. In June 2000 the navy deployed gunboats to force the Canadian oil company CGX to remove its rigs from waters at the mouth of the Corantijn that are claimed by Suriname. The army numbers only 1,400, the navy 240 and the air force 200.

Suriname, economy

GNI: US $761m. (2001); *GNI per caput:* $1,810 (2001); *exports:* $437.0m. (2001); *imports:* $297.2m. (2001); *currency:* Suriname gulden, guilder or florin, plural guilders; US $1 = 2,650.00 guilders at 31 May 2003.

In 2001 agriculture accounted for 11.7% of Suriname's gross domestic product (GDP). Only 0.3% of the land is arable, 0.06% under permanent crops, 0.1% permanent pasture and more than 80% forest and woodland. The main crops are rice, **bananas** and oil palm. Cattle are mainly kept as draught animals. Fishing is a significant activity. Large logging concessions have been granted despite environmental protests, but as yet little has been exported. The main mineral resource is **bauxite**. The principal industry is the processing of bauxite into alumina and finished aluminium. The main energy source is petroleum, discovered in 1981, a small proportion of which is exported. Main exports are rice, bananas, **sugar**, oranges, and shrimp. Principal imports are food and beverages, fuels, basic manufactures and road vehicles. In 2000 Norway was the greatest purchaser of exports, followed by the USA and the Netherlands. The USA was the main supplier of imports, followed by the Netherlands and Japan.

A history of serious economic mismanagement has left the country heavily indebted. Annual GDP declined by 2.4% in 1999, when inflation reached 98.9%. It declined again, by 0.1%, in 2000, but rose by 2.1% in 2001. About one-half of the population is estimated to be living in poverty.

T

Tegucigalpa

Tegucigalpa, capital of Honduras, is situated in an intermontane basin in the southern highlands of the country. Founded in 1578 as a mining settlement, it became the capital in 1880. Its population in mid-2001 was estimated at 1,089,200.

Tobago

Tobago, the smaller of the two islands making up the Republic of Trinidad and Tobago, with an area of 300 sq km (116 sq miles), is situated in the Atlantic Ocean some 32 km to the north-east of Trinidad. In mid-2001 it was estimated to have a population of 54,100. It was first settled by the Dutch in 1628 but was afterwards in French hands for a century until captured by Britain in 1762 and ceded in 1763. With the collapse of the **sugar** industry in the 19th century it was attached to Trinidad in 1889.

Torrijos Herrera, Omar

Lt-Col Omar Torrijos Herrera, 1929–1981, *de facto* leader of Panama in 1968–78, was one of the two leaders of the 1968 coup that overthrew President Arnulfo Arias. Once in power, in 1969 he exiled his colleague, Col Boris Martínez, and within months had begun a radical assault on the entrenched oligarchy that had dominated Panama since 1903, notably by a programme of land reform. In 1972 Congress elected him as President for a six-year term. His anti-Americanism made him enemies in Washington, but his pragmatism enabled him successfully to negotiate the 1977 Canal Treaties with President Jimmy Carter, by which Panama gained control of the Canal in 1999. In 1978 he chose not to run for re-election. He died in an air crash in 1981.

Tourism

Most Caribbean states have experienced the growth of large-scale tourism. This is an obvious strategy for an area caught between the emergent trading blocs of the **North American Free Trade Agreement** and the **European Union**, which have sought to protect their own producers at a cost to their traditional Caribbean suppliers. Tourism in the region represents only a small percentage of tourism world-wide, but it is far greater than that experienced in other parts of the Third World. The number of visitors to the Caribbean each year is in excess of the total population of the region. This anomaly is most marked in the cases of the long-established tourist destinations, the Bahamas and Bermuda, but other islands are catching up. By the 1990s the Dominican Republic was the most popular destination in the Caribbean, with 1.9m. stopover visitors in 1994.

In a region where unemployment is a key problem, tourism is a major source of jobs on many of the islands. The most extreme case is the Bahamas where more than one-third of the official labour force are directly employed in the tourist industry. Direct employment of locals is for the most part low paid, unskilled and seasonal. Many more work in the informal sector in activities connected with tourism such as providing transport or selling souvenirs.

Trades Union Congress (TUC), Guyana

The sole national trade union confederation in Guyana, founded in 1940 and merged with the Federation of Independent Trade Unions in 1993. It comprises 16 affiliated trade unions.

Leadership: Norris Witter (Pres.)
Address: Critchlow Labour College, Woolford Ave, Non-pareil Park, Georgetown
Telephone: 226-1493
Fax: 227-0254
E-mail: gtuc@guyana.net.gy

Trades Union Congress of Jamaica (TUCJ)

The second largest trade union confederation in Jamaica, the TUCJ is affiliated to the Caribbean Congress of Labor and the International Confederation of Free Trade Unions and has some 20,000 members.

Leadership: E. Smith (Pres.)

Address: 35 Sutton St, POB 19, Kingston
Telephone: 922-5313
Fax: 922-5468

Trinidad and Tobago
Republic of Trinidad and Tobago

Trinidad is a large island at the end of the chain of the Lesser Antilles, and lies in the Caribbean Sea, enclosing, with the coast of Venezuela, the Gulf of Paria. It is separated from the mainland at its closest point by only 11 km (7 miles). Tobago, a much smaller island (approximately 300 sq km, or 116 sq miles), lies to the northeast of Trinidad.

Total area: 5,128 sq km (1,980 sq miles); *capital:* **Port of Spain**; *population:* 1,296,000 (2001 estimate), 40% of 'East Indian', 40% of African and 18% of mixed descent; *official language:* English—other languages spoken include Hindi, Chinese, Spanish and a local French Creole; *religion:* Christian (Roman Catholic 30%, Anglican 11%, other Protestants 14%), Hindu 24%, Muslim 6%.

Constitution: Since 1976 Trinidad and Tobago has been a parliamentary republic within the **Commonwealth**. The bicameral Parliament consists of a Senate of 31 members appointed by the President and a House of Representatives of 36 members elected by direct universal suffrage for up to five years. The President is indirectly elected by an electoral college consisting of the members of parliament, and appoints the Prime Minister, whose Cabinet is collectively responsible to parliament.

History: Trinidad was named by **Christopher Columbus** on his third voyage in 1498, but Spanish settlement did not begin until 1592, when the island was incorporated in the presidency of Nueva Granada. After 1776 Spain encouraged settlers from French possessions but in 1797 Trinidad was captured by Britain and formally ceded by Spain in 1802. Owing to the power of the French planter class Trinidad did not have an elected Assembly and elected members were introduced to the Legislative Assembly only in 1925. Trinidad and Tobago, which had been attached to Trinidad in 1889, attained full self-government in 1961 and independence in 1962.

Latest elections: In the general election held on 7 October 2002, the People's National Movement (PNP) obtained 50.7% of the vote and 20 seats, and the United National Congress 46.6% of the vote and 16 seats. The Government was formed by the PNP led by Patrick Manning.

International relations and defence: Trinidad and Tobago is a member of the United Nations, the **Organization of American States**, the Commonwealth, the **Caribbean Community and Common Market**, and the **Rio Pact**. In 2002 the Trinidad and Tobago Defence Force consisted of an army of 2,000 troops and 700 coastguards.

Trinidad and Tobago, economy

GNI: US $7.8m. (2001); *GNI per caput:* $5,960 (2001); *GNI at PPP:* $11m. (2001); *GNI per caput at PPP:* $8,620 (2001), rank 77; *exports:* $2,258.0m. (2001); *imports:* $2,998.9m. (2001); *currency:* Trinidad and Tobago dollar (TT$), plural dollars; US $1 = TT$6.269 at 31 May 2003.

In 2002 agriculture accounted for 1.5% of Trinidad and Tobago's gross domestic product (GDP), manufacturing industry for 7.2% and the petroleum sector for 26.3%. Some 14.6% of the land is arable, 9.2% under permanent crops and 2.1% permanent pasture. The main export crops are **sugar** and **cocoa**. The fishing industry is small. The only significant mineral resources are petroleum and gas. The principal industries are the manufacture of methanol and ammonia, and the production of steel, cement and glass. The main energy sources are petroleum and, since 1994, gas.

Main exports are refined petroleum products and chemicals. Principal imports are fuels and consumer goods. In 1999 the USA was the greatest purchaser of exports, followed by Latin America, Japan and Canada. The USA was the largest supplier of imports, followed by Latin America and Canada.

Rapid economic development began with the steep rise in petroleum prices in 1973, but with the fall in prices in the 1980s GDP fell by an annual average of 6.1% in 1982–87. However, though the unemployment rate rose to over 20% and real wages fell, the National Alliance for Reconstruction Government avoided the worst consequences of the crisis through strict adherence to a structural adjustment programme and was able to reschedule its debt at the beginning of the 1990s. There followed a moderate economic recovery during the 1990s boosted further by the steep rise in oil prices since 1999. Average annual GDP growth in 1990–2001 was 3.5%. GDP grew by 5.0% in 2001 and by 3.2% in 2002. However, the rate of inflation also rose, from 3.5% in 2000 to 5.6% in 2001. The rate of unemployment was 12.2% in 2001.

Trinidad and Tobago Chamber of Industry and Commerce

F. 1891; the Chamber has 291 members.

Leadership: Michael Arneaud (Pres.), David Martin (CEO)
Address: Chamber Bldg, Columbus Circle, Westmoorings, POB 499, Port of
   Spain
Telephone: 627-6966
Fax: 637-7425
E-mail: chamber@chamber.org.tt
Internet: www.chamber.org.tt

Turks and Caicos Islands

The Turks and Caicos islands consist of two groups of islands, islets and cays, some 40 in all, lying in the Atlantic to the south-east of the Bahamas and 145 km north of Hispaniola. The two groups are separated by the Columbus or Turks Island Passage.

Area: 430 sq km (166 sq miles); *capital:* Cockburn Town (on Grand Turk); *population:* 19,000 (2001 estimate), approximately one-half 'belongers' of African descent; *official language:* English (Creole is also spoken); *religion:* Protestant 40%, Baptist 18%, Anglican 16%. Methodist 12%, Church of God.

Constitution: Under the British Overseas Territories Act of 2002, the Governor represents the Crown and presides over both the Executive Council and the House of Assembly. He himself is responsible for defence, external relations, internal security, the judiciary, audit and the appointment of public officials. The Executive Council consists of the Chief Minister, chosen by the Governor as the leader of the political party most likely to command a majority in the Legislative Council and four other ministers appointed by the Governor from the elected members of the Legislative Council, as well as three members ex officio: the Financial Secretary, the Chief Secretary and the Attorney-General. The Legislative Council consists of the Speaker, the three ex officio members of the Executive Council, 13 members elected by residents over the age of 18 and three members who are nominated, one on the advice of the Chief Minister, one on the advice of the Leader of the Opposition and one at the Governor's discretion.

History: The islands were a dependency of Jamaica until its independence in 1962. They then became a separate colony, but were administered from the Bahamas between 1965 and 1973. In 1976 a pro-independence party gained power and agreement was reached with the United Kingdom in 1980 that the islands would be granted independence, but so far no government has chosen to exercise this option.

Latest elections: At the general election held on 24 April 2003 the ruling People's Democratic Movement won seven of the 13 seats on the Legislative Council; the results in two of these, however, were challenged by the opposition Progressive National Party (PNP), and in June 2003 the results were declared void by the Supreme Court. The subsequent by-elections gave both seats to the PNP, and on 15 August Michael Misick of the PNP was appointed Chief Minister and formed a new government.

International relations and defence: The United Kingdom government is responsible for both.

Economy: Until 1964 the principal export was salt produced by the solar evaporation of sea water, but the industry has now almost ceased. Fishing for lobster and conches forms the mainstay of the export economy. There is no significant agriculture on most of the islands and most foodstuffs have to be imported. In recent years there has been a substantial increase in the tourist industry, which is concentrated on the island of Providenciales and caters mainly for US visitors. The expansion of offshore finance, however, led to the islands being blacklisted by the OECD in 2000, though they were removed in March 2002 when they were judged to have made sufficient progress in tightening up their financial regulation.

U

Unidad Nacional (UN)
National Unity

Peruvian centrist political alliance founded in 2000 to support the presidential candidature of Lourdes Flores, who came third in the first round of the 2001 elections, with 24.3% of the votes cast. The alliance also won 17 seats in the Congress.
  Leadership: Lourdes Flores (Leader)
  Address: Calle Ricardo Palma 1111, Miraflores, Lima
  Telephone: (1) 224-2773

Unidad Nacional de Trabajadores Salvadoreños (UNTS)
National Unity of Salvadoran Workers

El Salvador's largest trade union confederation, founded in 1986.
  Leadership: Marco Tulio Lima (Leader)
  Address: Calle 27 Poniente 432, Col. Layco, Apdo 2479, Centro de Gobierno El
        Salvador, San Salvador
  Telephone: 225-7811
  Fax: 225-0558

Unidad Revolucionaria Nacional Guatemalteca (URNG)
Guatemalan National Revolutionary Unity

F. 1982 as an umbrella organization to co-ordinate the efforts of four armed guerrilla movements: the Ejército Guerrillero de los Pobres, the **Fuerzas Armadas Revolucionarias**, the Organización del Pueblo en Armas and the **Partido Guatemalteco del Trabajo**. Its political wing was called the Representación

Unitarida de la Oposición Guatemalteca. In December 1996, with UN mediation, the URNG signed a definitive peace agreement with the government, bringing armed action to an end. Demobilization of the guerrillas began in March 1997 and was completed within two months.

In the following month the URNG applied for provisional recognition as a political party. The formalities of registration were completed in December 1998 and the party contested the presidential and congressional elections of November 1999 in alliance with two other parties, winning 12.3% of the votes and 9 seats.

Leadership: Abla Estela Maldonado Guevara (Sec.-Gen.)

Address: Avda Simeón Cañas 8-01, Zona 2, Guatemala City

Telephone: 288-4440

Fax: 254-0572

E-mail: prensaurng@guate.net

Internet: www.urng.org.gt

Unión del Centro Democrático (UCeDé)
Union of the Democratic Centre, Argentina

More right-wing than centrist, the UCeDé is a conservative party standing for a free-market economy and a reduced public sector. Originally a coalition of eight small centre-right parties, the UCeDé was formed in 1980 under the leadership of Alvaro Alsogaray, who had held an important position in the post-1976 military government. In the October 1983 elections the party won only two seats in the Chamber of Deputies, Alsogaray receiving only 0.3% of the presidential vote. In order to improve its chances in the Federal Capital of **Buenos Aires** in the November 1985 elections, the UCeDé formed the 'Popular Centrist Alliance' coalition with the Capital Democratic Party (PDC) and Federalist Centre Party (PFC). The vote for the alliance increased to 3.5% of the national vote.

Although Alsogaray was elected as the UCeDé presidential candidate in June 1988, the party leadership at the same time decided to support the campaign of the Peronist **Partido Justicialista** (PJ), hoping thereby to raise the UCeDé's profile. This strategy led to the party polling 9.5% of the national vote, giving the UCeDé nine seats out of the 127 that were contested in the May 1989 elections. Alsogaray came third with 6.4% of the presidential vote. In May 1989, with Alsogaray as its candidate, the party polled 6.4% of the presidential vote, placing them a disappointing third overall. The party's legislative vote was only 2.6%, increasing only slightly, to 3.0%, in 1995. However, with the accession of President **Menem**, the party was invited to participate in government, Alsogaray's daughter, María Julia Alsogaray (b. 1943), becoming a member of the Cabinet. After the change of government in 1999 she came under attack and was arrested in August 2003, charged with mishandling public funds. The UCeDé supported the unsuccessful candidature of Menem in the presidential election of 2003.

Leadership: Alvaro Alsogaray (Pres.)

Address: Av. R. S. Peña 628, P. I. Of. 2, 1008 Buenos Aires

E-mail: bucd@hcdn.gov.ar

Unión Cívica Radical (UCR)
Radical Civic Union, Argentina

As Argentina's largest centrist/moderate left party, the UCR has been the dominant mainstream opposition to the Peronist **Partido Justicialista** (PJ). The party was founded by Leandro N. Alem in 1890, when the radical faction split away from the mainstream Civic Union and led an unsuccessful revolt against the Conservative government. One of the party's main demands was the enfranchisement of all adult male Argentines, and it did not participate in any elections until 1912, when that demand was met. In 1916 the UCR formed its first government and remained in power until 1930, when President Hipólito Yrigoyen, nephew of Alem, was ousted by a military coup. After losing both the 1945 and the 1951 elections to the Peronists, the UCR suffered internal problems which culminated in a dramatic split in 1956, caused by the nomination as the UCR's presidential candidate of Arturo Frondizi of the Intransigent faction, who was favourable to some co-operation with the Peronists. Frondizi became the candidate of the newly formed UCR Intransigente (UCRI, later the Partido Intransigente) and, with assistance from the Peronists, won the presidency in 1958.

The conservative wing of the party, led by the former UCR presidential candidate Ricardo Balbín, formed the People's UCR (UCR del Pueblo—UCRP) in 1956, which was to become the official UCR in 1972, when a court ruling awarded it the sole right to the name. The UCRP supported the military coup against Frondizi in 1962 and in the subsequent elections of 1963 the UCRP's candidate, Arturo Umberto Illía, was elected as President. He was himself overthrown in 1966 in another military coup which was supported by the UCRI. Balbín stood again in the 1973 presidential elections for the now renamed UCR and was heavily defeated by Peronists in both the April and September polls.

In 1981 the UCR helped to form a five-party democratic alliance opposed to the latest military junta (in power since 1976), which called for the restoration of democracy. Following the deposition of the military regime in 1982, UCR candidate Raul Alfonsín won a major victory in presidential elections in October 1983. He took 317 of the 600 seats in the electoral college, receiving 51.8% of the electoral college vote. The UCR also won a majority of Chamber of Deputies seats (129 out of 256) but only 16 of the 48 Senate seats and seven of the 24 provincial governorships, including the Province of Buenos Aires. Inaugurated in December 1983, Alfonsín proceeded to make good his election promises of reorganizing the armed forces and putting an end to the cycle of political instability and military intervention. Over half the military high command was forced into retirement and members of the military juntas since 1976 were prosecuted for murder, torture and abduction, some being sent to prison. However, after uprisings in a number of army garrisons in April 1987 and amid persistent rumours of an impending coup, Alfonsín introduced the law of 'Due Obedience', dropping all prosecutions against lower-ranking army and police officers indicted for human rights violations.

Spiralling inflation and a highly unstable economy forced Alfonsín to relinquish power to **Carlos Saúl Menem** of the PJ in July 1989, five months before the expiry of his presidential mandate. Two months earlier Menem had comfortably won presidential elections in which the defeated UCR candidate was Eduardo César Angeloz. The UCR became the main opposition party, and in February 1990 Angeloz refused an invitation from President Menem to join his Cabinet. Instead, he called for all political parties to sign a pact under which a plan for effective government would be drawn up to preserve and consolidate democracy in an extreme social and economic crisis. Such proposals, and the UCR's criticism of government policies, did not improve the party's electoral performance. In the 1991 mid-term elections the UCR lost five Chamber seats, its strength thus falling to 85 seats, while in the gubernatorial elections the UCR retained only three governor-ships. One of the victims of this poor showing was Alfonsín himself, who, following strong criticism from within the UCR, resigned the party leadership in mid-November 1991. Upon his resignation, Alfonsín announced the formation of an internal faction within the UCR, the Movimiento por la Democracia Social, which called for the defence of traditional UCR democratic principles. The eventual outcome was his re-election as party leader by an overwhelming majority in November 1993. In the 1995 presidential elections, the party's nominee, Horatio Massacesi, came a disappointing third with 17.1% of the vote. However, in legislative balloting the UCR retained the second highest Chamber representation with 69 seats.

The UCR contested the 1997 legislative elections in an alliance (*Alianza*) with the Frente del País Solidario (Frepaso) which won 45.6% of the popular vote compared with 36.1% for the PJ. Although the PJ secured 118 seats compared with the *Alianza*'s 110, the balance of power shifted to the *Alianza* and smaller provincial parties which collectively held 29 seats. In presidential elections held in October 1999 Fernando de la Rúa, the *Alianza* candidate, defeated Eduardo Duhalde of the PJ, thus ending a decade of Peronist domination of the presidency. De la Rúa and his Frepaso running-mate, Carlos 'Chacho' Alvarez, took 48.5% of the popular vote compared with 38.1% for Duhalde. In simultaneous legislative elections, in which 127 of the 257 Chamber seats were contested, the *Alianza* won 63 seats, increasing its representation in the Chamber to 127 seats, two seats short of an overall majority.

In 2000 the government of President de la Rúa, and the stability of the UCR-Frepaso alliance, were shaken by a corruption scandal in which ministers were accused of having bribed legislators in order to secure the enactment of labour reform. However, it was a new collapse in confidence in the economy which began in late 2000 which eventually forced the resignation of President de la Rúa in December 2001. The party seemed so discredited that two of its presidential candidates chose to run in 2003 as independents. However, Ricardo López Murphy, who had served as Minister of Defence and, briefly, as economy minister under de la Rúa, came a creditable third with 16.35% of the votes cast.

Leadership: Fernando de la Rúa (Pres.), Horacio Francisco Pernasetti (congressional Pres.)

Address: Alsina 1786, 1088 Buenos Aires

Telephone: (11) 449-0036

E-mail: info@ucr.org.ar

Internet: www.ucr.org.ar

Unión Industrial Argentina (UIA)

Argentine Industrial Union

Argentine association of manufacturers, representing the industrial sector, f. 1979. Its predecessor, the Confederación Industrial Argentina, was founded in 1973 but dissolved by the military government in 1977.

Leadership: Osvaldo Rial (Pres.)

Address: Avda De Mayo 1147, CP 57, Buenos Aires

Telephone: (11) 4124-2300

Fax: (11) 4124-2301

Unión por Panamá (UPP)

E-mail: uia@uia.org.ar
Internet: www.uia.org.ar

Unión por Panamá (UPP)
Union for Panama

Political alliance formed to contest the presidential elections of 2 May 1999, comprising the Partido Arnulfista (PA), Movimiento Liberal Republicano Nacionalista, Cambio Democrático and Movimiento de Renovación Nacional. Its presidential candidate, Mireya Elisa Moscoso (PA), widow of former President Arnulfo Arias, won 44.8% of the votes cast and was elected. In the Legislative Assembly, however, it won only 33.7% of the votes and 24 of the 71 seats, the rival **Nueva Nación** alliance taking 41 seats.
Leadership: Mireya Elisa Moscoso (President of the Republic)

United Democratic Party (UDP)

Conservative political party formed in Belize in 1974 by the merger of the People's Development Movement, the Liberal Party and the National Independence Party. It first achieved a majority in the House of Representatives in 1984, when Manuel Esquivel became Prime Minister. In March 2003 it obtained 45.6% of the votes cast but won only seven of the 29 seats.
Leadership: Dean Barrow (Leader), Elodio Aragon (Chair.)
Address: South End Bel-China Bridge, POB 1898, Belize City
Telephone: 227-2576
Fax: 337-6441
E-mail: info@udp.org.bz
Internet: www.udp.org.bz

United National Congress (UNC)

Social-democratic political party founded in Trinidad and Tobago in 1989. In the general election of 6 November 1995, it won 45.8% of the vote and 17 of the 34 Trinidadian seats, and was able to form a government with the support of the two members from Tobago. Its leader, Basdeo Panday, had in 1976 founded and become leader of the United Labour Front, a mainly 'East Indian' party with trade union support, and was Minister of External Affairs in the government of N. A. R.

310

Robinson, until his dismissal in February 1988 and subsequent expulsion from the National Alliance for Reconstruction.

Leadership: Basdeo Panday (Leader, Prime Minister)
Address: Rienzi Complex, 78–81 Southern Main Rd, Couva, Trinidad
Telephone: 636-8145
E-mail: info@unc.org.tt
Internet: www.unc.org.tt

United Nations Development Programme (UNDP)

Programme instituted by the United Nations General Assembly in 1965 to help countries achieve a sustainable level of human development. Five members from Latin America and the Caribbean sit on the 36-member Executive Board, and there are UNDP representatives in 24 countries in South America, Central America and the Caribbean.

Leadership: Mark Malloch Brown (United Kingdom, Administrator)
Address: 1 United Nations Plaza, New York, NY 10017, USA
Telephone: (212) 906-5295
Fax: (212) 906-5364
E-mail: hq@undp.org
Internet: www.undp.org

United States Virgin Islands

The US Virgin Islands are situated at the north-eastern end of the chain of the Lesser Antilles, separated from the British Virgin Islands by a narrow channel. There are some 68 islands, islets and cays, but only the larger islands are inhabited.

Area: 347 sq km; *capital:* Charlotte Amalie (on St Thomas); *language:* English (Spanish and Creole are also spoken); *population:* 108,612 (2000 census), 80% black and 15% white; *religion:* Christian (Baptist 42%, Roman Catholic 34%, Episcopalian 17%).

Constitution: The islands are an unincorporated territory of the USA. Executive power is vested in a directly elected Governor and legislative power in an elected assembly of 15 senators. The islands send one (non-voting) representative to the US Congress.

History: The islands were settled by Denmark in the 17th century and remained under Danish rule until bought by the USA in 1917 to avoid them falling into the hands of Germany. Limited self-government was granted in 1954.

Latest elections: In elections to the Senate held on 5 November 2002 the Democrats won eight seats, the Independent Citizens' Movement two and independents five.

International relations and defence: The USA is responsible for defence and the conduct of foreign policy.

Economy: The main source of income and employment in the islands is tourism. Ninety per cent of all trade is conducted with the USA. The giant petroleum refinery on St Croix has operated below capacity for many years and the alumina processing plant closed in 2001.

Uruguay

República Oriental del Uruguay—The Eastern Republic of the Uruguay

Uruguay is situated on the north bank of the Río de la Plata estuary, between the east bank of the River Uruguay and the Atlantic Ocean, adjoining Brazil to the north-east.

Area: 176,215 sq km (68,037 sq miles); *capital:* **Montevideo**; *language:* Spanish; *population:* 3,341,521, mainly of European descent; *religion:* Roman Catholic 75%, Protestant 2%.

Constitution: Under the 1966 Constitution, the Republic has an executive President who is assisted by a Vice-President and an appointed Council of Ministers. Legislative power is vested in a National Congress consisting of a 99-member Chamber of Deputies and a 31-member Senate (30 senators plus the Vice-President, who presides over Senate business but is also permitted to vote). The President and Vice-President are elected for a five-year term by direct universal suffrage on a run-off system. The President cannot be re-elected. Under a constitutional reform passed in 1996, parties must choose their presidential candidates by open primary elections that take place simultaneously for all parties on the last Sunday of April of the year of the presidential election. Senators and deputies are elected by proportional representation for fixed five-year terms. Senators are elected from a national constituency and deputies from the 19 departmental (provincial) sub-divisions. Under Uruguayan electoral law, the electorate votes in congressional elections for factions within each party itself. Parties usually present a large number of lists of candidates for the two chambers of parliament and congressmen represent both their faction and their party. Congressional party discipline necessitates co-ordination between the party's factions. Provincial (departmental) elections take place in May of the year following the general election. Voting is compulsory for all citizens from the age of 18.

History: The independence of the Eastern Republic of the Uruguay was recognized in 1830 after a period in which its territory was the subject of a dispute between Argentina and Brazil. Internal politics were then dominated by the struggle between the liberal Colorado (red) (PC) and conservative Blanco (white) (or National, PN) parties, giving rise to civil wars throughout the 19th century. The Colorados held power continuously from 1865 to 1958 before giving way to the Blancos. However, in 1904 **José Batlle y Ordóñez** successfully broke the cycle of violence and ushered in a new era of stability and social reform. Having visited Switzerland, he became a strong advocate of collegial government. The first collegiate government, introduced in 1919, broke down when Colorado President Gabriel Terra dissolved Congress and assumed dictatorial powers to combat the Great Depression. In 1951 a national referendum ushered in a second period of collegiate government. However, after nearly two decades of economic stagnation, the presidency was restored in 1967. This change came too late, however, to cut short the rise of the **Movimiento de Liberación Nacional**, generally known as the *Tupamaros.* Any illusion that Uruguay could remain 'the Switzerland of Latin America' in a continent increasingly ruled by dictatorships was shattered when in 1971 laws curtailing civil liberties were introduced to give the army a free hand. Two years later, in 1973, the armed forces took power. Though they retained a figurehead civilian President, Juan María Bordaberry, who was an admirer of the Spanish dictator Franco, they dissolved Congress and replaced it with an appointed Council of State. Although by 1976 the military promised a return to democracy, their regime of terror continued, with an estimated 6,000 political opponents imprisoned and subjected to torture, of whom some 900 died.

. With an eye on eventually transferring power to a civilian government, the military regime drafted a new Constitution that was intended to guarantee the army's influence in all matters of national security. This was rejected by a plebiscite in November 1980. Amidst mass protests, demonstrations and strikes and an economic crisis, the military finally agreed to elections being held in November 1984. These were won by the Colorado candidate, Julio María Sanguinetti. His Government was marked by a major controversy over whether an amnesty should be granted to all military and police personnel accused of human rights infringements, which was finally approved in a referendum in April 1989. Then, when the first fully free elections since the coup were held in November 1989, the Blancos emerged as the winners, with their leader, **Luís Alberto Lacalle Herrera**, becoming President.

Latest elections: In the first round of voting in the presidential election held on 31 October 1999, Tabaré Vázquez, former mayor of Montevideo, leading the Encuentro Progresista-Frente Amplio (EP-FA) left coalition, obtained 38.5% of the vote, compared with 31.3% cast for **Jorge Batlle Ibáñez**, who had secured the nomination of the ruling Colorado Party over Luís Hierro López, candidate of outgoing President Julio María Sanguinetti. Former President (1990–95) Luís Alberto Lacalle Ibáñez of the centre-right PN, received 21.3% of the vote (the worst performance in its history for his party) and Rafael Michelini, of the moderate left Nuevo Espacio, only 4.4%. However, in the run-off contest held on 28 November Vázquez, who appeared to have successfully reassured financial sectors that he would maintain the 'American Switzerland', was decisively defeated by Batlle, whose formal coalition with the PN gave him 54.1% of the vote, compared with 45.9% for Vázquez. In the Senate the results were: EP-F. 12 seats, Colorados 10, PN seven, Nuevo Espacio one; and in the Chamber: EP-F. 40 seats, Colorados 32, PN 23 and Nuevo Espacio four.

International relations and defence: Uruguay is a member of the United Nations, the **Organization of American States**, the **Latin American Integration Association**, the **Southern Common Market**, and the **Rio Pact**. There is no compulsory military service. The all-volunteer army numbers 15,900, the navy (including coastguard) 5,700 and the air force 3,000.

Uruguay, economy

GNI: US $19.2m. (2001); *GNI per caput:* $5,710 (2001); *GNI at PPP:* $28m. (2001); *GNI per caput at PPP:* $8,250 (2001), rank 79; *exports:* $2,294,557m. (2000); *imports:* $3,465,809m. (2000); *currency:* peso uruguayo, plural pesos uruguayos; US $1 = 27.85 pesos at 31 May 2003.

In 2001 agriculture accounted for 6% of Uruguay's gross domestic product (GDP), industry for 16.6% and financial services for 11.1%. Some 7.3% of the land is arable, 0.2% under permanent crops and 76.8% permanent pasture. The main agricultural activity is the rearing of cattle and sheep for the production of beef and wool; the dairy sector also produces for export. Wheat, maize, rice, **sugar** cane, barley, potatoes and sorghum are grown mainly for local consumption. The main mineral resources are marble (27 varieties) and other construction materials. The principal industries are meat and dairy processing, and manufacture of beverages, chemicals and textiles and clothing. All oil, gas and coal have to be imported.

Main exports are meat and wool. Principal imports are fuel and mineral products, electrical, electronic and other machinery (including car parts) and chemicals. In

2000 Brazil was the greatest purchaser of exports, followed by Argentina. Argentina was the greatest purchaser of imports, followed by Brazil and the USA.

Low world prices for meat and wool culminated in crisis for Uruguay's traditional ranching sector at the end of the 1990s, and a prolonged economic downturn began in 1998 under the consecutive impact of Brazilian devaluation, recession in Argentina and an outbreak of foot and mouth disease. Then, in 2002, the collapse of the Argentine economy caused a heavy run on Uruguayan banks. By the time emergency funding arrived the Government had had to devalue the peso and sustain a steep rise in the national debt, which stood at 90% of GDP at the end of the year. In May 2003, however, the Government was able to renegotiate about one-half the outstanding debt on favourable terms. Annual GDP growth in 1996–98 averaged 5%. GDP declined by 2.7% in 1999, by 1.4% in 2000, by 3.1% in 2001 and by 10.5% in 2002. The rate of unemployment in late 2002 stood at a record 20%.

Uruguay Round

The 'Uruguay Round' was the name given to the eighth and final round of negotiations concerning the revision of the General Agreement on Tariffs and Trade. It took its name from the meeting in Punta del Este, Uruguay, in 1986 at which negotiations formally commenced, the outcome of which was the formation of the **World Trade Organization**.

V

Vargas Llosa, Mario

Jorge Mario Pedro Vargas Llosa was born in Peru in 1936. He worked as a journalist and broadcaster before publishing his first novel, *The Time of the Hero* (1963), which describes adolescents striving for survival in the hostile environment of a military school and which showed the strong commitment to social change characteristic of his early work. His best-known works include *The Green House* (1965), *Aunt Julia and the Scriptwriter* (1977), and *The War of the End of the World* (1981). He won the Cervantes Prize in 1994. His later work reflects a growing conservatism in face of the conflict tearing Peru apart and in 1990 he ran for the presidency of Peru, but he was successfully presented as the conservative candidate and defeated unexpectedly in the second round by **Alberto Fujimori.**

Velasco Alvarado, Gen. Juan

Juan Velasco Alvarado (1910–1977), was born in Castilla, Piura, to a working-class family. Having trained as an Army NCO at Chorrillos, he won a place at the Escuela Militar and graduated top of his class as an officer in 1934. He graduated to staff rank at the Escuela Superior de Guerra in 1945–46 and was rapidly promoted to become brigadier-general in 1959. After a posting as military attaché to France in 1962–64, he held increasingly senior posts until as chief of the army's general staff in 1965–67 and commander of the army 1967–69 he led a successful coup against the Government of President **Fernando Belaúnde Terry**.

As President of a Revolutionary Government of the Armed Forces, Velasco resumed diplomatic relations with Cuba, which together with the Soviet Union came to Peru's assistance after the catastrophic **earthquake** of 1970. He presided over a series of left-wing reforms, including the expropriation of the large coastal estates, the nationalization of key industries and the systematic planning of state investment in industry, the expansion of the fishmeal industry and workers' participation in management. An aneurysm of the abdominal artery cost him his right leg in 1973, and in August 1975, when already terminally ill, he was deposed in an internal coup by Gen. Francisco Morales Bermúdez, who restored good relations with the USA and reversed many of Velasco's reforms.

Venetiaan, Runaldo

Runaldo Ronald Venetiaan has been President of Suriname since 2000. In 1991 his Nieuw Front (NF) coalition won the first election in the country to be monitored by the **Organization of American States** and he became President for the first time (1991–96). His Government curbed the armed forces, persuaded the Dutch government to resume economic aid and in 1994 implemented a structural adjustment programme that had been approved by the **International Monetary Fund**. The reforms, though officially successful, caused widespread hardship and in 1996 the NF was defeated. However, amid rapidly rising inflation and serious economic crisis Venetiaan was again elected in 2000 and between 2000 and 2003 restored good relations with the Netherlands and tackled the country's serious drugs problem.

Venezuela

República Bolivariana de Venezuela

The Bolivarian Republic of Venezuela is situated on the north coast of South America, bounded on the north by the Caribbean Sea, on the east by Guyana, on the south-east by Brazil and on the south-west by Colombia. Its name, 'little Venice', refers to the coastal settlement sighted by the first Spanish explorers. Seventy-two Caribbean islands, islets and cays are included in the national territory, though the northernmost, the Isla de los Aves, 565 km north of the mainland, is disputed by other Caribbean states.

Area: 912,050 sq km (352,144 sq miles); *capital:* **Caracas**; *language:* Spanish (several indigenous languages are still spoken); *population:* 22,688,803 (2001 census), 2% Amerindian, 67% mestizo, 21% of European descent; *religion:* Roman Catholic 86%, Protestant 2%.

Constitution: A new, Bolivarian Constitution was promulgated on 30 December 1999. The legislature, the single-chamber National Assembly, is directly elected by universal suffrage. Executive power is vested in a President directly elected for a six-year term. The country is divided into 22 states, a Federal District (Caracas) and 72 federal dependencies.

History: After the disintegration of Gran Colombia, Venezuela had a very turbulent history in the 19th century. Then, between 1899 and 1945, power was held continuously by four soldiers from the state of Táchira. Under the second of these, the dictator Juan Vicente Gómez (1908–35), oil was discovered and Venezuela replaced Mexico as the major oil-producing state of Latin America. When Gómez died, power passed constitutionally to his son-in-law, the Minister of War, Gen. Eleázar López Contreras, who was elected as President for the term 1936–41, and he, for the first time in Venezuelan history, relinquished power to an elected successor, Gen. Isaias Medina Angarita.

In October 1945 Medina was overthrown by a military coup, which established a military-civilian junta, led by **Rómulo Betancourt**, founder of a social democratic movement called **Acción Democrática** (AD). As interim President (1945–48), Betancourt carried out several important changes, in particular establishing that in future Venezuela would receive one-half of revenues generated from the sale of petroleum. In 1948 he handed over power to an elected successor, the distinguished novelist Rómulo Gallegos. The Gallegos Government passed an agrarian reform law, but in only a few weeks was deposed by yet another soldier from Táchira, Lt-Col Marcos Pérez Jiménez. AD was dissolved and in 1950 the military head of the ruling junta was kidnapped and murdered. Pérez Jiménez refused to accept the result of fresh elections and in December 1952 assumed dictatorial powers. Despite his much-feared secret police, his corrupt lifestyle made him so unpopular that he was overthrown in a popular uprising, aided by dissident military elements, in 1958. Elections were held and Betancourt was elected for the term 1959–64.

Until 1994 Betancourt's AD and the rival Partido Social Cristiano, or Comité de Organización Política Electoral Independiente (COPEI) alternated in power through free elections. As elsewhere, however, the world recession of the early 1980s had an adverse effect and, with the large debt accumulated in the years of prosperity, recovery was painful. In 1993 the incumbent President, Carlos Andrés Pérez (also President 1974–79), was successfully impeached on corruption charges and later imprisoned for two years. He had already become extremely unpopular on account of high unemployment and reductions in public expenditure and two abortive military coups revealed the extent of the threat to democracy.

However, Venezuela's political system survived this severe crisis and, in 1994, Dr **Rafael Caldera Rodríguez** (President in 1969–74), though disowned by his party, was returned to the presidency at the head of an independent coalition. In 1998 voters again rejected both of the historical political parties which had shared power since 1958. Instead, the nationalist **Hugo Chávez Frías** was elected President. Chávez had been implicated in two abortive coups against the civilian government in 1992 and had spent time in jail before being pardoned in 1994. Fighting a skilful electoral campaign, Chávez avoided making many political commitments. However, after taking office he successfully rallied support for the election of a new Constituent Assembly and the dissolution of the existing legislature. He even offered to mediate between the Government and rebels in neighbouring Colombia. He was re-elected to the presidency in July 2000 and since then has taken vigorous steps to address Venezuela's persistent economic problems.

Latest elections: On 30 July 2000 President Hugo Chávez Frías, running as candidate of the **Movimiento V República** (MVR), in alliance with the Movimiento al Socialismo (MAS), was elected to a new six-year term under the new Constitution, having received 59.7% of the votes cast, compared with 37.7% for his former colleague, Lt-Col (retd) Francisco Arias Cárdenas. Claudio Fermín, a former mayor of Caracas, of the newly founded Encuentro Nacional received only 2.7% of the vote. However, though the MVR took 93 and the MAS six of the 165 seats in the new National Assembly, AD emerged as the second largest party in the legislature with 32 seats; the remainder being divided thus: Proyecto Venezuela eight, COPEI five, Primero Justicia five, Causa Radical three, indigenous three, others 10. The MVR won 12 and the MAS three of the 23 state governorships and a division later opened up in AD as the secretary-general, Timoteo Zambrano, attempted to oust the party leader, Henry Ramos Allup.

International relations and defence: Venezuela is a member of the United Nations, the **Organization of American States**, the **Latin American Integration Association**, the **Andean Community of Nations**, and the **Rio Pact**. It has unresolved boundary disputes with both Colombia and Guyana. Traditionally oriented towards the USA, relations have deteriorated since 1998. In 2002 the army numbered 34,000, the navy 18,300, the air force 7,000 and the National Guard 23,000. Compulsory military service is selective and varies in length by region; in 2002 there were 31,000 conscripts enlisted, about half of them in the army.

Venezuela, economy

GNI: US $117.2m. (2001); *GNI per caput:* $4,760 (2001); *GNI at PPP:* $138m. (2001); *GNI per caput at PPP:* $5,590 (2001); *exports:* $30,948.1m. (2000); *imports:* $14,584.2m. (2000); *currency:* bolívar (B), plural bolivares; US $1 = 1,598 bolivares at 31 May 2003.

Venezuela is the world's sixth largest oil producer and the only member of the **Organization of Petroleum Exporting Countries** in the western hemisphere. The petroleum industry, which was nationalized in 1975, provides four-fifths of government revenue. In 2002 agriculture accounted for less than 5% of Venezuela's gross domestic product (GDP). Some 2.8% of the land is arable, 0.9% under permanent crops, 20.0% permanent pasture and more than 50% forest and woodland. The main crops are maize, palm oil and **sugar**. Livestock include cattle and chickens. The main mineral resources apart from petroleum are coal, iron ore, **bauxite** and gold; zinc, **copper**, lead, phosphorus, nickel, diamonds, silver and uranium are also found. The main energy source is electricity, two-thirds of which is generated by hydropower and one-quarter of which is illegally diverted.

Main exports are petroleum and petroleum products. Principal imports are machinery and road vehicles, basic manufactures and chemicals. In 2001 the USA was the greatest purchaser of exports, followed by Colombia. The USA was the main supplier of imports, followed by the Netherlands Antilles and Brazil.

In the 1990s the government pursued a policy of maximizing oil production, thus ending two decades of steady decline, and in 1997 production averaged 3.2m. barrels per day (b/d). This policy was reversed in 1999, when world prices were at their lowest since before 1973, and Venezuela's reduction of 650,000 b/d contributed to the steep rise in world petroleum prices to more than $30 dollars per barrel by 2003. The policy triggered a petroleum workers' strike in 2002 which prejudiced the government's plans for expansion of petrochemicals and severely damaged the economy. Since 1997 tourist numbers have declined sharply, owing to the perception of unrest, and 90% of tourists who do travel to Venezuela confine their visits to the island of Margarita. GDP grew by 6.4% in 1997, contracted by 0.2% in 1998 and by 6.1% in 1999. It grew again, by 3.2%, in 2000 and by 2.7% in 2001, but the crisis of 2002 resulted in a decline of 8.9%. Liberalization of the foreign exchange market in 1989 was followed by persistently high inflation, this peaking at 103.2% in 1996 when a 'crawling peg' system was introduced. Inflation then fell slowly and had declined to 12.5% in 2001 when the 'crawling peg' was abandoned. In February 2003 the bolívar was pegged to the dollar at US $1 = 1,600 bolivares. The official rate of unemployment was 19.3% in May 2003, when it was estimated that 86% of the population were living in poverty. However, the informal sector is estimated to account for 52% of all employment.

W

Washington Consensus

The term 'Washington Consensus' was first used in 1992 by John Williamson, of the Institute for International Economics, to describe how, by that time, the model of development which claims that there is only one road to prosperity and that it lies through the operation of the free market, impeded as little as possible by national boundaries, had become generally accepted. The liberalization of trade and the free market had already become accepted values for US policy-makers, but in the post-Cold War era they were unquestioned by international institutions, including financial institutions, with the consequence that countries in Latin America, and elsewhere, were expected to follow a specified pattern if they were to receive loans from the **International Monetary Fund** or the **International Bank for Reconstruction and Development**.

Willemstad

Willemstad, chief town and capital of the Netherlands Antilles, is situated on the south coast of the island of Curaçao. Founded in 1634, it was in earlier times an important centre for slave trafficking and retains much of its Dutch colonial architecture. With the building of the oil refinery in 1918 it enjoyed a further spell of prosperity. Its population was estimated at 125,000 in mid-2001. Willemstad is notable for having the oldest synagogue in the western hemisphere, now the Reconstructionist Shephardi Congregation Mikvé Israel-Emanuel, founded in 1732.

Williams, Dr Eric

Eric Eustace Williams (1911–1981), first Prime Minister of independent Trinidad and Tobago, 1962–81, studied at Oxford (where he received his doctorate) and Howard Universities, before returning to Trinidad to found, in 1956, the People's

National Movement and lead the struggle for independence, initially as part of the West Indies Federation and in 1962 as an separate state. The country's substantial oil reserves helped fund a strong educational system and a well-developed welfare state, but his last years in office were overshadowed by economic crisis.